Mayo Clinic

Its Growth and Progress

The brothers Mayo
Charles Horace and William James

Mayo Clinic

Its Growth and Progress

By

Victor Johnson, Ph.D., M.D., D.Sc.

Emeritus Director, Mayo Foundation for Medical Education and Research and Mayo Graduate School of Medicine

VOYAGEUR PRESS

First published by Voyageur Press
9337 Nesbitt Road, Bloomington, MN 55437

ISBN 0-89658-037-7

First Edition
5 4 3 2 1

Contents

Part II. The Mayo Clinic Grows

Illustrations

Preface

Since Helen Clapesattle's book *The Doctors Mayo*, published in 1941, there has been no complete coverage of Mayo Clinic history. There have been biographies of staff members and accounts of developments in specific sections or departments. In *Mayo Clinic: Its Growth and Progress*, the author recounts the history of the entire institution and its affiliated hospitals over the last forty years.

For Part I, The Clinic Revealed (early 1940s), the author relied much on the Clapesattle volume. This was supplemented with his complete survey of the institution when he decided to accept the Clinic appointment. As executive officer of the American Medical Association's Council on Medical Education and Hospitals, one of his responsibilities had been to evaluate advanced medical education programs in institutions seeking AMA approval. This experience enabled him to realize Mayo's superior graduate medical training efforts and accomplishments.

In Part II, The Mayo Clinic Grows (early 1940s to late 1960s), the author recounts much of his personal experience as director of the Mayo Foundation for Medical Education and Research, and as director of the Mayo Graduate School of Medicine. He participated directly in much of the Clinic's planning, development, and accomplishments in addition to directing the graduate education of doctors seeking to become medical specialists. He sat on numerous Clinic committees, including its leading administrative body, the board of governors.

Important, also, were personal contacts and discussions by the author with section heads, departmental chairmen, research leaders, fellows in graduate training, secretaries, and many other employees. The various relationships of the Clinic to the national and international scene were made more clear to the author via his intimate relationships with the American Medical Association and the World Medical Association, on some of whose committees he continued to serve.

For Part III, The Mayo Clinic Today (1982), the author recounts important events following his retirement from the Clinic in 1966. For much of this he relied on minutes of significant Clinic meetings of staff, divisions, or other groups. Annual reports provided much valuable information. All of these were freely available to the author in a variety of Clinic locations. There were numerous conferences with Clinic personnel from executives to clerks.

Various Clinic publications were also most revealing. These included the *Mayo Alumnus,* a quarterly publication with eleven thousand copies distributed to alumni all over the world as well as locally. And there was *Mayovox,* with twelve thousand copies published monthly for the entire Clinic family, from staff physicians to all other employees. Much information was also derived from the Clinic's scientific publication, the *Mayo Clinic Proceedings,* which has a worldwide subscription list of ninety thousand. Help also came from the hospital publications *Rochester Methodist Hospital News* and Saint Marys' *Caring*.

Most important in developing such an account is to share in the basic spirit of the Mayo Clinic by living in it, sensing and absorbing the institution's wholehearted devotion to patient care, medical education, and scientific research. According to Dr. W. Eugene Mayberry, chairman of the board of governors of the Mayo Clinic, "Progress in the practice of medicine at the Mayo Clinic . . . has evolved through deliberate consideration of a single question: 'What is best for our patients?' "

No account of the Clinic's activities would be complete without appreciation of the spirit of the Mayo Clinic, which does not treat the disease of a patient, but treats a patient with a disease.

Bibliography

The major published sources of information were the several Mayo Clinic periodicals: *Collected Papers of the Mayo Clinic and Mayo Foundation, Mayo Alumnus, Mayo Clinic Proceedings, Mayo Today, Mayovox,* and *Proceedings of the Staff Meetings of the Mayo Clinic.* Also helpful was Rochester's newspaper, *The Post-Bulletin.*

Additional sources of information were these journal publications or books:

American Journal of Medicine
American Journal of Physiology
American Review of Respiratory Diseases
American Review of Tuberculosis
Annals of Biomedical Engineering
Annual Review of Physiology
Blood
British Medical Journal
Clagett, O. T. *General Surgery at the Mayo Clinic,* Rochester, Minnesota, 1980
Clapesattle, H. *The Doctors Mayo.* Minneapolis: University of Minnesota Press, 1941.
Encyclopaedia Britannica
Federation Proceedings

Gastroenterology
Hospital Progress
Hilton, C. *Be My Guest*. Englewood Cliffs, N. J.: Prentice-Hall, 1957.
Journal of the American Medical Association
Journal of Arkansas Medical Society
Journal of Aviation Medicine
Journal of Medical Education
Journal of South Carolina Medical School
Mayo, C. W. *The Story of My Family and My Career*. New York: Doubleday & Company, 1968
Minnesota Medicine
New England Journal of Medicine
Psychiatric Annals
Resident and Staff Physician
Silber, S. J. *Microsurgery*. Williams & Wilkins, 1979

PART I.

The Clinic Revealed

This section recounts the status of the Mayo Clinic and its hospitals with regard to patient care, medical education, and scientific research in the early 1940s. The author became acquainted with all of this when he accepted the appointment as director of the Mayo Foundation for Medical Education and Research. For the first several months, he spent alternate weeks in Chicago and in Rochester. In Chicago he terminated his work with the American Medical Association and helped train his successor. In Rochester he had no responsibilities except to become acquainted with the vast Mayo enterprise. To learn all that went on, visits were made to major divisions as well as to small corners. His understanding of the Clinic and of the origins of its activities was materially assisted by the account of the University of Minnesota historian Helen Clapesattle in her important book *The Doctors Mayo*, published in 1941.

CHAPTER 1

Introduction to the Clinic

First View of Rochester

Here in the rural calm of southern Minnesota, without a scenic wonder or historic shrine in sight, was a city of thirty thousand inhabitants that had an annual transient population of ten times that number. For here in this little town on the edge of nowhere was one of the world's greatest medical centers, to which people come from the ends of the earth for treatment and instruction.

These reflections were in the author's mind on his first trip from Chicago to Rochester. He had been asked to speak to the Mayo staff about the anticipated postwar needs for the training of physicians in the various specialty fields of medicine. Approaching the city by plane, he was amazed at the skyline of this country town, revealing the beautiful Plummer Building, the hospitals, and the hotels. Before he ever saw the Mayo Clinic, its image was firmly imprinted on his mind, with its enviable reputation in medical practice, teaching, and research.

Aware as he was of the Clinic's performance record, he was not fully cognizant of its spirit and philosophy. He delved into these. Dr. James Priestly, a great surgeon and an equally great leader in Mayo Clinic activities, stated that the aims of the brothers Will and Charles Mayo in establishing the Clinic were:

> To offer to all who came, both the sick and the well, medical care of the highest standard through a coordinated and integrated group practice of medicine, conducted with the highest principles of ethics which have guided private physicians through the years;
>
> To offer opportunities in graduate medical education to outstanding young men and women of medicine through fellowships in the Mayo Foundation aimed at a higher competency in the practice of medicine and its various specialties, preparation for teaching and a knowledge of medical research, as a means of contributing to improvement in the standards of medical care in the country and in the world;
>
> To advance and enlarge knowledge and skill in medicine and the sciences related to medicine through continuing research toward a broader understanding of man in health and disease and of diagnostic and therapeutic measures applicable to disease;
>
> To attain these objectives in medical practice, medical education, and medical research, upon the ideal that our first obligation is to our patients, no one of whom shall be asked to pay a charge beyond his means, with no financial benefits to any staff member or officer or employee beyond a reasonable annual compensation and with only such returns to the institution as will safeguard the future.

And according to Dr. Howard Gray, "The Mayos and their associates were determined that income, beyond a reasonable remuneration for the staff members, should be returned to those from whom it came—the sick; . . . They came to the decision that this could best be done through teaching and research." All was as Dr. Will Mayo philosophized, "We are the custodians of the sick man's dollar."

While the Mayo brothers ran the institution extremely well, they felt strongly that their responsibility was equally great to train successors who would carry on the task as well as they had done. Dr. Will once said to Dr. Louis Buie, head of proctology, "Buie, you should run your department so that if you died tonight things would run as well tomorrow without you."

In the words of Dr. Thomas Magath of pathology,

> The development of the Mayo Foundation is of course one of the most significant things in medical history not only here but in the world. It was the first graduate school of medicine—as contrasted to postgraduate schools of which there were hundreds—to be established. As a result of this we had the establishment of medical specialties and boards for certifying specialists. These developments were of universal importance.

At a somewhat later date, the *Encyclopaedia Britannica*, in one of its medical-health annual publications, cited the Mayo Clinic as "the standard against which all other clinics are judged." And,

> Every profession has its paragons, every area of human endeavor its meter sticks against which the accomplishments of others are measured: medicine has its giants, too, but none stands taller than the Mayo doctors and the

> Clinic they founded. The Mayo Clinic is such a world medical treasure that if it did not exist, it would be necessary to invent it—and today, at least, that would probably be impossible.

Several of the Clinic's permanent staff were well known to the author in joint enterprises concerned primarily with the education of medical specialists. The author was the secretary of the Council on Medical Education and Hospitals of the American Medical Association, with responsibilities to assist medical educational institutions to maintain high standards at all levels of medical education in our country and, to some extent, abroad as well.

At the level of hospital and university training of physicians desiring to become specialists in internal medicine, surgery, pediatrics, or whatever, the author functioned in close collaboration with national specialty organizations, such as the various national boards in this and that field, and also with the Advisory Board for Medical Specialties and many others. It was in such work at national levels that he came to know well such prominent Mayo doctors as Arlie Barnes, cardiology; Frank Krusen, physical medicine; Ralph Ghormley, orthopedics; Byrl Kirklin, radiology; Louis Buie, proctology; not to mention Russell Wilder, one of his teachers in medical school. He had also taught physiology at the University of Chicago Medical School to Drs. Minot Stickney, Herman Young, and others presently on the permanent Mayo staff.

Besides its concern with the quality of medical education at all levels, the AMA's Council on Medical Education and Hospitals was also immersed in wartime concerns. How could the country produce more physicians of high quality when half the doctors of the country were in military service?

But never content with immediate problems, the council probed the future as well. What should be done with the countless physicians who had entered military service before completion of training and who desired to become competent specialists?

The council estimated that immediately after World War II it might need double the normal peacetime opportunities for advanced training beyond the internship. Because the council wished to verify this estimate, in collaboration with a number of national organizations and agencies, civil and military, the American Medical Association conducted a survey of postwar educational desires of military medical officers. Questionnaires were sent to some three thousand medical officers selected at random, representing all age groups, all military services, and all theaters of operation. About a thousand officers replied, and about half of these indicated they would seek further training of more than six months in one or another of the specialty fields of medicine.

Manipulating and extrapolating these figures to cover all physicians in military service, it was concluded that immediately after the war the AMA would need training places for nearly double the peacetime numbers, at least for a few years. This confirmed the estimate made before the objective study. The results applied only to specialty training; in addition, many officers indicated a desire for review or refresher course training. It was the council's responsibility to disseminate all this information to appropriate universities, hospitals, and national organizations engaged in the advanced training of physicians. Naturally, one of these was the great Mayo Clinic.

And so the author was requested, along with Lt. Col. Harold L. Leuth, assigned by the army as a collaborator of his, to present these concerns at the Mayo Clinic. Knowing the Clinic fairly well in his mind, it was nevertheless overwhelming to know it with his eyes as well. The author surmised that his invitation to speak at Rochester was only in part to hear about investigations and recommendations for postwar medical educational needs. He was certain that the call to Rochester was also for the Clinic people to see who and what Dr. Victor Johnson was and whether he was worthy of consideration as a successor to Dr. Donald Balfour, who was near retirement as director of the Mayo Foundation for Medical Education and Research.

And so it was. Soon after this visit, they offered him the position. Balfour had been at Mayo for some forty years, serving in various capacities and eventually as the foundation's director. He was highly respected, deeply admired, and much loved. Voicing complaints against the consequences of aging, he once said:

> As I get older, there are three things I forget; first, I forget people's names, although I remember their faces; second, I even forget their faces; and third–mm-ahem-uh–I forget what that is!

There followed several discussions about the directorship with a number of Clinic executives. These included the incomparable Harry Harwick. At one of these sessions, when the author's potential salary was mentioned, he pointed out that for a time he had to travel back and forth between Rochester and Chicago to wind up his affairs with the AMA while also learning more about his responsibilities in Rochester. So he asked for some three thousand dollars annually more than the salary mentioned.

"But of course!" said Harry.

In the author's former work at estimating the quality of a medical school being surveyed for the council, he usually first examined the school's financial budget. From this he could often anticipate weaknesses that were confirmed in further investigation. He asked Harry if he might see the Mayo budget. This was not to assess the quality of the institution, which he knew was of a most superior order, but it might help him understand the full nature of the manifold activities of the Clinic.

"We have no budget," said Harry.

The Clinic's Hometown

Rochester, Minnesota, derived its name from Rochester, New York. George Head, whose hometown was the New York city, built a log house here in 1854, establishing the settlement which later became Minnesota's Rochester in a charter of incorporation granted by the Minnesota Legislature in 1859. Soon after this, Dr. William Worrall Mayo moved from LeSueur, Minnesota, and made his residence here. Shortly, he became the leading physician and surgeon in Olmsted County, as well as the father of two sons.

When the two Mayo brothers were born, the village had a population of fifteen hundred. Subsequently, there were increases of several thousands of inhabitants per decade. By the time of the author's arrival in 1947, there were nearly thirty thousand people living here. Mayo doctors had contributed significantly to these population numbers. To the young children of Clinic staff members, all adult males bore the name "doctor." These were Dr. Jones and Dr. Smith. These children knew no one named "mister." There was no Mr. Brown or Mr. Gray. One Mayo doctor said, "My kids even call the garbage man 'doctor.' "

And besides the human inhabitants, there were Canadian geese wintering on Silver Lake. This phenomenon was a result of Rochester drawing cool water from Silver Lake for a power plant and returning heated water, keeping the lake mainly ice-free all winter. Eventually, the winter goose population reached twenty-five thousand, or almost half the human population. Among the waterfowl were some so-called giant Canadian geese, the largest geese in the world, weighing usually twelve to fourteen pounds, but sometimes even reaching twenty pounds, and with a wing span of about six feet. This giant goose was thought to have become extinct in 1920. Then some forty years later, biologists were shocked by the discovery of this bird, not on some distant Canadian prairie, but in the heart of Rochester.

All this started way back with Dr. Charlie Mayo, who began raising a flock of captured Canadian geese on his estate near Rochester and providing them with food. Eventually the geese, like the Mayo Clinic, became big business in Rochester. Merchants near the lake who sell two-pound bags of shelled corn are able to sell upwards of two tons of corn during a single month to natives and visitors who feed the geese. Each October these great flocks of birds come from the north, sweeping across the skies. They stay until late March. But these migrants are not entirely an asset to Rochester. At one time, area farmers complained that Silver Lake geese had eaten more than eight thousand dollars' worth of crops from their fields in a single month. But the geese remain, like the thousands of patients, as permanent migrants to Rochester.

Regarding the weather, we may aptly quote a Mark Twain weather forecast made for New England but equally applicable to Rochester: "Probable nor'east to sou'west winds varying to southard and westard and eastard and points between; high and low barometer sweeping round from place to place; probable areas of rain, snow, hail and drought, succeeded or preceeded by earthquakes with thunder and lightning."

Particularly in the town's center, amid the tall Clinic buildings of today, Rochester is indeed a windy city. The winds sweeping across miles of open prairie impinge on the high structures and rush with increased velocity down the streets, like a wide river encountering upthrusts from the bottom and dashing down narrowed channels.

On one occasion an embryo internal medicine fellow from the Deep South looked out of his bedroom window on his first real winter morning in Rochester. He beheld the ground covered with some five or six inches of snow. He returned to bed, muttering gleefully, "Nothing will be moving today. No patient can get to the Clinic!"

University Relations

While considering the offer to join Mayo, as well as during his early months there, the author studied that giant medical enterprise with its magnificent patient care facilities and its relationship to the University of Minnesota. The Mayo Foundation for Medical Education and Research became a department of the university's graduate school back in 1915. There were compelling motivations for this alliance, both in Rochester and in Minneapolis.

President George Vincent of the university bemoaned the fact that success in medical specialty practice depended almost entirely on natural ability rather than on organized training. There was no systematic advanced medical education in existence anywhere. Vincent and graduate school dean Guy Stanton Ford saw in the collaborative enterprise the possibility of "a graduate school which will stand absolutely alone in the sphere of medical education in America."

And in Rochester, the brothers Mayo determined to devote excess Clinic earnings to helping the sick through the advancement of medical education and the pursuit of research. The enterprise in Rochester would be financed entirely from Mayo Clinic income, at no financial cost to the university. So the funds to support the educational and research activities came from fees paid by patients. This did not mean that the charges to patients were excessive. It did mean that many dollars which might have gone into the pockets of Clinic doctors were used otherwise. In one study many years later, it was revealed in the Consumer Price Index that Mayo fees during inflation rose less rapidly than did the general medical-service portion of the index.

Lofty though these aspirations were, the objections were multiple. Helen Clapesattle cited some of those which were raised:

> Since it would be impossible in practice to separate the activities of the Mayo Foundation from those of the Mayo Clinic, the university would actually be affiliating itself with a private partnership. Because the partners as incorporators of the Mayo Foundation were, through the scientific directors, to control the appointment of teachers and expenditure of funds, the University Regents would in effect be granting to a private enterprise, a rank equal to that of the medical school. If they gave such privileges to one group they must grant them to any other that asked, and medical education in the state, so lately centralized at great cost, would again be dispersed, more widely and weakly than ever before. . . .
>
> Advanced medical education would overshadow undergraduate work and check the development of the medical school. And then in the future, when the Mayo Clinic deteriorated to mediocrity as the critics said it surely would when the Mayo brothers died, the university would be saddled with the responsibility for maintaining it and would have to divert to legislative appropriations intended for the medical school.

The Hennepin County and Ramsey County medical societies in Minneapolis and St. Paul passed emphatic protest resolutions and persuaded groups in the general Rochester area to do likewise. A bill forbidding the enterprise was introduced into the state legislature.

One of the several pamphlets depicting the evils of the plan was entitled "A Phantom Gift and a Trial Marriage." The phantom gift was the proposed Mayo endowment to the university, the entire income of which was to be spent in Rochester. Nothing would go directly to the university, which was the unwilling bride of the trial marriage.

Translating some of the high-sounding objections into simple English, many physicians and educators thought the whole scheme to be mere advertising for the Mayo Clinic's medical practice.

But wisdom and foresight and courage prevailed. President Vincent's dream of the systematic training of medical specialists in Rochester and Minneapolis became a reality, truly anticipating a major development not only in the training but also in the identification of specialists in this country. The Clinic and the university became pioneers in the distinctly

American system of advanced education of physicians for specialty practice, sponsored eventually by the American Medical Association, the American boards in the numerous specialties of medicine, the American College of Surgeons, the American College of Physicians, and other official agencies. In Rochester, the sick man's dollar would be returned to the sick by the superior education of specialists and the fruits of medical research.

For some time after the university/Clinic alliance some doubts still lingered regarding the wisdom of this unprecedented union. The board of regents of the university, in 1921, requested a committee of distinguished figures in American medicine to investigate and report. Dr. Frank Billings of Chicago, Dr. Victor Vaughn of Ann Arbor, and Dr. J. M. T. Finney of Baltimore pronounced their verdict:

> The University of Minnesota possesses in the Mayo Foundation an asset which is not equalled in any other university in the world. [We wish] . . . to avoid every form of exaggeration, but if there be anywhere a graduate medical school comparable in all its details with the Mayo Foundation, [we do] not know of its existence.

This encouraging encomium was considered by the leaders of the enterprise to be more a challenge for the future than a judgment of the efforts of that day.

Until the Mayo Foundation was established, graduate school education in clinical medical fields leading to an M.S. or Ph.D. degree did not exist. One might earn an advanced degree in physiology, biochemistry, or anatomy, but nowhere was there systematic training in clinical medicine or surgery leading to an academic degree beyond the M.D. That phase of medical education originated entirely with William and Charles Mayo and the University of Minnesota.

On the author's arrival in Rochester, there were some five hundred physicians in training to become specialists. They came from a majority of the medical schools of the United States and from some abroad. They were designated as fellows and were like residents in other training institutions. But Mayo fellows were different from residents in that there were opportunities in Rochester for meeting the requirements for the M.S. or Ph.D. degrees, which many sought. These degrees were in the name of the clinical department of the fellow's major field, such as pediatrics or obstetrics.

Such advanced academic degree requirements included research in one of the basic medical sciences such as physiology or pathology. A thesis based on original investigations was prepared and was subject to approval not only by the Mayo Foundation administration but also by appropriate faculty members and committees of the university in Minneapolis. The final examination for a degree was given by a joint committee of Mayo and Minneapolis faculty members. All this was strongly fostered by Dr. Donald Balfour.

Academic appointments to the permanent Mayo staff, from instructor to professor, were based on the same rigid requirements that obtained in any university department, medical or otherwise. Final confirmation of the Mayo recommendations for faculty appointments or promotions were made by the university after discussion in a joint committee.

And thus there came to fruition the Mayo conviction that the care of the sick, which was always the primary function of the institution, could be most effective only if it is combined with the teaching of young physicians and with investigation into the problems of health and disease.

Mayo Association

The financial ramifications of an institution as tremendous as the Mayo Clinic have always been perhaps as complicated as the diagnosis of disease and the treatment of patients. But the principle guiding the management of these money matters was as simple as it was lofty. There would be no shareholders or individual owners of the Clinic or personal profit to anyone from its earnings. Everyone, every doctor or other employee in the Clinic, would be on salary. This even included the Mayo brothers, William and Charles. The financial arrangements were such as would ensure perpetuation of the institution beyond the lives of any individuals. All institutional profits must be devoted to medical education and research. The professional staff must forever consider themselves the custodians of the sick man's dollar.

These principles guided the establishment of the Mayo Foundation as part of the University of Minnesota. In about 1917 the Doctors Mayo made personal gifts to the university totaling $2 million. This was the entire personal savings of Will and Charlie. Earnings from this contribution soon elevated the endowment to $2.5 million. The original deed of gift contained these words:

> The fund shall be known as the Mayo Foundation for Medical Education and Research. The principal of said fund perpetually shall be kept invested and reinvested, and all the net income therefrom perpetually shall be used for the purpose of graduate medical and surgical instruction and research, to be carried on by and under the direction of the university.

After due consideration, the Mayo Association was formed. Known in its earlier years as the Mayo Properties Association, it was a charitable organization made up of twelve trustees serving without compensation. The trustees included the Mayo brothers, Drs. William Plummer, Starr

Judd, and Donald Balfour, as well as that remarkable Harry Harwick. Harry was an astute administrator and business executive, but he never allowed business or money matters to distract him from the Mayo ideals, motives, or principles. Referring to the organization of Mayo Association as "another real milestone," Harwick also stated:

> Members of Mayo Association are honored by the acceptance of Mr. Kingman, Mr. Fitzgerald and Doctor Wilbur to serve as public members of the Association. We deeply appreciate the willingness of these men to take time out of their busy schedules without compensation to bring us their judgment and counsel in achieving the objectives and purposes of Mayo Association.
>
> This change in organization structure, in my opinion, brings to further fulfillment the intent and ideals of the Doctors Mayo and their associates in establishing the Mayo Association as essentially a public trust. It was the thought of the Doctors Mayo, which they often expressed, that the sick man's dollar should be returned to him in the form of better medicine through medical research and the training of better doctors.
>
> The relationship between the University of Minnesota and the Mayo Foundation, which has prevailed for many years, has been most constructive and the University has been unfailing in its support of medical education and research in the Mayo Foundation. It has been a most pleasant and inspiring association.
>
> This charge marks another real milestone in the development of the three related institutions, the Mayo Clinic, Mayo Foundation and Mayo Association. I am confident that present and future members of the Association will be united and untiring, as in the past, in their efforts to elevate the standards of the practice of medicine and of medical education and research.
>
> Above all, what will be accomplished in the future, as has been true in the past, will depend upon the united efforts of a strong and devoted staff of the Mayo Clinic dedicating their lives to the advancement of an ideal in medicine.

The Mayo Association was charged with

> aiding and advancing the study and investigation of human ailments and injuries, and the causes, prevention, relief and cure thereof, and the study and investigation of problems of hygiene, health and public welfare, and the promotion of medical, surgical and scientific learning, skill, education and investigation, and to engage in the conduct and to aid and assist in medical, surgical and scientific research in the broadest sense . . . No part of the net income of this corporation, or of its properties or assets upon dissolution or liquidation shall ever inure to the benefit of any of its members, or of any private individual.

To this board the Mayo brothers transferred the ownership of absolutely everything: all their accumulated cash and securities and all the property of the Mayo Clinic, including all present and future buildings with their total contents, from x-ray machines down to pencils and paper and test tubes. The association was to receive and manage all the income of the Clinic after payment of salaries and expenses.

Within five or six years the property values reached $5 million and the securities of the Mayo Association became $5.5 million. The Mayo Association also owned properties, including the Clinic buildings. These had increased in value tremendously, as had the cash and securities of the association. Permanent staff now numbered well over two hundred, and there were some five hundred fellows in graduate medical training.

All Clinic salaries had to be approved by the association to avoid anyone accumulating more than enough for a reasonably good living and old age security. The Mayo brothers did not wish a staff member to be able to keep his children on the beach in Miami when they ought to be working.

The acceptance of funds from sources outside the Clinic was frowned on. There was a tradition that the Clinic should live within its income from patient fees and Mayo Association investments. Not only were funds not requested, but outside offers of funds were considered with great hesitation. From the author's experience in physiology and the deanship at the University of Chicago Medical School, he could scarcely comprehend this ultraconservative viewpoint. How drastically the Clinic view was to change in future years!

Government support was accepted for construction and operation of the acceleration laboratory of the Mayo Clinic aero-medical unit and for high-altitude research, beneficial to fighter pilots during the war. This exception to the rule emanated from the Clinic's intense desire to participate in the war effort. There was also government support for the Mayo medical unit of the war, culminating in the unit's stations in New Guinea and the Philippine Islands. And the Army Medical Corps selected the Mayo Clinic as a training center for newly recruited medical officers in a number of medical and surgical fields. The Clinic's conservative policy was also penetrated by personal gifts from Dr. Donald Balfour. He contributed funds used mainly to assist in sending fellows to national meetings to present papers.

One early contribution to the Clinic's program came from a strong-minded gentleman from a western state, whose Clinic bill was sixty dollars. He said the services he had received were worth only thirty dollars, which was all he paid on leaving, in the year 1933. Years later he sent the Clinic seventy-five dollars, which he said would cover the thirty dollars he really still owed the Clinic, plus allowance for interest and inflation. But he was told that the Clinic was unable to decide the present value of inflated dollars and it did not charge interest on bills due. The westerner was told that his extra forty-five dollars would go into one of the Clinic's research funds or to the Clinic welfare fund, which is used for destitute patients.

Another early bequest to the Clinic came from an elderly bachelor who died at St. Louis, Missouri, in 1949. His will read:

> After payment of all my debts and funeral expenses, I give, devise and bequeath my entire estate, consisting of real, personal and mixed property of every description and wherever situated, to the Mayo Clinic in the city of Rochester, Minnesota, to be used for any purpose that the officers of said Clinic team deem desirable.

This donor of his modest life savings had never been in Rochester. His action was prompted by an experience of a good friend of his who did visit Rochester and the Mayo Clinic. This friend had an operation, and his total Clinic bill had been eight hundred dollars. To pay this, he had borrowed the money, with his farm as security. In paying the Clinic, he had mentioned the source of his money. Naturally, the Clinic had returned the eight hundred dollars, stating that no one had to mortgage his farm to pay a Clinic bill.

Within two decades all this was to change radically, with usually successful efforts to obtain millions from whatever sources seemed promising, emulating universities, colleges, hospitals, and research institutions everywhere.

CHAPTER 2

Care of Patients

The Clinic

Before the name Mayo Clinic was ever used, the Mayo brothers and early associates had medical facilities in the Ramsey Building, where Massey's store is now located, at First Avenue and Second Street Southwest. In 1901 they moved their offices across the two streets to the old Masonic Temple, where they functioned for fourteen years. This building was destroyed by fire in 1916 and soon replaced with a new building, which today still houses the Masonic Temple as well as the Weber & Judd Drugstore.

The name Mayo Clinic first came into being with the construction and operation of the Red Brick Building in 1914, called Plummer's folly by some local residents. Here began the Mayo brothers' pioneering concept of group medical practice. It was mentioned that "this large new building was the final answer; surely it would take care of all patients for all-time-to-come." In that year 30,632 patients visited the Clinic.

The "all-time-to-come" was of brief duration. In just ten years the annual number of patients coming to the Clinic was doubled, necessitating the planning and construction of the Plummer Building. The structure was named for its designer, who was also a noteworthy Mayo clinician. About Dr. Henry Plummer, Dr. Will once said that the hiring of Dr. Plummer—at the turn of the century—was the best day's work he ever did for the Clinic.

On the author's arrival in Rochester in 1947, about 220 members of the Clinic staff and faculty of the Mayo Foundation provided for some 135,000 patients, the medical care of whom has always been the major function of the entire Mayo organization. For this there was the Plummer Building and the affiliated hospitals. The old Red Brick Building now was used mainly for diagnostic laboratories and research facilities.

Seeing the Plummer Building for the first time, the author ventured that if Plummer were as good a physician as he was an architect and designer, Mayo would know none better. He was just that. The living memorial to Plummer was dedicated and occupied in 1928. It was said that "with the Plummer Building the Mayo Clinic emerged as a distinct institution." Complete with all its equipment, it cost the Mayo Properties Association three million dollars. At its dedication Dr. Will stated:

> The object of this building is to furnish a permanent house wherein scientific investigation can be made into the causes of diseases which afflict mankind, and wherein every effort shall be made to cure the sick and the suffering. It is the hope of the founders of this building that in its use the high ideals of the medical profession will always be maintained. Within its walls all classes of people, the poor as well as the rich, without regard to color or creed, shall be cared for without discrimination.

There are fifteen stories of rich Sierra limestone, elaborate terrazzo floors, carved bronze front doors and elevator doors, terra-cotta ceilings, and hand-carved oak walls. Here are incorporated some of the best features of a castle or cathedral. The building is crowned with a bell tower more than four stories in height. Says Helen Clapesattle:

> In the tower that tops the building hangs a carillon of 23 bells cast in the famous foundry of Croydon, England. For years Doctor Will had wanted for Rochester a set of bells such as he had heard in other cities, and the new building gave him a chance to gratify this wish. Day in and day out the bells ring the hours, and for half an hour three times a week Rochester seems to hush while the carillonneur sends hymns and folk songs through the sky into the farthest hotel and hospital room in town.

May we pass for a moment from piety to frivolity? A man strolling in Mayo Park while the carillon was sounding its lofty music stopped before another man seated on a bench.

"Isn't that music simply glorious?" he asked.

"Sorry, I didn't hear what you said."

After some repetitions the seated man said, "I just can't hear a word you're saying on account of them darn bells."

Combined with the remodeled Red Brick Building, the Plummer Building provided ample facilities for patient care, in a measure equal to the beauty of the structure. There were waiting rooms, examining rooms, offices, laboratories, and all needed chemical and other supplies.

Patients coming to Rochester for the first time were motivated by the Clinic's reputation but often had no concept of the magnitude of the institution, even in those remote days. Newton Holland, a Rochester restaurateur, was stopped on the street by an obviously new arrival, who asked about the location of the Mayo Clinic. Pointing to the Plummer Building, Holland said,

"That's the Clinic, there."

"I know," the visitor answered impatiently. "But which floor is it on?"

Some four decades after its construction, the Plummer Building was designated a Registered National Historical Landmark by the United States National Park Service, and in the same year (1970) it was declared a State Historical Site by the Minnesota Legislature.

The pressure of patient demands continued, resulting in the construction of the Clinic Annex at the site of the present Damon Parkade. It housed neurology, the new psychiatry unit, and other departments formerly located in Plummer. This move provided needed areas for the general nonspecialist sections.

The passage of years was soon to demonstrate the fragility of the adage "adequate for all-time-to-come." Voiced first regarding the Red Brick Building, it soon was to be rendered equally false as pertained to Plummer.

Henry Plummer was a superior thinker, clinician, and architectural designer. Dr. Will Mayo stated that he was "the best brain the Clinic ever had." Yet he was afflicted with a degree of absentmindedness in matters of minimal importance. Helen Clapesattle recounts these episodes:

> He always ate his lunch at the same restaurant and always ordered the same meal, so that sometimes when he sat talking overlong his waitress would clear away the table and a second girl coming by would bring him his order all over again. And he usually ate it, forgetting he had had one lunch. His table companions never knew whether their conversation would end up on a Cook's tour or on the fine points of Italian marbles. But they could be fairly sure they would have to pay the check, for Plummer never remembered it. There are half a dozen versions of the story that once when he was host to a visiting doctor at lunch he took so little notice of the check that the guest finally paid it himself. But when the waiter brought the change Henry Plummer picked it up, with a vacant thank-you.
>
> One day he sold his car to one of his young assistants and the next morning listened with great interest to the young man's excited tale of its disappearance the night before. Suddenly Dr. Plummer started for the door with a queer look on his face and in half an hour came back to explain sheepishly that the car was in his garage. He had driven home in it, forgetting that he'd sold it.

Hospitals

Hospitals were as essential as the Clinic diagnostic buildings, which provided no facilities for bedding patients or conducting surgery. Saint Marys Hospital came into being. A devastating tornado struck Rochester back in 1883, and the father of the Mayo brothers requested some Catholic teaching sisters to help treat the injured. Mother Alfred was in charge of these sisters. She came to America from Luxembourg "to teach the Indians," building and staffing schools in the Midwest. She became a central figure in Rochester's hospital history. Her name was appropriately perpetuated decades later when it was given to the elegant Alfred unit of Saint Marys Hospital. In her early years she arrived at the compelling conviction that her order should build a hospital in Rochester. This came to pass. In 1889 the Sisters of St. Francis constructed Rochester's first hospital, with twenty-seven beds, two operating rooms, and three surgeons—William Worrall Mayo and his two sons, Will and Charlie. The cost of the original hospital was twenty thousand dollars. It had "beautiful floors of curly maple." In its first three years the hospital and its staff of three served a total of 655 patients medically and surgically. Less than a century later, many more than this number came to the Clinic every day.

At first, Rochester's Protestant doctors refused to join the Protestant Mayos in working with "papist" nurses. Later they began using the hospital only as a place to leave the dying. Soon the sisters ruled that all their patients must be examined by Mayo physicians, making them the hospital's executive staff, and this arrangement continues today.

In Rochester, hospital growth has always been as perpetual as that of Clinic facilities. In the half century preceding 1941, seven additional structures were added. The Joseph Building of 1922 was named after the first Saint Marys administrator, Sister Mary Joseph Dempsey. This was termed "the most up-to-date surgical pavilion in the entire world." The large seventh medical building ultimately bore the name Francis Building, after the thirteenth century St. Francis of Assisi (Italy), who also provided the name for the Sisters of St. Francis. On the author's arrival in Rochester the hospital had grown to 845 beds and sixteen operating rooms, with all the necessary laboratory and other facilities. The staff of nurses and other employees totaled about 580.

The ideal and ambition of Saint Marys was once expressed by the Right Reverend Patrick Heffron, bishop of Winona, who said, "We have the best surgeons in the world, the best sisters in the world, and why can't we have the best hospital in the world?"

But throughout all the growth and changes there is one thing which has persisted unchanged at Saint Marys Hospital—"the spirit of compassion evident in the quality of care given and in the unending dedication to the motto—'And He healed all!' "

And Saint Marys Hospital was supplemented. Throughout Mayo

Clinic history there has persisted an intimacy between the Clinic and the Kahler Hotel enterprises. Adequate hotel provisions were virtually as indispensable as were Clinic and hospital facilities for the multitudes thronging to Rochester. Initially John Kahler and subsequently the Kahler Corporation were mainly responsible for this facet of Rochester growth. In fact, Kahler was as intimately involved in hospital development as in hotel construction and management. Hotel and hospital soon became intimately intertwined.

Originally the Colonial was a hotel mainly for convalescent patients. It was opened in 1915 and for a time it was not owned by Kahler. In a year, a needed addition was built, and soon after this, with its 230 bedrooms, it was converted into a hospital and purchased by John Kahler, embarking on a remarkable adventure in patient care. The Mayo Clinic now had available the Colonial Hospital, supplementing Saint Marys.

Like the Colonial, the Worrall Building was not initially designed as a hospital but was aimed primarily at providing training and living quarters for nurses. It was purchased by the Kahler Corporation in 1919 and converted to the Worrall Hospital of some 130 beds. Its name was derived from the father of the Mayo brothers, Dr. William Worrall Mayo.

But this was still not enough for John Kahler. Traveling in Europe, he encountered a number of combined hotel-hospital structures. Why not combine the Kahler Hotel in Rochester with hospital facilities. Done! There emerged a "triple-plan-Kahler," consisting of a 210-bed hospital, 3 operating rooms, a 150-bed convalescent unit, and a 220-room hotel, all under the same roof. Hospital beds in the Kahler Hotel were maintained until 1952.

So now Mayo had downtown hospital facilities to supplement those at Saint Marys, and located conveniently close to the Clinic buildings. At this time there was no Rochester Methodist Hospital. There were the Colonial, the Worrall, and the Kahler hospitals, with a total of nearly six hundred beds. These, plus the operating rooms and laboratories, were sufficiently ample, along with Saint Marys' more than eight hundred beds, to meet the needs of the 135,478 patients who came to the Mayo Clinic in 1947–sufficiently ample, that is, for an all-too-brief period.

CHAPTER 3

Research Advances

For years there was no specified research center or unit at the Clinic. Research occurred wherever there were patients to treat and young doctors to train. Laboratories primarily for diagnosis and therapy were located in multiple areas of the Clinic and hospitals. These provided such research facilities as were needed for the isolation of the thyroid hormone and cortisone, for rapid diagnosis of surgical tissue, for the first American blood bank, and for the development of the postanesthesia recovery room, to mention but a few of the notable research advances made.

But progress in research is limited unless there are facilities for laboratory experimentation on animals. There is no greater justification for this assertion than is found in the history of the discovery of the cause of diabetes in Germany and its control by insulin in Canada. Much of this work was done on dogs. As a conservative estimate, more than 100 million years of human life have been saved since the ultimate discovery of insulin in the late 1920s. All this we owe largely to experimentation on dogs.

At Mayo, where to keep such animals – dogs and cats and guinea pigs and rats and more? For a time there were animal quarters on the roof of one of the Clinic buildings. More were maintained in the basement of Saint Marys Hospital, and eventually some were housed in the barn on Dr. Louis B. Wilson's farm. Indecision arose, according to Helen Clapesattle:

> The development of independent research based on experimentation came . . . slowly because it was less urgent, and because Doctor Will was of two minds about it. Incidental investigations immediately related to some clinical or surgical problem he considered legitimate, but he could not decide how far beyond that the Rochester group ought to go. After all, they were engaged in the private practice of medicine; they were not an endowed or state institution.

But Drs. Henry Plummer and Louis Wilson forced on Dr. Will the recognition of the truth of their contentions that an experimental research program was essential to the vitality of the institution, that it would broaden the horizon of staff members, and that it would prevent the practice of medicine from being limited to existing knowledge. Dr. Wilson was director of the Clinic laboratories, devoted primarily to patient care and study. When he considered building a barn on his farm to keep experimental animals, he requested a Mayo gift of five hundred dollars for its erection. This request was granted.

Physiologist Frank C. Mann entered the scene. This tremendous leader in the Clinic's experimental research program was dedicated to medicine and surgery from childhood.

> By the time I was six years old I had determined to be a doctor, and with my broken-bladed pocket knife I attempted to dissect, before burying them, various parts of the fowl and animals that had died on our farm. In addition, my father taught me to assist him with the necessary obstetrical duties required by our registered sheep, and with other similar tasks having to do with farm animals.

During medical school at the University of Indiana, he worked in physiology, mainly at night and on weekends, for some two years. Here he assisted in laboratory work, taking courses and carrying on research. His first visit to Rochester, of one day's duration, followed a scientific meeting at the University of Minnesota, where he was impressed by a Mayo Clinic exhibit. He later sought and was appointed to a fellowship in surgery at the Clinic, with the understanding that he could carry on some research work in the Clinic's laboratory for experimental surgery and pathology.

Soon after Mann made his surgery application, Dr. Wilson telegraphed and offered him the position of chief of the laboratory in which he hoped to work. The stipend offered him looked big at the time, but "it currently would be little more than the monthly payments on an automobile." Mann commenced his Clinic appointment on April 10, 1914.

Eventually Dr. Charlie offered Mann space for experimental animals on his farm a few miles south of Rochester. There were some forty acres in a lovely little valley. New kennels for animals were built, and a veterinarian was provided to look after the animals. For some time the farm was used only for housing experimental animals, with the actual research procedures carried out in town. But Mann insisted that it would be better if there were research facilities at the farm where the animals were located. Dr. Will eventually acceded to Mann's insistence, and work on a new research laboratory was begun in 1922.

Unhappily, when this eighty thousand dollar structure was nearly completed, it was burned to the ground. Some claimed this was an act of opponents of animal experimentation, but this was never proven. At any rate, the building was reconstructed on Dr. Charlie's farm two years later. This was the Institute of Experimental Medicine of the Mayo Foundation. Here, under Mann's direction, research on animals was conducted for some two decades. Work was carried out in experimental medicine and surgery, physiology, pathology, biology, bacteriology, biochemistry, physics, and parasitology. Drs. Charles Code, Earl Wood, and Edward Lambert were among the chief investigators.

Mann was greatly assisted in this project by the veterinarian Dr. Carl F. Schlotthauer, who came to the institute about when it was completed. He tells us:

> On my first day in Rochester I received several calls. The most interesting one was a call late in the evening to go to Dr. Alfred Adson's farm . . . and deliver a calf. I found, however, that the cow had a torsion of the uterus which I was unable to correct, and that the calf could not be delivered naturally. Doctor Adson and I on the following day delivered the calf by cesarean section.

One of Schlotthauer's major responsibilities was to procure animals to be used in experimentation. This was no mean task in those days. He set up a system for procuring dogs locally, but he had to discourage anyone from bringing in a stray or stolen dog.

> We developed an affadavit form of sales slip for the purchase of dogs. On this slip is a description of each dog purchased, and its kennel number and also the address of the person bringing it to the Institute. Such a sales form was signed before a notary public by the person selling the dog. This record assured that we would always know the source of each dog in the kennels and that none would become lost in the pack. We never bought dogs from minors. This system of buying was very effective. We were able to obtain as many dogs as were needed, and we were not subjected to open criticism by persons or groups opposed to the use of dogs for medical research.

A large number of fellows of the Mayo Foundation were assigned regularly to the institute as assistants or to carry out independent research that would form the basis of a thesis for an advanced degree. In most instances such laboratory work was a supplement to the fellow's major training program in some clinical field.

In due time the institute became outdated, and its experimental functions were transferred to the new downtown Medical Sciences Building in the early 1950s. The institute building itself was eventually demolished. But the institute area remains functional as quarters for experimental animals. It still functions in this capacity as the Institute Hills Farm. This serves not only as a base for experimental animals but also for carrying out large-scale experiments. The animal quarters are abundant. Here have been kept baboons, pigs, cats, dogs, guinea pigs, rabbits, goats, horses, donkeys, cows, and even bears.

The Thyroid Hormone

One of the greatest of Mayo's many great names was Edward C. "Nick" Kendall. Kendall's reputation as a physiologist was well known to the author at the University of Chicago. And now he came to know the man himself and more about his work on ductless glands. Such endocrine glands transmit the chemicals or hormones they produce directly into the bloodstream instead of into ducts which carry the secretion products to the site of their work. The salivary glands send their digestive juices into the mouth. The hormones of the endocrine glands are carried by the blood to all areas of the body and may produce effects on body parts from head to toe.

This is the case with the thyroid hormone, whose main action is to regulate the rate at which all the body cells burn their fuel and perform their various functions. This hormone also governs the rate of growth in children, as well as their mental development.

The thyroid gland had been Kendall's primary interest when he first came to the Clinic in 1913. He had been working on this project elsewhere for some time. Until then, only one of the ductless glands had yielded the secret of its secretions to investigating biochemists. This was the medulla, or inner core, of the adrenal glands, lying above the kidneys. Its hormone, adrenaline, yielded its secrets to the investigations of Johns Hopkins pharmacologists way back in 1901.

The hormone adrenaline was relatively easy to extract from the adrenal glands of animals. To extract hormones from some of the other endocrine glands is much more complicated. For example, it took some thirty years to isolate insulin, the hormone of the pancreas, which prevents diabetes, a fatal of illness if untreated with the hormone.

For the thyroid hormone it took four years and four months of Kendall's time to isolate thyroxine, in 1914, in a form which could be used to treat patients whose thyroid glands functioned inadequately.

Since the thyroid hormone regulates the rate at which the body burns its fuel, it was necessary to devise some means of measuring the rate of this combustion. What is the normal rate of such burning of body fuel and how can we determine if the combustion rate is too slow or too rapid? Kendall suggested that the Clinic get Dr. Walter Boothby from Harvard to do just that. Boothby came and solved the problem.

Over a period of years he and his associates measured the rate of fuel combustion in thousands of people, including Clinic patients, nurses, Rochester citizens, or anyone else willing to submit to the measurements of the basal metabolism rates (BMR) as determined in the BMR machines. These machines determined standards for the normal rate of basal metabolism at all ages and what low levels or high levels of combustion of foods were abnormal. Boothby explained the process for laymen as follows:

> The ten-minute test is a collection of flue gases to see how much oxygen you are taking out of the air and how much carbon dioxide you are putting in. The air you expire is analyzed in terms of heat and compared to a normal standard. We have made the most extensive tests recorded anywhere to determine this normal standard.
>
> By measuring the expired air we find out whether, let us say, one, two or three Bunsen burners are working in your body. If it is one, your thyroid is functioning too little; if it is two, you are normal; and if three, your thyroid is overactive and you may have a goiter. Thyroid hormone causes food to burn rapidly. You may have too hot a fire and you burn out your boiler. If the fire is too slow you must be treated with thyroid hormone. If the fire is too rapid you probably need surgery, removing part of the overactive thyroid gland.

Regarding such treatment, Kendall recalls:

> Treatment of patients with the hormone of the thyroid gland in crystalline form produced astonishing results. Two outstanding cases concerned a girl ten years old and a woman in her fifties. The girl was 37 inches in height and weighed 37 pounds. Both somatic and mental growth were retarded. Her picture was taken, showing her infantile-looking face, while she was holding her doll. She received therapy with the thyroid hormone and was sent home for six months. She had grown four inches and had changed mentally into a bright, responsive person. At the end of a year she returned again. She had grown two more inches, and when her picture was taken in the dress she wore originally, the long sleeves came only to the elbow, and the hem was above the knees.

And there was another case:

> The woman had been sent to the Clinic by a judge in Illinois. She was accompanied by her sister and a nurse. She had been diagnosed as mentally incompetent. If this finding was confirmed by the Clinic and a hopeless prognosis given, the judge would assign her to an institution and divide her estate among her relatives. The patient was found to be suffering from myxedema (retarded thyroid gland function). Her skin was

> dry and scaly, her face was puffy, and she had a vacant, stupid expression. Administration of the thyroid hormone abated the edema, brought back her usual keenness of mind, and restored her to her former activities.
>
> These patients were presented at a meeting of the Clinic staff. They were dramatic and convincing evidence that biochemistry could be of practical use in clinical medicine.
>
> In 1916 I was asked to present a paper at the plenary session of the annual meeting of the Federation of American Societies for Experimental Biology, in New York City. It was a satisfaction to comply. The title of the paper was 'Isolation in Crystalline Form of the Iodine Containing Compound of the Thyroid Gland.' The chairman of the meeting was Dr. Simon Flexner.

This tremendous contribution to the health of mankind was as much deserving of a Nobel Prize as any medical discovery you might name. But apart from a Nobel Prize, the thyroxine achievement of Kendall did receive due recognition. During the 1964 Mayo centennial year the American Thyroid Association met in Rochester, holding a symposium to note the fiftieth anniversary of the isolation of thyroxine.

For the young institution which had given Kendall a home, the thyroxine achievement in 1914 added a new dimension to what was still essentially a surgical practice. The prestige of this event weighed heavily in favor of the establishment of the Mayo Clinic as we now know it. Magnificent though this achievement was, it was exceeded some decades later, this time actually resulting in a Nobel Prize being awarded to Kendall and his chief associate Dr. Philip Hench, for their isolation of cortisone.

Kendall's Cortisone

The magnificent scientific and medical contributions of Dr. Edward Kendall would in themselves have brought renown to the Mayo Clinic even were there no other research activities in the institution. Some years after his isolation of the hormone of the thyroid gland, he diverted his attention to the adrenal glands. Each of these paired structures, lying just above the kidneys, is really two glands. The interior portion, or medulla, secretes adrenaline. This hormone is most useful to the organism, but it is not essential for the maintenance of life. The outer covering layer of these glands, called the cortex, secretes into the blood hormones without which man and many other animals cannot survive.

Man's eyes began to be opened regarding the indispensability of the adrenal cortex by the British investigator Thomas Addison, working a full century before Kendall. He presented a paper entitled "On the Constitutional and Local Effects of Disease of the Suprarenal Capsules" (1855). In this paper he described what is now known as Addison's disease.

He described this fatal deficiency of adrenal cortex activity as causing a progressive anemia, bronze skin pigmentation, severe weakness, and low blood pressure. We know now that the adrenal hormone is related to a considerable number of other bodily activities, including the metabolism of food, kidney function, and the maintenance of proper balance in the concentration of the salts of sodium and potassium in the blood. We know, as did Addison, that untreated adrenal cortical deficiency has a mortality of one hundred percent.

During the following decades, innumerable investigators in many lands sought means of controlling Addison's disease. Experimental work on dogs was widespread. Removal of the adrenal glands of dogs produced the disease, with death in a few days. Researchers sought means of prolonging life in such animals mainly by injecting various chemical extracts of adrenal cortex tissue.

How little the average American knows of these lifesaving endeavors in contrast to his extensive knowledge of man's life-expending activities during this century: the Vietnam War, the Spanish-American War, and World Wars I and II!

In the early 1930s considerable progress was made in prolonging the lives of animals surgically deprived of their adrenal glands. Various products of unknown nature were extracted from the adrenal gland cortex and administered to experimental animals deprived previously of their adrenal glands. Success eventuated. Such extracts also prolonged the lives of human beings suffering from Addison's disease. But no one knew the chemical nature of these effective gland extracts until Kendall's work.

Throughout these efforts, Kendall functioned primarily as a chemist. Testing his findings was the responsibility of Dr. Philip Hench, assisted by a number of others, including Dr. Randall Sprague. Some five or six years after Kendall commenced this work, he and his colleagues isolated what proved to be the vital hormone called cortisone and determined its chemical composition.

For use during his work it was stated that "Doctor Kendall holds some kind of record for securing adrenal glands (of animals), for he has used tons of them in his experiments—and it is only one of the most heartening facts in the story of the Clinic that the Mayos and their successors have been willing to support such studies financially."

Success in the isolation of the hormone cortisone came in the 1940s. Now Addison's disease is controlled by the administration of Kendall's purified product. Initially cortisone had to be injected into patients. Somewhat later effective preparations were devised which could be taken by mouth, with lifesaving results. This may be contrasted with insulin, the lack of which hormone from the pancreas produces often fatal diabetes. There is yet no antidiabetes product which can be taken effectively by mouth, except in very mild cases of diabetes. Throughout his lifetime, a diabetic may inject himself with insulin tens of thousands of times.

There will be more to tell later about Kendall and Hench and their award of the Nobel Prize for the isolation and analysis of cortisone.

Surgical Tissue Diagnosis

A surgeon has opened the abdomen of an anesthetized patient. He exposes the tumor that had been revealed in previous x-ray studies. How shall he proceed properly with the operation? This immediate problem can be solved only by having answers to such questions as these: Is this tumor really cancer, or is it benign? Is it some kind of infection? What is it?

Until such questions could be answered, proper surgical procedures could not continue. Truly enough, the very appearance and feel of the tumor frequently supplied the answers. But all too often only a microscopic examination of the tumor could tell the surgeon how he should proceed. Unfortunately such microscopic studies as were available at the turn of the century might take hours or even days. In the meantime, here was the patient undergoing surgery.

All this was unsatisfactory, especially to Dr. Will Mayo, expert as he was in diagnosis. "Before proceeding properly with my surgery I want to know the microscopic appearance of this tumor." So he prodded the Clinic's recently acquired pathologist Dr. Louis B. Wilson: "I wish you would find a way to tell us surgeons whether a growth is cancer or not while the patient is still on the operating table."

The chief difficulty was to prepare and harden a piece of soft tissue removed by the surgeon so that it could be cut into slices thin enough for microscopic examination. Available chemical techniques for this took far too much time. Freezing of tissue to permit cutting thin slices had been tried elsewhere, as a substitute for chemical methods, without much success. Wilson invaded this challenging area, accompanied by Dr. William C. MacCarty, another surgical pathologist. Rapid freezing of tissues was not too difficult, but proper staining to facilitate accurate observation of the tissue slides was a problem that they sought to solve. This took weeks and weeks of study, using many animal and human body studies.

By 1905 the technique was so well ordered that it took only five minutes and sometimes less to report the pathology of the tumor sample, while the patient still lay on the operating table. Dr. Will pronounced enthusiastically:

> The quick examination of sections of living tissue . . . enables the microscope to guide the surgeon's knife for the benefit of the patient in a manner as fundamentally different from the examination of mummified dead tissue, several days after the operation, as the work of the operating surgeon differs from the anatomist's dissection of the cadaver.

Some years later MacCarty, reviewing nearly fifty thousand cases of surgery, found that about eighteen percent of these required microscopic diagnosis. It was stated:

> The examination of fresh tissues during the progress of the operation is of almost as great value for the information it gives the surgeon concerning the nature of inflammatory processes, especially in tuberculosis, as it is in relation to malignant cancer processes. In either case it is indispensable to the surgeon who would give the best possible service to the patient.

The rapid freezing of a bit of tissue removed by the surgeon was done in a specially designed chamber in which there was also a device for cutting tissue slices thin enough for microscopic examination after staining. The slide was passed into an adjacent room, where a diagnosis was made by one competent in surgical pathology. This microscopic diagnosis was transmitted by a speaker system to the operating surgeon, who then proceeded to do what was indicated by the diagnosis: remove the benign tumor or extend the surgery further as indicated for a malignant tumor.

The laboratory for such tissue diagnosis was so located that it was readily available to surgeons in several nearby operating rooms. And from the time the surgeon removed the tissue sample until the pathologist told him the diagnosis, no more than three to five minutes had passed.

Revolutionary though this procedure was, it had a significant drawback. It required the attendance of a staff pathologist adjacent to the operating room, removing him from his pathology laboratory where the work load was demanding. Wilson sought assistance in the person of Dr. William C. MacCarty to help overcome this obstacle.

Eventually there was developed a procedure involving the use of closed-circuit television. This necessitated the presence in the operating room of only a technician. The television camera was set up in the operating room, suspended above the patient. When the surgeon exposed the tumor, a picture was transmitted to the pathologist away in his own laboratory. From this alone he might well be able to tell a good deal about the nature of the tumor. He could also advise the surgeon by wire just where to take a sample from the tumor for making a microscopic study. This sample was quickly frozen, sliced thin, and stained. Again the television camera came into play, transmitting the microscopic picture to the pathologist, who could then make an accurate diagnosis. Informed of this via a loudspeaker telephone, the surgeon could then proceed with the operation. Only a few minutes elapsed between the time of the surgeon's exposure of the tumor and the pathologist's diagnosis.

Eventually the use of this ingenious and valuable device was discontinued. This was primarily due to the multiplicity of operating rooms that came into being, which would necessitate installation of too many such machines. The procedure was replaced by the operating surgeon sending tumor samples to a nearby laboratory. Here a competent pathologist had sufficient work to remain permanently busy. He was not called to the surgery area away from his main laboratory; his main laboratory was adjacent to surgical operating rooms. Frozen sections and microscopic slides were rapidly made, and the pathologist reported his opinions to the operating surgeon by a loudspeaker system.

A bit more about Wilson and MacCarty. When the University of Minnesota and Mayo Clinic liaison was established, Dr. Wilson became the first director of the Mayo Foundation for Medical Education and Research. MacCarty collaborated with Dr. John Lundy in the establishment of America's first blood bank. The MacCarty name is distinct in Mayo history because of William's tremendous contributions to the field of fresh tissue diagnosis during surgery. In addition, this is the only Clinic family (even to 1980) in which father, son, and grandson successively became members of the Mayo Clinic permanent staff: William C. in surgical pathology, Collin S. in neurosurgery, and Robert L. in diagnostic radiology.

Anesthesia

The control of pain in surgical operations has been a pressing problem for centuries. Sir Francis Bacon, more than three centuries ago, opined, "I esteem the office of physician not only to restore health, but to mitigate pain and dolors." The author once ventured to write about pain in one of his *Buenos Aires Herald* columns, under the title "Pain is Good." It is not pleasant, but it often serves the purpose of indicating where correctable trouble may lie in the body.

Merely to list all the pain relievers, perhaps commencing with the use of alcohol centuries ago, would be something of an undertaking. Some of these were pressure on nerves or blood vessels, nitrous oxide, chloroform, opium, and curare. These might be administered by local injections, breathing, spinal or intravenous injections, or rectal infusions. Although ether anesthesia was first described by Valerius Cordus in 1540, it was not effectively used for many decades.

Naturally an institution like the Mayo Clinic had to be particularly versed in the multiple problems of anesthesia. The leading figure here was Dr. John Lundy, whom Dr. Will met at a Seattle medical meeting in 1923. Dr. Will was impressed by Lundy's belief in the possibilities of progress in this field and invited him to come to Rochester as head of anesthesiology. He came.

Lundy was particularly interested in the matter of inducing surgical anesthesia by intravenous injections. Such anesthesia was particularly desirable when the surgeon employed cautery or diathermy, during which the heat might cause ether fumes to explode. Increased use of the method was retarded by the lack of suitable anesthetic agents. In a few years and with much labor, Lundy developed the safe and effective use of various barbiturate derivatives for intravenous anesthesia. By 1941 the barbiturate sodium thiopental was used on nearly thirty-two thousand Mayo surgical patients.

Lundy also worked extensively on inducing anesthesia in limited areas of the body without affecting regions not involved in the patient's problem and without total unconsciousness. Among a number of such projects was his extensive development of spinal anesthesia by injections into the spinal canal. This was especially useful in surgical operations carried out in areas in the lower half of the body. He also devised relatively simple machinery to measure and reveal at once to the operating surgeon the patient's heart rate and blood pressure, thus eliminating the necessity for assistants to repeatedly make such measurements directly on the patient.

Lundy was never in active military service, but he contributed to that effort by more than his discoveries. Groups of medics were sent to Mayo by the military to be trained in anesthesiology by Lundy. His talents and industry in teaching not only army officers but Mayo Foundation fellows as well were as tremendous as his many other accomplishments.

In the course of his regular responsibilities, he would pass from one surgery room to another to see how things were progressing. By some extrasensory perception, on entering an operating room, he would know at once if there were troublesome developments, without inquiring or having the difficulty narrated.

America's First Blood Bank

The loss of blood in accidents and fighting of all kinds, including war, goes back in history to the origin of man. Attempts to replace the loss were usually unsuccessful until the present century. Blood loss was not the only stimulus to attempt transfusions of blood from one person to another. There were instances in which blood from a child was injected into an aged person with a view to retarding the aging process or even restoring youthfulness. On one such occasion it was stated that the old man became ill, the child died, and the "physician" fled. Then there is the account of the police arresting a medicine peddler selling eternal youth pills derived from blood. And behold, he was one of those repeat offenders—a man had been arrested for the same offense in 1780, 1845, and 1912.

All too frequently in transfusions the blood (actually the liquid plasma) of the donor giving the blood would destroy the red blood cells of the recipient, or the reverse: the recipient's plasma would destroy the red cells of the blood injected into his veins, usually with serious or even fatal consequences.

At the turn of the century, Karl Landsteiner, Nobel laureate, showed how transfusions could safely be made. Following much investigation, it was demonstrated that for transfusion purposes, one's blood might lie in one of four categories, which were called blood groups or types. It was shown, for a potential recipient in one of these groups, in just what blood group the donor's blood must be for a safe transfusion. In every transfusion the recipient's blood group and the donor's blood group must be determined.

Here again we encounter Dr. John Lundy. He was in charge of these blood group determinations and of blood transfusions at Saint Marys Hospital. Lundy kept a list of potential donors in each group, or tested blood donors at the time the transfusion was to be done. In any case, the donor had to be present at the time of transfusion. His blood was drawn and immediately injected into the patient.

For some decades after Landsteiner's blood grouping work, there was no storage of blood to be used for transfusions. Enter Lundy. He had an idea. Although this idea was to become of tremendous importance in the future care of patients, it was first voiced with no more fanfare than a casual "good morning" to Dr. W. C. MacCarty, head of surgical pathology. Lundy said, "Mac, may I store some blood in your laboratory refrigerator?" This blood had been treated to prevent clotting and placed in a bottle with its blood group number written on the label. And so in 1935 the first blood bank, at least in North America, was established in Saint Marys Hospital in Rochester. The Cook County Hospital in Chicago began such a service a year later. Today every hospital deserving the name has a blood bank. There is no need now to have the donor at the patient's bedside. Just get the proper bottle from the blood bank and transfuse.

Very soon after 1935, only about twenty percent of blood transfusions were made with fresh blood drawn from a donor at the time of the procedure. About eighty percent of some six thousand transfusions in 1947 were made with blood from Lundy's blood bank. In due time the complexities and improvements of blood banking were greatly multiplied.

The Postanesthesia Recovery Room (PAR)

The postanesthesia recovery room is a hospital ward located near surgical operating rooms and accommodating about a dozen patients. Immediately following surgery, patients are taken to the PAR instead of being returned to their own private or semiprivate rooms, which might be scattered over a large area of the hospital. Only after the patient has fully recovered from anesthesia does he return to his regular hospital bed.

The advantages of the PAR are numerous, and they are of utmost importance. These rooms save lives, and time and money. Trained personnel are immediately available to each and every patient still unconscious encountering trouble, whether it be from hemorrhage, vomiting, respiratory obstruction, or shock, which often occurs soon after rather than during an operation. Furthermore, in such rooms there is at hand all the needed facilities to cope with the problems: intravenous apparatus, suction devices, oxygen tanks, blood for transfusion, drugs, and whatever. By contrast, a patient sent to a more or less distant room in a hospital lacks the readiness of such personnel and facilities.

And who started all this? Again it was Dr. John S. Lundy, chief of anesthesiology at Mayo. Two stimuli prodded him, both related to World War II. An army hospital he visited in 1941 had such a ward for postoperative care, concentrating in one place patients who after surgery might need catheterization, change of dressings, intravenous injections, and other special nursing or medical care. At Mayo, as elsewhere in this wartime, there was a serious nurse shortage, so it was impossible to provide adequate care for postoperative patients if they were distributed throughout the hospital.

On March 17, 1942, the first patient was taken to the newly established PAR at Saint Marys Hospital, the first of its kind in civilian hospitals of this country. Born, as this procedure was, of wartime emergency, it has remained a standard peacetime practice to this day, not only in Rochester but in all well-run hospitals of the country.

Here we have but one of several examples that might be mentioned in which a wartime emergency situation contributed a significant advance in the care of patients and the saving of life, time, and money. According to Dr. Lundy, "The value of having such a place to send anesthetized patients until they are awake now is very important owing to the scarcity of nurses and hospital personnel. This, in addition to the better care that the patient receives in the PAR makes it one of the most valuable facilities in the hospital."

Tuberculosis

Tuberculosis of the lungs has been a scourge of mankind throughout history. Effective treatment of this infection is relatively recent, thanks a good deal to Mayo. Not long ago the best treatment available consisted of a good diet and complete bed rest. The story today is the bright light of day contrasted with the past's black night. Much of this may be attributed to the Mayo Clinic's Drs. William Feldman, H. Corwin Hinshaw, Frank C. Mann, and O. T. Clagett.

Dr. Clagett and colleagues attacked the problem surgically. They worked at the Mineral Springs Tuberculosis Sanitarium, not far from Rochester. Their aim was to collapse affected areas of the lungs by removing ribs. Jim describes his first operation:

> We resected the first three ribs and closed the incision. Ten days later . . . we reopened the wound and removed the next three ribs. Fortunately we had a beautiful result. The removal of the first six ribs collapsed the pulmonary cavity and the patient made a rapid recovery, his sputum turned negative (i.e. there were no tuberculosis germs) and in a few months he was able to return to his family and occupation.

Clagett continued this successful procedure for many years. And then came chemical treatment to kill the invading bacilli. A scientist at Rutgers University, Dr. Selman Waksman, had discovered and isolated a germ-destroying chemical which he called streptomycin. But he had inadequate facilities available for studying the drug, so he sent some of it to his Mayo friend Dr. Feldman, who had become interested in possible drugs that might be effective in combating tuberculosis. The Mayo team worked on guinea pigs, which are particularly susceptible to injected tubercle bacilli. Such artificially infected animals invariably die if untreated.

In a number of experiments they infected a group of guinea pigs with the bacilli. Half of these were untreated and half were given injections of streptomycin over a period of time. The results were all that an investigator might pray for. Dr. Feldman stated:

> Tuberculous disease in untreated animals was widely disseminated and in most instances destructive. Among the animals that had received streptomycin the reverse was true, evidence of the disease being absent or barely detectable.

But what about tubercular human beings? Why not try? A twenty-one-year-old tubercular girl at nearby Cannon Falls, and later in Rochester, was selected as the first human being to be injected with this drug in November of 1944. According to Dr. Clagett, who collaborated in the case:

> The disease spread quite rapidly and it became apparent that this young girl would die of tuberculosis unless her disease could be brought under control. No human being had ever been treated with streptomycin. We didn't know what the dosage should be or what toxic effects there might be. We did know that streptomycin could cure tuberculosis in guinea pigs and that the girl would die if we didn't do something. Nowadays the Federal Drug Administration would not allow a human being to be treated with a drug so little was known about. However, we didn't have so much regulation in those days and were desperate to help this young patient. Treatment with streptomycin was begun. The patient began to improve in a few days. Treatment was continued for six weeks. The dosage and length of treatment were matters of pure guess. The patient completely recovered and has remained alive and well.

At that time there were literally millions of people throughout the world who were afflicted with tuberculosis, urgently needing treatment to avoid death. Today the disease has been practically eliminated as a real problem from most parts of the world, thanks to streptomycin and a number of other antituberculosis drugs. Thanks to streptomycin, yes. But profound thanks more particularly to Feldman, Hinshaw, Clagett, and Mann.

It must be added that there are other factors involved in the decline of this disease. Among these, according to Dr. David Carr, are "better housing, better nutrition, isolation of patients who might spread the disease to others, and elimination of the more susceptible people by Darwin's law of the survival of the fittest."

CHAPTER 4

World War II Participation

Active Military Duty

The efforts of the Mayo Clinic during World War II extended well beyond providing multitudes of individual physicians to become medical officers. Considerable research was carried out in the field of aviation medicine to assist fighter pilots. And there was also the military medical Mayo unit organized by Mayo's Dr. Charles W. Mayo, better known as Chuck.

On the morning of Pearl Harbor, Dr. Mayo was at a medical meeting in St. Paul. He tells us, "I have an imperishable recollection of the moment when I heard the news; for me it came from the hoarse cry of a newsboy selling papers on the street. I remember thinking, 'I'm 43, that's still young enough to go.' "

But merely thinking that he might go was entirely insufficient for Dr. Mayo. The Clinic should do more than simply release staff members for military duty. "The best plan, it seemed to me, was to recruit an entire staff of nurses and doctors at the Clinic and present ourselves as a package to the Armed Forces."

He returned to Rochester and commenced at once on this voluntary enlistment program. The idea was enthusiastically approved and gratefully accepted by the armed forces. It became known as the Mayo unit. Actively associated with Dr. Mayo in this enterprise was the surgeon Dr. James T. Priestly. Extensive conferences in Washington resulted in the

Mayo unit being activated and posted at a staging area in Charleston, South Carolina. Mayo, as a lieutenant colonel, was named director of the unit. Initially, there were sixty-five doctors and seventy-five nurses from the Clinic. These numbers required supplements of many other doctors, nurses, and technicians, all to be properly trained. The project required many months.

When the total organization and military training were complete, they were moved off to the front, nearly two years after Pearl Harbor. What front? They had no idea, but presumed it might be the European theater. But no. They were sent to San Francisco, shipped across the Pacific Ocean, and ultimately found themselves in New Guinea. The Mayo unit, often called there the Mayo Clinic, was organized into two units. One, under now Major Mayo, functioned at Nadzab, and the other, under Dr. Priestly, worked at Finschhafen, both toward the eastern end of New Guinea. This region was a hot spot in Japan's ravaging warfare—largely by air. Some time after General MacArthur fulfilled his promise to return to the Philippines, the units also moved there, where they functioned for the remainder of the war.

In the European theater there was no Mayo unit, but there were numerous Mayo physicians. A number of them were on hand at the time of D-Day, announced in a June 6, 1944, news flash: "Under the command of General Eisenhower, allied naval forces, supported by strong air forces, began landing allied armies this morning on the coast of France."

On this day, the Clinic's Dr. Howard Andersen had a particularly exciting but dangerous time aboard the United States destroyer *Corry*, which escorted airplane carriers and hunted submarines. Andersen's only major surgery at sea was on a rescued enemy submarine commander. H-Hour of D-Day designated the planned frontal attack from the sea, hours after paratroopers had been landed in France. H-Hour for the *Corry* and for Andersen was 6:30 A.M., Tuesday, June 6, 1944. But Andersen beat this deadline by one hour. At 5:30 A.M. he was dressing a shoulder wound amidships. There was an explosion of either shells or a mine, which ripped the *Corry* almost in two, practically blowing it out of the water. Andersen was hurled the width of the ship, but he fetched up bruised but whole. He worked on the fractures and burns of the wounded, who were then packed into one life boat and one life raft. The medical team and the captain walked off the deck of the sinking ship into chilling fifty-degree water. Still under fire, beaten by the surf, turning blue with cold, most of them were in the water over two hours before being picked up. About a day later, what remained of the *Corry*'s crew, including Andersen, were back in England. Eventually he was awarded a Bronze

Star for his work on D-Day. At war's end, he returned alive and well to his Clinic post in the section of thoracic diseases.

Even back in Rochester the war efforts were in force. The Army Medical Corps selected the Mayo Clinic as a training center for newly recruited medical officers in a number of medical and surgical fields. The army sent groups of eight or ten surgeons to Rochester every three months. Dr. Clagett, active in the field of thoracic surgery training, stated:

> Obviously, the Mayo Clinic could not provide much experience or training in the field of thoracic trauma that these surgeons might encounter in military service, but we did do our best to organize a series of lectures and seminars on all aspects of thoracic surgical problems and their management. In addition to these lectures and seminars, the services of the Clinic library were available and the men assigned to us were given lists of selected articles on thoracic trauma to study. They also observed surgery and made postoperative rounds. All of the young surgeons assigned to us had good training in general surgery previously and were very receptive to our efforts to teach them what we could about thoracic surgery.

The author was too young for active military duty in World War I and too old during World War II. He could not serve in the military medical services because he was never licensed to practice medicine. This he never needed in his activities of teaching, research, and administration. But he did aid the armed forces. He was consultant to each of the three surgeons general of army, navy, and air force. His function was to assist in recruitment and training of medical officers, and he holds valued certificates from the three services attesting to this assistance to them.

And besides all its war-related efforts, the Clinic had its civilian practice to maintain. More than one hundred thousand patients came to Rochester in each of the war years, or about three hundred per working day. This was more than in any prewar year. With its great reduction in staff members, this imposed a tremendous burden on Clinic physicians, as the surgeon Dr. Clagett recalls:

> I believe my longest surgical list in one day was 23 major operations. Lists of 15 to 20 operations daily were almost routine. I remember one day I had a list of 19 operations. A visitor in the gallery spoke to me in the course of the day and said, "I am the medical officer who examined you at Fort Snelling and turned you down as unfit for active military service. I think I made a hell of a mistake." I can remember times when I had as many as 90 patients on my surgical service at St. Marys and another 40 at Colonial Hospital the same time. The postoperative rounds, dressing wounds, administering fluids, writing orders for postoperative care and all the other details involved a tremendous task for all those involved.

After V-E Day (May 8, 1945) the Clinic's war efforts intensified against

Japan, and the Mayo unit in the Philippines worked harder than ever—until the end. Dr. E. S. Judd, son of one of the first surgical associates of the brothers Mayo, was with the unit. He recalls hearing a radio message from the Philippines to Japan, advising the government to withdraw people from certain specific areas, because those regions would soon be completely devastated by a tremendously destructive new weapon in our possession. The actual time for this attack was even announced. The Japanese paid no attention.

At 8:15 A.M. on August 6, 1945, the first atom bomb was dropped on Hiroshima, Japan's seventh largest city. This destroyed everything within a radius of a mile and a half, with some seventy-one thousand immediate fatalities. Just three days later the event recurred in Nagasaki, a city somewhat larger than Hiroshima, with an even greater death toll and a destruction of some half of the city.

How well the Pope may have called this an inhuman engine of destruction and banned its use. A Pope did say just this, but not of the atom bomb. His statement referred to the newly introduced weapon known as the crossbow and was uttered in the twelfth century.

The author recalls how close, but uninformed, a neighbor he was to Enrico Fermi during his first successful chain reaction at the University of Chicago, giving birth to the atom bomb. V-J Day, the complete surrender of Japan, came less than a month after the Hiroshima bombing.

Aviation Research

Early in the war, a number of Clinic scientists became interested in the effects of acceleration in relation to aviation. The air force was also intensely interested, since pilot blackouts—loss of vision or even loss of consciousness—would occur if a plane took too sharp a banked turn. Again this threatened when a pilot, after dropping a bomb, would pull out rapidly from his dive, suddenly directing his plane upward.

Originally, Mayo physicians and researchers were interested in the environmental physiology of air travel under peacetime conditions. Then, as war intervened, American fighter pilots found that their German counterparts were able to fly higher and could better withstand the rapid acceleration of banked curves and dive-bombing pullouts. If our pilots were to compete successfully, new protective devices were needed most urgently. Mainly with government support, a Mayo building was constructed in the early 1940s at the site of the present Medical Sciences Building. This building was named the Acceleration Laboratory of the Mayo Aero-Medical Unit.

In this unit there was a high-altitude chamber to simulate conditions in planes flying thousands of feet above the earth's surface. Here labored Drs. Walter Boothby, Randolph Lovelace, and Arthur Bulbulian, and others. More spectacular was the human centrifuge, more appropriately christened the Big Wheel, to serve the studies primarily of Drs. Earl Wood, Edward Lambert, and Charles Code. The motivation for all this effort was well stated by Dr. Code:

> I think there was a prominent desire on the part of the Mayo Institution to play a role in the war effort of World War II. There was a tremendous feeling of loyalty to our country at the time; a tremendous feeling that we were right, and a tremendous feeling that our enemy, composed of Hitler and Mussolini, were affronts to civilized man that they should be done away with.

For many years, Walter Boothby had been interested in man's use of oxygen, including that of an aviator at high altitudes, where getting adequate oxygen was a problem. With his colleagues, working in the high-altitude chamber, he eventually (in 1939) developed a pilot's mask solving the problem of getting adequate oxygen to a pilot. This became known as the BLB mask, from the names of Boothby, Lovelace, and Bulbulian. Air force pilots used this mask on military missions. It was also extremely useful in the management of civilian hospital patients needing oxygen therapy.

The Big Wheel

Mayo's Big Wheel, or human centrifuge, was the first of its kind in the nation. Its construction resembled two opposing spokes of a wheel rather than an entire wheel. The subject under study sat at the outer end of one spoke, which was about eighteen feet from the center, or hub, of the wheel. Rapid rotation of the machinery exerted pressure on the subject, pushing away from the center not only the entire body, but the inner contents of the body as well. This was just like the action of gravity, but multiplied a few times by the centrifugal force of rapid rotation.

Much of the interior of the body consists of relatively soft tissue whose shape might be altered by such multiplication of gravity. But it is the liquid blood which can be most easily moved or otherwise affected by gravity or centrifugal force. So the studies dealt mainly with what happens to the body's blood and its circulation.

When the subject's head was in a position oriented toward the axle of the rotating wheel, with feet away from it, the blood content of the abdomen and legs and its circulation there increased. And the flow of blood was decreased to the upper parts of the body, including the brain. These arrangements and motions duplicated what happens in a pilot's body and bloodstream when he turns or banks sharply or rapidly pulls upward after dive-bombing. In effect, the rotation of the wheel multiplies gravity by two, three, four, or more times, exactly as a pullout does. In either case, the reduced blood supply to the retina of the eye causes loss of vision or blackout. The inadequate blood supply to the brain causes complete unconsciousness.

What might be done about this?

The position of the pilot in a plane or the subject in the centrifuge can reduce or negate the danger. The Clinic investigators stated:

> Changes in the position of the pilot can be used to shorten the distance between the various parts of the body. In the prone or supine position, the vertical distance between heart and brain is zero and centrifugal force does not reduce the arterial pressure at head level. In this position man can withstand maintained forces in excess of 12 times gravity without occurrence of unusual symptoms. The practical difficulties flying a plane in the prone or supine position are numerous, although many have been overcome by mechanical aids.
>
> The possibility has been investigated of accomplishing partial reduction of the hydrostatic distance between head and heart by having the pilot's seat tilted backward at an angle of 45° to 60°. This was found to be an effective means of increasing gravity tolerance, but was not found practical in conventional aircraft. On the other hand, pilots are able to accomplish some reduction in heart/brain distance by crouching forward in their seats. This procedure was used extensively by German pilots. While all these postures effectively increase tolerance, the necessity for the pilot to assume an abnormal position to avoid blacking out restricts his activity in the cockpit and, as a rule, decreases his efficiency in combat.

What else, besides the pilot's posture, might be done to avoid blackouts during rapid turns or rapid ascents after dive-bombing? There were numerous attempts to solve the problem with antiblackout suits, constructed so as to diminish the pooling of blood in the abdominal blood vessels and swelling the veins of the legs with blood. Such studies were carried out under United States Navy auspices for some years even before the war. A number of such suits were developed. All the suits were tested early in the war, some in combat, and were found to provide protection against blackout; but because they were complex, cumbersome, and uncomfortable, they were not generally accepted by pilots. They did, however, demonstrate the desirability of providing antiblackout protection for pilots and thus stimulated further development of suits.

Eventually the problem was solved by the Mayo physiologists Earl Wood, Edward Lambert, Edward Baldes, and Charles Code, employing the Big Wheel in their investigations. They eventually designed a suit which was not only antiblackout, but was immediately accepted by fighter pilots. The suit, properly inflated, provided proper pressure on the calf and thigh of each leg as well as on the abdomen. Combat reports gave conclusive proof that these suits offered American pilots a definite margin of superiority over Germans and Japanese alike.

For this work, and for further productive studies of similar problems carried on after the war, the Aero-Medical Aswsociation granted Dr. Lambert the first Arnold D. Tuttle Award for "distinguished service in aviation medicine," and Dr. Wood was named to the lifetime post of career investigator by the American Heart Association. This career provided financial support throughout his professional life.

CHAPTER 5

Appointment Accepted

All of that which has been recounted took place at the Mayo Clinic before the author first visited the great institution. He studied and pondered all this while considering the Clinic's offer to make him director of the Mayo Foundation for Medical Education and Research. He eventually accepted the great challenge, with the concurrence of his wife, Dr. Adelaide. He began spending part of the time in Rochester and part in Chicago with Dr. Donald Anderson, who had been selected to replace him at the AMA post as secretary of the Council on Medical Education and Hospitals. This was in the year 1947.

One of the author's last tasks in his AMA position was to participate in its television Health Education Program.

> I was to discuss the pumping of blood by the heart. I had a very small instrument which when held on the chest over the heart of my subject, transmitted to viewers the sounds of the beating heart. In those early days of television the walls and ceiling of the room were fairly covered with bright lights. These were not only bright, but hot. Discussing my upcoming telecast with the TV operator in this sweltering environment, he looked at my small instrument for picking up heart sounds.
>
> "I don't know just what this is," he said, "but you better keep it well covered in your hand. Some of its delicate parts might be injured by the heat from these lights. The temperature in the room may rise to more than 125°!"

For this enterprise the author was awarded a certificate "in grateful appreciation for constructive and friendly cooperation in the Health Education Program of the American Medical Association. . . ."

Regarding the move from Chicago to Rochester, the author recalls,

> During the period of terminating my work with the AMA in Chicago and introducing myself to the complexities of the Mayo Clinic and the Mayo Foundation, my wife Adelaide was also arranging for the move to Rochester. She had done very well in psychiatry over the years since we took our physiology Ph.D. degrees together and later finished medical school. While taking her psychiatry residency under Dr. Adolph Meyer, at Henry Phipps Institute in Baltimore, she was an instructor in psychiatry at Johns Hopkins Medical School. Back in Chicago, while pursuing psychoanalytic studies and investigations, she was at various times psychiatrist on the faculty of Chicago's Institute for Juvenile Research, assistant professor of criminology at the University of Illinois Medical School, lecturer in psychiatry at the University of Chicago, consultant psychiatrist of Chicago's United Charities, staff member of the Institute for Psychoanalysis, and advisor to the United Charities of Chicago.
>
> The demands upon her contributions to psychiatry involved considerable travel also. She functioned for a time as lecturer in psychodynamics at the University of Nebraska. She was lecturer in psychiatry at Smith College School of Social Work in Northampton, Massachusetts, and served as a trustee of her alma mater, Rockford College, which awarded her an honorary Doctor of Science degree in 1947. What excited us most about this occasion was that at the same convocation, the honorary Doctor of Laws degree was awarded to none other than Enrico Fermi, of atomic bomb fame. I informed him that when he was carrying on research in his laboratory—really a handball court at Stagg football field—I was working nearby in physiology at the University of Chicago. At that time I was in complete ignorance not only of what he was doing, but even of his very existence.
>
> Coming to Rochester, Adelaide was immediately taken on the psychiatry staff, with a University of Minnesota faculty appointment in the Mayo Foundation as associate professor. I believe she and I were the first wife and husband physicians to achieve appointment on the Mayo Clinic permanent staff.

Psychiatry was then rather new in Rochester, founded in the late 1940s by Dr. Frank Braceland. The need for such a service was generally recognized. None other than internist Dr. Rynearson once stated that "all physicians will agree that at least 50%—or do I hear 90%—of our patients are in our waiting rooms because of what life has done to them, rather than because of organic disease. . . . The physician can't send all of these to a psychiatrist for consultation; there are too many patients and far too few psychiatrists."

And so the Johnsons both became part of the Mayo Clinic and Mayo Foundation and University of Minnesota.

Part II.

The Mayo Clinic Grows

This section records the major Clinic developments during the two decades (1947–1966) when the author functioned first as director of the Mayo Foundation for Medical Education and Research and later as director of the Mayo Graduate School of Medicine. During this period there were tremendous advances in patient care, medical education, and scientific investigation.

Important events and developments were open-heart surgery, kidney transplants, the Nobel Prize, the Mayo and Harwick buildings, and so very much more, terminating in the celebration of the Mayo Centennial year in 1964.

CHAPTER 6

Graduate Training of Physicians

When Dr. Donald Balfour concluded his directorship of the Mayo Foundation for Medical Education and Research in 1947, there were 551 fellows in training, many of whom were just retired from military service. Mayo was engaged in training more residents to become medical specialists than any other institution in the entire world. To train these graduate medical students, there was less than half that number of permanent Clinic staff members. This staff, with some 2,000 paramedical and other employees, had the major responsibility for caring for the 135,478 patients who came to the Clinic that year. Additionally, there were some 600 nurses and other employees at Saint Marys, Worrall, and Colonial hospitals. Altogether, then, there were about 3,400 people who cared for forty times that number of patients. And where did all this occur? In New York? Chicago? London? Paris? No. It all transpired in a small community with a permanent population of less than thirty thousand–Rochester, Minnesota.

Mayo Foundation Fellowships

Exactly what is a Mayo Foundation fellow? A good definition is,

> A fellow who sees patients is a young physician who is a medical school graduate, has served an internship, is licensed to practice medicine, and is in advanced training to become a specialist. He has been selected from

> many who compete for appointments as fellows of the Mayo Foundation, because of his superior professional and personal qualifications. He comes to Rochester as a competent physician. He leaves a qualified specialist. In most other training institutions he was called a "resident."
>
> His three or more years of fellowship training, under the supervision of the Mayo Clinic staff and the Mayo Foundation faculty is nationally recognized as meeting the educational requirements of the various American Boards, which certify as to competence of physicians to practice a specialty of medicine. Mayo fellows are the cream of the crop of young physicians from the medical schools of this country and from the best medical schools abroad.

Evaluation of the potential of an applicant for training at Mayo was made with intensive care. It was felt that the best single objective measure of an appointee's promise was probably his class standing in medical school. About one fourth of the appointees were members of Alpha Omega Alpha, or AOA, the medical school honor society to which only the very top medical students were elected. Nearly two thirds of the new fellows ranked in the upper third of the medical school class.

The Clinic regularly made appointments to applicants from virtually every medical school of this country, as well as from the best medical schools abroad and in Canada. In 1955 only seven medical schools in the United States had no representatives on the fellowship roster. Each year more than 2,000 young medical school graduates inquired about appointments. Preliminary screening reduced this number to about 600, who were invited to submit applications. Of these, some 150 were selected annually.

The training program was primarily clinical, in an outpatient section seeing new patients, at the hospital bedside, in the surgical operating rooms, or wherever else doctors and patients came together.

Fellowship assignments would eventually be made in a total of some one hundred services or subdepartments, called sections, in all the various fields of medicine and its subspecialties, the several areas of surgery, as well as pediatrics, obstetrics, dentistry, and laboratory sciences. For virtually every fellow in a clinical field, this training was supplemented with laboratory training and research, leading possibly to a thesis and an academic master's degree from the University of Minnesota.

All of the training programs were approved by such national agencies and organizations as the American Medical Association, the American College of Surgeons, the American College of Physicians, and the national boards in all the specialty fields of medicine. In fact, most of Mayo's training programs were in operation prior to the development of most American boards. The boards in internal medicine and in surgery were organized in 1936 and 1937.

On behalf of the Association of American Medical Colleges, Dr.

Stanley Dorst stated,

> In our opinion, the Mayo Foundation of the University of Minnesota represents an important part of the graduate medical education of the country and continues to be worthy of recognition as a graduate school of medicine and an institutional member of the Association of American Medical Colleges.

Not representing a formal approving agency, a group of visiting British university vice-chancellors stated that "they had never before viewed so significant and arresting an enterprise in medical care and graduate medical training."

The regular fellowship training program involved three years in internal medicine and the medical specialties and usually four years in surgery and its various specialty fields. It was felt necessary to provide even more advanced training. Suppose that a three-year fellow in internal medicine developed a special interest in functions and disorders of the gastrointestinal tract. There should be advanced training available in this specialty. So there was prepared for him an advanced selective gastroenterology program lasting an additional year or two following the basic three-year program. A comparable fellow in surgery might require a total five or six years training if his special interest oriented him to orthopedic surgery.

An early example of this development was the advanced educational program in the circumscribed area of thoracic or chest surgery, organized and supervised by Dr. O. T. Clagett. In the expanding advanced fellowship program, there were soon a total of sixteen such programs. In internal medicine alone there were eight such advanced fellowships in allergy, cardiology, gastroenterology, hematology, nephrology, peripheral vascular diseases, pulmonary diseases, and rheumatology. These fellowships attracted good applicants from other training institutions and also encouraged the Clinic's superior fellows to remain longer, useful to them and to the Clinic. They also provided a promising source of especially well-trained permanent staff members. About five percent of the fellows followed these advanced programs. In some fields this medical educational development was distinctly of Mayo origin.

At the same time, Mayo sought to prevent trainees and even the staff from becoming so highly specialized that they lost sight of the patient as a whole. The problems presented by a patient do not always fit entirely into a narrowly limited field. Trainees should be adequately informed about medicine as a whole as well as about rheumatology alone, or cardiology, or gastroenterology.

The most vital ingredient of the educational program was the work with patients. This was supplemented with educational courses similar to those which occur in medical school but at an advanced level. There were seminars, conferences, lectures, and demonstrations. At any one time there might be eighty such courses regularly available to fellows, covering the whole vast sweep of modern medicine. One or several such "Educational Courses Open to Fellows" was held every weekday from morning into the evening. This program of organized classroom teaching was probably excelled nowhere.

It is revealing to review the nature and the dizzying number of these offerings on a typical day, say Monday, taking place in the various clinical, hospital, and laboratory units of the Clinic complex. Naturally, a given fellow could and should attend only a very few of these courses, depending on his special interests and his available time.

7:30 A.M. Orthopedics fracture conference; surgical pathology conference.

8:00 A.M. Conferences on dermatology, proctology, ophthalmology, dentistry, and oral surgery; demonstrations of eye pathology; conference on child psychiatry.

10:00 A.M. Lectures and demonstrations in anatomy.

12:45 P.M. Conferences on physiology problems.

1:00 P.M. Seminars and conferences on pathological anatomy.

2:00 P.M. Laboratory demonstrations in physiology; demonstrations of surgical specimens.

3:30 P.M. Clinical urology conference.

4:00 P.M. Conference on physiology.

4:30 P.M. Report on cases and current literature in dentistry and oral surgery.

7:00 P.M. Clinical lectures; anesthesiology.

Recall that this was only a Monday listing. Early Tuesday morning began conferences on cardiovascular and renal diseases, on gastrointestinal disorders, and so on throughout each week. Many available courses were necessary if fellows in various specialties were to be provided with a well-rounded picture of the huge and growing store of medical knowledge.

Each general and special Clinic section had at least one informal seminar per week, mainly for its own fellows. The quality of such seminars was largely determined by the enthusiasm and interest of the staff. Outstanding seminars were those in which staff and fellows in several clinical and laboratory fields collaborated.

Also, each year there were more than a dozen guest lectureship performances by experts from outside Rochester. Important among these was the Donald Church Balfour Visiting Professorship, named in honor of the former director of the Mayo Foundation. It was quite appropriate that the first of these (in 1961) should be Dr. Owen Wangensteen, chairman of the department of surgery at the University of Minnesota Medical School.

The staff realized that excellent as this organized teaching program might be, it could not replace the combination of teacher and pupil and patient. The most effective training in medicine is that in which one staff member relates his experience and knowledge to one fellow regarding one patient. But with the excessive demands of patient care on the time of fellows and staff, this must be amplified by classroom exercises.

Supplementing the fellowship training program provided in Rochester, there were also developed off-campus assignments in which some fifteen or twenty fellows per quarter were assigned elsewhere to supplement the Clinic's training. Such assignments were made for three or more months, with six as the most common. These assignments included the fields of anesthesiology, dentistry, neurosurgery, obstetrics, ophthalmology, pediatrics, plastic surgery, psychiatry, general surgery, and basic medical sciences.

It was felt that however good the training program might be locally, it could often be strengthened by such supplementary experience in other institutions in which are encountered differences in patients seen, in approaches to medical problems, and in institutional practices and procedures. Affiliations extended from New York to California, from St. Paul to Memphis.

Before effecting such an affiliation, a careful survey was made of the institution to ensure that fellows would receive a quality of training consistent with Mayo standards, particularly as regards a proper balance between competent, adequate supervision and independent responsibility. In almost every instance the off-campus hospital was affiliated with a medical school and the chief of the service involved was a faculty member.

In a number of these arrangements, trainees of the affiliated institutions came to Rochester for some special experience in exchange for Mayo fellows going there.

A senior fellowship adviser program was started. This provided for senior fellows helping and advising new fellows just arriving in Rochester, as a needed supplement to whatever staff members or the Mayo Foundation personnel might provide. It was a valuable project of the education committee of the association of fellows, aimed at helping newcomers adjust to the complexities of Mayo's vast enterprise. The who, what, when, where, and why of Mayo was explained in informal discussions between the advanced fellows and the new appointees. All this referred not so much to the professional and scientific Clinic activities as to the multiplicity of personal problems. Should I buy a house? What are

Rochester's recreational opportunities? How do I decide to which of the 130 weekly conferences I should go? How can I plan to learn about teaching in addition to medical practice? Who do I seek to discuss problems arising in my relationship with staff or patients? This arrangement was also a learning experience for the senior fellowship advisors, since it taught them how they might in later life deal with trainees under their supervision.

The need to provide adequate housing for fellows was challenging, particularly for those who were married and had children. There was a painful housing shortage in the years directly after World War II, since there had been virtually no residence construction during the war years. And every train, plane, and bus brought more former servicemen back home to Rochester, including numerous fellows returning to complete their training.

For some time the "Graham Addition" quonset huts had been available, but replacement was needed. The Homestead Village, southeast of Rochester, was devised to include 102 living units, partly for new staff, but mainly for married fellows. Each of these contained a living room, dining room, kitchen, and utility room on the first floor, two bedrooms on the second floor, and storage space in the attic. There was adequate heating, gas for stoves, and electricity. The cost to the Clinic was about $10,000 per unit, or a bit over $1 million for the entire project, which became available in the late 1960s.

The Clinic's Responsibility

Some thinking about the tremendous educational enterprise once prompted the foundation's director to declare:

> As part of a great university, the Mayo Foundation shares the responsibility of training men and women to do the world's medical work and to advance knowledge through research . . . The desire, the need to teach, is as old as the profession of medicine. The Hippocratic oath of antiquity admonishes the physician not only to care well for his patients, but to teach the art and practice to the young aspiring to become physicians. In no other profession is the urge to teach more compelling than in medicine. In truth, the very word "doctor" means "teacher."

Mayo Foundation House

A considerable asset to the educational program was the availability of the Mayo Foundation House, where frequent lectures, discussions, seminars, and presentations of scientific papers took place. Here there was a sizable lecture room, named Balfour Hall, as well as ample dining facilities. Meetings of staff and fellows were often preceded by a meal. Purely social gatherings also took place here.

This magnificent structure, located a few blocks west of the Mayo Building, was the former home of Dr. Will Mayo. The presentation of his home was his last gift to the Mayo Foundation. Regarding this, Dr. Will stated (in 1938):

> We have no desire in any way to dictate or control the manner in which this adventure in education shall be carried out. It is for the younger people to meet the conditions of their generation in the way that appears to them to be wise and best. We only hope that Mayo Foundation House will be a meeting place where men of medicine may exchange ideas for the good of mankind.

Dr. Will's hope was amply fulfilled. Two decades later, in one single year, the house was entered by 15,029 persons, including many times by the same individual, of course. In that year, 3,985 attended seminars and 934 listened to lectures.

A uniqueness of Mayo Foundation House is that it has retained much of its character as a home while serving the thousands of persons who use it as its donor intended: as a fruitful meeting place for physicians to increase their knowledge of medicine.

Private Patients in Medical Education

In the advanced graduate training of physicians, the Mayo Clinic made this tremendous contribution: advanced training can be done in a medical institution that treats private rather than only charity patients. It was generally felt by medical educators that surgery in particular could be taught successfully only in charity hospitals. The Mayo Clinic has always believed that technical operative competency can be acquired by an assistant who is an integral unit in an operative team and who later, as a first assistant, does significant portions of many operations. Such a mosaic pattern of personal operative experience may equal or even exceed the practical experience of a resident who does complete operations, as occurs in a traditional residency in a charity hospital. In due time the author ventured the opinion:

> It now appears that perhaps our system of teaching surgery on private, paying patients, may well point the way for advanced education in surgical fields elsewhere in this country. An eminent eastern university surgeon, who had been an adverse critic of our system, recently wrote to the Clinic essentially as follows: "My charity patients are decreasing to the extent that my residency training program is jeopardized. Please tell me how you train surgeons on private patients." And with the phenomenal expansion of hospital and surgical insurance coverage, charity patients are

dwindling and pay patients are rapidly becoming more numerous. Almost inevitably, a pattern similar to ours will become increasingly the rule.

Fellowship Tidbits

These fellowship tidbits are recounted by the author:

Altogether, I suppose I was involved in the appointment of some 3,000 fellows for training with us. One of these stands out above the other 2,999. When I was Dean of Students in Biology and Medicine at the University of Chicago, my many duties included the unpleasant one of dismissing failing students after due warning. Early in World War II, I had to tell a sophomore medical student – let us call him Willston – that he must leave medical school because of continued poor work. He left school, entered the Air Force and became a fighter pilot.

Years later, here in Rochester, there came to my desk an application for a fellowship appointment and a request for an interview. It was from Willston! Telephoning my friend, Dr. Joseph Mullin, then Dean at the University of Chicago, I learned that Willston had flown in some 50 bombing missions over France and Germany and was decorated by the Air Force. He was never wounded. Based on his war record, he was readmitted to the University of Chicago Medical School. He had now performed most creditably.

So I again met Willston for the interview he had requested. I had already arranged for the approval of his appointment with the proper committees. The last time I had talked to him I had dismissed him from medical school. This time, as we shook hands, I could say, "Doctor Willston, I am pleased to inform you that you have already been admitted to a Mayo Foundation fellowship."

I was responsible for the selection of the first colored physician ever to have his fellowship application approved. He was a graduate of Wayne Medical College in Detroit. He applied in orthopedic surgery. I got the application approved by the Section of Orthopedics and the Medical Graduate Committee. I felt that all this was sufficiently unusual to warrant taking the matter before the Board of Governors of the Mayo Clinic. They also approved.

I still had some concern about the matter because at that time there were very few colored residents in Rochester. So I wondered a bit about the life and activities of the appointee and his family outside the Clinic and the hospitals. "But we'll help them," I thought. So I sent him the formal letter of appointment to an orthopedics fellowship. He replied, "Thank you very much, but I have already accepted an appointment to a residency in Detroit."

Eventually there were black fellows at Mayo, and no significant difficulties developed. One of the early ones was Dr. Victoria Nichols in obstetrics and gynecology. She stated that a patient never refused to be put under her service because she was black. But one female patient refused her services because the doctor turned out to be a woman.

The author also recalls:

> The farthest away long-distance telephone call I ever got in Rochester was from an Army installation in Korea. I knew that the Surgeon General of the Army, my good friend "Army" Armstrong, was in Korea at the time. The call must be from him, I ventured. But not at all. It was from a fellowship appointee who wished to know if it would be OK with me if he reported for duty with us a week late. I helped pay for this telephone call via the Internal Revenue Service.

Mayo fellows and their spouses were active in Rochester's stage performances. An orchestra composed of fellows and staff came into being. They appropriately named themselves the Notochords, combining the medico-scientific name for the embryonic precursor of man's backbone and the phonetic suggestion of music. They played at numerous occasions involving Clinic people, such as dances, parties, celebrations, and whatnot.

Besides individual participation in Rochester Civic Theater productions, the Clinic itself engaged in a manner of theater staging. There was an elaborate performance at each of the annual Clinic Christmas parties for staff, employees, and fellows at the Mayo Civic Auditorium. In one sequence, a patient of the Clinic was portrayed at various stages of her progress through the Clinic. While sitting waiting, she knitted a wide woolen scarf. At the onset the scarf was about two or three inches long. Before she finished, it had reached a good six feet.

CHAPTER 7

Research by Fellows

Some research experience was included in most all clinical training programs. Most fellows carried out research investigations in some basic science such as physiology, pathology, or biochemistry, even though their major interest and training schedules were in a clinical field such as internal medicine, surgery, pediatrics, or whatever. Such research almost always culminated in a thesis for a master's degree and sometimes even the doctorate of philosophy. These theses were evaluated not only by the medical graduate committee in Rochester, but also by appropriate scientists in the graduate school of the university in Minneapolis. Academic degrees also involved examinations jointly administered by the Clinic and the university. Such fellowship endeavors were by no means exceptions to the rule. They were the rule, the normal, the expected.

A far larger proportion of Mayo fellows took master's degrees than was true in the clinical departments at the university in Minneapolis. At a meeting of the joint medical graduate committee, representing both areas, a Minneapolis member inquired, "Why do so many Rochester fellows seek the master's degree?" The reply:

> While our fellows are not required to seek a degree, they are encouraged to do so. They find themselves in an atmosphere which encourages investigation and which values the prestige of a higher academic degree as a significant educational supplement to a course of training for the practice of a medical specialty.

Completing a master's thesis should constitute an intellectual experience which can be attained only by carrying out and reporting a series of scientific experiments and observations. Important ingredients of this experience are (a) the recognition and formulation of a problem, (b) a definition and determination of the scope of the problem, (c) the development of a promising plan of attack, (d) the making and accurate recording of observations, (e) a critical analysis of data accumulated, (f) the drawing of conclusions and the recognition of valid versus unwarranted conclusions, (g) the presentation of this scientific experience in the form of a concise but adequate paper, and (h) an extensive familiarity with the literature of the field.

In describing the requirements for a thesis, the term *contribution to knowledge* is frequently employed. In a master's thesis such a contribution is necessarily very minor in most instances. A real, if modest, contribution to knowledge may be an increment of additional evidence bearing on a rather widely accepted concept which may not be thoroughly established. It may be a clarification or amplification of the well-known. It may provide, not the solution of a problem, but a suggestion for a new attack on an unsolved problem.

Even though most fellows who sought the master's degree would devote their futures to clinical medicine and not primarily to research, the experience of their investigative work at Mayo should be of true worth in their future clinical activities. They should have learned the difficulty of making even a minor contribution, the magnitude of labor required to establish a new conclusion, and the necessity for caution and conservatism in drawing conclusions. They should have learned how to evaluate critically the published works of other investigators.

Some one hundred fellows per year usually qualified for master's degrees and about five for the doctorate of philosophy. Regarding this aspect of Mayo's fellowship training program, Dr. C. A. Owen remarked that fellows should

> tackle one minute part of the whole field, but in that part to become without a peer, to become truly an authority. Fellows should write a paper that a reader cannot help but accept as a definitive statement on the area concerned.

Research by fellows was reflected not only in theses for higher degrees but also in the presentation of papers at national meetings and in publications in scientific journals. Both such projects are enthusiastically encouraged by the Clinic faculty. In one prime year (1961) there were forty papers presented by fellows at national meetings from Seattle to Miami, from New York to Los Angeles. Meetings attended by fellows, at many of which they presented papers, included meetings of the American College of Surgeons, the International Congress of Dermatology, the Association for Research in Ophthalmology, the American Medical Association, the Society for Pediatric Research, the Neurological Society of America, the American Thyroid Association, the American Rheumatism Society, the American Society of Hematology, the American Physiological Society, the American Heart Association, the American Society for Clinical Pathology, the American Academy of Orthopedic Surgeons, the American Association for Study of Liver Disease, the Congress of Neurological Surgeons, and the Conference on Engineering in Medicine and Biology.

It was ventured by the author that

> to present a paper at a national scientific meeting for the first time is an exciting experience. The fellow gains confidence in speaking, appreciates the necessity to be clear and concise, compares the quality of his work and presentation with that of others, and sees in person the great names he has encountered in the literature. The stimulus to continue in some investigation is perhaps the most important consequence of participation in such meetings.

A great deal of the expense involved for attendance at national meetings by fellows was provided by the Balfour Fund. Over the years this fund provided an opportunity for hundreds of fellows to broaden their educational experience and to advance their careers. By providing financial support for fellows to attend national meetings, the Balfour Fund has contributed materially to Mayo's educational effort.

As for publication of research findings in scientific journals, it may be noted that in 1953 there were 218 published papers bearing the names of 156 fellows, in over half of which the fellow was senior author. One fellow in every four was a scientific author in that year. In 1965 there were 194 fellows who were authors or coauthors in 288 published papers.

Awards were made to fellows for superior activity in the various fields of medicine, primarily in research but also for excellence in clinical performance. These honors were bestowed at annual awards convocations, held usually in Balfour Hall of Mayo Foundation House. Candidates for awards were nominated by members of the Clinic staff, and final decisions were made by the medical graduate committee, assisted importantly by the advisory committee on awards. There was involved not only the distinction of being selected but a cash prize as well. In one typical year there were nineteen recipients, involving a total monetary value of about seventeen thousand dollars. These might be for "the best thesis in surgical research," "excellence in the field of internal medicine," or "the best thesis or original piece of research in orthopedic surgery," to cite but a few instances.

These prizes included the Alumni Award, the Staff Memorial Award, the Randall Travel Award, the Hench Scholarship Award, the Faucett Memorial Award, the Carman Fellowship in Roentgenology, the Judson Daland Award, the Howard K. Gray Award, the Edward Starr Judd Award, the Noble Foundation Awards, the Postgraduate Medical Travel Award, the J. Arnold Bargen Award, the A. Ashley Rousuck Fellowship, the Neurological Travel Award, and the R. K. Ghormley Award.

Some thoughts on research as an essential ingredient of post-internship training and, to a degree, even in undergraduate medical education were included in an address the author gave at the Second World Congress on Medical Education, held in Chicago in 1959.

> It is evident that training and experience in scientific investigation are essential at an early stage in the education of the physician who intends to continue to carry on research. But there is also much value of participation in research as part of the experience of a student who may not again work in a research laboratory, who has no intention of conducting further clinical investigation or who will never write another scientific paper. Some training in research can contribute enormously to the education of such a physician engaged entirely in clinical responsibilities, as is necessarily the case with most physicians.
>
> Past research experience by a physician who is now fully engaged in clinical practice sharpens his judgment and enhances his evaluation of research by others. "Medicine, a lifelong study," requires the physician to keep abreast by reading the journals and listening to scientific papers . . . Experience in research warns against the pitfalls of inadequate numbers of observations, faulty controls, inaccurate measurements, the intrusion of chance, the inherent variability of biological material. Engagement in research enhances the physician's judgment of conclusions reached in medical papers he reads, sensitizes him to inadequacies of evidence, increases his wariness of exaggerated claims, tempers his acceptance of enthusiastic predictions.

Research also develops in a physician an alertness to apparently inconsequential or insignificant details. Such details may be invaluable in the diagnosis and treatment of a patient. A noted example of attention to unexpected detail in research is that of Sir Alexander Fleming in his discovery of penicillin. The magnitude of his discovery of this bacteria destroyer was hardly apparent from his description of an experimental accident of vast moment.

> While working with staphylococcus variants, a number of culture plates were set aside on the laboratory bench and examined from time to time. In the examination these plates were necessarily exposed to the air and they became contaminated with various microorganisms. It was noticed that around a large colony of the contaminating mold the staphylococcus colonies became transparent and were obviously undergoing destruction.

This "contaminating mold" destroying bacteria on Fleming's culture plate became known as penicillin. It has become a major factor for destroying bacteria infecting human beings.

And in clinical practice, attention to small details, often apparently unrelated to the patient's main complaint, may be most significant. Dr. Plummer noted that the whiteness at the end of a clean fingernail becomes more extensive in overactivity of the thyroid gland. An orthopedist entering a room to see a new patient often ascertained important information by the manner in which the patient rose from his chair to shake hands. A few pinpoint, purplish red spots might point to a heart problem. Anesthesiologist Lundy, on entering an operating room, could sense at once if something were wrong. As Helen Clapesattle states:

> Some educators object to requiring all medical graduate students to attempt research because they think nothing worthy of the name can be done in six months. Besides, they say, it is absurd to think a man cannot be a good surgeon or internist without the ability to do original research. But others, including most of the Minnesota faculty on both campuses, believe that if a subject of proper scope is selected, the fellow can accomplish enough to give him an introduction to research techniques and problems, enough to make him wary of accepting as gospel everything he reads in medical journals. In the process some men discover an unsuspected interest in scientific investigation. In the laboratory experiments of their undergraduate days, they worked only for the correct answer printed in their laboratory manuals; in graduate research the problem is theirs to solve, the unknown answers theirs to find.

CHAPTER 8

Recruitment of Fellows

For a few years after World War II there were ample numbers of medical school graduates seeking such training as was offered at Mayo. Many physicians in the military medical corps had had little or no training beyond the internship. At Mayo it was the policy to assure former trainees who entered military service that their fellowships could be resumed immediately on discharge. Also, there were many appointees who went to war before arriving in Rochester, who were also assured of training positions when military duty ended. All in all, Mayo had made such promises to 580 fellows and appointees.

American Applicants

And there was a plethora of new applicants. In one year alone there were twenty applicants for every one place in surgery and fifteen for each internal medicine position. But all too soon the discharged medical officers throughout the country finished their training. Then applicants for training at Mayo and elsewhere were drastically reduced. Plethora became deficiency. The number of residencies offered in the country was well in excess of the numbers seeking advanced training. In 1954 there were about twenty-two thousand residency positions available in the United States. This was enough to provide every medical school graduate with three years of advanced training. But only about one half of the country's interns sought advanced training. Any top-notch applicant in any field could select any place he wished to train, with assurance that he would be accepted. It was indeed a buyer's market. But matters went relatively well at Mayo. Whereas in the country at large only seventy-eight percent of residency positions were filled, the Clinic managed to appoint ninety percent of its needs, despite the policy to select only superior applicants. How was this done?

To attract superior applicants, an outstanding training program was essential. This was certainly true at Mayo. But how transmit this truth to potential applicants? Simple words would be inadequate. Mayo possessed an effective recruitment program. To all appointees, before their arrival, were sent the weekly Clinic bulletin, the *Mayo Clinic Proceedings*, recording research results, as well as *Mayovox*, the Clinic's bimonthly newspaper for all staff and employees and their families. They even received Rochester's daily general newspaper, the *Post-Bulletin*, partly to inform the spouses of appointees about life in the city. Appointees were bound to show much of this to their associates and friends, who might also become applicants.

In addition, some foundation and Clinic activities that drew recruits were not designed specifically for recruitment purposes but developed as parts of the educational programs. Clinical clerks who came to Mayo for a quarter's work from various medical schools would themselves learn about Mayo's superior advanced medical education program. And they would inform their classmates. To potential applicants the Clinic's superiority was also demonstrated throughout the country by Mayo fellows presenting papers at national scientific meetings. And when Clinic fellows were assigned to other institutions on off-campus assignments, they functioned in part as missionaries of the message. There were organized visits to Rochester by medical student groups. It was also felt that many visiting medical school faculty members and section guests carried away favorable impressions that they might impart to their own medical students. Thousands of Mayo alumni over the country and the world, many on medical school faculties, would also spread the word. Recommendations to prospective applicants from enthusiastic former fellows exerted a tremendous influence. Almost without exception, applicants implicated former fellows as a major determinant in their selection of Mayo for their advanced medical training.

These devices were accessory to the primary recruiting influence: the high quality of the training program. All efforts at seeking fellowship applicants would soon fail if the educational programs did not keep pace with or provide leadership in the forward march of medicine, science, and education.

It must be remembered that the successful recruitment of superior fellows also meant the maintenance of a superior Clinic permanent staff, since most of the staff was derived from the fellowship group.

As it has been with so many challenges to Mayo, this recruitment problem was managed with gratifying results. During the years 1950 to 1964 the fellowship roster increased from 488 to 657, a thirty-five percent increase compared with a twenty-four percent increase at this educational level in the country at large. During this period there were about 30,000 residents in thirteen hundred training institutions of the country, of which more than 600 trainees were in Rochester. This meant that one in fifty United States residents were at Mayo. It also meant that one in fifty of the country's future specialists received their advanced training at the Clinic.

Foreign Appointees

The Mayo organization has always felt that just as it was obligated to treat patients from anywhere in the world, it should also provide advanced medical education to qualified medical school graduates from any country. The major difficulty here was to evaluate the qualifications of foreign graduates. To meet this difficulty, the American Medical Association, along with other national medical organizations, established the Educational Council for Foreign Medical Graduates (ECFMG). The author was pleased to be involved in this venture as a member of the AMA's Council on Medical Education and Hospitals before his coming to Rochester.

The ECFMG established and conducted annual examination procedures in many foreign countries. Foreign graduates seeking advanced training in the United States took such examinations, which tested not only medical knowledge but also the command of the English language. No foreign graduates were appointed to a Mayo fellowship without proper certification by this body. ECFMG approval also rendered a foreign medical graduate eligible to seek licensure to practice medicine in many of our states.

Before the adoption of the ECFMG principle, Mayo was once grossly deceived. Appointed was a fellow with an M.D. from a Greek medical school. He presented a superior academic record, excellent recommendations, and a good command of English. But at the Clinic he performed atrociously. After several severe, ineffectual warnings, he was dismissed after only a few months. He returned to Greece. Some years later the

Foundation got a letter from him that said,

> I am dying of leukemia and I wish to make peace with my conscience and with God. I must confess to you that I never went to medical school. All my credentials and papers were forged. To help save my soul, will you forgive me?

Early in the 1950s there were fellows from thirteen schools in the following nine countries: Belgium, England, France, Iceland, Ireland, Italy, Mexico, South Africa, and Sweden. Such numbers increased so that in 1959, 93 of the 575 fellows came from elsewhere than the United States and Canada.

Not long after World War II, about one third of all interns and residents in the country at large were foreign medical graduates. There were even more in New York City, where forty-eight percent were from abroad. At the Mayo Clinic less than seventeen percent of the fellows came from medical schools outside the United States and Canada.

Objections were raised by medical schools throughout the United States to the appointment of so many foreign graduates for advanced training. Their own graduates encountered difficulties in securing appointments for advanced specialty training because of competition provided by the number of foreign applicants. Also, practicing physicians in communities throughout the country disliked the competition provided by foreign doctors settling permanently in their areas. In about 1974 the realization dawned that nearly half of the physicians newly licensed in the United States were foreign medical graduates.

Pressure from numerous sources (not including Mayo) induced Congress to enact the Health Professions Educational Assistance Act in 1976, which limited to two years the duration of a foreign medical graduate's stay in a United States hospital providing postgraduate medical training. Although difficult to obtain, there might occasionally be an extension to three years. Two years was too short a period for most clinical specialty training programs but was sufficient for research experience or training in a subspecialty such as cardiology for a foreign medical graduate already well-trained in internal medicine.

Consequently, one aspect of Mayo's contributions to the world's health was markedly diminished. A great reduction occurred in the number of foreign medical graduates who were trained at the Clinic and who then returned to their native land to dispense a superior quality of medical specialty care. And Mayo staffing also experienced a bit of difficulty. A. R. Hanson, chairman of the Clinic's division of education, regretted that "if you have an outstanding foreign medical graduate and you want to put him on the Clinic staff, you can't, because he won't be able to gain permanent immigration status."

Language Problems

But even with limiting foreign appointments to those properly certified, an occasional difficulty was encountered. An ECFMG-certified fellow from France got into trouble with some women patients who stormed to the admissions desk to rage about his insults. He was a good physician and a pleasant young man. Investigation revealed that like any good doctor taking a patient's history, he asked each one about her main complaint or main trouble. Unhappily, his French pronunciation of *ai* in *main* altered his inquiry to "Tell me all about your MEN trouble."

CHAPTER 9

Supervision of Fellows

Administration

The medical graduate committee in Rochester was charged with all the responsibilities related to fellowship training. If anyone were to name the dozen or twenty most important people in all Mayo activities, it would essentially be a list of those who have served on this committee. The names would progress from Barnes and Clagett and Code, to Welch and Wilder and Wallaeger. Closest to the foundation's director were those serving as assistant or associate directors of the Mayo Foundation, later entitled the Mayo Graduate School of Medicine. These were successively Drs. Stan Olson, Ken Corbin, Ray Pruitt, John Welch, and Drew Miller. And there was the most able assistant, Russ Hanson.

There were various important Mayo Foundation committees. The committee on admissions evaluated fellowship applicants. The university academic committee evaluated staff qualifications for academic appointments and promotions. The advisory committee on awards selected fellows performing meritorious research. The committee on educational and research facilities evaluated and recommended improvements in laboratories and meeting places. The educational program committee was concerned mainly with the lecture and seminar programs. The university relations committee sought to further strengthen the union with Minneapolis colleagues. The committee on Mayo Foundation House dealt with the use of this facility by the several thousand who entered it each year.

University Relations

The criteria for university faculty appointments and promotions for Mayo staff members were more rigorous than in an undergraduate medical school faculty because the Mayo staff is a graduate medical school faculty, which demands research productivity of a high order of originality and significance, especially at the professorship level. Effectiveness in the teaching of fellows was a secondary criterion, but one which also carried considerable weight.

Excellence as a practicing physician, so basic to the operation of the Mayo Clinic, was only a minor consideration for faculty status. The most demanding problem faced by the university academic committee was a sound evaluation of the significance of the research conducted by the staff member. Did he play a leading role in the planning and execution of the research? Did the research contribute in an important and basic manner to a better understanding of health and disease? The emphasis was on quality rather than quantity of research. The research contributions expected for faculty appointment and promotions, might have been summarized as follows:

Instructor: Has he made a significant beginning in research?

Assistant professor: Is he well on his way in investigation?

Associate professor: Has he made contributions of considerable basic scientific importance?

Professor: Is he generally recognized as an authority of national or international reputation, a leader in the advancement of knowledge in his chosen field of specialization?

The qualifications for academic appointments and promotions of staff members were annually reviewed. Each year the academic committee seriously considered for promotion every staff member whose academic status had not changed in the preceding four or five years. Recommendations were discussed in Minneapolis by the joint medical graduate committee, with members from Rochester and Minneapolis. The discussions reached were acted on finally by the university administration. As an example of these procedures, in the year 1960 the Mayo medical graduate committee received a lengthy report of recommendations from its university academic committee, Dr. O. T. Clagett, chairman. This report listed the qualifications of 167 staff members. Of these, 43 were finally recommended to the university, which agreed with Mayo on all but two.

Eventually the university granted Mayo the privilege of independently appointing instructors and making promotions to assistant professorships without these time-consuming joint committee meetings. Reported were simply the actions of the medical graduate committee along with such supporting material as bibliographies of the staff members concerned. The university graduate school never contested these recommendations, but simply verified the appointments.

With university approval, there were also adopted in Rochester appointments as clinical associate professors and clinical professors. Requirements for appointments and promotions in the clinical category were less rigorous as regards research productivity. This arrangement did allow deserved recognition of a staff member's contributions in clinical research. The Clinic was authorized by the university to make such appointments on its own initiative. Promotions to associate professor and full professor, without the clinical designation, still required sessions of the joint medical graduate committee. Eventually, the clinical designation at all levels was discontinued.

In a single typical year (1962) there were sixty-five faculty appointments and promotions: eleven professors, sixteen associate professors, thirteen assistant professors, and twenty-five instructors.

So in every sense Mayo was a university graduate school of medicine, with full national and international recognition as such. This status was unique in the country. The Clinic and hospitals and laboratories and research and education were part of the University of Minnesota, yet independent of the University in many respects, especially financially. The university's valued accomplishments, via Clinic efforts, cost the university nothing in dollars.

More and more, as regards teaching and research, Mayo and the university became a single family. Common professional and scientific interests brought together the members of the faculty from Rochester and Minneapolis in many state meetings, such as meetings of the Minnesota Society of Internal Medicine, the Minnesota Surgical Society, the St. Paul Surgical Society, the Minnesota Heart Association, the Minnesota Society for Clinical Pathologists, the Minnesota Academy of Medicine, and others. Voluminous informational data were submitted from Rochester to Minneapolis for inclusion in official publications of the university. An annual report was prepared, listing all the scientific papers published by the Mayo staff. This appeared as a sizable segment of the university volume entitled *Publications of the Faculties.* Information was also provided regarding the Mayo Foundation's offerings in the graduate school, department by department, for inclusion in the bulletins of the university and its graduate school. The biennial report of the president of the university incorporated an account from the Mayo Foundation, summarizing important developments and accomplishments.

There could be listed an imposing array of intimate contacts between Rochester and Minneapolis personnel. There were common examinations of candidates for higher degrees, joint meetings of the graduate committees, visits of the senior medical school class (and later, the sophomore class) to Rochester, interchange of faculty lectures, interdigitation of educational programs in the basic sciences, and representation of the Mayo Foundation in the university senate.

The University of Minnesota Senate amended its constitution in 1957 to provide for direct Mayo Foundation representation. According to the university's constitution, the senate "shall have legislative authority over educational matters concerning the University as a whole . . . [and] shall have the power to enact statutes for the government of the students in those relations with the University which affect the University as a whole." The university units represented in the senate were sixteen in number, from agriculture to technology. And now there was added the Mayo Foundation, with four representatives on the university senate. The first of these were Drs. Charles Code, Raymond Pruitt, William Remine, and Victor Johnson. So Mayo became involved not only in its own affairs but also in those of the university as a whole. And at one time the Clinic also had representation on the university's major ruling body, the board of regents, in the person of Dr. Charles W. Mayo, who even became president of the board for a time.

In Rochester there was a considerable degree of academic autonomy, such as the appointment of fellows who were university graduate students, design of the educational program, and assignment and supervision of these projects. Such autonomy illustrates the university's confidence in the quality of Mayo's educational operations. In all relationships with the university, none of the Clinic's activities have ever had financial support from state funds or from the general university budget.

One reflection of the shared endeavors of Mayo and the university was an award from Mayo given to retiring university president, Dr. James L. Morrill. A scroll was presented to him at a dinner in Minneapolis given by the university faculty to honor Morrill. The text read:

> To James Lewis Morrill, President of the University of Minnesota, 1945-1960, the Faculty of the Mayo Foundation for Medical Education and Research and the Staff of the Mayo Clinic acclaim his vigorous leadership and scholarly vision which have guided the University into new dimensions of greatness, and with all his spirited good humor and warm understanding which have endeared him to the hearts of men.

Educational Grants

Time was when outside grants for the education of fellows were not accepted. But later Mayo not only accepted but actively sought such support, and with unbelievable success. In 1956 there were outside grants for clinical and research training of fellows from fifteen sources: American Heart Association, American Psychiatric Association, Bernard Baruch, Linwood D. Keyser Fund, Minnesota Department of Public Welfare, Minnesota Heart Association, National Fund for Infantile Paralysis, National Institute of Arthritis and Metabolic Diseases, National Institute of Mental Health, National Institute of Nervous Diseases and Blindness, National Research Council of Canada, Rockefeller Foundation, United States Air Force, United States Navy, and United States Office of Vocational Rehabilitation. In the one year of 1962, grants from outside sources totalled $485,293 for the training of more than eighty Mayo fellows.

The Vitamin Foundation of New York established a three-year, fifteen thousand dollar fellowship for postgraduate training in nutrition. This they named the Russell M. Wilder Fellowship, in honor of his many major contributions in the fields of nutrition and metabolism as a Clinic staff member. The Edward John Noble Foundation provided leadership grants seeking to encourage trainees to become leaders in their fields. There were also travel awards for fellows, including the Howard K. Gray Fund for surgical trainees to travel and visit leading medical centers and "thus to continue their graduate and postgraduate training through observation of the methods of others."

In accepting such outside training grants, it was always insisted that the trainees must be selected by Mayo and not by the granting agency. And such trainees must be responsible only to Mayo for evaluation of their work.

Regular fellowship stipends from the Clinic itself were rather modest for the average trainee. In 1959 the monthly stipend was elevated to two hundred dollars and a few years later it rose to three hundred dollars per month for first-year fellows, with increases beyond the beginning of training.

Governmental Relations

Throughout its training and research activities Mayo has always had rewarding experiences with the United States government and its various departments and agencies, including the military services. These were always cooperative enterprises, with never any governmental dictation regarding what the Clinic should do or how to do it.

At one stage, advocates of socialized medicine called for intervention of the government in all aspects of medicine. The author recalls an incident when a famous senator from a nearby state addressed the assembled medical students of a great midwest university in the early 1950s. Although the author was well beyond medical student days, he was in the audience listening to the man expound on the benefits of socialized medicine, of which he was an ardent advocate. The senator said:

> When you who are freshmen have graduated, you will all be employed by the United States Government. By then we will have socialized medicine in this country and you will be part of it. I have studied this plan thoroughly and am convinced of its desirability and also its immanence.
>
> As a senator, I have listened to all the arguments pro and con, including, naturally, the views presented at Senate hearings on behalf of the American Medical Association, which naturally opposes the socialization of medicine.

The author was tempted to arise and say:

> Twice, Mr. Senator, I have testified before the Senate committee considering this project, on behalf of the American Medical Association. You are a member of that committee. At neither of these sessions were you present.

But he did not arise; he did not say it.

CHAPTER 10

Care of Patients

Much of this account has dealt with research and education, to which everyone has been ardently devoted, from the Mayo brothers on through the decades. But the first goal of the Clinic is the care of the sick, although it is generally recognized that this end is best met if coupled with education and research. Only in such a complex combination can there be the best in diagnosis and treatment.

Patients came not only from the United States, but from the world over. Figures are often more revealing than words, and statistics more enlightening than phrases. To say a man is six feet tall and weighs two hundred pounds presents a more accurate picture than a paragraph of description. During the author's stay in Rochester (1947–1966) patient visits increased from over 135,000 annually to nearly 200,000, or from about 2,600 per week to about 3,800. Staff physicians and scientists nearly doubled, from over 200 to almost 500. In the year 1961, for the first time in Clinic history there were more than 1,000 physicians at work, including staff and fellows.

Mayo's two millionth patient arrived in September of 1954. This was a thirty-two-year-old married woman from Liberal, Kansas, who was referred to the Clinic for diagnosis of a suspected allergy. This occurred nearly sixteen years after patient number one million. And then came patient number three million: five-year-old Elaine Beatty of Hazel Park,

Michigan, with an optical problem. This registration stimulated something of a celebration, with a welcome to Rochester by Mayo officials, an Easter basket of sweets for Elaine, and a luncheon at Kahler's Elizabethan Room. Elaine made Mayo Clinic history and captured the hearts and fancy of almost everyone she encountered. As for patient number four million, one may ask—who, whence, why, and when? One may guess only at the *when*. It should be sometime in the 1980s.

Outpatient Services

To care for these great numbers, in the mid-1960s, the Clinic had more than thirty special fields of medicine and surgery, located mainly in the Plummer and Mayo buildings, besides the extensive hospital facilities. There were eleven laboratory disciplines devoted to diagnostic problems as well as research. Here the largest numbers of staff were in physiology and pathology. Eight other related services included the Clinic library and the section on publications. This listing does not include the multitude of Clinic committees, numbering over thirty; it refers only to the major fields of activity, from anesthesiology to veterinary medicine.

Dr. James Priestly stated that growth in size

> has been a by-product of growth in ability and accomplishment and not a primary objective. Our primary objective must always be quality. Growth in size but not maintaining high quality would be a serious error. On the other hand, a determined effort not to grow larger, even though quality can be maintained, would be contrary to our past and inimical to our future. True, as we get larger there are more problems. But when growth stops, a plateau is reached and the aging process is likely to become dominant.
>
> Our objectives should be so high that they are never fully achieved, thereby providing continuing incentive . . . In evaluating our excellence we should compare ourselves with the best.

Regarding the future in education and research, Dr. Drew Miller ventured, "We should consider the next 50 years of the Mayo Graduate School of Medicine just as much a challenging venture as the past 50 years has been a colorful history."

Occasionally a Mayo-bound patient, usually from abroad, would deplane at the other Rochester, in New York State. Proceeding to the airport information desk he would inquire,

"How do I get to the Mayo Clinic?"

He was handed a printed card telling him the Clinic was about seven hundred miles westward. The card also contained information about airline flights to this mecca. Geographical blunders are not limited to foreigners seeking the Mayo Clinic. Driving west years ago, the author and his wife found themselves in Boulder, Colorado, near Denver.

"Just how do we get to the famous Boulder Dam?" they asked.

"Keep driving southwest about six hundred miles until you reach Las Vegas, Nevada. There they will tell you how to get to the dam."

In the late 1960s a study was made of the manner in which Mayo Clinic patients travel to Rochester so that the Clinic might recommend improvements in the schedules of airlines and other transportation facilities. Questionnaires were answered by more than four thousand patients who came to Rochester during a two-week period. They came from forty-six states, the District of Columbia, Canada, four Central American countries, eight countries in South America, and several other foreign countries. Nearly seventy percent (about three thousand) came by their private automobiles, and eighteen percent came by airplane. The remaining, about twelve percent, came by bus, combined train and bus, and private planes or limousines. Many patients voiced complaints that there was a complete lack of direct train service to and from Rochester. This fault has never been corrected. This survey revealed one real puzzler: a patient from Hawaii listed his means of transportation as a private automobile.

Patients coming to the Clinic from abroad over the years were numerous, requiring interpreters. There resulted the establishment of the language department. In its annual report for 1965, this department stated that in that year they received requests for interpreters speaking Arabic, Chinese, Czechoslovakian, French, German, Greek, Hebrew, Hungarian, Italian, Korean, Persian, Polish, Portuguese, Spanish, Russian, Turkish, Vietnamese, Yiddish, and Yugoslavian, a total of nineteen languages. The language department staff could itself manage the Italian, Portuguese, and Spanish, the last being the most common language needing interpretation. For the remaining languages the department used on-call interpreters, who were called on temporarily when needed. Some of these were Clinic fellows or their spouses, nurses, other employees, and non-Clinic Rochester people—wherever they could be found. Not often requested, but important when needed, were the services of two local women who could communicate with the deaf by sign language. The interpreter assisted the patient in registering and gave other needed assistance during the course of the examinations, translating the physician's questions for the patient and the patient's replies for the physician.

Interpreters not only may be needed when the examining physician first deals with the patient but must often be available at the time special examination procedures are carried out later.

Philomena DeJohn, supervisor of the language department, stated

Early on a Monday morning the scene at the Language Department desk resembles an open-air market. An average of 15 to 20 new foreign patients, many with several family members, are speaking any number of foreign languages simultaneously.

Clinic gastroenterologist Dr. Lloyd Bartholemew stated,

> When you first start working with an interpreter it may seem that things go a little slower because of the intermediary, but once you become accustomed to working with them, you see that they really know the patients and it goes almost as rapidly as if there were no language barrier.

The entire operation of the complex Clinic machinery and the functioning of its staff in practice, education, and research is the responsibility of the chief administrative body, the Mayo Clinic Board of Governors. This body of eleven staff members was first organized in the early 1920s. The term of service is six years. The Board nominates new members or reappointees, who require confirmation by the Mayo Association and also by the voting staff of the Clinic. In this it is essentially a democratic body. Its one-time chairman Dr. S. F. Haines stated that this "democratic method of solving our problems is an essential part of our structure." And as Dr. M. B. Coventry opined, "You and I and the person sitting next to you are the Mayo Clinic."

The administrative committee, the personnel committee, and the research administrative committee are subcommittees of the board. But in addition, the board and its subcommittees are assisted in carrying out their many functions by some twenty-five other committees of the Clinic and the graduate school. Membership in these bodies consists of staff members with special interests in one or another field of Mayo's trilogy of practice, education, and research. Board of governors chairmen in recent times were successively: Drs. A. R. (Arlie) Barnes, S. F. (Sam) Haines, J. T. (Jim) Priestly, and L. E. (Emmerson) Ward.

Apart from the complications of diagnosis and treatment, the registration of patients, correlation with previous visits, and directions about what to do or where to go next were rather complicated. This required not only skilled employees, but more and more complicated machinery. Joe Fritsch, commonly called Joe Clinic, combined brains and machinery. He was stationed just inside the entrance to the Plummer Building, prior to the erection of the Mayo Building. He gave directions to entering patients inquiring where to go. Joe memorized the correlation between a given patient registration number and the exact year that number was assigned the patient. Occasionally, while listening to a patient's question, he would surreptitiously glance at the registration folder held by the patient, noting the name and number.

"You should go to the desk on the seventh floor, Mrs. Brown."

"Mrs. Brown? How do you know my name?"

"I remember you very well, dear lady. You first came here just seven years ago!"

The decision of the Clinic's board of governors to adopt a five-day workweek was made in the mid-1960s after intensive study and deliberation of what effect this might have on patient care. After a year's test it was decided that there was no evidence to indicate that quality of medical care was in any way adversely affected by the change. And patients were not inconvenienced. In fact, one member of the Clinic's administration noted that "fewer people have commented on the Clinic's Saturday morning closing than previously expressed surprise that we were open."

Saint Marys Hospital

In one sense the growth of Saint Marys Hospital was a bit less complicated than was true of the scattered, though effective, downtown hospitals in the early years. Around the original twenty-seven-bed hospital built in 1889 there was plenty of land for expansion. Addition after addition was built: in 1893, 1898, 1903, 1908, 1912, 1922 (the Joseph Building), 1941 (the Francis Building), and 1956 (the Domitilla Building). Each of these was tied directly into the parent structure so that there has always been one hospital with numerous connected wings.

In the late 1960s the Saint Marys Alfred Building neared completion. It was appropriately named after Mother Mary Alfred Moes, founder of the original Saint Marys. The size of this ten-story building came as a surprise, with its total of 204,000 square feet of floor space, or about one half of a square city block. Equally surprising was the extent of Clinic and foundation involvement in the project. In this joint Saint Marys-Clinic project, about one third of the space was Clinic, manned by Clinic staff and paramedical employees. Included here were facilities for these numerous sections and enterprises: therapeutic radiology and housing of a cobalt 60 telemetry unit (a cobalt bomb), tissue transplants, expanded laboratory for electroencephalography, the Clinic's blood bank, expanded radiology facilities, quarters for experimental animals, a conference room for Clinic use, a cardiology laboratory, laboratories for anesthesia research and surgical investigations, and an expanded unit for gastroenterology.

The major activity in the gastroenterology unit was research aimed at elucidation of the causes of abdominal diseases and their treatment. Studies centered on the structure and function of all parts of the gastrointestinal tract, as well as the liver, the biliary systems, and the pancreas. Each staff member in the unit carried out a number of studies, frequently in collaboration with other members of the Clinic staff. Projects completed or underway numbered more than one hundred.

This research program was supported in part by National Institutes of Health grants, as was also the extensive training program in gastroenterology. There was also outside grant support for the actual construction of that portion of the Alfred unit which was devoted to research. Dr. William Summerskill, in charge of this unit, stated that these impressive facilities were "no greater than are needed in an institution which has commitments to education and research as well as patient care." The number of patients with gastrointestinal disorders seen at the Clinic exceeded the number with any other single complaint. Summerskill voiced the hope that this unit might become the prototype for other new facilities for research based primarily on the study of patients—so-called clinical research. This hope was ultimately fulfilled with the development of still other patient-oriented studies. Clinical research at Mayo has a distinguished past, a productive present, and a promising future.

Apart from some outside financial help, these Saint Marys Hospital ventures were largely self-financed, with Mayo help. Funds came from paying patients and from bond issues. But there was also considerable aid from outside sources. One request for such aid was made to the National Institutes of Health for about two million dollars to cover a five-year period. The reply from NIH was interesting. The grant application was approved, but notification of this approval was coupled with a statement of regret that "no funds are available to pay for this deserving application. If additional funds become available in the future, the award will be made."

Recalling these developments years later, Sister Generose Gervais, the hospital administrator, remarked, "The growth of the Mayo Clinic and Saint Marys Hospital is something of a fairy tale. Why should a famous Clinic and a famous hospital grow up in a small unknown midwestern town?"

The distance between the Clinic and Saint Marys necessitated establishment of a shuttle service for the benefit of staff, fellows, and other personnel with interests and responsibilities in the two places. There had been far too many requests to the Clinic's general service, "Can you take me to Saint Marys?" Station wagons were employed, operating every fifteen minutes all day long. They also included the Medical Sciences Building in their tours. Ease of travel between the Clinic and the hospital made it convenient for a staff consultant to make an extra trip to see a patient or to look in on a research project. A fellow on hospital assignment felt more inclined to come downtown for a lecture or seminar or to spend an hour in the library.

Saint Marys Hospital, although Roman Catholic in origin and management, has always maintained the policy of keeping its doors open to all persons, regardless of race, creed, sex, color, financial status, or religion. All persons received the same care and essentially the same accommodations. The measure of the patient's medical needs determined his care and treatment. Financial status was not considered.

Throughout all these out-of-this-world developments one could scarcely pronounce the words *Saint Marys Hospital* without hearing the echo *Sister Mary Brigh*. She came to Rochester in 1925 and eventually became the chief administrator of the hospital, in which position she remained for more than twenty years. Modest and reserved, she moved mountains while seeming only to be dusting the table. Much of the hospital's phenomenal growth and effectiveness in the care of the sick must be credited to Sister Mary Brigh. After retirement, she still continued to function in various emeritus capacities.

It would probably be impossible to find anywhere a Roman Catholic hospital, operated by sisters of the faith, where there is such a deep appreciation of ideals and goals such as those of the non-Catholic Mayo Clinic. All were completely at one in the conviction that superior medical care necessitated an equal dedication to research and education, regardless of religious faith.

The nonsectarian status of the Clinic was once questioned by the experience of a participant in a tour of the Clinic. The tour leader introduced himself, "I am Luther Boie." One of the visitors was astonished, for what she heard was, "I am a Lutheran boy."

Radial Hospital Concept

For all the patient facilities provided by Saint Marys to meet the needs of the Clinic patients, it was felt that a new hospital was needed immediately adjacent to the Clinic. This would replace the nearby Worrall, Kahler, and Colonial hospitals. Discussing this project over luncheons, perhaps twice a week, were the world-renowned thoracic surgeon Dr. O. T. Clagett and some of his close associates, such as Drs. Edward Weld, Herbert Schmidt, and Oliver Beahrs. A new idea emerged. Clagett states:

> We thought it should be possible to design a unique type of hospital that could be more attractive and efficient than existing hospitals, and came up with the idea that a round hospital with rooms on the outside and nursing services in the center would provide the privacy desired for patients and avoid numerous trips down long corridors for nurses and attendants.

Eventually the term *radial* replaced the term *round* as more descriptive of the units in which the patients' rooms "radiated" from the centrally located attendants and nurses station, like short, blunt spokes of a wheel. A patient's call for assistance, by an over-the-door light and a buzzer, was immediately made known to the central desk. There was privacy for patients but no necessity for numerous trips down long corridors by nurses and attendants. The Clinic administration, always ready to test promising concepts, determined to experiment with the idea. It was decided "to build an experimental unit to prove the merits of the round concept." Funds were provided by the Ford Foundation and the Hill Family Foundation. The Simmons Bed Corporation designed some special beds, and the Ohio Chemical Corporation provided some hospital room equipment.

Tom Ellerbe of the St. Paul hospital-designing firm of Ellerbe Company was skeptical of the idea at first, but he soon cooperated. A radial unit was constructed in 1957 in back of the old Colonial Hospital. The unit was connected with the main hospital by an overpass, providing easy passage back and forth. There were twelve beds, which seemed sufficient to provide for the projected studies. The radial unit proved a great success. Hospital administrators and architects came from all parts of the country to observe its functioning. Ellerbe Company began to incorporate the radial idea into their planning of hospitals to be built across the land.

The board of trustees of the Rochester Methodist Hospital, which now owned the Colonial, became equally enthusiastic. They began considering a new, large hospital to replace the Colonial, Kahler, and Worrall hospitals. This was to be built with due consideration for the radial plan, now a nationwide concept.

Rochester Methodist Hospital

The downtown group of Rochester hospitals has had a somewhat variable history. Back in 1915 a building originally designed as a hotel was converted into the Colonial Hospital by the Kahler Corporation, marking the beginning of this company's combining of hotel and hospital facilities for Mayo patients. Very soon this corporation added another hospital when they built the Worrall Hospital, named after William Worrall Mayo, father of the Mayo brothers. There were also hospital beds within the Kahler Hotel itself. This hospital trio, along with Saint Marys, provided reasonably adequate facilities for some thirty-five years. There were about 230 beds in the Colonial, 130 in the Worrall, and 210 in the Kahler Hotel.

The Kahler discontinued hospital functions in the early 1950s. Dr. Charles W. Mayo recalls, "I can now order a delicious meal on the exact spot where I once removed gallstones, a circumstance which does not affect my appetite in the least."

Then the Rochester Methodist Hospital came into being as a distinct corporation, affiliated with the General Board of Health and Welfare Ministries of the Methodist Church. It purchased the Colonial and Worrall hospitals from the Kahler Corporation with a down payment of six hundred thousand dollars. An important figure in this development was Harry Blackmun, then legal counsel to the Mayo Clinic and later a Justice of the Supreme Court of the United States. Blackmun made the initial overtures to the Methodist Church for this venture. He wrote the original articles of incorporation for the Rochester Methodist Hospital. So now the Clinic had two great hospital organizations—Saint Marys and Methodist.

The early years of the Rochester Methodist Hospital, with its separate units, were difficult. There was overcrowding, and the facilities became worn and obsolete. A new modern facility was needed and planned. In the meantime the idea of radial hospital units had been developed and tested by Dr. Clagett and colleagues. This must be an integral part of any new construction. And it was. The plans called for an expenditure of fourteen million dollars, of which the government contributed more than six million dollars.

The beautiful new Rochester Methodist Hospital was completed in 1966. It had 558 beds and 30 operating rooms. About half of the beds were in the new radial units, in which patients' rooms opened directly on the centrally located attendants' and nurses' stations, like short spokes on a wheel. In one such unit, for example, thirteen patient rooms accommodating twenty-seven patients, radiated from the central station. The hospital also had old-fashioned corridor units. Patients not acutely ill and not needing much attention sometimes found the old style a little more private and quiet.

The inevitability of perpetual growth of everything related to the Clinic was reflected in the words of Justice Harry Blackmun. At the Methodist Hospital dedication exercises he said, "The hospital came into being because the sun was meant to shine and because the hospital was meant to be . . . But now that we have the new building let us not lose the spirit of the old buildings."

Related Services

The diagnostic and therapeutic facilities of the Clinic and the operating rooms and beds of hospitals were basic to the medical care of patients. Equally necessary in the kind of unexcelled practice carried out were the laboratories in the various basic sciences. Enumerating these is similar to naming the departments in an undergraduate medical school. There were all of these: anatomy, biochemistry, biophysics, clinical pathology, electrocardiography, electroencephalography, microbiology, pathology, pharmacology, physiology, radiology, surgical pathology, and surgical research. Indespensable as these activities are in the clinical practice of medicine, they are equally necessary in the other two components of the Clinic's triad: teaching and research. This Mayo trilogy of medical practice, education, and scientific investigation must forever stand unbroken.

CHAPTER 11

Special Educational Opportunities

In the very early years of the Clinic's history, medical students from a number of schools came to the Clinic during summer vacation to observe various activities. At first this occurred mainly in laboratory fields. This practice was particularly encouraged by Dr. William MacCarty, who came to Mayo as head of the section of surgical pathology in 1915. Gradually, and with staff encouragement, medical students came to observe in various clinical fields as well.

Medical Student Clerkships

In the medical schools of the country, assignments of students for study and experience in clinical fields with patients were called clerkships. These included quarterly assignments to clerkships in medicine, surgery, obstetrics, and the rest. Clerks took patients' histories, made physical examinations, and ventured tentative diagnoses, working under the direction of interns, residents, and faculty members. Why not establish such medical school clerkships here at Mayo, even though we had no complete medical school? This was done. Describing such programs to a number of medical schools, it was soon arranged with the deans of several institutions for them to give regular medical school credit for such work done at the Clinic by their students. These medical schools accepted

Mayo's reports and grades for credit toward the M.D. degree. In the 1961 Mayo Foundation report to the Clinic, the author stated:

> Increasingly, medical schools are providing for elective quarters which may be spent away from the parent medical school. We now offer training programs for such students in clinical as well as laboratory fields. During all of last year we had 40 such students; this summer there were 23, the largest number in any quarter so far. They came from 15 medical schools: Baylor, Emory, Harvard, Jefferson, Johns Hopkins, Maryland, McGill, Minnesota, Northwestern, Pennsylvania, Rochester, New York, St. Louis, Stanford, Tulane and Women's Medical College. They worked in biochemistry, dentistry, dermatology, medicine, neurology, pathology, pediatrics and surgery.
>
> Scholarships from the Alumni Association of the Mayo Foundation and endowment funds provide a modest stipend to these medical students to help defray expenses. Medical school deans are regularly notified of this educational opportunity for their students.
>
> This project accomplishes several purposes. The medical student provides a teaching opportunity to our regular fellows which they welcome with enthusiasm. The deficiency of our program of limited teaching opportunity by fellows is partially corrected by the medical student program, if only to a modest degree. This program also acquaints the medical student with our fellowships, so that he may not only himself apply for an appointment in due time, but presumably he also tells his fellow medical students about his experience.
>
> We know that medical students are enthusiastic about this experience from the written comments requested from and submitted by each medical student, appraising his experience with us. The students found their work "extremely rewarding." They were impressed by "the amiable and enthusiastic atmosphere," "the exciting team effort on behalf of the patient," "the infectious spirit of cooperation," "the academic excellence of the staff" and "the willingness to teach." They "felt welcome as a questioning student" and were "surprised at the attention paid by the staff to the opinions of students."

As foundation director, the author was later able to report that in 1965 there were eighty-one medical student clerks at Mayo, and "in the past six years there has been a total of more than 200 clerks at Mayo from two-thirds of the medical schools of the United States."

Originally the Clinic's clerkship programs were elective courses, chosen by the students themselves, with the dean's approval. But soon medical students were assigned to Mayo by the deans of a few schools as a required rather an elective course. In this manner the Mayo Clinic was actively engaged in undergraduate medical education a full decade before the opening of the Mayo Medical School.

Assistant to Staff

There was always a careful evaluation of a graduate fellow's performance every quarter of the year. A letter grade and amplifying comments were submitted by the fellow's staff supervisor and transmitted to the Mayo Foundation office, where detailed records were kept on every fellow. The foundation could virtually list the class standing of all these graduate students. The very top third-year fellows were offered extensions of their appointments with increases in both stipends and responsibilities. These fellows were sufficiently outstanding to be considered of potential staff caliber. Indeed, most of the Clinic's permanent staff were recruited from this source.

This system was adopted in the late 1940s, and such appointees were entitled assistants to the staff. In the early years of this program about ten fellows per year were so designated. More than half of these subsequently became permanent staff members. Few fellows declined the offers of assistantships to the staff. There was one notable exception.

Tom did superior work clinically and in research. As he neared completion of his three-year training, he was offered an assistantship to the staff in dermatology, citing the real possibility of a permanent staff appointment a bit later.

"Thank you very much," he replied, "but I think my ultimate ambition would be more likely served if I accepted the position offered me at the Medical School of the University of Oregon."

"And what might be that ultimate ambition?" the author asked.

"I want to be head of dermatology at my alma mater, Harvard University."

This utterance from an M.D. about four years out of medical school was preposterous. He certainly was offbeat, despite his superior performance at Mayo. No, he was not offbeat. A few years later Dr. Thomas B. Fitzpatrick became head of the department at Harvard, as Wigglesworth Professor of Dermatology and chief of dermatology at Massachusetts General Hospital in Boston.

Internships

Throughout the country, the internship was a year of hospital training after finishing undergraduate medical school. In theory it was to enable the medical graduate to put into practice what he learned in medical school. This experience was required for licensure to practice medicine in all states of our country. The Council on Medical Education and Hospitals of the American Medical Association established requirements that must be met by hospitals to warrant approval for internship training and maintained a list of all the country's hospitals meeting such standards, as determined by detailed inspections and surveys.

For decades at Mayo, appointees to the Clinic's graduate training program must first have completed internships in approved hospitals. Why not incorporate this educational experience into the Clinic's medical training program? This was done. In a rather elaborate developmental program there were organized both "straight" internships in the various specialty fields and also "rotating" internships providing combined experience in the various major fields of medicine. Mayo's internship program was considered the first step in a program of graduate education and was integrated with subsequent advanced training in the various medical specialty fields of medicine at the residency or fellowship level. Thirty-one medical school graduates commenced internships at Mayo in 1969.

But internships in the entire country were moving toward extinction, which culminated in 1975. Here Mayo encountered something unique in its history. Almost every project ever embarked on would grow and expand with increasing complexity. The internship died. But more realistically it did not die, but was wedded to the residency program.

Almost all of the states of the country still required one year of hospital training beyond the medical school for licensure. This was not an internship but a first year of residency training, often referred to as G-1, or graduate year one. To become certified as a specialist by the various American boards, the internship was no longer required, so medical school graduates could immediately enter specialty training residencies or fellowships. At Mayo some of the appointees already had had a year of residency training elsewhere, but some had come to Rochester directly after medical school graduation.

War Dangers Continue

There was war in 1950—Korea. Some five years before this, Korea was divided into a northern Communist area and a southern republic. Subsequently, north attacked south. Supported by the United Nations and United States troops, General MacArthur helped the south, ending in a truce after three years. In this effort more than 33,000 United States soldiers were killed and 103,000 wounded.

Soon came more war—Vietnam. Like Korea, this country was divided into its Communist north and republic south. And just four years after the Korean truce the Vietnam North attacked the South. Later this country sent troops and bombers to help the south, the total of United States forces numbering some 550,000. By the time our troops were withdrawn, we had lost some 43,000, and there were 306,000 wounded. And the cost of this war to the United States was estimated at nearly $148 billion.

Let us recall that Russia was involved, since we fought against their allies, the communists, in both North Korea and North Vietnam. All this was rather far away. But then came the Cuban crisis, very near home. Cuba's Castro and Russia's Kruschev were pals. Russia aided Cuba against efforts to overthrow Castro. There was the Bay of Pigs in 1961. Cuban refugees were trained in Central America. The United States aided in this and transported anti-Castro forces to Cuba, protected by United States destroyers. This effort was a complete failure.

Meanwhile, Russia was sending atomic missiles to Cuba and forming missile sites there. President Kennedy warned that the Soviet Union was establishing missile bases in Cuba to provide possible atomic bomb strikes against the Western Hemisphere. We imposed quarantines, and the president bluntly implied that the United States was ready to meet threats to this hemisphere with measures up to and including war.

The purpose here is not to recount American military history. But all this terror impinged itself on all Americans and all Rochester and all the Mayo Clinic. What should be done? An atomic bomb explosion would immediately kill everyone within miles. The Clinic could do nothing about this. But there were dangers other than those at the site of the explosion. Atomic radiation carried by dust or otherwise could seriously injure or even kill people dozens of miles away. Should the Twin Cities be bombed, Rochester could be affected disastrously by atomic fallout. It was necessary to devise and stock fallout shelters as retreats for civilians after an atomic bomb explosion some distance away. To meet this need the Clinic appointed a disaster committee to cooperate with the various government agencies involved.

"Overall community shelter planning has assigned a quota of 31,714 men, women and children to the Franklin Complex in downtown Rochester, of which the Mayo Clinic buildings are a part."

These underground shelters included the subways of the Clinic buildings, which in themselves could provide for more than two thousand refugees. The Clinic, with government help, managed stores to meet the needs of sheltered thousands. At one time, six huge trucks rolled up to the Damon Building, unloaded their cargos, and drove away. This mass of material had nothing to do with Mayo's chief function—the care of the sick. It related rather to the threat of international thermonuclear warfare. The shipment came from the United States Civil Defense Agency. Its 233,958-pound cargo contained 3,641 cases of biscuits, 667 sanitary kits, and 107 packages of medical supplies.

Staff members were encouraged to lay in emergency supplies in their own homes to carry to fallout shelters if needed. Emergency supplies consisted of canned foods, blankets, candles, and the like. Some of the staff built their own personal fallout shelters. Russ Hanson had one dug deeply in his own backyard. It was well equipped for sleeping and contained stores of food, water, and other essentials. Fortunately, the Cuban crisis was resolved in late 1962, and the fallout shelters were never used.

All these war dangers necessitated medical education of a special kind. But medical education of any special kind has always been a Mayo forte. The Clinic joined the Medical Education for National Defense (MEND) program. Its aim was to acquaint medical institutions and their staffs and students with problems to be met in military service or in emergencies here at home. All of the country's eighty-seven undergraduate medical schools eventually participated in MEND. The Mayo Graduate School of Medicine was the only participating graduate school.

Even before the military units of the government established MEND, the Mayo Clinic had established a committee for disaster planning under the leadership of Dr. J. C. "Jack" Ivans. Its responsibility was to coordinate Clinic activities with other local, state, and national efforts to prepare for a variety of possible disaster situations. The committee cooperated with many like-minded people and institutions such as hospitals, law enforcement agencies, governmental bodies, and the military. Dry runs of disaster possibilities were held; weaknesses in planning were unearthed and strengthened. Through all this the Clinic was somewhat ahead of the story when the government established MEND.

Included in Mayo's MEND program was a series of lectures on these subjects: thermonuclear weapons and their effects, principles of medical care in mass emergencies, principles of wound healing, management of thoracic and abdominal injuries, management of injuries to the head and the extremities. Among the MEND projects, now hard to believe, was the requisitioning of some portable two-hundred-bed hospitals. These amazing units were complete down to the self-contained x-ray equipment and power plants. Wherever such a "hospital" might be needed in the Rochester area, it would be transported in one large van. The entire contraption needed only two thousand cubic feet storage space and weighed just 13½ tons.

Not everyone was convinced of the value or necessity for MEND. Some of the country's doctors complained that they already had all they could do in caring for their own patients. Some medical educators protested heatedly that medical students already had too much to learn in four years. There were a few who would dismiss the whole project as merely "playing soldier." But a growing number of physicians saw such training and preparation as essential. Should thermonuclear war be precipitated, tens of millions of American civilians would be sitting squarely in the front lines. The medical problems would be appallingly unlike anything American medicine had ever encountered.

Then there was also SEND—Staff Education for National Defense—covering all aspects of this tremendous problem, including the nature and effects of nuclear missiles. It was pointed out that one-megaton bomb was equivalent to one million tons of TNT; elapsed time for the nuclear reaction was one-millionth of a second; temperature within the explosive volume would reach several million degrees; the pressure of this exploding volume was several million pounds per square inch. Brightness after seven thousandths of a second might be thirty times as bright as the sun, even at a distance of sixty miles. Glare in the sky in early dawn might be visible up to four hundred miles away, and the heat wave could cause burns on exposed skin up to twelve miles away.

Active in planning and developing these educational programs were several Clinic staff members, chief of whom was Dr. C. A. Owen. It was recognized that although Rochester would probably never be a primary target area, the Civil Defense Agency designated Rochester as a definitive treatment area for fifty thousand seriously injured or ill patients. Fortunately, none of these disasters eventuated, but the Clinic tried to be ready for them.

Sometime in the mid 1960s there was a rather extensive SEND tour with a group of about thirty people, including a few from the Clinic, but mostly deans and representatives of other medical institutions. The tour included San Antonio, Texas, and San Diego, California. Participants learned something about pressure chambers, pressure suits for pilots, inflatable field hospital units, and many other military developments. Tanks, ships, airplanes, submarines, and helicopters performed for the group. The tour ended in San Diego Harbor aboard a United States airplane carrier. This carrier's deck acreage could accommodate both the *Queen Mary* and the *Queen Elizabeth*. Here, among other things, was demonstrated a helicopter rescue of men floundering in the open sea.

The author's wife, Maria, accompanied this SEND tour, and together they returned by train from California to Rochester. As they left their breakfast table in the diner, there, sitting alone, was California's former governor Ronald Reagan. Maria recognized him as one of her heroes in long-ago movies and TV shows. They stopped at Reagan's table and introduced themselves. He was most cordial. He autographed the dining car breakfast menu, "To Maria with best wishes." Later, somewhere in New Mexico, the train stopped to have the windows cleaned, and passengers got off to walk alongside the stopped train. The Johnsons encountered Reagan again:

> Fortunately I was carrying my movie camera and asked Reagan if I might take some film of him and Maria. He readily agreed. Maria was a bit nervous as he took her arm and said, "Relax and smile now, Maria, you're with me in the movies now."

Numbers of staff members were on active duty in various parts of the world. One instance deserves special mention. A young but very able consultant received orders for active duty in Seattle. At the Mayo Foundation office he explained that he had no objections to active military duty. He expected it. But he explained that his wife had an emotional problem related primarily to troubled relationships with her parents. Under treatment at the Clinic she was making excellent progress.

"But I am ordered to active duty in Seattle. My wife's parents live there. She will lose all she has gained if we go to that city."

In a telephone call to his friend "Army" Armstrong, the surgeon general in Washington, the author explained the situation frankly. Armstrong was agreeable to making a change of assignment. When his new assignment arrived, the consultant complained, "I am now ordered to San Diego. My wife's family spends the winter in nearby La Jolla!"

So there was another telephone call to the surgeon general. Intensely amused, Armstrong said, "O.K., we'll send him out of the country." So the young staff member was ordered to occupied Germany, where he and his wife spent a most satisfactory two years.

Mayo Clinic Library

The deep roots of the Mayo Clinic library may be traced back to William Worrall Mayo, father of the two Mayo brothers. His wife once stated,

> The doctor had one weakness. It was for book agents. He knew and loved good books. Oh, many a time I planned to buy a dress for Trude or something for the boys or the house, only to have a book agent come to town and tip over my bucket of milk.

The Clinic library, as such, was begun in 1907 in a room of the offices of the father and his two sons in the old Masonic Temple Building. Dr. Will once reminisced, "I can see father now, standing on a wooden chair, reaching up to take books down or, with one book under his arm, another held between his knees, looking into the pages of a third." From their father the brothers learned the profound respect for the printed word that marked their entire lives. Very soon a separate library was constructed adjacent to the offices and connected with a corridor.

When the Red Brick Building came into being in 1914, the four-thousand-volume library collection was moved to its fourth floor. Library contents grew with a rapidity comparable to the increase in patient visits, so that when the Plummer Building was completed in the late 1920s, the Clinic library was moved to its present location on the twelfth floor, expanding eventually to include space on the eleventh, fourteenth, fifteenth, and sixteenth floors. By the mid 1950s there were ninety-five thousand volumes in the stacks. Journals numbering more than two thousand were received regularly by purchase, by exchange for the *Mayo Clinic Proceedings*, or by outright gift.

In addition to the medical staff of the Clinic and fellows of the Mayo Foundation, others served by the library were members of the State Hospital staff, student nurses, nurse anesthetists, physical medicine and occupational therapy students, Rochester Junior College students, visiting physicians, as well as Clinic patients.

Initially the library was under the direction of Maude H. Mellish, who also did editorial work involved in the publication of papers by staff members and fellows. And later, for nearly three decades, the major factor in the library's growth and management was Thomas E. Keys. He was a historian, scholar, and author as well as a librarian. After some lesser library posts, he became chief librarian in 1946, following his military service, much of which was at the Army Medical Library in Cleveland. Even the military recognized his expertness in library matters and granted him promotions from first lieutenant to lieutenant colonel.

In addition to the massive holdings of the library, there were notable special features. For example, it was generally recognized that the library collection of Russian periodical medical literature was the largest in the United States. There was an impressive collection of rare books, resulting largely from Tom Keys' increasing efforts. He also directed matters leading up to and during the thirty-ninth annual meeting, in Rochester, of the American Association for the History of Medicine, which was dedicated to "promote research, study, interest and writing in the history of medicine."

Eventually, Jack Key became chief librarian, following Tom Keys. What an anomalous transition—from Keys to Key. They were entirely unrelated. No surprise would emerge from a Johnson succeeding a Johnson, with scores of such names to be found in Rochester, but Keys to Key was indeed unique.

The Clinic's library was not among the nation's largest. A number of medical school libraries in the United States contained more volumes. But as to quality, like so much at Mayo, the library ranked with the world's best.

A significant unit of the library complex was devoted to the history of medicine. Headquarters and collections were located on the Plummer Building's fifteenth floor, vacated by the movement of the Mayo Graduate

School of Medicine headquarters to the new Harwick Building. Librarians in the historical unit handled the antique volumes with reverent hands, deeply aware of the responsibility of preserving these books, some of them centuries old. The three thousand volumes date back for ages. The oldest volume is dated 1479, prior to Columbus's discovery of America, when Serapin the Younger wrote, *Liber Aggregatus in Medicinas Simplicibus,* which translates approximately to *Book of Writings on Plain Medicine.* In charge of this historical collection was Ruth Mann, daughter of Dr. Frank Mann, Mayo's early and great medical scientist. Ruth Mann was also in charge of the activities of the Clinic's history of medicine society, arranging its monthly meetings.

Historical data relative to Mayo became voluminous. The Clinic's historical committee became responsible for the "acquisition, arrangement and orderly preservation of any items which have sound and permanent historical value." The committee became convinced that Mayo needed someone to supervise the tremendous backlog of archives. And so Clark W. Nelson became the Clinic's archivist. He had had service with the federal government's National Archives and Records Service. And what, precisely, is the job of an archivist? Nelson considered himself as having two primarily Mayo Clinic assignments: (1) the preservation and protection of permanently valuable items such as papers, letters, documents, citations, honors, early professional instruments, and the like; (2) the making available of these items to individuals and groups of the Clinic, medical scholars, and others with a legitimate interest in medical history.

Nelson felt strongly that it is a misconception of the function of archives as only "places where things are kept. Archives should be places where historically valuable information is kept both for its historic interest and practical use."

As with all else at Mayo, the library expanded tremendously over the years, so that eventually it contained nearly a quarter of a million volumes. There were thirty-four hundred journal subscriptions. Weekly, more than one thousand volumes circulated. Among the numerous library services was the production of photocopies of scientific articles. In one recent year about two million pages were photocopied, mainly for Clinic staff members, who may use this service in lieu of taking a volume from the library. Requests for photocopies also come from libraries located elsewhere in the country. Usually the distant library request is made on behalf of a physician in that locality.

CHAPTER 12

Research Accomplishments

To adequately record the research achievements of Mayo would require a considerable number of volumes rather than a mere chapter in this one volume. In fact, by 1957, Clinic and foundation authors had published more than twenty-one thousand medical and scientific papers, as well as more than one hundred books. Let us attempt to summarize a few of the major accomplishments.

Open-Heart Surgery

The problem of defects in the interior of the heart in newborn infants has challenged medicine for decades. Many of these are septal defects, or openings in the partition between the right and left sides of the heart. The right side of the heart contains venous (or "impure") blood from the body generally. The left side contains oxygenated (or "pure") blood from the lungs. A partition, or septum, normally separates the left and right halves of the heart completely. A septum defect, or hole in this partition, results in mixing the venous and oxygenated blood. Thus the heart pumps this mixture out to the entire body. The results may be serious or even fatal if the hole in the heart's interior partition is rather large.

The surgical repair of defects of this kind and size elsewhere in the body is relatively simple. But not so in the pumping heart, filled as it is with moving blood. How might the heart be emptied of blood so that it can be opened surgically and the defect repaired, while still providing the patient's body with an adequate supply of blood during the surgery? A solution to this problem challenged Dr. John Gibbon, a surgeon at Jefferson Medical College in Philadelphia. He said:

> The ultimate objective of my work has been to operate inside the heart under direct vision . . . In the presence of a septal defect, shunting the flow of blood around one side of the heart with a pump will not provide a bloodless field for operative closure of the defect. An apparatus which embodies a mechanical lung, as well as pumps, enables you to shunt blood around both the heart and the lungs, thus allowing operations to be performed under direct vision in a bloodless field within the opened heart.

Machinery was needed to continue both the pumping action of the heart and the functioning of the lungs, removing carbon dioxide and providing the blood with oxygen–a heart-lung machine. What a challenge! But it was met. All the venous blood about to enter the heart was shunted into the heart-lung machine. Here a pump pushed the blood into an artificial lung device for oxygenation and carbon dioxide removal. Then another pump directed the "pure" blood into the arteries. Of the mechanical lung in his machine, Gibbon said, "This presents far more difficulties than pumping blood. I am sure that the most efficient apparatus for performing the functions of the lungs has not yet been devised."

But this also came, thanks in large part to Mayo. Dr. John Kirklin, a native of Rochester and son of Mayo's chief radiologist, became a Mayo heart and lung surgeon after completing a five-year fellowship in surgery in 1950. He shared the goal of Gibbon, to be able to operate inside the heart. His chief collaborators in this epic enterprise were pediatrician Dr. James DuShane and physiologist Dr. Earl Wood, who stated, "I think we are on the verge of a new era in cardiology."

Of course, other surgeons, pediatricians, physiologists, cardiologists, and anesthesiologists also participated. Engineers were also required. The Clinic's section of engineering undertook the development of the heart-lung bypass apparatus, incorporating and improving on the essential features of the Gibbon device. The Mayo-Gibbon heart-lung machine eventuated. Many experiments on laboratory animals were necessary to achieve this goal before the machine could be used on human patients. On a patient's bloodless heart it was also necessary to stop the heartbeat during surgery. This was done using proper chemical preparations. Employing the mechanical substitute for man's heart and lungs, Kirklin recalls:

> Early in 1955 five patients were identified for the initial use at the Mayo

> Clinic of a pump-oxygenation for cardiac surgery. They were selected after careful review of a large number of patients who needed open operations for otherwise ultimately fatal heart disease, for which no other kind of surgical treatment would be possible. Each family was told that we would use a new and hitherto unproven method with which we had extensive laboratory but no clinical experience. We explained the risks, imponderables and possible benefits of the operations. The first operation, repair of a large ventricular septal defect in a 5½-year-old child, was performed on March 22, 1955. Our plan was to proceed with the other four operations even if the first patient died, so great was our confidence in the methods we had developed in the laboratory work. In spite of temporary dislodgement of the arterial line during bypass, the first operation was successfully done and the patient's postoperative course was uneventful.

The first eight of Kirklin's patients provided the material for the world's first publication concerning a group of patients operated on employing the Mayo-Gibbon heart-lung machine for mechanical bypass of the heart and lungs. Dr. Kirklin stated:

> In a series of operations upon eight patients who had severe congenital heart disease, each with symptoms of advanced severity indicating poor prognosis, the mechanical pump-oxygenator system adequately maintained the patients during the period of perfusion. Use of this system established excellent conditions for precise, unhurried cardiac surgery. The foregoing facts demonstrate the usefulness of this technique in the surgical treatment of certain abnormalities of the heart and great vessels.

Reviewing past events leading up to this success, we note that three years earlier, Kirklin and Earl Wood presented to Mayo's sciences committee "a proposal that they had had under consideration for some time, calling for the production and experimental use of a mechanical heart for certain types of cardiac surgery."

This inaugurated events leading eventually to John Kirklin being designated as "the chief architect of open-heart surgery," and Earl Wood as having "laid the foundation for open-heart surgery at Mayo."

The teamwork involved in such surgery is astonishing. There are clinicians, cardiologists, radiologists, clinical pathologists, anesthesiologists, residents, nurses, dietitians, bypass machine operators, social workers, and perhaps more. Years later, Dr. Dwight McGoon stated that each of these "holds a key post. The cardiac surgeon plays a major part, but even with the training, hard work and discipline that he must master, he is but a leader and not a soloist."

Eventually it became routine for the surgeon or cardiologist to notify social service when an appointment for heart surgery was made.

> Social Service immediately writes to the parents giving information which answers anticipated questions: how long they may expect to be in

Rochester; how long the child will be hospitalized; probable cost for medical care and living expenses. She offers to arrange for inexpensive living quarters if this is desired and to help "in any way we can." The parent (most often only one parent accompanies the child) is asked to come to the Social Service section the day the child is registered at the Clinic and close contact is maintained during the stay here.

The assistance given may include serving as banker (depositing the funds the parent has brought or sent ahead, receiving and paying bills for hospitalization and living quarters); arranging reservations for the return home; enlisting help of Travelers' Aid and airline stewardesses to provide wheelchairs, rest facilities, low salt diets. Certainly one of the most important things the social worker does is to provide a sympathetic ear to a worried parent.

When, as is often the case, neither parent or patient speak English, the Language Department arranges for an interpreter to bridge the communication gap.

May we pass for a moment from the sublime to the ridiculous? Dr. James DuShane, the pediatric cardiologist collaborating in these epic investigations, complained to a group at some luncheon:

> I am annoyed at getting these repeated requests and forms to fill out from "Who's Who in America." They want me to tell all about my past history and what I have accomplished in life. It is entirely too much bother. I won't do it.

"Jim," the author said, "you will do it. If ever you forget the exact date of your wedding anniversary all you need to do is look it up in *Who's Who.*" The name James W. DuShane now appears in *Who's Who in America.*

But to return from the ridiculous back to the sublime, let us look at this heart-lung machinery in a bit more technical detail. Blood from all the body enters the right side of the heart via two great veins, the superior and inferior venae cavae. After opening the chest, these veins are attached to a tube which carries all this blood into the Mayo-Gibbon machine, aided by a suction device in the apparatus. A similar arrangement carries blood into the machine from the veins in the muscles of the heart itself. This mixed blood from the entire body, including the heart muscles, enters a chamber which takes the place of the right side of the heart.

A pump in the machine simulating the action of the heart's right ventricle pumps all this blood into the artificial lung or oxygenator. Devising the artificial lung machinery was the most challenging task in the whole investigation. It is necessary that all this blood be spread in very thin layers exposed to oxygen-rich air. So in the machine, all the pumped blood was spread over some fourteen wire-mesh screens, each screen being twelve by fourteen inches in size. Thus every tiny droplet of blood was exposed to the air of the oxygenator to exchange its unwanted carbon dioxide for needed oxygen. Then another pump, simulating the heart's left ventricle, returned the freshened blood through a tube leading into the patient's left subclavian artery, thence to circulate throughout the entire body except lungs. For all this necessary movement of blood the heart-lung machine had three separate pumps.

The tremendous efforts behind Dr. Kirklin's first open-heart surgery operation are left unspoken when the first five and one-half-year-old girl was referred to simply as "alive and well."

The heart-lung machine is used not only during operations involving opening the heart. It is necessary also in operations involving the coronary arteries lying on the outer surface of the heart ventricles. Eventually there were five or six operations per day involving this machinery. In 1973, the Clinic celebrated the ten thousandth of these heart operations. All this happened during the eighteen years since Dr. John Kirklin did the first historic open-heart operation.

The first nationwide TV hookup to be originated in Rochester was a demonstration of all the techniques and machinery involved in open-heart surgery. This was the first of a twenty-six week series called *Medical Horizons*. The audience was estimated at six to nine million people.

Overactive Parathyroid Glands

The endocrine glands, which secrete their hormones into the blood, can become overactive as well as underactive. The hypophysis, inside the skull, secretes a hormone regulating growth. When this gland is overactive, excessive growth results and the patient may become a husky, eight-foot-tall giant. The thyroid hormone controls the rate at which the body burns its sugar, among other things. When this gland becomes overactive, the body fires flame up. The patient is hot and sweating and hungry and weak. He is nervous and excitable. The pancreatic hormone controls the blood sugar level. While underactivity produces diabetes, overactivity causes the sugar concentration of the blood to fall, leading to convulsions, unconsciousness, and death. All these conditions can be duplicated in experimental animals by feeding or injecting them with excessive amounts of the proper hormone.

The two small pair of parathyroid glands are embedded in the back of the thyroid gland in the neck. Their hormone controls the body's management of calcium, including its incorporation into bone. When these glands are underactive, the calcium level of the blood falls, the muscles twitch, and death occurs unless treatment is administered.

In overactivity of these glands, or hyperparathyroidism, calcium is withdrawn from the bones, causing weakening and fractures, and the excess of calcium in the blood may produce kidney stones. There may also be psychiatric disorders, stomach ulcers, and pancreatic derangements.

Among the numerous Mayo doctors achieving worldwide distinction there appears the name of Dr. F. Raymond Keating. Among his many investigations were studies on hyperparathyroidism, its recognition, diagnosis, and treatment, as well as the normal functioning of the glands. All this is far more complicated than this simplified account. The diagnosis, especially of mild abnormal function, is by no means easy.

Surgery is the only acceptable final treatment, removing some of the overactive glands. Yet the patient may be too ill to permit immediate operation. Keating sought and found ways of administering medical care until the patient's condition improved sufficiently to endure surgery. Says Keating:

> Primary hyperparathyroidism is a disease of astonishing variety, both in severity and in its mode of clinical expression. It is encountered in patients with no symptoms whatsoever, as well as in patients with involvement of the skeleton or urinary tract. High blood calcium remains the principle clue for identifying cases and in most instances the principle criterion for diagnosis; hyperparathyroidism can usually be defined as hypercalcemia (high blood calcium levels) for which alternative explanations have been excluded. Nevertheless, in some patients the calcium levels are borderline, equivocal or within the normal range. In such instances a battery of other procedures is used, which in the aggregate is only partially helpful. Careful clinical judgment with consideration of all the evidence and all alternatives is required; the diagnosis is not only a clinical one. The treatment is surgical, but like the diagnosis, is difficult and not without risks.

Epilepsy

> Convulsive disorders among children are common and of varied course. Any physician in general practice, any pediatrician, and physicians specializing in other fields may be called on to treat a child with convulsions. The seizure may indicate an underlying serious condition or it may in itself be dangerous to life. It must be remembered that it is a symptom and not a disease, and it demands that immediate attention be given the child, followed by a thorough investigation as to the origin of the attack.

This statement was pediatrician Dr. Haddow Keith's introduction to his account of convulsions in children (1963). It is often difficult or even impossible to determine the basic cause of the epilepsy, with its frequent convulsions and unconscious states. Many disorders within the brain or affecting the brain can cause this malady. Even though the basic cause may evade detection, it is important to treat the epilepsy itself, even if this is only a symptom of an unknown defect. Not only are the fits very upsetting to one's daily life, but they might even terminate fatally.

Early in the century it was learned, not at the Mayo Clinic, that fasting might reduce convulsions. One observer stated that of his twenty-six patients only four had epileptic seizures after fasting ten days. But obviously treatment by fasting is necessarily limited in duration. Why not examine the various consequences of fasting in anyone, even a normal person? Perhaps some chemical change in the body might be the effective factor in controlling the convulsions. The Clinic's Dr. Russell Wilder found the answer.

Ordinary fats eaten are either stored in the body or burned to give off only carbon dioxide and water, plus heat and energy. For such fat combustion it is essential that carbohydrates such as sugar be burned simultaneously. "Fats burn in the flame of carbohydrates." Without this accomplishment, the fat combustion is incomplete, resulting in much of the fat breaking down into what are called ketone bodies. And in periods of fasting, with limited burning of carbohydrates, ketone bodies are also formed from fats. So Dr. Wilder thought that perhaps the beneficial effects of fasting in epileptic patients might somehow be the presence of these ketones in the body fluids and tissues.

Numerous investigators pursued this idea. Very important among these was Mayo's Keith, who worked at the project for many years. A diet that causes much of the eaten fat to produce ketone bodies was developed. Essentially this was a high-fat diet. Using this ketone-producing diet controlled the disorder in many epileptics. Along with these investigations on human beings, there was also much work on experimentally produced convulsions in dogs.

In his book on the subject published in 1963, Haddow Keith reviewed the effects of the ketogenic diet on 530 patients who cooperated in the diet treatment program. Nearly one third of these became well with no attacks, and about one fourth were definitely improved. This meant that there were good results in more than one half of those treated. In the remainder the diet proved ineffective.

Although this was not nearly as successful a result as obtained in treating diabetes with insulin, it was a most noteworthy achievement.

Early Cancer Detection

The most common death from cancer in women is when it occurs in the breast. The second most common is from cancer of the cervix, or neck, of the uterus. Cancer of the breast commonly reveals itself by the patient or her physician feeling a lump in the breast, although such lumps are by no means always malignant. But in early cancer of the uterine cervix there may be no lump palpable on vaginal or other gross examinations. And the patient may have no symptoms or complaints referable to the uterine area. This early cancer was designated preclinical, meaning that it was not detectable clinically by the usual tests or examinations.

Mayo's surgical pathologist Dr. David Dahlin pursued an extensive elaboration of the findings of George Papanicolaou, who had developed Pap smears. Dahlin found (in 1943) that carcinoma growing on the uterine cervix emitted free cancer cells that could easily be collected in a smear, and their cancerous nature could be identified microscopically. It was demonstrated that the material thus shed from the surfaces of cervical carcinomas was just as good for cancer diagnosis as material derived from the interior of advanced cancerous growths.

Employing this information, a program for the detection of preclinical carcinoma was developed at Saint Marys Hospital by Dahlin and associates beginning in 1948. At first such cervical smears were made only when requested by gynecologists. Soon the cervical smear became part of the routine examination of all women seen in the section of obstetrics and gynecology. Largely at Dahlin's insistence, this procedure was expanded so that cervical smears were made routinely on all women of age twenty-five or over who registered at the Clinic for any complaint whatsoever, however unrelated to the uterus the patient's complaint might be. Dahlin perfected the techniques necessary and trained the technicians to process the smears and keep the records.

The lifesaving results of these inspired efforts were remarkable. In the ten-year period to 1958 a total of over 90,000 cervical smears were made. In these, 678 preclinical cancers of the cervix were discovered, leading to lifesaving surgery which would never have been considered without the background of these elaborate researches.

Another area in the Clinic's development of early diagnosis was in the field of lung cancer, by microscopic examination of the patient's sputum, including secretions of the trachea, or windpipe, and its branches to the two lungs. This work was conducted by the Clinic's pathologist Dr. John R. McDonald with a number of coworkers, starting in 1947. McDonald was stimulated in this effort by similar studies carried out elsewhere than in Rochester.

Challenging problems were the procuring of samples of the proper origin, excluding mere saliva from the mouth, and the preparing of samples properly for microscopic examinations. All this was most complicated. The researchers found that a malignant tumor located in any part of the respiratory system was likely to produce cancer cells in the sputum. In fact, they stated that a positive finding in examination of the sputum was to be expected in about three fourths of patients with cancer in the respiratory tubes or bronchi.

Recall that the original observations on such early detection of cancer of the uterine cervix and cancer of the lungs were made elsewhere than at the Mayo Clinic. This by no means diminishes the importance of the contributions of Dahlin and McDonald in these two areas of research.The Mayo investigators carried on studies that were as essential as the original discoveries. First, in all such cases there must be a thorough confirmation of the initial findings. Then techniques for carrying out the process must be improved and perfected. Staff members and technicians must be properly trained to carry them out.

And also the procedures must be done on hundreds or even thousands of patients to be sure that the best has been obtained in both methods of diagnosis and forms of therapy. The Mayo Clinic so adequately provides this requirement. In 1951 there were about three thousand patients coming to the Clinic every week, presenting almost innumerable varieties of human ailments. And this mass of necessary material was coupled with Mayo's endless devotion to determining the causes, diagnosis, and treatment of human diseases, regardless of the staff time and financial support required.

Just as one example, Dahlin learned which was the best one of at least seven different methods that had been proposed for securing the best uterine smears and preparing them properly. And McDonald was involved in inducing the Minnesota division of the American Cancer Society to support the training of technicians to function properly in the procedures. Examples could be multiplied regarding the contributions of Dahlin and McDonald toward meeting the challenge of early detection of cancer of the uterus and lungs.

Control of Cancer

Cancer continues to be medicine's major problem. It is astonishing that science has discovered so much about the cause and control of many diseases, with only limited success with this dread affliction. Tuberculosis, once a scourge of mankind, is eliminated from the civilized world. Insulin administration has permitted millions of diabetics to live reasonably normal lives. We can perform surgery on the human heart and transplant kidneys. Even heart transplants have been performed. We know about the microscopic structure of the body cells, how chromosomes transmit heredity, and all the events occurring when a body cell reproduces by dividing into two. We have learned much about cancer, but know too little about how to control it, except by removing the growth by surgery or destroying it by radiation therapy.

Suppose you had been asked this question some decades ago: Which do you think will come first in the future, complete control of cancer or earthly humans safely making a round trip to the moon, with a stop on that sphere?

In the year 1966 it was estimated that a diagnosis of cancer would be made on some 570,000 patients in the United States. Of every six of these persons, two could be saved. This figure might be raised to three by means of early diagnosis and treatment. The remaining three would be patients suffering from types of cancer whose control awaits the results of intensified research in the future.

At Mayo, a diagnosis of cancer was made on about six thousand patients annually. Each year about nine thousand patients with cancer diagnosis returned for checkups or further treatment. The combined figure of fifteen thousand represented about eight percent of all patients registering at the Clinic in 1964. Naturally such patient numbers also meant that a proportionately large number of Clinic consultants were involved. Actually there were twenty-two Clinic sections or departments involved in some aspect of cancer diagnosis, treatment, or research. These cancer efforts were integrated by the section of clinical oncology, headed by Dr. Harry F. Bisel. There was also an oncology society composed of some fifty Clinic staff members with a special interest in cancer, meeting monthly at Mayo Foundation House, along with scientists visiting Rochester.

Major studies at the Clinic were on various drugs that might extend the useful life expectancy of cancer patients who have not responded well to surgical treatment or radiation therapy. The long-term goal was to achieve the chemical control of cancer. Some twenty promising drugs were under investigation. These were mainly compounds that destroy cells or interfere somewhat with the growth of cancer cells. Dr. Bisel noted that "we speak of control rather than cure. Forty-five years ago diabetes was a fatal disease. Today it can in most instances be controlled—not cured—by insulin." The hope that a similarly effective drug might be found for cancer stimulates the endless testing of new compounds produced in laboratories of research institutions and drug companies. Dr. Bisel was asked whether he was at all optimistic about finding such a drug. The reply, "Yes. Only optimists specialize in clinical cancer research."

Support for such research was provided by various governmental and voluntary agencies, including the National Cancer Institute and the

American Cancer Society. In due time the Mayo Clinic was designated, along with fifteen other institutions, as a comprehensive cancer center by the governmental agency, the National Cancer Institute.

Kidney Transplants

The function of the kidneys is to remove various waste products from the blood to be eliminated in the urine. Like all other organs of the body, these are subject to disease and gradually extending destruction. Fortunately, the animal body is provided with much more tissue of various kinds than is needed to maintain health and life. Such margins of safety, of which we all have many, include paired organs such as the kidneys and lungs. One of the pair can carry out all the work required.

Even in such unpaired organs as the liver or spleen, merely a part of the organ can function adequately to preserve health when much of the organ is destroyed by disease or accident.

But despite such margins of safety, disease can destroy enough of the kidneys to cause death. In such an event, investigators asked, might it not be possible to remove surgically a patient's nearly dead kidney and replace it, by transplant, with a good kidney taken from a healthy donor? Again the margins of safety principle emerges. A healthy person who gives up one of his kidneys in such an event need have no worry about his own kidney function. His remaining one kidney can carry out all the functions required.

The Mayo Clinic surgeon Dr. George Hallenbeck, with a number of associates, including the kidney specialist Dr. James DeWeerd, bent themselves to the problem. Hallenbeck did his first kidney transplant in 1963.

The surgery involved is complicated compared with the removal of the appendix. The kidney arteries and veins of the patient must be well preserved to be properly attached to the arteries and veins of the transplanted kidney. And the duct carrying urine to the bladder must be properly placed. But first, solutions had to be developed for other than purely surgical problems: (a) where and how to secure a healthy donor willing to give up one of his kidneys, (b) how to keep the patient alive and relatively well until such a donor is found, (c) how to be sure that the transplanted kidney will not be destroyed by the recipient, just as that person's body fluids destroy other foreign invaders such as bacteria, or even transfused blood if the blood is drawn from one who is of the wrong blood group. Preventing destruction of transplanted kidneys has been a bigger problem than the surgery involved.

Finally, how is the life and functioning of the kidney to be transplanted maintained after its removal from the donor and before completely transplanting it into the recipient?

The world's researchers and surgeons solved these problems, thanks to such as Hallenbeck, and thanks to the Mayo Clinic's devotion to exploring new avenues into the unknowns of health and disease. Many were involved in the task: surgeons, kidney specialists, radiologists, anesthesiologists, surgical pathologists, investigators in experimental and anatomic pathology, microbiologists, veterinarians, and even psychiatrists, as the main team members. The challenge was great. Of the estimated one hundred thousand patients who die annually from kidney disease in the United States, at least eight thousand were considered suitable candidates for kidney transplants.

As might be expected, it was soon learned that the safest donor was found to be a member of the immediate family: father, mother, sister, or brother. This close relationship between donor and recipient was the best insurance against destruction of the transplanted kidney by the recipient's blood defenses against foreign tissue. In one early study at Mayo it was found that a kidney transplant from a near-blood relative was three times more likely to succeed than in cases of unrelated donors. And eventually drugs were developed that when given to the recipient would diminish the chances of destruction of the transplant. These drugs are called immunosuppressives; they alter the body's innate production of antibodies, which might otherwise attack the newly transplanted organ.

An important Mayo research development in this field involved the employment of horses stabled at the Clinic's Institute Hills Farm. Into the horses' veins were injected measured amounts of thymus gland tissue. Blood was later drawn from the horses and subjected to a many-step process in the Clinic's laboratories. The end product was a clear, sterile liquid serum. This material was injected into the kidney recipient before surgery and for several days afterward. It was found to overcome that major problem in all transplants—the rejection of the transplant by the body's natural defense mechanisms. Before its use on patients, this serum product from horses was elaborately tested on experimental animals, where it was demonstrated to delay rejection of organ and skin grafts on the animals. This was judged to be a useful supplement to other immunosuppressive drugs, such as azathioprine and prednisone.

And in due time tests were developed to determine the likelihood of transplant survival in any given instance of a potential donor and the recipient. In this test, blood serum from the recipient is mixed with white blood cells from the donor. If the recipient's blood has antibodies against the donor's white cells, a kidney transplant should not be carried out. This process somewhat resembles the tests which must be made to determine what blood transfusions are safe by employing the blood-grouping principle.

The need for donors far exceeded the supply. So why not use the kidney of someone who just died of an accident or a disease unrelated to the kidneys? This also was done. The Kidney Foundation of the Upper Midwest sponsored and administered a program where any person over age eighteen could sign a donor registration card indicating that after his death specific organs could be made available for transplantation. Another source for cadaver kidneys was through Mayo's participation in the United Network for Organ Sharing. Member institutions provide one another with donor kidneys.

Methods had to be devised which would ensure the survival of the kidney from the donor until it was completely transplanted, especially if there was some time lapse between securing the kidney and placing it into the patient's abdomen. Such time intervals were almost certainly to be the case where kidneys from cadavers were used. The problem was solved by pumping proper liquids through the isolated kidney to provide oxygen and other necessities and remove wastes from the living organ. Speed is necessary, since a donor kidney can be properly maintained for no longer than seventy-two hours. Kidneys for transplantation to Mayo patients have been flown to Rochester from medical centers in Oklahoma, Florida, Ohio, and Kentucky. During such transport, a perfusion machine pumps an oxygenated solution through the kidney to maintain viability of the kidney tissue.

But the main source of cadaver kidneys for transplant was in Rochester itself, at the Saint Marys and Methodist hospitals, where staff and facilities were on a twenty-four-hour alert to remove kidneys at the time of a patient's death.

Besides keeping the projected transplant alive, it was equally challenging to keep alive the badly diseased patient needing the transplant. For this, artificial kidney machines were developed. Blood from an arm artery flows into a system of cellophane tubes that lie in a bath of salt solution. Here waste products of the blood are eliminated, just as occurs in healthy kidneys. The blood then flows from the machine into an arm vein of the patient. Even in severe cases, such employment of the artificial kidney need not exceed a four-hour session carried out three times per week. During the process the patient's blood is treated (with heparin, usually) to prevent its clotting in the artificial kidney apparatus.

The Artificial Kidney

Mayo established an artificial kidney center in its Curie Pavilion. Here patients with complete kidney failure could be maintained by use of the artificial kidney device. This center concentrated, for the most part, on training patients to use the artificial kidney in their own homes until they could receive kidney transplants. Such training involved the patient coming to the center for a portion of every day of the workweek for a month. Samples of blood and of the waste liquid from the machine required periodic examination at the Clinic.

After such training, on the day before the patient is to leave the hospital, the equipment is transported to his home under the watchful eye of a skilled technician. After installation the equipment is tested to be sure it functions properly. On the following day the patient returns to his home accompanied by a nurse trained in the field, a technician, and a Clinic fellow.

Under these watchful eyes the patient carries out the procedure as directed, to make sure all goes well. Usually another person in the patient's home is also involved, learning how to insert a needle into an artery to lead blood into the machine and into a vein to return the cleansed blood to the patient. The patient is then left at home, using the machine for a four-hour period three times a week. Remarkably, the patient can carry out a relatively normal life. On an overall basis it was felt that patients so treating themselves at home made a better adjustment to the program than was the case with patients receiving this care at Clinic facilities. And in due time the patient might receive a kidney transplant.

To carry out the hemodialysis, or artificial kidney, program is financially very costly to the patient, but somewhat less so if it is done at home. If a patient were maintained at the Clinic by outpatient treatment for a ten-year period, the cost might approach two hundred thousand dollars. Maintained by home dialysis for the same period, the cost would be reduced to sixty thousand dollars including the initial cost of eleven thousand dollars for the equipment and training for its use. Financial aid may sometimes be had from private insurance or local service organizations.

Dialysis patients were by no means limited to local residents. They might reside not only elsewhere in Minnesota but also in Wisconsin, the Dakotas, Illinois, or Iowa. Each patient was instructed to visit his family physician once a month and return four times a year to Mayo's artificial kidney center. Tests were regularly performed to determine whether the patient-operated machinery was carrying out its assignments properly. Eventually, there were some one hundred Mayo patients carrying out such artificial functions at home.

Within a decade of the first Mayo kidney transplants in the early 1960s, of all patients receiving kidney transplants from living related donors, there was a ninety-five percent survival rate, and at least ninety percent of the patients returned to a fairly normal lifestyle. Of patients receiving kidneys from cadavers, seventy-six percent survived. In 1979 the Methodist Hospital marked the transplantation of the five hundredth kidney. Eventually, all the transplanted kidneys began functioning immediately; before the patient left the operating room the transplanted kidney was producing urine.

It is impossible to list all who have participated in this momentous enterprise, from Dr. George Hallenbeck's first kidney transplant in 1963 until the present time, when much of the work is supervised by Dr. Sylvester Sterioff, director of the Mayo organ and tissue transplantation program.

Peritoneal Dialysis

Some years after the development and use of the artificial kidney, an entirely new procedure was developed to supplement defective kidney function. In this procedure, the role of the kidneys in removing wastes from the blood is taken over by the abdominal peritoneum, which is the thin membrane lining the inner walls of the abdominal cavity; it also covers all the organs contained in the abdomen. This membrane, as is true of much of our body tissue, is provided with a profuse network of blood vessel capillaries. An appropriate sterile solution is introduced into the abdominal cavity. Blood wastes enter the solution from the peritoneal blood capillaries. In this process all the tiny abdominal wall blood vessels take over the functions of the capillaries of the kidneys, which have become ineffective in eliminating body wastes. And the abdominal cavity is, in a sense, a substitute for the urinary bladder.

All this is done after inserting a tube through the abdominal wall, providing a channel through which proper liquids can be introduced into the abdominal cavity from an overhead bag. After some six hours this liquid, with its body waste, can be drained through the tube into a container, and again the peritoneal cavity receives a new dosage of fresh liquid so that there is a continuous presence of the fluid in the abdominal cavity.

Patients are taught how to perform the procedure at home without being bedridden. The emptying and refilling procedure is carried out by patients every four to six hours in the daytime and every eight to twelve hours overnight. The exchange process of draining plus refilling can be carried out within a half hour. At any one time there are about forty-five patients on home peritoneal dialysis.

This process, which bears the impressive and expressive title of continuous ambulatory peritoneal dialysis, was begun in 1977 at the Austin

Diagnostic Clinic, the University of Texas, and the University of Missouri under the auspices of the National Institute of Health. Peritoneal dialysis we may contrast with hemodialysis, which refers to the employment of the artificial kidney device in which blood flows through the machinery. In peritoneal dialysis no blood leaves the body to be cleansed.

Hip Reconstruction

Over a number of years orthopedic surgeon Dr. Mark Coventry devoted his energies to the surgical treatment of the degenerative disease of the hip technically termed osteoarthritis. Occurring mainly in older persons, the chief complaint is pain and stiffness of the hip joint. Few if any human disorders cause more pain than arthritis. The aim in treatment is to eliminate or at least reduce the pain and to restore or improve the various leg movements taking place at the hip joint. Regarding the operation he devised, called osteotomy, or surgical cutting of the bone, Coventry stated:

> The advantages of osteotomy are very clear and definite. The operation is the conservationist's approach to surgery in osteoarthritis of the hip . . . There is no foreign material placed into the joint. There is a minimal postoperative disability period and minimal patient cooperation is necessary. Physical therapy, as such, is usually not required. But the foremost of the advantages is the high incidence of relief of pain as compared with other procedures.

Dr. Coventry's work continued about a decade, until 1964. Summarizing the total results, he said:

> Evaluation of the results is exceedingly difficult, because osteotomy is an operation designed to relieve pain, and relief of pain is hard to judge objectively.
>
> Of the 103 hips of patients who were traced for one year or more after the operation, 83 had good results and 20 had fair or poor results. A result was termed good when all, or almost all, of the pain was relieved and activity returned to normal. A result was considered poor or fair when the patient still had daily pain and was unable to carry out his regular activities. Improvement in deformity and lessening of limp were part of a good result.

Philosophizing on research in general, but more particularly on the design and execution of a clinical research project, Coventry voiced these thoughts:

> How is the subject for clinical research born? Who first conceives the idea—the experienced orthopedist, the internist who sees an orthopedic patient, the resident? Or do we always know? Does the spark strike when we see an entity the nature of which is obscure? Does the idea come from reading an article that stimulates recall to some of our own experiences? Is the thought generated from listening to others discuss certain matters privately

or at a meeting? Somehow or other the idea for a research project *does* come about. After the idea is born it is nurtured by reflection and discussion; it gradually emerges as an entity requiring investigation and ultimately the next phase of the research program gets underway.

Arthritis

There is another eventful historical account of Mayo Drs. Kendall and Hench, and cortisone, related to the affliction known as rheumatoid arthritis. In this disease there is an inflammation of various joints in the body, with pain, swelling, and limited motion. These workers became interested in this condition when they were also working at the adrenal gland hormone cortisone, which is necessary for life itself in the prevention of fatal Addison's disease.

Kendall as a chemist and Hench as a clinician worked for some two decades on rheumatoid arthritis, somewhat independently, but with frequent conferences. They found that cortisone had an enormous influence opposing the inflammation of joints in rheumatoid arthritis. Working with Drs. Charles H. Slocumb and Howard F. Polley, they administered cortisone to a patient in Saint Marys Hospital, beginning September 21, 1948. Within forty-eight hours the arthritis was appreciably improved and remained so as long as cortisone continued to be administered. Similar effects were found subsequently in four other patients with rheumatoid arthritis. And when cortisone administration was discontinued, all the evils of the arthritis recurred.

It was apparent that the beneficial effects of cortisone administration were not due to the patient having defective adrenal glands, as in Addison's disease. In that fatal condition there are no symptoms of arthritis. Cortisone apparently functions here as a curative drug rather than replacing a hormone defect as insulin substitutes in diabetes for deficient production of the hormone by the pancreas.

The pituitary gland, at the base of the brain in the skull, produces several hormones, one of which regulates adrenal gland secretion of cortisone. This is known as adrenocorticotropichormone or ACTH. Well, if cortisone controls rheumatoid arthritis, might not ACTH do likewise? This was first attempted in 1949, with results identical with those of cortisone.

In a preliminary report to physicians and other interested scientists, the beneficial effects on fourteen patients were presented at a weekly staff meeting of the Mayo Clinic. This account immediately stimulated great and widespread excitement among patients and public news media, as well as among medical scientists and physicians. This report, being fair-minded as in almost all Mayo Clinic accounts, did present some so-called undesirable effects as well as the beneficial consequences, all in appropriate perspective. However, as Kendall commented later, "The effective use of cortisone for anything was retarded for awhile by intemperate and unscientific extremes of exaggerated praise, bitter denunciation and emotion-laden criticism, but these reactions gradually were replaced by more reasonable attitudes."

Even today the discovery of the antirheumatic and other antiinflammatory properties of cortisone and ACTH is regarded throughout the world as a major milestone in medical history.

Blood Bank

Loss of blood in accidents or disease was originally the most important indication for blood transfusions and also the stimulus for storing the precious fluid in blood banks. But eventually numerous other conditions called for transfusions. They provided needed red blood cells for anemic patients. When there was a low concentration of proteins in the blood, there developed an imbalance between fluids inside and outside body cells. A donor's blood could provide the needed proteins. Faulty blood clotting after even minor injuries could be corrected at least partially with donor blood possessing a normal clotting time. In certain infectious diseases a patient's defenses against invading organisms could be improved by transferring to him blood from a donor having a normal concentration of antibodies. Transfusions were often helpful after severe burns, as well as in edema, with its undue collection of fluids in the skin and elsewhere. Lowered blood pressure in shock following trauma, even without significant blood loss, could be improved by increasing the total volume of the patient's circulating blood.

For all this, the Clinic has had to expand its quarters and personnel repeatedly. In 1963 the blood bank was moved into expanded and renovated quarters in the Plummer Building. In addition to this main unit, laboratories were located at Saint Marys Hospital and the Methodist Hospital. At this time Dr. Howard Taswell became the Clinic's blood bank director. He later achieved the distinction of becoming the president of the American Association of Blood Banks. As Mayo's blood bank director, Taswell succeeded Dr. Donald R. Mathieson, who had followed in the footsteps of Dr. Harry Seldon and of the great Dr. John S. Lundy, the father of American blood banking. Blood bank nurses, technicians, consultants, fellows, and clerical workers were abundant, soon numbering about fifty.

There was also a Clinic Blood Transfusion committee to advise on all problems and procedures relating to blood transfusions. Operation of the blood bank, procuring donors, and examination of blood took place in the clinical pathology laboratories. In this organization, administration of the blood bank was transferred from the section of anesthesiology, where all this complexity originated.

Then there was developed the procedure of using on a patient only a special part of the donor's blood. Dr. Taswell stated, "The concept of what a blood bank should do has changed. We're no longer concerned solely with collecting, storing and distributing whole blood. The present trend is to separate donor blood into its component parts and use the appropriate components for treating specific conditions." He noted that in modern blood banks as many as forty out of every one hundred transfusion used blood components instead of whole blood. This might include blood proteins, blood-clotting elements, or red blood cells, which have been separated from the liquid blood in a centrifuge.

The liquid portion of blood, or plasma, after separation of all the cellular elements, was often useful in itself. Plasma could be preserved and used with safety after prolonged storage, whereas whole blood should be used soon after storage. There was also dried plasma, with all liquid removed. This powder was kept in sterile condition, and could readily be dissolved again in sterile distilled water when needed – a great spacesaver in the blood bank storage areas, although its use declined after World War II.

Fresh-frozen blood plasma was also included in the blood bank for special purposes. Frozen blood can be stored safely in freezers for at least five years. By this process, very rare types of needed blood could be collected and stored for use whenever needed. Also, frozen blood could readily be shipped over long distances.

"Borrowing" blood was developed. Perhaps a pint of blood was taken from a donor. From this were separated various needed elements such as the liquid plasma, proteins, or blood-clotting elements. After such extractions, the remaining blood, with all its red blood cells, could be returned to the donor's blood vessels. Such "lenders" of blood expressed amazement at getting back this "borrowed" blood after only 15 minutes.

Another blood bank advancement was the introduction to the Mayo Clinic in 1964 of plastic bags for collecting, processing, and storing blood. These nonrigid containers were unbreakable and used much less storage space than glass bottles. They reduced the danger of air bubbles in transfusions and facilitated the separation of various needed blood components under sterile conditions.

One of the greatest demands on the blood bank was the open-heart surgery of Dr. John Kirklin and associates. In this operation the patient's and donor's blood bypassed the heart and lungs and traveled through a mechanical heart-lung bypass machine, leaving the patient's heart blood free for the surgeon to repair its defects. For each such procedure, about ten pints of freshly drawn blood were necessary. Only blood drawn on the day of operation could be used. During 1961 there were 521 such heart operations, requiring some 5,023 pints of donor blood, drawn within a few hours of its use.

The blood bank developed a tremendous need for blood donors. It was necessary for donors who supplied blood for cardiac surgery to come to the blood bank on the day prior to and on the day of surgery. Consequently, it was necessary that these donors be local residents. It was even more convenient if donors were from Clinic personnel.

At the time when Doctor Kirklin wished to increase his heart operations from four to five per week, the determining factor was whether the blood bank had sufficient donors. As to his performing one more operation per week, Doctor Kirklin stated that it would not be sufficient "to allow us to keep our heads above water as regards the clinical load, but it will help a little."

There were about twenty thousand transfusions administered at the Clinic in 1964, or about sixty-five each day. The Red Cross and blood banks elsewhere helped to supply this great need for donor blood. Sources outside Rochester provided blood for about half of the transfusions. But more local donors were sorely needed—from the Clinic staff, fellows, employees, and other Rochester residents.

Dispatching blood or its parts from the Clinic blood bank to the hospitals presented problems. It was thought that the pneumatic tubes which link the Clinic with the hospitals, might become a "mile-a-minute blood stream." The section of engineering (in 1964) cooperated with the blood bank in this venture to deliver blood rapidly to operating rooms, obstetrical delivery rooms, and emergency stations at Saint Marys and the Methodist. There was designed a metal container, which held a plastic bag filled with blood, for use in the tube system. It was determined that the blood itself suffered no harm in this sixty-mile-per-hour journey through the tubes.

Chilled blood in the refrigerators of the blood bank needed warming before transfusion. Cold blood from the bank was passed through a long coil of plastic tubing immersed in a hot-water bath. The blood then went through the needle placed in the patient's vein. However, this type of warmer reduced considerably the rate of transfusion, which was a serious disadvantage when rapid and massive blood replacement was crucial. There was available a microwave blood warmer for bottles. But in Mayo's bank, blood was kept in plastic bags. Taswell and collaborators proceeded to develop a microwave warmer for rapid heating of the blood in these bags. With this device, blood for transfusion could be warmed from the slightly above freezing temperature of the bank up to body temperature in just about one minute.

The wildest dreams were surpassed in the blood banking enterprise during the twenty-five years since anesthesiologist Dr. John S. Lundy asked permission to store some bottles of blood in Dr. MacCarty's laboratory refrigerator, thus initiating America's first blood bank. Lundy's achievements rank as lofty as those of anyone in the Clinic's history. Besides this primitive blood bank, he also established the first postanesthesia recovery room, developed new anesthesia procedures, supervised surgical anesthesia, and trained countless physicians and dentists in his speciality. In addition, he published hundreds of scientific papers.

On the national scene, Lundy held certificate number two of the American Board of Anesthesiology, which he helped to found and on which he served later as president. He helped to organize the American Society of Anesthesiologists and became a recipient of its Distinguished Service Award. He was involved in forming the American Medical Association's section of anesthesiology and soon became its chairman. He served many years as chairman of the committee on blood and blood banks and the committee on first aid and Red Cross of the Minnesota State Medical Association. Early in his career he organized the Anesthesiologist's Travel Club, which later became the Academy of Anesthesiology.

Basic Sciences

There are numerous Clinic departments not directly dealing with patients, such as physiology and biochemistry. A major aim here is to learn more about the functions and activities of body parts, ranging from organs to cells. Name any part of the body, from microscopic blood cells or nerve fibers to the gastrointestinal tract or heart, and you have named an area of research in the Clinic's basic science departments. A mere listing of recent research titles would constitute a long chapter of this book.

But the practical applications of many of these studies have been recounted, such as the development of the antiblackout suit, the heart-lung machine, the control of hormone deficiencies, the continuous recording of a patient's blood pressure, the kidney transplant, and very much more. Rare indeed is a Clinic advance in patient care which has not involved collaboration with one or another of the Clinic's basic science departments.

Publications

Naturally, all these efforts were incorporated into scientific publications. During one year alone (1955) over four hundred Clinic people had 629 papers published in a multitude of medical and scientific journals, or an average of more than two publications per workday. While these numbers reflected primarily the tremendous volume of clinical and investigative work carried out by Mayo staff and fellows, they also reflected the labors of the section of publications. Dr. Clagett describes the procedure:

> Every publication from the Mayo institution was critically reviewed, edited, and revised as necessary by members of the editorial staff before it could be offered to a journal for publication. This ensured that the paper was of reasonable length, that the material was presented in a coherent, easily understood manner, that all tables or graphic materials were accurate and had appropriate identification, and that all references to other literature were valid and the bibliography was complete in every detail. Unfortunately, many very good doctors and scientists do not really write well, but the editorial department of the Clinic ensured that papers published from the Clinic were of an extremely high quality. Editors of medical journals everywhere knew from experience that they could depend on the quality and accuracy of any paper from the institution whoever the author might be.
>
> It soon became apparent that graphs, charts, photographs, and illustrations could be used to enhance the effectiveness of medical papers and presentations, and gradually departments were developed to provide these visual aids. Medical artists were available to provide drawings of pathologic conditions or to depict the technical steps of a surgical procedure. The artists even came to the operating rooms to make accurate sketches which could later be completed to provide illustrations, and photographers with their equipment were available to provide both gross and microscopic representations of a great variety of material that could be used for teaching and illustration.

Over many years these contributions to knowledge were assembled in annual volumes of *Collected Papers of the Mayo Clinic and Mayo Foundation*. The first volume of reprints in this series appeared in 1911, edited by Maude H. Mellish. It aimed to provide an indexed repository of all scientific papers from the Mayo Clinic. Very soon the Mayo physicians and scientists published so many papers in journals that only a selected number could be reprinted in full in the collected papers. Some appeared in abstract or abridged form; many were listed by title only.

Initially the articles reprinted in entirety were directed mainly at the general practitioner—now called the family doctor—as well as at the general surgeon and diagnostician. This policy was later expanded so that the articles published pertained as well to the various medical specialty fields and the basic medical sciences. Only then could the full contribution of the research of the institution be expressed.

Later this annual work was published by W. B. Saunders and Company. Seven to eight thousand copies of the collected papers were produced each year. The supply of each volume was always completely sold. But eventually the mass of publications by the staff became all too great and the expense too excessive. *Collected Papers of the Mayo Clinic and Mayo Foundation* was discontinued in the late 1960s. But the objectives of this publication were retained.

The *Mayo Clinic Proceedings* took over. This was a monthly Clinic publication of considerable diversity. It evolved from the publication *Bulletin of the Mayo Clinic and Mayo Foundation*, begun in 1926, with an almost immediate name change to *Proceedings of the Staff Meetings of the Mayo Clinic*. This name was an accurate description of its contents. It was primarily for staff and fellows, containing numerous scientific presentations. The *Proceedings* carried at its masthead the statement that the publication was for the "information of members of the staff of the Mayo Clinic and fellows of the Mayo Foundation." However, there were requests for copies of the *Proceedings* from multitudes of physicians and scientists throughout the world, so that the mailing list grew to more than thirty thousand, including some six thousand individuals in seventy-six foreign countries.

To recapitulate the publication sequence: the *Collected Papers of the Mayo Clinic and Mayo Foundation* in 1911, the *Bulletin of the Mayo Clinic and Mayo Foundation* in 1926, and the *Proceedings of the Staff Meetings of the Mayo Clinic*, also in 1926.

On page one of volume one of the *Proceedings* we encounter the impressive title, "Mucosis Fungoides (Granuloma Fungoides) of the D'Emblee Type" by Dr. Hamilton Montgomery, then a fellow in dermatology and later a staff member in that field. Suffice it to say that this article dealt with the diagnosis and treatment of a complicated skin ailment.

Ultimately the *Proceedings of the Staff Meetings of the Mayo Clinic* became the *Mayo Clinic Proceedings* in 1964. By this time only a small proportion of the published material came from meetings of the staff. The *Proceedings* published results of medical and other scientific investigations by Mayo Clinic personnel. The only exception to this was the inclusion of some reports presented at Mayo Clinic meetings by physicians and scientists from elsewhere than Rochester. As the circulation of this publication multiplied into many thousands, the problem of financing the project became acute, since nothing was paid by most recipients of the issues, including staff members and alumni. A revolutionary policy was debated. Why not accept paid advertising in the publication? The decision again involved the issue of accepting or not accepting outside funds for Clinic enterprises. Editor-in-chief Dr. Edwin Bayrd stated:

> The maintenance of reader interest, the growth of the circulation and the erosive pressure of inflation have combined to increase production expenses to a point of significant cost . . . This has forced a reconsideration of principles and priorities. As an outcome of this it was decided to accept advertising for the first time in the 45 years of our journal's existence.

Advertising paid practically all the expenses involved in the monthly printing, which reached fifty thousand by 1971. The publication was given to staff members and was presented to librarians throughout the world. On request, it was sent everywhere to physicians, dentists, veterinarians, junior and senior medical students, medical librarians, and persons with advanced degrees in allied fields. About one fifth of the recipients lived outside the United States. Rochester's Whiting Press produced the bound volumes, employing a Swiss-made book binding machine that processed two thousand journals per hour.

Decades ago, Helen Clapesattle tells us, a surgeon friend told Dr. Will Mayo, "You ought to write more, make more reports to the profession, all of you." This most assuredly has been done. To do this, Dr. Will determined they must have expert supervision and assistance. This has been provided by the section of publications. Its members have shared with the writers the responsibility of making every publication which bears the words *of the Mayo Clinic and Mayo Foundation* a worthy contribution to scientific literature. Leadership in this enterprise has been provided by Drs. Richard M. Hewitt and Carl M. Gambill, as well as Dr. James Eckman, who represented the Clinic's committee on medical relations and publications.

CHAPTER 13

Honors to Mayo

Nobel Prize

A glorious occasion for the entire Mayo Clinic family was the awarding of the Nobel Prize to our Drs. Edward C. Kendall and Philip S. Hench in Stockholm on December 10, 1950. This award was for their lifesaving work on cortisone, a hormone of the cortex, or outer layer, of the adrenal glands. This hormone is necessary for life.

For Kendall and Hench the Nobel Prize outshone but did not lessen the significance of previous honors received for their work on the treatment of arthritis, involving the hormone of the adrenal cortex. Earlier they received the Passano Foundation Award. Regarding Kendall and Hench, the foundation directors stated, "It has been said by many research workers and clinicians that their contributions have opened an entirely new field for clinical investigation of many disease conditions yet to be conquered."

Kendall and Hench also received outstanding achievement awards from the New York Newspaper Guild. There was also a Research Corporation Award, the Lasker Award, the Chriss Award, and many others. Hench had several honorary degrees, including one from the National University of Ireland.

Their Swedish Nobel Prize certificate—with its tax-free cash supplement—reads:

> "För Deras Upptäckter Rörande Bijurbarkens Hormonen Derar Byggnad och Biologiska Verkningar." Or, "For their discoveries concerning the adrenal cortex hormones, their structure and biological functions."

Let us examine some of Kendall's recollections of this momentous event:

> Soon after the announcement of the Nobel Prize I received a request from Stockholm for a recorded acceptance of the prize that could be broadcast to the people of Sweden. The message was recorded in Rochester and airmailed to Sweden . . . When we arrived at the railroad station in Stockholm on December 8, I was surprised to hear my name on the public address system: "Doctor Kendall has arrived and here he is." Then the record made six weeks earlier was played. It sounded as if I were speaking "live" from the railroad Station.

Interestingly, this was the first use of public television in Sweden. Kendall continues his account:

> The scheduled program for Sunday, December 10, was long and arduous. In the morning the new and old Nobel laureates were taken to the nearby cemetery for a short ceremony during which a wreath was placed on the grave of Nobel . . . Above Nobel's grave some pine trees with long needles were heavily laden with a blanket of snow. As we stood with our hats off, a water-soaked, snowy avalanche fell with a muffled thud . . . .
>
> Sobering thoughts concerned the events of the immediate future. Only 11 Americans had been awarded a Nobel Prize in medicine and physiology during the preceding 50 years. Doctor Hench and I wanted to perform our part in the Nobel Festival without fault. The people of Stockholm realize that the annual award of the Nobel Prize is a unique event. The Concert Hall was filled to capacity (about 2,000), extra chairs were placed in the aisles, and 3,500 people watched the ceremony on television screens in two nearby auditoriums.
>
> All who attended the Concert Hall were in formal attire. This was true even of the photographers, of whom there were many. The Nobel Festival of 1950 was a solemn occasion. One was conscious of the continuity of the Nobel Foundation with its chain of awards that reaches back to 1901 and will doubtless continue even longer into the future. December 10, 1950, was a link in that long chain, but it was our day, the high point of our lives, and our emotions were deeply stirred.
>
> The recipient remained seated while his "sponsor" presented a short review of his work and explained why his contribution was considered worthy of a Nobel Prize. Following this presentation the recipient rose from his chair and received a personal citation from the sponsor. In each case the sponsor closed his remarks with the same formula. "I now have the honor of asking you to accept the Nobel Prize for 1950 from the hand of His Gracious Majesty, the King." Immediately thereafter, the orchestra played a short interlude while the recipient walked to the platform at the front of the stage, bowed to King Gustav VI, turned to the right, and descended a flight of steps to the auditorium floor. As each recipient reached the floor, the king rose from his chair in the center of the front row and advanced to greet him. When they met, each laureate received from

> the king a diploma and the gold medal enclosed in a tooled leather case. The king and the laureate engaged in a short conversation, the king returned to his chair, and the laureate passed to the flight of steps on the right side of the platform and ascended to the stage. When he reached the stage he turned to face the king, made a second bow, and returned to his seat.
>
> The time required for each recipient to accept the prize from the king was not more than two or three minutes.

When Dr. Arlie Barnes, chairman of the Clinic's board of governors, relayed to Kendall and Hench the pride felt by the entire Clinic staff at the honor they received, Kendall replied, "In the whole world, it could only have happened at the Mayo Clinic."

And Hench said, "Thanks, but the honor doesn't belong to me. It belongs to the Mayo Clinic . . . only wish Doctor Will and Doctor Charlie were here."

Some time before Kendall was to receive the award, he met a famous scientist who was certain that he too would be a recipient:

"I have been so recommended by a committee of the Royal Caroline Institute, so I am sure of it."

"Don't be too sure," replied Kendall. "I know about a man who was so recommended, but he did not get the prize."

"Who was that?"

"It was I," said Kendall. He was referring to his prize-deserving work on the thyroid hormone in 1914, when indeed he came near to receiving the award. It is most unusual for any scientist to have made two such prizeworthy discoveries.

Mayo's Dr. Bayrd Horton tells a story, "The Nobel Prize—Won and Lost":

> Dr. H. Milton Conner of the Mayo Clinic . . . had conceived the notion that patients with pernicious anemia could be treated successfully by feeding them large amounts of liver . . . In March 1926 he presented the results of this study before the Interstate Postgraduate Assembly . . . I attended the meeting and listened to Doctor Conner's report. He had marshaled his facts and presented them in a clear-cut manner. After he had finished speaking, a visiting professor from one of the midwestern universities got up and casually remarked, "Anyone who thinks he can treat pernicious anemia successfully by feeding patients liver must be out of his mind." Doctor Conner was so discouraged that he did not publish his observations . . . A few years later Doctors Minot, Murphy and Whipple were awarded the Nobel Prize for doing the same work.

Cortisone is similar to insulin in that when administered it controls the otherwise fatal Addison's disease, in which the adrenal glands fail to produce a sufficiency of the vital hormone. Likewise, insulin injections prevent death from diabetes, in which condition the pancreatic islets fail to produce enough hormone. In each case the hormone administrations do not cure the ailment—they control the condition.

While insulin therapy is limited to use by diabetics, the employment of cortisone has extended far beyond the control of the endocrine gland deficiency. Numerous useful compounds have been developed for patients other than those with Addison's disease. Within decades, cortisone became the parent of numerous widely used drugs, employed in the therapy for severe asthma, for some kinds of arthritis, leukemia, ulcerative colitis, and certain eye diseases. These compounds became a mainstay in a variety of mild or severe skin disorders. Manufacturers report a tremendous market for cortisone-related skin creams, ointments, sprays, and lotions employed for annoying skin irritations too minor to warrant a doctor's attention. Much of this material is sold over the drugstore counter without a doctor's prescription. So the Nobel Prize work of Kendall and Hench has not only led to the control of fatal Addison's disease but has aided adolescents to combat pimples.

Alfred Bernhard Nobel and his prizes are of universal interest. He was a Swedish engineer who amassed a tremendous fortune derived in large part from his studies and development of explosives, particularly nitroglycerine. Perhaps it was Nobel's conscience, prodded by his tremendous contributions to effective warfare, that prompted him to include a peace prize in these annual world-moving ceremonies and honors. The peace prize, he said, should be awarded "to the person who shall have done the best work for fraternity among nations, for the abolition or reduction of standing armies and promotion of peace congresses." He also said:

> Perhaps my dynamite plants will put an end to war sooner than your congresses. On the day two army corps can annihilate each other in one second all civilized nations will recoil from war in horror.

How futile! Decades later, Enrico Fermi, a nearby neighbor of the author's at the University of Chicago, developed the nuclear chain reaction that led to the devastating atomic bomb. Fermi was far too knowledgeable of human frailties and hostilities to venture such a forlorn hope as Nobel's.

A number of years after the Kendall-Hench awards, Rochester experienced another Nobel event. Gustavus Adolphus College, at nearby St. Peter, Minnesota, dedicated a new science center, Nobel Memorial Hall. The Mayo Clinic and Foundation served as hosts at a luncheon preceding the dedication, at which there were as guests more than thirty winners of the Nobel Prize from the United States. Following the events at the college, ten of these Nobel Prize recipients assembled in Rochester for a brief visit, including a dinner as Mayo's guests.

Of course, world-famed visitors to Rochester as patients or otherwise were by no means rare. We may include Presidents Franklin D. Roosevelt, Harry Truman, and Lyndon Johnson, as well as Emperor Haile Selassie of Ethiopia. The Clinic archives contain a picture of him touring the Clinic with his guards, escorted by Drs. Jan Tillisch and Victor Johnson.

We might also mention Jack Dempsey, the famous world heavyweight boxing champion. He made several visits to the Clinic for checkups and became acquainted with Dr. Balfour as well as with the author. For some time after his retirement from boxing, precipitated by Gene Tunney, Jack operated a restaurant in New York. Dr. Balfour recounted his visit to the establishment with some friends. After the meal, an argument arose as to the dinner bill.

"I want to pay," said Balfour.

"No, it is on the house," said Jack.

After a bit of persistent discussion, Jack put up his arms and fists in pugilistic style toward Balfour and demanded, "Do you want to make something out of this?"

Awards, Tributes, Merits

National and international awards for excellence in investigations were numerous. In one year alone (1958) the American Medical Association bestowed honor for six Mayo research exhibits at its annual meeting in San Francisco. Among those honored was Dr. Frank Krusen, who received the Distinguished Service Award, considered one of the highest awards of the medical profession. This was for his outstanding achievements in the rehabilitation of persons crippled by sickness or accident and for other great accomplishments during his professional career. Krusen had formerly been granted the Gold Key of the American Congress of Physical Medicine and Rehabilitation and the Physicians Award from President Eisenhower for outstanding contributions to the employment welfare of the physically handicapped.

The Billings Gold Medal, the highest award for its class, was granted to Dr. C. H. Hodgson and associates for x-ray studies of diseases of the lungs. Then there were two certificates of merit, one relating to studies on the value of blood smears in diagnosis and the other for accomplishments relating to diabetes. Honorable mention was bestowed for studies on bile pigments and also for an exhibit relative to the management of carcinoma of the rectum.

All this occurred at one session of the American Medical Association. Many more awards from the AMA were made in following years. There were still other recognitions of accomplishments of our staff.

Dr. E. J. Baldes was named Chevalier de l'Ordre National de la Légion d'honneur by the republic of France. Henri Bonnet, French ambassador to the United States, said to Baldes, "I am happy to congratulate you on this highly-deserved distinction which is granted to you by the French Government as a token of gratitude for the outstanding services you have rendered to medical science, especially by your research in the field of aeronautics, and for the constant friendship you have always manifested towards my country."

The University of Minnesota's Builder of the Name Medal was awarded to Dr. Donal Balfour, the second director of the Mayo Foundation for Medical Education and Research. At this occasion the president of the University, Dr. J. L. Morrill stated,

> Among the honors which it is the happy privilege and pleasure of the University of Minnesota to bestow from time to time is the Builder of the Name Medal, which is awarded in recognition of outstanding contribution to the ongoing program and welfare of the University . . . Needless to say, the members of the Board voted this medal for you with enthusiasm, for they are deeply mindful of all that your service has meant over the years to this institution . . . I know that I speak for your countless friends, both here and at Rochester, when I say that the honor that is involved is richly deserved.

As a matter of fact, Dr. Balfour's professional affiliations, as recounted at the time of his death in 1963, were almost endless. Besides his many activities at Mayo and in addition to memberships in local, state, and national medical societies, he was a member of the executive committee of the Advisory Board of Medical Specialties, a founder and charter member of the American Board of Surgery, president of the American College of Surgeons, chairman of the AMA's section of surgery, vice-president of the American Surgical Association, president of the Interstate Postgraduate Medical Assembly of America.

He received the Distinguished Service Award of the AMA and the Friedenwald Medal of the American Gastroenterological Association, held honorary fellowships in the Royal College of Surgeons of England, of Edinburgh, of Australia, and of Canada, received honorary doctorates from McMaster, Northwestern, Western Ontario, and Toronto universities and Carleton and St. Olaf colleges.

He held honorary fellowships in the Association of Surgeons of Great Britain and Ireland, the Royal Society of Medicine, American Gastroenterological Association, and National Academy of Medicine of France. He was also honorary member of medical and surgical societies of Argentina, Belgium, Chile, France, Greece, Hungary, Italy, the Southeastern Surgical Congress, Association of Military Surgeons of the United States, International Society of Surgery, and Pan American

Medical Association. He was one of the founders of the World Medical Association and a charter member of the World Health Organization and Central Surgical Association. One might also agree with the words of a friend, "He was the kindest man I ever knew."

Harry A. Blackmun was general counsel of the Mayo Clinic. After some nine years at Mayo, he was appointed a federal judge of the United States Court of Appeals for the Eighth Circuit. The day before he was sworn in, he was honored with an award from those who had worked most closely with him. They gave him a supremely appropriate gift—his first judicial robes. This appointment was succeeded eventually by Harry's appointment to the United States Supreme Court, where he still sits today.

While at Mayo he was highly respected, a legal scholar, reserved, a man of intellect and integrity. No arguments about such descriptions ever came from those who worked under him. In the words of one secretary, "He was thoughtful, considerate, sincere, interested and always concerned. Even when his desk was piled high with work, he always had time to say hello, to listen to everyone." Another secretary asserted, "He was exacting in his work and expected the same from his secretary. But he was so fair to the people who worked with him—if you did a good job he always complimented you, and he never hesitated to do so in front of other people."

Awards from abroad multiplied. Dr. Walter M. Boothby was honored with the order of Commander of the North Star by the king of Sweden. The Swedish Consul Gunnar Dryselius made the presentation "in the name of the King of Sweden, in appreciation for your work in aviation medicine."

Dr. Henry Meyerding was elected an honorary member of the French Society of Orthopedics and Traumatology. He has served as president of both the International Society of Orthopedic Surgery and Traumatology and of the International College of Surgeons.

Dr. Waltman Walters was elected an honorary member of the section of surgery of the German Society for Clinical Medicine "in recognition of his extraordinary influence on the development of abdominal surgery and in recognition of his continuous efforts to enlarge friendly relations among surgeons throughout the world."

Dr. O. T. Clagett informed his friends, "In the spring of 1968 I received a letter from the Royal College of Surgeons of England that I had been selected to receive the Sir Clement Price Thomas Medal and it was hoped that I would be able to come to London for the presentation. This medal was awarded only at intervals of three years and the basis of selection of the recipient was 'meritorious contributions to surgery.' It could be awarded to any surgeon in the world who in the judgment of the Council of the Royal College of Surgeons of England merited this honor. Being selected to receive this medal was and still is the greatest honor that I have received in my surgical career." But lo and behold, "In 1969 I again received a letter from the Royal College of Surgeons, this time announcing that I had been elected an honorary member of the College. According to the rules of the College the number of honorary members is limited to 50 and new members can only be elected when vacancies result from death of a previous honorary member. Obviously, membership in this College is one of the highest honors any surgeon can ever achieve."

Even in the light of such worldwide recognition, Clagett considered the celebration of "Jim Clagett Day" in Rochester to be one of the most rewarding experiences of his surgical career, two years after the Royal College event. During his years on the staff Jim had trained a total of 115 chief residents. At this occasion 110 were still alive and 100 of them came to Rochester to honor Jim. They came from all over the United States and Canada and even from Europe and South America. There were several scientific sessions and social gatherings. "That so many would return to honor their old chief was the most heartwarming experience a man could ever have."

Dr. James Eckman, an eminent historian of medicine, ultimately became senior consultant in the section of publications. He achieved membership in the British Museum Society and the Gutenberg Gesellschaft of Mainz, Germany.

Dr. Howard Gray was elected an honorary member of the surgical section of the Royal Academy of Medicine of England. The Clinic, the Rochester community, and medicine as a whole lost not only an eminent surgeon and teacher but a great and good friend with "Howdie's" premature death by drowning. The members of the Clinic's board of governors "recorded with deepest regret the untimely death of their colleague . . . Beyond his eminence in the field of surgery, Doctor Gray was a man whose fundamental philosophy was Christian consideration of others."

The American Academy of Achievement annually honored "men and women of exceptional accomplishment in the great walks of life." Among those so honored at the academy's "golden plate banquets" was Dr. Arthur Bulbulian. He was one of fifty outstanding persons in the fields of art, science, business, the military, and the humanities. Bulbulian was cited for his work in preparation of scientific exhibits and his part in the development of the oxygen mask employed by fighter pilots in World War II.

In the history of the great Mayo Clinic the name of Harry J. Harwick ranks equally with the greatest of the staff engaged in medical practice, teaching, and research. Not directly involved in any of these three activities, Harry played a major role in their growth and development. Space limitations in this book prevent a complete listing of his accomplishments. His education was limited to high school, but in his education of Clinic staff and other personnel he was an M.D., a Ph.D., and whatever else.

At age twenty-one he was induced by Dr. Will Mayo to leave his post at Rochester's First National Bank to become a bookkeeper, with the responsibility of developing a more efficient accounting and business system in medical practice. This occurred at about the time the words *Mayo Clinic* began to be used, mainly by visitors rather than by the practicing group of Mayo doctors.

An early assignment was to explore methods whereby earnings of early Clinic doctors would serve the objective of advancing medical care, teaching, and research rather than going into the doctors' pockets. The charitable corporation which resulted became known as the Mayo Foundation. Harry was one of its incorporators, a member, then secretary-treasurer, and finally chairman of the organization's board of trustees.

For many years he was secretary and later executive officer of the board of governors of the Mayo Clinic, which body directed the many activities of the institution. Scarcely any major development in the growth of the institution could be described without including Harry's name as a major participant, including the great building projects: the Red Brick building of 1914, the Plummer Building of 1928, and the present Mayo Building. And then, appropriately, there was the Harwick Building, dedicated in his honor. His efforts extended beyond the Clinic limits into many business, philanthropic, and social organizations, from organizing the National Association of Clinic Managers to the founding of the Rochester Golf and Country Club.

The Rochester Chamber of Commerce presented him a citation "for 50 years of extraordinary service to his community, its people and its institutions through kindly counsel, undeviating integrity and wise leadership, for which he now enjoys the high esteem and admiration of his fellow citizens."

At Harry's death in 1978, Dr. W. Eugene Mayberry stated, "Those of us who serve the Clinic in administrative and supervisory roles owe him a debt of gratitude. He showed us how to do our jobs."

Tribute was likewise paid him by the United States Supreme Court Associate Justice Harry Blackmun, formerly the Clinic lawyer:

> Under his guidance, the Mayo organization survived the ordeal of three wars, of the great depression, of the almost simultaneous departure of the two Mayo brothers. Yet here the institution still stands, certainly larger, hopefully stronger than ever, emblematic of what is good and worthwhile in medicine.

If one measures greatness by the ability to command loyalty, he was great. He could listen and ponder and decide and say no and yet retain the petitioner's respect and confidence because he had listened and because his judgment was known to be good and was so deeply respected.

It was said of another, and I think it can be said of him: "Not often in the story of mankind does a man arrive on earth who is both steel and velvet, who is as hard as rock and as soft as drifting fog, who holds in his heart and mind the paradox of terrible storm and peace unspeakable and perfect."

Dr. Charles William ("Chuck") Mayo was named from both his father Charles and his uncle William. After his education to the M.D. degree at the University of Pennsylvania, he came to Rochester for advanced training and became a member of the surgical staff at age thirty-three. He was active in administrative matters as well as in surgery, serving as a member of the Clinic's board of governors, chairman of the Mayo Foundation's board of trustees, and also a member, and ultimately chairman, of the Board of Regents of the University of Minnesota. He had an outstanding military career in command of a Mayo unit in New Guinea and the Philippines. He later served as an alternate delegate to the United Nations, as delegate to the World Health Assembly, as president of the American Association for the United Nations, and as personal representative of President Eisenhower for the coronation of the king of Nepal.

Chuck was a member of numerous national and international organizations, both professional and in other areas, ranging from an honorary fellowship in the Royal College of Surgeons of England to the National Council of the Boy Scouts of America. He was a founding member of the American Board of Surgery. He received honorary degrees from a half-dozen American colleges and universities.

Scientifically, he published nearly four hundred papers on medical subjects and a book, *Surgery of the Small and Large Intestine,* and functioned as editor-in-chief of the journal *Postgraduate Medicine.* With all his renown, he preferred to be known as Chuck, whether this be to a United States president, to a taxi driver, or to the multitudes of the sick for whom he cared and planned.

On his death in 1968, the accolades were numerous: President Lyndon B. Johnson, ". . . one of those rare men whose talents enrich the lives of men everywhere;" Vice-President Hubert H. Humphrey, ". . . a good friend and a fine public servant . . .;" Minnesota Governor Harold LeVander, "His contributions and those of his family to the fields of health and education are without parallel . . ."; Rochester Mayor Alex Smekta, "He was a man who could walk with kings and never lose the common touch." And there was the good Sister Mary Brigh, administrator of Saint Marys Hospital, "He meant a lot to all of us—as a surgeon, but particularly as a person."

There could scarcely be a more unusual award than that granted to Dr. Randall G. Sprague. This came in 1972 from the Joslin Diabetic Foundation. Randy was a diabetic. His condition was diagnosed when he was a fifteen-year-old high school junior in Chicago. At that time there was as yet no insulin. The only treatment available to him was strict dietary control with frequent "starvation" days. At that time most young diabetics died within a couple of years. And then came insulin from the Canadian investigators Banting and Best of the University of Toronto, who succeeded in their investigations to maintain life in dogs whose pancreases had been removed, by injecting them with pancreas extracts. And eventually such extracts became insulin, whose injections have saved the lives of millions of diabetics. Sprague became one of the first patients in Chicago to receive insulin, in 1922.

For this discovery Banting and Best and their associates were fittingly awarded the Nobel Prize. And what was Dr. Sprague's award from the foundation named for Dr. Joslin, a pioneer in the treatment of diabetes? It was a certificate attesting to his having lived "50 courageous years" with the disease diabetes. And there was a medal appropriately depicting a marathon runner bearing a torch. At that time there could be found only twenty-five diabetics in the United States who had survived for fifty years. Randy estimated that he had injected himself with insulin some thirty-three thousand times. It was as routine as brushing his teeth.

At the Clinic, Dr. Sprague became a staff member after completing a fellowship in medicine and was soon head of a section. Quite naturally his specialty was endocrine diseases, including diabetes. Among the awards he received for his scientific contributions to understanding metabolic diseases, including diabetes, were the Victory Medal from the Diabetic Fund of Boston, the Banting Medal, and later the Banting Memorial Award of the American Diabetes Association. He also served as president of this association.

Until his retirement and up to today Sprague appears the picture of health and strength and vitality and good humor, thanks to his daily injections of insulin and his inimitable fortitude.

Few names are as revered at the Clinic as that of Dr. Russell M. Wilder. During his long and brilliant career he was awarded some of the highest honors of his profession. He had his premedical, medical, and scientific training at the University of Chicago. After some ten years on the staff at Mayo he returned to the University of Chicago to become professor and chairman of the department of medicine in 1929. He was adored by the medical students there, of which the author was one in those days. There was an amusing experience with him. As a junior medical student, the author spent a quarter as a clinical clerk in Wilder's department. He recalls, "One day I was in a room at Billings Hospital taking the history of a most conceited lady, whose high esteem for herself defied description. As we talked and I took notes, a nurse entered the room and asked this snooty lady to roll up her sleeve."

"What for?" the patient demanded.

"I must take some blood from you. We have to make some tests."

"You will not! The only person who may draw blood from me is the head of the department!"

Russell Wilder had probably not drawn blood from a patient's vein in twenty years.

At the University of Chicago all were tremendously disappointed when after his two-year sojourn there, he returned to Mayo to become professor of medicine in the Mayo Foundation and head of the Clinic's department of medicine. Wilder was the first Clinic staff member who was taken back on the staff after resigning and leaving for a post at another institution.

Throughout his career Wilder's major interest was in diabetes. Before the discovery of insulin he was responsible for the care of diabetic patients and did extensive research on the dietetic treatment of this disease. After the discovery of insulin he was one of a small committee of experts called to meet in Toronto to plan the clinical evaluation of the newly discovered product. He stated that he would never again experience a thrill equal to that occasion.

Wilder contributed more than 250 papers to medical and scientific journals. He authored the books *Clinical Diabetes Mellitus and Hyperinsulinisim* and *A Primer for Diabetic Patients.* He was director of the National Institute of Arthritis and Metabolic Diseases of the United States Public Health Service. He was made a master of the American College of Physicians. The American Diabetes Association conferred the Banting Medal on him, and the University of Chicago awarded him the Distinguished Service Medal and also the Howard Taylor Ricketts Award. The American Medical Association honored him with the Joseph Goldberger Award. There was even an award from the American Bakers' Association recognizing his activities in promoting enrichment of white flour and bread with vitamins.

He was a member of a large number of professional organizations and served terms as president of the American Diabetes Association and president of the National Vitamin Foundation. He served on the editorial boards of the *Journal of Nutrition,* the *Archives of Internal Medicine, National Reviews,* and *Public Health Reports.*

Fellows assigned to his service, as well as his staff associates, derived much impetus for their investigative projects from Wilder's consuming interest in research. He was known for his generosity in giving ample credit to his research collaborators, including fellows and staff members.

The recognition of Dr. Edward Rynearson as "the greatest doctor in the world" was another historic event of great moment. Eddie was attending a scientific meeting. He and a number of others were seated about a large round table during a period of relaxation. Conversation turned toward discussion of the truly great of medical history. Someone ventured to question, "And who would we consider to be the greatest doctor in the world today?" Without hesitation, Eddie said, "I am. And I can prove it."

He had a bellboy get a plain postcard on which he wrote a simple query such as, "I would like your help." He addressed the card to "The Greatest Doctor in the World," and assured them all he would receive this card, which he asked the bellboy to post. The federal postal authorities go to great extremes to try to deliver poorly addressed mail. They pondered awhile, and then it occurred to them that probably the great Mayo Clinic may know who the greatest doctor in the world might be. The Clinic's mail clerk who received the inquiry thought at once, "This looks to me like one of Rynearson's stunts." Eddie got the postcard.

Primarily for research accomplishments, more than one hundred of the Clinic's staff were cited in *Who's Who in America* in the early 1960s.

From time to time the role of the Mayo Foundation's director was to grant awards. None of these gave him more pleasure than the citations he gave to two of the Mayo Foundation's office supervisors. They truly represented the manner in which nonmedical workers in the Clinic were completely at one with the medical staff and administration. At the retirement of Isabel Farr, the author ventured,

> Through the years Miss Farr has represented a continuity in the Mayo Foundation, providing an immediate source of encyclopedic knowledtge of the Foundation, the University and the Clinic, which has been invaluable to those who have come from other fields to assume Foundation responsibilities. Her deep devotion to her duties and to the institution have permitted her to assist each successive officer of the Foundation with unswerving loyalty.

And on the death of Alice Schmid:

> Her loyalty to the institution found its finest expression in her intense devotion to the interests of the fellows, past and present. She knew them all, and their families, as well as their trials and triumphs. Let an alumnus of years ago enter the office, and she would call him by name, mention his field of medicine, and chat about the present activities of his fellowship contemporaries.

> She will be sorely missed by her many friends in Rochester, and across the nation. It may be said of the great map in the Mayo Foundation office, showing the present locations of many hundreds of alumni: "This map shows where Alice Schmid's friends live."

There was the dedication of a shrine to honor the Mayo brothers—the Mayo Memorial in Rochester's Mayo Park. This event appropriately occurred during the same month as the opening of the new Medical Sciences Building in 1952. The memorial honored Mayo's past; the building predicted future accomplishments. Statues of Drs. Will and Charlie were created by James Earle Fraser, showing the two brothers in their surgical gowns—their working clothes. They stand in front of a massive granite block or dais, and they rest on an even more massive granite base. In their immediate foreground is a large semicircular amphitheater to seat spectators at celebration events. The two brothers look on a long tree-lined mall at the far west end of which is a statue of their father, William Worrall Mayo.

Contributors to the expense of the Mayo Memorial were a multitude of men, women, and children from all the professions and pursuits, as well as people who gave anonymously. All contributors wished others to see and appreciate what they had known of the personalities and lives of these two world-famous but kind and friendly doctors.

An elaborate afternoon program included a Clinic carillon recital of many of the musical favorites of the brothers and renditions by the Rochester Municipal Band. A thousand-voice choir sang "Now Let Every Tongue Adore Thee" and "America the Beautiful." Attending and participating in the program were Minnesota's Governor C. Elmer Anderson, Dr. Walter Judd, former fellow of the Mayo Foundation and later United States congressman from Minnesota, and also Judge Vernon Gates, president of the Mayo Memorial Association. Hundreds and thousands of friends, admirers, and followers of the community's most illustrious sons attended the occasion.

The entire geographical arrangement was such that the father, William Morrall, was represented in his statue as looking toward his sons, in whom he placed great faith. The sons, facing west, looked toward their father, whom they considered their greatest teacher and guide, and beyond him to the Mayo Clinic, which they created in an effort to better serve humanity. In the brothers' faces one may read courage, resolution, understanding, sympathy, nobility, and poise. The viewer might realize he is in the presence of something greater than himself with a feeling of awe and reverence.

Much of this account is from the words of Judge Vernon Gates, who also stated:

No one can contemplate these statues in this beautiful setting without being inspired by them. The Doctors Mayo will take on a new significance to those who view the statues.

The doctor will think of the accomplishments of the Mayos in the practice of medicine and the tremendous stimulus they gave to medical education.

The scientist will think of their programs of research, and training of men skilled in research, and their advocacy of the scientific spirit.

The educator will think of their intense interest in improving education, of Dr. Will's long service on the Board of Regents of the University of Minnesota, and of Doctor Charlie's services on the Rochester School Board, and as a trustee of Carleton College and of Northwestern University.

The statesman will think of the services the two brothers and their assistants rendered to their country in time of war.

The historian will think of their impact upon modern civilization and the manner in which they helped to change the course of medical history and to usher in a new era in the treatment of patients, the education of physicians and the pursuit of research into the unknown.

The resident of Rochester and vicinity will think of the love of the two brothers for their home community and of their constant efforts to make of it a better place in which to live and work, of their friendliness, kindness and helpfulness and loyalty.

The person without any special frame of reference will think of them as the 'good physicians' and be thankful that they spread the gospel of better training for physicians throughout the world.

The youth will think of the way they met the challenge of life and will find inspiration in it.

CHAPTER 14

The Wide World

Alumni

The major responsibility of the Mayo Clinic is to care for the sick. In a very real sense this care of the sick is not limited to patients coming to Rochester. Mayo alumni carry the high Mayo standards of medical practice to much of the entire world. Here we must again resort to figures, which are sometimes boring but often necessary. The outcome of a baseball game may be summarized in a variety of descriptions of what has happened. But the final score of Chicago Cubs 9 and Cincinnati Reds 5 often relates more than such accounts. Let us resort to numbers also in the account of Mayo alumni.

In 1966 there were listed 4,400 alumni, including 396 on the Clinic staff. These were located in 828 cities and towns in all the states of the Union. In eleven states there were over 100 alumni: California (actually with 580), Florida, Illinois, Michigan, Minnesota, New York, Ohio, Pennsylvania, Texas, Washington, and Wisconsin. About two percent of all the practicing medical specialists in the country were Mayo alumni.

Mayo was represented in eight of Canada's eleven territories. Not yet penetrated by Mayo trainees were only New Brunswick, Northwest Territories, and Yukon. Alumni may be found in 45 Canadian cities.

Traveling to the rest of the world we find 257 alumni in 138 cities of fifty-one countries. It is surprising to note that the number of alumni in the U.S.S.R. and East Germany is zero. But Mayo contributed to a high quality of medical care in some 1,000 cities and communities of this earth.

While medical care is the first responsibility of the Clinic and its worldwide alumni representatives, one must repeatedly recall the remaining two of the Mayo triad: education and research. In medicine, these two are inseparable. Good teaching cannot be conducted except in an atmosphere of inquiry, of questioning, of research. A university has just two functions: to disseminate knowledge and to increase knowledge. The Clinic fully believed that if it should fail in teaching and research, its world renown in clinical medicine and surgery would tumble.

Alumni have adhered to this Mayo principle of correlating their practice with teaching and investigation. A survey revealed that some forty percent of Mayo alumni held academic appointments in more than one hundred training institutions in the world. Here in the United States alumni made up two percent of all part-time faculty members and one percent of all full-time staff. Mayo supplies the country's medical schools with more part-time faculty members than any other of the nation's thirteen hundred residency training programs. Abroad, Clinic graduates hold faculty appointments in twenty-seven countries.

Besides contributing to a high level of practice and to teaching and research in their own localities, Mayo's alumni also continue to serve their mother institution. By example, in their labors, and by word of mouth, they convey the institution's high status to prospective trainees who anticipate appointments for advanced medical speciality training. Without being requested to do so, Mayo alumni have been active and effective in fellowship recruitment efforts.

National Activities

Besides their diverse activities and responsibilities in Rochester, the Clinic staff was most active in national medical and scientific organizations. This refers not to presentations of papers at scientific meetings or mere membership in various associations, but to functioning actively in the operation of various societies and their committees. Among the most important of the country's organizations relative to specialized medical practice are the various American boards. For each specialty in medicine or any of its branches there is a board, such as the American Board of Obstetrics and Gynecology. Each board has essentially two functions: first, to evaluate and approve institutions offering training in its field, acting jointly with the American Medical Association and other involved bodies;

second, to assess the qualifications of physicians trained at these places who wish to be designated as specialists. No physican claiming to be a child specialist was recognized as such unless he was certified by the American Board of Pediatrics. Many Mayo staff members functioned actively as members of one or another of these American boards. Naturally, each of Mayo's many specialty advanced training programs has the full approval of the respective American board.

Foreign Service

The major aspects of the Clinic's service to the world at large are its treatment of patients from everywhere and its training of medical specialists for most countries of the earth.

And there were other foreign services provided by Mayo doctors, notably in Vietnam and Thailand. Actually, such services were based on individual interests, not on Mayo support. The Clinic was involved simply by giving leaves of absence to interested staff members. Financial support came from American and British philanthropic enterprises. And there was an AMA-sponsored Volunteer Physicians for Vietnam program. Various United States governmental agencies were also involved.

The magnitude of need for medical support in Vietnam was startling. For upward of fourteen million civilians in the country there were fewer than two hundred physicians, a ratio of 1 doctor for 70,000 people, as compared with a ratio in the United States of 1 doctor for 780 people. Drs. Joseph M. Kiely and Albert B. Hagedorn eventually received Certificates of Humanitarian Service from the American Medical Association for their Vietnam work.

And there was also Thailand, a country of thirty-five million people, suffering also from lack of physicians and medical facilities. Cardiac surgeon Dr. Dwight McGoon conducted a session of several weeks in Bankok, teaching local doctors about cardiac defects and also about heart surgery. At Siriraj Hospital, McGoon implanted a pacemaker in a heart patient–the first such operation in the country. McGoon once stated, "The United States can help greatly by sending more teams of medical and surgical specialists to the Far East for educational purposes. One such team can train a large number of doctors more economically than would be the case if the doctors individually visited the United States for postgraduate training." During McGoon's Thailand visit there were eight open-heart operations performed.

A major leader and active participant in these foreign services has always been Mayo's eminent orthopedic surgeon Dr. Mark Coventry. He stated, "Except for emergency situations, ultimately it is our teaching that is effective. Results can be achieved in underdeveloped countries by teaching them to teach others in their countries." The Foreign Service Corps eventually extended its services to Caribbean and Central American countries.

Irish Adventure

When the author resigned as secretary of the Council on Medical Education and Hospitals to assume the Mayo post, the AMA house of delegates appointed him to membership on the council itself. The council was composed of national leaders in medical education who held private full-time positions in various institutions throughout the country. During these years a number of foreign medical schools sought approval by the AMA. Such approval rendered their graduates eligible for advanced training in institutions certified in the United States.

One such school was Trinity College in Dublin, Ireland, with branches in Cork and Galway. The school is now known as University College, Dublin. To survey and evaluate medical schools abroad was far too difficult, time-consuming, and expensive in most instances. However, some of the members of the AMA's council attended the first World Conference on Medical Education at London in 1953. The author was vice-president of the conference. Since Dublin was nearby, three or four of the council representatives arranged to survey the school after the world conference closed.

> We soon concluded that the medical school did not warrant AMA approval. There were serious defects. The first two years of their program, in the basic medical sciences, were excellent. But for the third and fourth years Trinity College assigned their students to several hospitals in Dublin and elsewhere in Ireland. During these junior and senior years the school itself had little or no control or direction over the kind or quality of the educational program. The hospitals were virtually independent of the medical school. Some of these hospital training programs were not very good.
>
> We explained the seriousness of these defects to the school authorities and informed them what they must do to correct this fault if they still wished approval by us. They were far from happy.
>
> Some 15 years later I chanced to meet a surgeon from Dublin at a medical gathering on the Spanish Mediterranean Island of Mallorca, where we then lived, after my Clinic retirement. We got talking about medical education. He seemed pleased to explain:
>
> "We now have an excellent medical school in Dublin. For this our thanks are due in part to some representatives of the American Medical Association who inspected our school years ago. They pointed out some serious defects. We were not at all pleased with their evaluation of us. But eventually we studied their recommendations, thought them sound

and put them into action. Thanks to all this we now have a super medical school in Dublin."

Scarcely controlling my amusement and pleasure, I forced myself to confess that I was one of those AMA representatives who carried out the survey and made those recommendations. He was overwhelmed with astonishment.

CHAPTER 15

Policies and Organization

Financial Grants

A revolution in the policy of accepting or even seeking outside financial support was announced in 1956 by Dr. Samuel F. Haines, chairman of the Clinic's board of governors. He stated:

> After careful consideration of all angles of this matter, the Board has agreed that, in the interest of maintaining reasonable charges to our patients, and in order not to limit or restrict the productiveness of our staff in contributing to the advancement of medical knowledge and to the improvement of medical care, the traditional policy of nonacceptance of grants in support of research should no longer be maintained.
>
> Few, if any, medical institutions have been able financially to support large teaching and research programs by their own efforts, nor could this Clinic have done so without the support of Mayo Association.
>
> However, even with this support, it is becoming increasingly difficult to satisfy increasing demands for research facilities, to maintain a large educational program—and to do this in a time of increasing costs—unless we are to increase our charges to patients, or accept grants from outside funds.

As to the Clinic's pride of its long and perhaps unique record of financial independence, Dr. Haines noted, "It would be unfortunate if we were to limit our research productiveness only in order to maintain our pride in this accomplishment.

> Grants will be sought only for those research projects which are carefully screened by our Sciences and Research Administrative Committees, for we must be even more circumspect about spending money obtained as grants than about spending our own money.

In retrospect, it is amazing that no financial support from outside was involved in research resulting in such momentous Mayo accomplishments as the country's first blood bank, the isolation of the hormones thyroxine and cortisone, open-heart surgery, and kidney transplantation, to mention only a few.

Under this new policy, one of the earliest grants came in support of the development of the round or radial hospital unit, in which patients' rooms radiated from the central nurses' and attendants' stations. For this, in 1957 there was a grant of $75,000 from the Ford Foundation and an equal amount from the Hill Family Foundation.

An early major grant of $214,350 was made by the John A. Hartford Foundation of New York to study the possibel surgical correction of a congenital heart defect known as common ventricle. This condition is characterized by the absence of the wall which separates the two pumping chambers in a normal heart. The multidisciplinary study was headed by Dr. Gian Pastelli, head of cardiovascular surgical research. His team included Dr. Dwight C. McGoon, head of cardiovascular surgery.

In the area of medical education, outside supporting grants were not particularly revolutionary. In the year following the Clinic's decision to accept such grants for research, the author could report as follows regarding grants for education:

> The financial support of fellows from outside is not new. For a good many years we have had fellows who have received no stipend from the Mayo Foundation, but have been provided fellowship and scholarship funds from such sources as military services, private foundations of either regional or national character, and civilian government departments.
>
> Funds are now available for fellowship stipends in physical medicine (Office of Vocational Rehabilitation) and in psychiatry (National Institute of Mental Health). We are also reasonably certain of support in neurology (National Institute of Neurological Diseases and Blindness). These programs are in clinical fields in which national shortages of specialists have been found to exist and encouragement of physicians to enter the specialty has been desirable. The support of a number of fellows in laboratory fields is also involved in certain grants under consideration.
>
> There are now some 30 clinical fellows at work here supported by the American Heart Association, American Psychiatric Association, National Institute of Mental Health, National Institute of Neurological Diseases and Blindness, Office of Vocational Rehabilitation, Minnesota Department of Public Welfare, Minnesota Heart Association, United States Air Force, Navy, National Research Council of Canada, Rockefeller Foundation, Lynwood D. Keyser Fund. This program is advancing, though deliberately and conservatively.

> Fellows at work here under outside grants . . . must be responsible to the Mayo Foundation and its faculty for all aspects of their performance . . . They must be, in every sense, fellows of the Mayo Foundation, despite the source of their funds.

Mayo Board of Development

The seeking of outside funds became intensified in the late 1960s with the creation of the Mayo Board of Development, under the initial chairmanship of Dr. Kendall Corbin, a former associate in Mayo Foundation activities. The sole but challenging function of the board was to seek outside financial support from private sources for Mayo programs of medical education and, primarily, research. The board's thinking was often in millions, or more millions. The results were stupendous. By 1967, fifty percent of the total research effort of Mayo institutions was supported from extramural sources. Dr. John Shepherd stated:

> Most of us have recognized that the support from outside has been essential for the continued development of our research as an institution and has kept us competitive with others in an increasingly competitive world.

Anticipating research expenditures for 1969, Dr. Emmerson Ward stated that these would reach about $9.7 million, of which Mayo funds would provide about $5 million and outside grant funds about $4.7 million.

Industry Day was held at Mayo on November 19, 1970. Here were assembled, according to G. Slade Schuster, "The most distinguished and influential group of corporate officers ever to be assembled in Rochester." The aim was to inform these national figures of Mayo's needs, and to hear their response. Former United States President Lyndon Johnson, a member of the new Mayo Foundation Board of Trustees, stated, "We want to put the muscle of business behind this kind of program."

Bert S. Gross, finance committee chairman of Minnesota Mining and Manufacturing (3M), announced that his company had voted a $500,000 gift and that an additional $700,000 had been contributed by International Business Machines (IBM), Merck and Company of Rahway, New Jersey, and the First National Bank of Rochester.

A year later that National Institutes of Health announced a contribution of $3 million for Mayo's clinical cancer center, located in the Curie Pavilion of the Damon Building. Under this grant, investigations were to be carried out on diseases and treatment of blood disorders such as leukemia and myeloma, on malignancies of the gastrointestinal tract, including the liver and pancreas, and on cancer of the prostate, breast, and lungs. Much of this work was carried out under the direction of Drs. Murray N. Silverstein and Hugh R. Butt. Dr. David Carr was also involved.

The promise of effective results in these investigations was due not only to the high caliber of the people involved but also to the fact that the Mayo Clinic is one of the largest centers in the world for diagnosis and treatment of cancer. Some sixteen thousand patients with all types of cancer were being seen annually at the Clinic, and at any one time more than sixty thousand patients with cancer were being followed. Establishment of the Clinic cancer center would provide opportunity to coordinate better the care of these patients and to collect and analyze the large amount of data which might in the future aid in earlier diagnosis and more effective treatment.

In the year 1971 the National Heart and Lung Institute awarded the Mayo Foundation a $2.1 million grant over a five-year period for etablishing a center for research, especially in the field of arterial disease, or artherosclerosis, a condition in which fatty materials are deposited on the inner walls of arteries, restricting the flow of blood to body parts. Depending on what arteries are affected, this may cause disabling or fatal heart disease, stroke, or inadequate blood flow to arms and legs.

Preparation of grant applications was, and still is, a major undertaking. The application for the Clinical cancer center grant involved preparation of twenty-seven protocols, each outlining in detail the problem to be investigated, the objectives of the research, the methods to be employed, and the budgetary needs. Of course, such preliminary thinking meant that as soon as the grant was awarded, there was little delay in getting the programs under way. Throughout succeeding decades the board of development multiplied its fund-raising successes.

New Mayo Foundation Board

Just as new building construction and staff expansion are always inevitable in Rochester, so also subject to change was the administrative organization of the Mayo enterprise. Many years ago the Mayo Properties Association became the Mayo Association, which held the ownership of all the Mayo Clinic property and financial assets. All Clinic income, after payment of salaries and expenses, went into the association's assets to be used mainly for education and research. And then in the mid-1960s the new Mayo Foundation Board of Trustees replaced the Mayo Association, taking over all its functions. In addition, this new body was charged with seeking outside funds to supplement the efforts of the board of development. With these nominal and functional changes, the former Mayo Foundation for Medical Education and Research was renamed the Mayo Graduate School of Medicine. In summary, the old Mayo Association became the new Mayo Foundation and the former Mayo Foundation was renamed Mayo Graduate School.

An entirely new aspect of this Mayo Foundation was the inclusion of non-Clinic public members on its board of trustees, supplementing the Clinic family members, consisting of all members of the Clinic's board of governors. Initially there were three public trustees: Edmund Fitzgerald, president of Northwestern Mutual Life Insurance Company in Milwaukee, Henry S. Kingman, president of F&M Savings Bank of Minneapolis, and Dr. Dwight S. Wilbur, clinical professor of medicine at Stanford University and former member of the Clinic family. The first chairman of the foundation's board was G. Slade Schuster, a longtime, outstanding administrator of the Mayo Clinic. Gradually the number of public board members was increased until there were six in 1969, along with nine from the Mayo Clinic.

Included in the public members were now Supreme Court Justice Warren Burger, Dr. W. Clarke Wescoe, chancellor of the University of Kansas, and Lyndon B. Johnson, recently retired president of the United States, who expressed willingness to interrupt his retirement of only a few weeks. He called his Mayo trusteeship "an honor and an opportunity." Included also was Atherton Bean, chairman of the executive committee of the board of directors of the International Milling Company of Minnapolis. More public members were named in later years.

The first woman to be elected as a public trustee of the Mayo Foundation was Dr. Hanna Gray, a historian and an administrator of Yale, Howard, and Northwestern universities. She was appropriately described as "one of the most upwardly mobile women in academia" and ultimately became the first woman president of the University of Chicago.

Considering the importance of computers at the Clinic, it was most appropriate that there was elected as a trustee, Thomas J. Watson of International Business Machines. Cooperation between Rochester's IBM facilities and Mayo has been of inestimable importance in the patient care operation of the Clinic. Without computers, the patient care would be tremendously hampered.

Atherton Bean became the second chairman of the Mayo Foundation Board of Trustees in 1969, succeeding Slade Schuster. Among Bean's reminiscences are these:

> The first time I was here [at Mayo] was years ago. The next time there was this acute situation and I came in as an emergency patient. I got here say two-and-one-half hours after a telephone call to the Clinic, and do you know when I entered the doctor's office, there was my medical record from 30 years ago on his desk!
>
> I was of course aware of the Clinic's worldwide reputation. But it seemed to me that the members of the Clinic were not as conscious of the real

> public position of the Mayo institutions as I thought they should be. There was even a tendency toward aggressive independence.

Regarding the role of the public members of the board of trustees Bean stated:

> I think you have come to realize the responsibility of your very special position in the development of American medicine. Mayo is a model of successful group practice, and as the world becomes more conscious of this type of practice it will become more generally acceptable. The problem is to make available knowledge of the mechanisms by which this institution has been able to serve hundreds of thousands with skill and compassion.

The public member "can say some things which might seem self-serving if they were said by a member of the Mayo staff. For instance, in general people do not really understand that Mayo institutions have been 'public' for 50 years in that all moneys have been applied to public purposes. They must be told this."

And he also asserted, most appropriately, "I have enormous respect for Slade Schuster and the job he has done. I feel quite an unworthy successor."

At this time the nine Clinic members of the board of trustees of the Mayo Foundation for Medical Education and Research were Drs. O. H. Beahrs, J. W. DuShane, J. T. Priestly, W. G. Sauer, J. M. Stickney, and L. E. Ward. The board also included J. W. Harwick (Harry's son), R. P. Kingsbury, and G. S. Schuster.

The enormous task of the board, assisted by the Mayo Board of Development, can be better understood by noting that some fifteen years later (1979) the annual expenditure at Mayo for education, research, and building construction and remodeling totaled more than $70 million. This translates into about $200,000 per day, or $2.50 per second for the entire 365 days and nights of the year. Note that these sums do not include expenses for patient care.

In one of the annual reports of the Mayo Foundation it was stated that

> the willingness of the Mayo Clinic and Mayo Foundation to respond to the needs of society is more evident today than ever before. This willingness extends beyond the care of Mayo patients to broader areas of concern such as the right of all people to optimal medical service, the training of physicians and allied health professionals, the advancement of medical knowledge, and the responsibility of private citizens and organizations to help solve the nation's problems in medical and health care.

One foundation trustee chairman was Stephen Keating of the Twin Cities Honeywell Corporation. He ventured that the world belongs to risk takers and that Will and Charles Mayo took enormous risks in their time to become world leaders in medicine and "I feel strongly that Mayo must continue to demonstrate leadership in medicine . . . that it must set an example to lead others."

Expanded Ventures

Expanding medical care programs raced with the multiplication of patients, staff, and fellows, with new building projects, and with increased numbers and complexities of mechanical machinery.

There was an expansion of the work in child and adolescent psychiatry. The organization of the section of general psychiatry was a relatively late Clinic development, although we know that considerable attention to patients' emotional problems was given by many staff members before this section was established in the 1940s. For a number of years child psychiatry did little more than provide advice at the request of pediatricians requesting help. There was little specific children's psychiatry treatment or teaching. This was changed under the leadership of Dr. J. G. Delano, consultant in pediatric psychiatry, and a four-year training program was established in child, adolescent, and adult psychiatry. In the late 1960s there was established the adolescent psychiatry service in the Methodist Hospital's Colonial Building. Patients served in this unit were in the high school and college age bracket, from fifteen to twenty-one years of age. The duration of patients' stay here ranged from a few days to a few weeks. This new hospital service broadened the educational experience of fellows. In addition to fellows majoring in psychiatry, all pediatric fellows spent some time here, usually one quarter.

The long-established section of dental and oral surgery expanded to include orthodontics, prosthodontics, and periodontics. And what might these be? Orthodontics seeks to prevent or correct irregularities of the teeth and jaws resulting in faulty occlusion. Prosthodontics employs various artificial appliances, such as bridges, to restore and maintain oral function that has been upset by missing teeth. Periodontics refers to diagnosis and treatment of diseases of the bone and soft tissue in which teeth are embedded. All this has long been attended to in the private practice of expert dentists throughout the country. It now became a limited Mayo Clinic function. But it must not be assumed that Mayo wholeheartedly entered into this practice. Staff members in the special dental fields were limited, by design. Patients who came to Mayo for other medical complaints may require dental care related to their main problem. Such needs could be met. But the Clinic was not set up to care for patients whose main complaint was dental, and a great deal of work in dentistry was caring for members of the staff and their families.

Then there were various allied health services. Considerable education was required in fields related to medicine for those who worked with physicians in the care of patients. Nurses come to mind first. At the beginning of the century medical care was provided by a doctor-nurse team in a one-to-one ratio. By the late 1960s this ratio became one to thirteen, with one doctor to thirteen in supportive health roles, including nurses. Mayo must train such health aides. Clinical laboratories that employ technicians have developed their own on-the-job training programs. Needed also were educational projects for nurse anesthetists and for technicians and supervisors in such fields as physical therapy, electrocardiography, electroencephalography. Medical secretaries and desk attendants needed special training.

Many such allied health sciences programs were undertaken, largely under the direction of Dr. Gerald M. Needham. The original intent of such education was to train personnel to fill the Clinic's needs, but soon it developed that many of those trained here took positions elsewhere. So these programs in allied health sciences and techniques trained students for work not only in Rochester but elsewhere, just as the Mayo Graduate School of Medicine taught physicians to become specialists either for the Clinic staff or to practice elsewhere in the world.

The school of physical therapy was particularly well developed. In 1969, of the forty graduates of this two-year training program, five remained at Mayo and the remainder went to other localities to employ what they had learned.

The section of clinical pathology was by no means new, but characteristically, it became expanded and more complex. Pathology itself is a very old subject. It literally means the study of the essential nature of diseases and especially the structural changes produced by disease, involving microscopic studies. In earlier times pathology really meant studying parts of the body after death at autopsy to try to determine the exact cause of death. Then came surgical pathology, involving the study of body tissues removed at the time of operation.

In the term *clinical pathology* the *clinic* portion is derived from the Greek *klinikos,* which means "of a bed." This then was the study, not of dead bodies, but of sick patients in bed. The work in this area has so increased that it eventually included microbiology, dealing with microscopic evidences of life and disease, and biochemistry, the chemical aspects of health and sickness. Also, some aspects of physiology were involved, as in the performance of tests to determine pregnancy or the body's basal metabolic rate.

Dr. C. A. Owen stated that organisms pathologists study vary in size from viruses too small to be seen with an ordinary microscope to animals longer than a whale—tapeworms. These living beings have a head about the size of a pinhead, but their bodies may be from twenty to eighty feet long.

Microbiologists may secure for study test material of the throat, the rectum, the blood, the spinal fluid, or elsewhere, from patients with an undiagnosed acute illness suspected to be caused by a submicroscopic virus, such as in mumps. In one of the tests, materials are injected into mice. The symptoms produced in the mice indicate the presence of a harmful virus. Much further investigation is needed to establish just what virus this might be. As in every Clinic activity, this work dealing with diagnosis and patient care was supplemented with extensive teaching and research.

The primary purpose of the new section of occupational health was to serve the needs of the multitude of general employees of the Clinic. In the past employees were served by staff physicians scattered throughout the various sections of the institution. Dr. Bruce Douglass, in charge of the venture, stated:

> In no instance is it planned or considered desirable to urge an employee to sever his relations with his present Clinic physician in favor of the new health service. Rather it is our hope that the new department will gradually gain confidence among employees and that in rendering good service with minimal delay we will attract employees for their annual examinations.

The section was also involved in examining new employees for job fitness. The magnitude of this responsibility is reflected in the numbers involved. By the mid 1960s there were nearly three thousand nonmedics working at the Clinic in various capacities. This number did not include employees of the affiliated hospitals with their many hundreds of nurses and other employees. The aim of the section of occupational health was to standardize employee care, improve records systems, and save time for the employee who sought medical aid and advice.

And then came the Argonne National Laboratories (ANL). In the metalurgical laboratories of the University of Chicago the world's first controlled nuclear chain reaction occurred under the leadership of Enrico Fermi. Immediately after the war, which Fermi's discoveries helped to conclude victoriously for us via the atom bomb, studies on radioactivity were continued, with goals basically scientific instead of destructive and killing. The ANL was established and operated with supervision by the University of Chicago under contract with the United States Atomic Energy Commission. Located some twenty miles southwest of Chicago, the ANL comprised some one hundred buildings in which functioned approximately thirty-seven hundred permanent employees, including one thousand scientists and engineers.

The University of Chicago established the Associated Midwest Universities, which helped operate the project. To such affiliates all the findings of ANL were made available. The Mayo Clinic became one of the thirty-one members of the Associated Midwest Universitites by meeting its qualifications as having "demonstrated active interest in basic science research by offering graduate research programs of good quality leading to doctorates in at least three of the broad fields of biological sciences."

The goals were to promote, encourage, and conduct research in many branches of science, including but not limited to nuclear science. Among the cooperative efforts were studies on the radioactive contents of bones in patients with bone cancer and adequate protection of personnel dealing with radioactive materials such as x-rays.

Collaboration with ANL consisted essentially of exchange of pertinent information. Also, Clinic staff members could visit ANL and participate in their programs. Staff members or fellows had the opportunity to spend some months there in research or observation. In turn, Argonne staff members visited Mayo to present various pertinent findings of their laboratories. So not only did the Clinic support the ANL by membership in the Associated Midwest Universities organization, but Mayo participated actively in its program. Regarding this fruitful cooperation, Mayo's Dr. A. L. Orvis stated, "Our use of the unique talents and resources of ANL and the ANL use of our unique talents and resources will result in a furtherance of knowledge which we all seek."

Arctic Adventures

And then there came the adventure in Alaska, located some three thousand miles from Rochester. Four of the Clinic staff flew to Alaska to conduct heart clinics at Anchorage, Fairbanks, and Juneau-Sitka in a program sponsored by the Alaska Heart Association in cooperation with the Alaska Department of Health and Welfare, the Alaska Crippled Children's Association, and the Minnesota Crippled Children's Association. Mayo's primary purpose was to provide the special examinations necessary to determine whether or not patients with heart ailments were suitable candidates for heart surgery. Some twenty-five percent of the nearly two hundred patients examined in a five-day study were recommended for heart surgery or further study. Most of these were Eskimo or Indian children, in whom there was found to be a high incidence of both congenital and acquired heart disease. Some of the children came to the Clinic or to other United States institutions for treatment.

In addition to their work with patients, Clinic personnel gave lectures, took part in seminars, and demonstrated techniques to the Alaskan physicians who participated in the various examinations. Besides the Mayo Clinic, other United States medical schools were involved in this Alaska program, which was initiated by Stanford University School of Medicine.

Mayo also functioned a bit in Greenland. From time to time, under an agreement with the military, it sent a few competent advanced fellows for a period of some six months service at the Thule air base and research station. This was entirely a volunteer program so far as fellows were concerned. Such volunteers were probably intrigued by the idea of spending some time in this arctic wilderness. The author once received a telephone call from Thule, with voices as clear as if from the Kahler Hotel. The words came partly over the Distant Early Warning (DEW) line established to warn the United States or Canada of hostilities coming to us from over the arctic region – from Russia, perhaps. Message transmission had to be clear under such circumstances. Negating its name, Greenland, this island is the foundation for over one-half million cubic miles of ice on its ice cap.

It is amazing to note all these supplements to the basic Mayo activity of a doctor serving a patient. To accomplish these multiple programs within and beyond the Clinic, elaborate administrative organization was essential. In the early 1960s there were seventeen Mayo Clinic committees involved in such supervision, plus seven committees related to graduate medical education. Dozens of Clinic staff members served on committees, mostly on a part-time basis, supplementing their major functions in patient care, education, and research.

Mayo Philosophy

From time to time the author ventured to formulate the philosophy of the Mayo Clinic basic to its multiple endeavors:

> We will continue to exist only as long as we provide superior educational opportunities for fellows. A wholehearted devotion to the practice of medicine, to diagnosis and therapy is not enough to sustain the world eminence of the Mayo Clinic. Our concern with medical care must be flanked, as in the stained glass window of Balfour Hall, on the one hand with education, and on the other hand, with research. We must embrace the credo of the University of Minnesota, paraphrased, that, through education, men of medicine are ennobled by an increased understanding of health and disease, and we must maintain a dedication to the advancement of learning and the search for truth.
>
> These admonitions to teach and to investigate are not flights of academic fancy in superior disregard of patients, histories, laboratory tests, x-rays, operations and transfusions. The hard practical fact is that, without teaching and research, we will not have patients. Unless our teaching is vigorous, inspired and sustained, we will not attract superior fellows. Without such fellows our source of staff potential is limited, and the quality of the institution will deteriorate. Equally, a devotion to the advancement

of knowledge by research is necessary for the most effective employment of existing knowledge in the care of patients. The staff member who is indifferent to teaching responsibilities and unconcerned with investigation, is indifferent and unconcerned regarding the future of the Mayo Clinic.

Organized teaching cannot and must not substitute for the intimate teacher-pupil relationships of the Clinic and hospital services in the day-by-day work of caring for patients. It is here that every staff member must continue as he has in the past to be keenly aware of his personal responsibility for teaching. A good teacher is essentially a generous man who wishes to share his experiences with younger men eager to learn. He is a mature man who is gratified by the growth of his pupils even if in that growth the student approximates or even eventually exceeds the stature of the teacher. The good teacher must identify with the student, and although he should be intolerant of negligence, he must be encouraging when mistakes are made unwittingly. Impatience is a cardinal sin in teaching; fortunately this is very rarely encountered at this institution. Coldness and lack of sympathy are occasionally rationalized by the teacher as a reflection of scientific objectivity. Scientific objectivity is entirely compatible with warmth of understanding of the student by the teacher and with a sympathetic human approach to the patient by the clinician.

These are matters for thoughtful concern by every one of us. Our teaching at the bedside, in the operating rooms, and in the Clinic sections must always constitute our major teaching effort. An ever-continuing emphasis upon such teaching will further strengthen our educational program and will foster in the minds of even more of our fellows, a keen desire to participate in the academic life of the great medical teaching institutions of this country.

"The University of Minnesota possesses in the Mayo Foundation an asset which is not equalled in any other university in the world." This statement in 1921 signed by Frank Billings and other outside-Mayo experts is not only a judgment. It is equally a challenge to achieve. We are not immodest if we are gratified with our contribution to an improved quality of medical care in this country and in other areas of the world through our fellowship program. We may be excused if we are proud of our productivity in increasing medical and scientific knowledge through research. But we may not be excused if we are sometimes tempted to forget the axiom that, without excellent education and sterling research, we would be just another group of ordinary doctors, doing moderately well.

In our research, we must never lose sight of the fact that our peculiar asset, perhaps our major asset, is the tremendous volume of clinical material available for study. Occasionally, one hears the criticism that we do an insufficient amount of so-called "basic" research. I disagree. That basic research which is done is good, but we would be missing an opportunity unequalled anywere else if we did not orient our research primarily toward the patient. If it be true that basic research in physics, chemistry and physiology can result in great practical good for mankind, it is equally true that the more applied variety of research can add significantly to our basic knowledge of man and nature. The very practical study of astronomy was born of man's habit of travelling the ocean and his desire to know where he is. This practical approach has profoundly changed our

> fundamental concepts of the world and the universe. Similarly, our applied medical research is contributing to "pure science." Experiments aimed at alleviating a painful disease have added materially to our basic knowledge of endocrine functions and interrelationships. Experiments conducted for diagnostic purposes have greatly increased our information on the dynamics of the circulation. In disease, nature performs experiments. If we read those experiments correctly, much may be learned about the science of man. The research productivity of the Mayo Clinic and Mayo Foundation is of such quantity and quality as would warrant pointing with pride by any medical school or institution in the world.

A phrase frequently used by one or the other of the two Mayo brothers was "my brother and I." Originally, this was a mere habit of speech of two boys growing up together. But in time it reflected the idea of the necessity for doctors to work together as a team. Their father once stated, "No man is big enough to be independent of others." The Mayo brothers fostered a cooperative activity–physicians and scientists and students working together for the benefit of the patient. This concept even penetrated to general nonmedical employees. One person ventured, "I do not work *for* the Mayo Clinic; I work *with* it." As Dr. Jan Tillisch once stated to a group of fellows:

> The principle implied in the words "my brother and I" became a cornerstone of this institution . . . You will soon realize that one individual practically never does the entire job. The care of patients is a joint effort of many individuals–the clinician who makes the examination, the radiologist who reads the x-ray films, the laboratory man who performs, and in many cases interprets the tests, and the surgeon who may ultimately furnish the definitive care.

The Mayo Clinic was cited as "the standard against which all other clinics are judged" in one edition of a medical and health annual published by the *Encyclopaedia Britannica*. The Clinic was designated as "the symbol of what doctors can do when they put the needs of the patient before all other considerations . . . The patient who arrives in Rochester for treatment or diagnosis discovers an atmosphere of total involvement in the healing arts; the interaction of the best in medical technology and human skills . . . Everyone from physicians and therapists to the aides that change the linens in the examining and treatment rooms, exudes compassion and everything at the Clinic from the record rooms with the bustling staff of blue-smocked workers to the tasteful nonthreatening decor seems designed to increase efficiency and put the patient at ease."

The Clinic knew that it must look not merely look back at superior past accomplishments but ahead to the challenge of the future. Mayo's philosophy, as phrased by Walter Pater, "must lie . . . in the maintenance of a kind of candid discontent, in the face of the very highest achievement." The past solution of a challenging, baffling problem in medicine or in any science provides no excuse for future inertia. However great past achievements might be, there are always still further advances to be made.

In one of his most moving stories, "The Apple Tree," John Galsworthy refers to the necessity in life for a union of the practical and the ideal. He speaks of "the apple tree, the singing and the gold." At Mayo, the apple tree is the care of patients. The singing is the communication of knowledge, skills, and inspiration to our fellows. And the gold is the better understanding of people in health and in illness, acquired in the collaborative research efforts of staff and fellows. To borrow from Winston Churchill: "The minds of men to whom study is open, are refreshed and enlarged and there is a quickening of the human spirit."

CHAPTER 16

Expanded Facilities

The Damon Complex

In a medical operation as tremendous as the Mayo Clinic and its hospitals and laboratories, it is also necessary to meet nonmedical needs of the thousands of patients who come to Rochester. Hotel requirements were amply provided by the Kahlers. Facilities for parking cars were also essential. This need was met, at least partially, by the construction of the Damon Parkade, across the street north of the Mayo Building. Opened in 1962, this structure accommodated 417 cars, but provision was made so that, if necessary, the ramp could be expanded to handle 660 vehicles. The name of this large unit is derived from Hattie Damon, wife of Dr. Will Mayo. But a building bearing such a name should assuredly be more than a parking ramp. And so it was.

Mayo Museum

The Damon complex also housed the Mayo Foundation Museum of Hygiene and Medicine, located elsewhere since its establishment back in 1935. Strangely enough, the museum had its origin partly in Chicago. It all began back in the early 1930s when the Clinic and foundation were invited to send an exhibit to the Hall of Science of the 1933 Chicago World's Fair. This display centered around the "transparent man," a life-sized and detailed model of man brought here from Germany's famed Dresden Medical Museum.

By the time the Chicago exhibition ended, the Mayo brothers and Dr. Balfour were receptive to the thought of a continuing medical exhibit in Rochester. This was established and quartered in the old Central School, on the site of the present Mayo Building.

The new museum in the Damon complex contained many exhibits displaying parts of the human body, normal and diseased, as well as medical and surgical procedures corrective of disease defects. The aims of the museum designers, headed by Dr. A. H. Bulbulian, were several. It sought to show visitors something of the intricacy of the human body; to help them understand better the problems faced by physicians; to explain in nontechnical language, with the aid of models and diagrams, why certain surgical procedures are necessary and how these are performed; to stimulate those who might make careers in medicine and allied professions; and to relate something of the history of the Clinic.

Attendance has always been remarkable, not only by patients and their families but also by various student and other groups visiting Rochester primarily to see the displays. In the first twenty-eight years after its establishment the museum attracted some 2,300,000 visitors, or about 2,000 per week.

Here we see another example of the Mayo dedication to education. The Clinic is devoted not only to teaching its fellows seeking to become specialists, but also to enlightening the general public in matters of health and disease. And here again Mayo's teaching extended well beyond Rochester. A number of the museum exhibits were displayed at Chicago's famous Museum of Science and Industry, which requested the exhibits as loans.

Curie Pavilion

The Curie Pavilion was established in the subway of the Damon Parkade. In this unit are carried out all kinds of radiation therapy, primarily for cancer patients. Included are two quarter-million-volt x-ray machines and two cobalt therapy devices, as well as a six-million-volt linear accelerator. To house such tremendous machines, an underground location was desirable. Also, it was necessary to ensure that damaging radiation not escape to the outside. For this precaution each treatment room has walls four feet thick consisting of concrete and much lead. The ceilings and floors are similarly constructed. Treatment-room doors are largely lead, covered with wood for appearance' sake. Each weighs half a ton. You must be strong to open such a door. How else could all this be done, except underground?

Prior to opening the pavilion, radiation therapy was administered at the Curie Building, which was located east of the Kahler Hotel. At the time of moving this project the staffs at Curie daily treated some 150 patients, six days per week. Dr. D. S. Childs was in charge of all of this work. The Curie Building was eventually demolished and was replaced by the Kahler East Hotel. But the underground Curie Pavilion remains.

Whence the name Curie? At this time every other building or unit in the Mayo complex bore the name of someone directly in the Mayo family. There are the Plummer, Mayo, and Harwick buildings, as well as Balfour and Judd halls. Marie Curie was a French scientist interested in substances producing various types of radiation. In 1903 she and her husband Pierre shared in the Nobel Prize in physics for the discovery of radioactivity. And in 1911 Marie was awarded a Nobel Prize in chemistry "for her services to the advancement of chemistry by the discovery of the [radioactive] elements of radium and polonium." What an accomplishment for a woman, or for anyone, to receive two Nobel Prizes! Mayo's Dr. Kendall came close to this, but ended with only one.

Dr. Charles W. Mayo met Marie Curie in Paris in 1925. At that time Charles was conducting a European tour on science and medicine for some one hundred physician members of the Interstate Postgraduate Assembly of North America. He conferred on her an honorary membership in the assembly. Marie Curie did visit America, but she never came to Rochester. However, her name is honored forever in the Curie Pavilion.

Mayo Building

All too soon it became apparent that the magnificient and large Plummer Building was quite inadequate to meet the needs of the unbelievable skyrocketing of the number of patients seeking Mayo medical care. By the early 1950s there were twice as many patients coming to Rochester than when the Plummer Building was built. Dr. A. R. Barnes, chairman of the Clinic's board of governors, stated:

> Inadequate physical facilities have increased the effort required of the staff to care for the growing numbers of patients seeking its services. Although all in the institution have lent every effort with complete unselfishness to preserve the high standards of service, of which we are justly proud, nevertheless the results of this overload have been such as to cause increasing concern for the preservation of the fundamental ideals, traditions and objectives of the institution.
>
> I believe that construction of new facilities is a necessary precondition for full freedom of operation of the institution, and when combined with appropriate administrative policies of the Mayo Clinic, the Mayo

Foundation and the Mayo Association, will result in a full realization of the resources of the staff in the practice of the art as well as the science of medicine, the full capitalization of our great opportunities for the training of younger physicians and a liberalization of conditions for those among us able and eager to conduct scientific investigations.

Factors such as these, combined with many others, were carefully weighed by members of the Board of Governors before they arrived at their unanimous decision to recommend construction of the new building.

And "Mr. Mayo Clinic," Harry Harwick, voiced:

During my association with the Clinic, there have been three occasions upon which it became necessary for the governing board of the Clinic to make a grave decision regarding plant enlargement.

The first occasion was in 1910, when, after much study and with considerable apprehension, it was decided to build the "Red-Brick Building" occupied in 1914. The second came in 1924, when it became necessary to consider construction of what we now know as the 1928 [Plummer] building. This decision also occasioned much apprehension on the part of the Board, the staff and, indeed, the entire community.

Each of these decisions was made necessary because of the demand of the public for the professional services of the institution.

The Clinic has now reached another very grave decision. The patient load has increased to the point not only far beyond the expectations of those who planned the 1928 building, but also well beyond the point where patients can be efficiently served with concurrent advantage to the great existing opportunities and resources in graduate medical education and research. Therefore, after several years of concentrated study by the Building Committee and the architects, decision has now been reached to build a new Clinic building as rapidly as possible.

Regarding the capital necessary to invest in such a plant, Harwick said that this "is an investment more adequately safeguarding the future of the Clinic than are securities or money in the bank . . . This is fundamentally an investment in ourselves . . . The staff of the Mayo Clinic cannot stand solely upon the achievements of the past, great as they have been. This milestone marks an opportunity for the future to make a great and lasting contribution to the history of an ideal in medicine—the Mayo Clinic." It was strongly felt by all that the Clinic could not stand still. Mayo must go ahead or fall back.

Where was the new structure to be? West of the Plummer Building was a square block of land surrounding a relatively small but important structure, the Mayo Foundation Museum of Hygiene and Medicine. Here was the location—a site with its own history. It was felt by some that probably the only unhappy thing about new buildings was that you often had to tear down old ones. The old building preceding the museum was a structure dating back to 1866, when the Rochester community voted to build an impressive new school on a vacant lot. The Central School soared to five stories. It was really only four, "but proud citizens cheated a little and counted the basement." It was the tallest structure in town. This huge and imposing school cost Rochester some seventy-five thousand dollars. A news reporter stated that "the site embraces two-and-one-half acres, and when graded and ornamented with trees, grass, plants and walks and surrounded by a neat iron fence . . . the school ground will be ample and efficient."

In the early 1930s the ground and buildings were purchased by the Mayo Association, the school was razed and the Mayo museum built. And now the museum must be torn down and its contents moved elsewhere—actually, into the Damon complex—to make way for the new Mayo Building.

The Korean War colored the thinking and caused some hesitation now and then. But the Clinic went ahead despite once again hearing such World War II expressions as *allocations, priorities, shortages,* and *military necessity.* And the new building came to be—a ten-story, fifteen million dollar Mayo building, which housed virtually all the Clinic sections dealing with all patients on their first entrance into the Mayo Clinic. The entire new building was air-conditioned.

A patient first arriving at the Clinic would probably be seen initially at one of the dozen or more sections of general medicine and surgery on the three upper floors, staffed by about one hundred consultants assisted by nearly as many trainees. On the other floors were located staff and fellows in some twenty special fields of medicine and surgery, from dentistry and dermatology to proctology and urology.

A typical floor contained some eighty rooms, including doctors' offices, for examining patients. In the secretarial suites there was sufficient space for consultants to give dictation. A large, comfortable patients' waiting room was centrally located; patients here could readily hear themselves being paged from the work areas where receptionists and other Clinic personnel were stationed. From here the various workers could clearly see signal lights from the doctors' offices and the patients' examining rooms.

The Building committee stated, "A typical floor of the new building is more than twice the size of a typical Plummer Building floor, plus all the added features that do not exist at Plummer, such as seminar rooms, service areas, secretarial suites and staff rooms for the exclusive use of Clinic consultants." The primary purpose of the staff rooms was to provide "between patient" working quarters for the staff members.

There was the 167-seat assembly room in the subway, named Judd Hall, after Dr. E. Starr Judd, a Rochester resident who had his M.D. degree from the University of Minnesota, interned at Saint Marys

Hospital, and was first assistant to Dr. Charlie until 1904, when he was appointed head of one of the Clinic's sections of surgery. He later became head of the Clinic's surgical staff.

The Harry J. Harwick Room on the second floor was "dedicated to one who brought to his task basic understanding of life, of the people he was to work with and of the pattern he was to shape—an understanding broad enough to encompass many points of view and wise enough to blend them into final unity."

Elevators for patients were supplemented with elevators for the Clinic staff. Characteristically, ample space was provided for more patient elevators in the future, when the building might be further pushed upward toward the sky. On the extensive first floor were lounge facilities for patients just arriving, the business office where patients paid their bills, as well as facilities and equipment and personnel for registering new patients, who were arriving at the rate of about 450 per working day.

In the new Mayo Building the group practice of medicine was carried out on an enormously expanded scale. Most medical historians agreed that one of the greatest contributions of the Mayo brothers and the Clinic was the demonstration that group practice could be carried out successfully on private patients as well as in charity hospital wards. In group practice the special skills of all branches of medicine can be brought to bear at one time on the problem of each patient.

The Plummer Building, released of its magnitude of activity related to patients, now contained various specialty diagnostic laboratories, the entire section of physical medicine and rehabilitation, research facilities, medical publications offices, the rare book room, facilities for retired Mayo physicians, the expanded Mayo Graduate School of Medicine offices, and the Clinic's grand library.

Let us review the Clinic's building history as related to patient load. The original Clinic building—the five-story Red Brick Building—was constructed in 1914, with 30,000 patients coming to the Clinic that year. It was generally felt that "this surely would take care of all patients for all-time-to-come." Within fourteen years the patient visits had more than doubled, so the Plummer Building eventuated. "This surely would take care of all patients for all-time-to-come." By 1950 there was another doubling of patient visits annually, to more than 140,000. Mayo must build still more. With construction of the original ten-story Mayo Building it was *not* considered that "this surely would take care of all patients for all-time-to-come."

In architectural design, the Clinic has been consistently inconsistent. There was first the Red Brick Building, then the rich-toned Sierra-stone Plummer, and now the Mayo Building, with its plain marble and aluminum exterior. The interiors also differed considerably, from the combination of art and function in Plummer to the combination of simplicity and efficiency in Mayo.

This is by no means a negative criticism of the Mayo Clinic or its building planners. We may learn from the past, but we must not be bound to it. Maintenance problems and functional efficiency must override the limitations of artistic traditions. And variety is the spice of life.

Many people wondered if changes in architecture and ornamentation for the new Clinic building meant that the Plummer Building was dated and less worthy than the new project. Art consultant Warren Mosman was emphatic on this point, stating that the Plummer Building "is a very fine example of the architecture of the 1920's. You can feel the loving care and thought and sensitive feeling that went into it. It is at once beautiful and functional, and the materials have worn beautifully. Walk into the lobby and it is as fresh and new as the day it was built. It is proof that with careful, intelligent choice of materials, a building keeps its flavor for long periods of time."

Why, then, wasn't the new building to be in the same general style architecturally and artistically? The builders explained that there were several reasons. Such interior decorative features as the intricate inlaid mosaic and tile or the exterior masonry and brickwork could no longer be duplicated, because the artisans and craftsmen of the 1920s were no longer available. More important, builders had learned more about how to use such building materials as glass, aluminum, floor and ceiling coverings, heating and ventilating systems. Such architectural advances were put to extensive use in the new building.

Which was better—the old or the new? Neither is better, the builders said. Both were right for the style and the period. Both served the same purpose: to help make a building which would be pleasant to visit and in which to work.

In his tale "Doctor Ox's Experiment" Jules Verne encountered a similar problem in viewing a colossal structure combining a great variety of architecture and period designs. His conclusion: "It had required . . . years to build it and it has conformed successively to the architectural method of each period."

And in the words of Victor Hugo, "Great edifices, like great mountains, are the work of ages. It is frequently the case that art changes while they are still in progress. The new art takes the structure as it finds it, encrusts itself upon it [and] assimilates itself to it." Hugo also ventured that "the trunk of a tree is unchangeable, the foliage capricious." Here at Mayo the trunk of the tree is devotion to medical care, research, and education. The foliage is the architectural design of the buildings.

Regarding the architecture of the Mayo Building, which extended the foundations down to solid rock to permit future construction, Harry Harwick said, "We can still expand – straight up." This likewise came to pass, with eight additional stories being added to the lower ten in the late 1960s.

Summarizing, the Red Brick Building was for 30,000 patients annually, the Plummer for 76,000, the original Mayo for 146,000, and the top Mayo floors for 200,000. Where do we go from here? Who knows?

There was speculation and guessing by people regarding the relative heights of the Mayo and Plummer buildings, located across the street from one another. Which was taller? Neither the eye nor the camera could answer this question. To satisfy this curiosity an observation was made from the very top of the Mayo Building, sighting the top of Plummer with a level. The Plummer Building is taller, expressed in inches.

The Harwick

During the half century to 1959, 2,228,924 patients had come to the Mayo Clinic. The tons of medical records, including x-ray films, from this vast number required considerable space, which was disseminated in various locations, including the Plummer Building and the Medical Sciences Building. All this should be in a single, readily available unit. Such a building would also free the badly needed space where these materials were stored at the time.

So the Biometrics Building was planned and was completed in the early 1960s, located just southwest of the Mayo Building. It was financed in part by the United States Public Health Service. On its completion, the task of moving more than a half-century's accumulation of records was no mean problem. It was estimated that this would require more than nine hundred trips with flat cars, each carrying fourteen or fifteen drawers of patients' records.

It was soon determined to rename the Biometrics Building. It became the Harwick Building, honoring Harry J. Harwick, that giant in the Clinic's development and operation. With his genius for choosing able associates, Dr. Will, in 1908, sought the services of the twenty-one-year-old Harry, then a teller at Rochester's First National Bank. He was to take charge of all the nonmedical activities and responsibilities of the Clinic. When he asked Dr. Will what his salary would be, Will asked what his bank wage was. When Harry told him it was $50 per month, he was told, "Your salary here will be $75."

Harry has said, "The first and perhaps greatest lesson I learned was that of teamwork. For 'my brother and I' was no mere convenient term of reference, but rather the expression of a basic indivisible philosophy of life."

In World War I, Harry decided to enlist in the hospital unit being organized at Mayo for overseas duty. While he was filling out his application papers, Dr. Will entered his office and asked what he was doing. When Harry told him, Will said:

> Tear them up. We're declaring you essential. Somebody has to stay home and do this side of the work, Harry. Tear them up.

Harry tore them up and stayed home.

In his forty-four years of service, Harwick held a number of highly responsible posts, including those of secretary, treasurer, and then chairman of the Mayo Association, executive officer of the Clinic's board of governors, chief of administration, purchasing agent, and business manager. To Dr. Will, Harry Harwick was his heir apparent as the executive head of the Clinic. About the naming of the building, Harwick said:

> This is a significant day for me.
>
> I feel very humble and grateful to be honored in this manner by the Mayo Clinic, which, next to my family, has been the absorbing interest of my life.
>
> I hope that this building may long serve as a useful part of the institution, made great by the high ideals and dedication of its founders and their associates and by those still dedicated to these ideals.

Interestingly, Harry had lived for a time years ago in a rented house at the very site of the Harwick Building. His daughter Margaret was born there.

The foundations of buildings constructed to house Mayo facilities were usually planned so as to permit later additions atop the original structures. The foundations of the first ten stories of the Mayo Building permitted the later addition of another eight floors after only about a decade. This occurred likewise with the Harwick Building because of the increasing need for storage of records and x-rays and for installing IBM computers. There was also need for a Clinic cafeteria "to give Clinic men and women a pleasant place in which to share the noontime break."

The Mayo graduate school offices needed more space also, crowded as they were on the top floor of the Plummer Building. So in 1965 offices, record space, and meeting rooms were provided on the top floor of the Harwick Building for the administration of the Mayo Graduate School of Medicine. This new name replaced Mayo Foundation for Medical Education and Research, since the latter term was now employed otherwise.

Medical Sciences Building

Although the Institute of Experimental Medicine was most productive in providing experimental research facilities, it had one considerable disadvantage. Located some five miles from the Clinic, it was inconvenient for investigators with other responsibilities in the downtown Clinic area. There must be a research unit in town near all of the other Clinic buildings. Where should this be? Space was available at the site of the acceleration laboratory of the Mayo aero-medical unit, which contained the Big Wheel, where Dr. Earl Wood and collaborators conducted aviation research and developed the antiblackout suit for fighter pilots in World War II. In this three-story aviation research building there was no general research space, only a number of storage areas.

The large downtown Medical Sciences Building resulted, only a short walk from the other major Clinic units. Ample space was provided for experimental laboratories, machinery, and quarters for the smaller experimental animals such as dogs and cats. The Big Wheel remained at the base of the building for many years. There were laboratories and other facilities in fields that included anatomy, pathology, biochemistry, biophysics, physiology, orthopedics, and surgical research. Included also in the building was the section of engineering, where special laboratory equipment was custom built for Mayo scientists. There was also the surgical instrument shop and storage space for clinical x-ray films. The Medical Sciences Building brought together in one modern, conveniently located structure many of the laboratory facilities needed for medical education and research. It also increased the opportunities for collaboration between scientists in the building and clinicians working with patients in the nearby Clinic buildings.

The dedication ceremonies in September of 1952 were elaborate, fitting to the Clinic's medical research history and presaging the momentous discoveries to come. Among the participants in the dedication proceedings was Dr. Owen Wangensteen, professor and chief of surgery at the university; he was a Mayo fellow in surgery nearly three decades earlier. There was also Dr. Lester Dragstedt, chief of surgery at the University of Chicago, where he had been one of the author's medical school teachers. The principal address was by Dr. Vannevar Bush, holder of some twenty honorary degrees.

In the dedication of the Medical Sciences Building, much attention was paid to the sizable assembly room for lectures and demonstrations, named Frank C. Mann Hall after Mayo's famed research pioneer. During the ceremonies Dr. Wangensteen stated:

> We are met today to honor a man whose contributions to medicine are an important legacy to humanity. For almost 40 years, Frank C. Mann has labored unrelentingly at his consuming tasks. Original observations, new interpretations of functions of organs, novel technics and masterful clarifications have sprung from his fertile mind. No one who has enjoyed the privilege of visiting Frank Mann at work could fail to observe the great

> care with which he planned and executed a program of experimentation. Imagination, the capacity to observe, superb surgical skill, dissatisfaction with anything less than precision technics, rare intuitive qualities of analysis and judgment, profound interphase knowledge, patience, enthusiasm, zeal and complete devotion to his tasks—these are some of the qualities that destined the work of Frank Mann for greatness. And through his workshop, over these many years have gone a large number of graduate students from the various medical specialties who have participated in his labors and have come under his influence. The seed that was sown when Frank Mann was brought to the Mayo Clinic to head up the Division of Experimental Surgery has reaped a rich yield, and the harvest is still incomplete.

And from Dr. Dragstedt was heard:

> It is both a privilege and a pleasure to have a part in the dedication of this splendid hall in memory of the man who has played such an outstanding role in the development of experimental surgery and physiology in this country. While Pavlov was perhaps the first to emphasize the importance of surgery as a method for the investigation of fundamental problems in physiology and medicine, the life and work of Frank C. Mann have provided the best example of the successful use of surgery in biologic research. In this accomplishment he has provided both a stimulus and a challenge to surgeons the world over to take their places in the army of scientific investigators.

About the structure itself, one of its planners stated, "After all, this is a remarkable building—one of the most remarkable in this region, perhaps in the country." The Minnesota Society of Architects agreed, granting the architecture a "meritorious award for excellence in design." There was another noteworthy feature; an employee affirmed by count that there were 620 doors in the building.

In planning and constructing the building, care was taken to protect the Big Wheel while building operations proceeded above it and below it.

Practically inactive for more than a decade, the Big Wheel came to life again in 1959. A new series of investigations was begun at the request of the United States Air Force. These studies related again to changes in the circulation of blood at high-speed flying, with safeguards against harm. They promised potential application to rocket and space flight. It was also felt that information derived from these studies might increase understanding of the mechanisms by which the heart and blood vessels maintain adequate circulation of the blood during other types of stress encountered in everyday living or in diseaes. For some of this work, Dr. Earl Wood received the Eric J. Liljencrantz Award of the Aerospace Medical Association for outstanding research in aerospace medicine, in 1963.

Scarcely any major research development at the Clinic could have eventuated successfully without collaboration with the Medical Sciences

Building investigators. One is inclined to view open-heart surgery or kidney transplants as surgical ventures. But for these tremendous contributions to knowledge and care of the sick, machines developed and perfected in the building were essential.

There was much work on the physiology of blood circulation and of respiration. Instruments and techniques were developed for studying the functioning of the heart and the circulation of blood. There was the new method for direct, continuous, and accurate recording of blood pressure, including a true picture of the rapid fluctuations in arterial blood pressure with each heartbeat. For such determinations Wood and Lambert employed what is called the strain gauge manometer, still used today on human hearts and arteries.

Perhaps the first mammalian blood pressure measurement was made by Stephen Hales 250 years ago. He inserted a tube into a neck artery of a tightly bound reclining horse. This tube was connected with a ten- or twelve-foot narrow glass tube held vertically. The horse's blood rose in the tube to a height of more than eight feet. This was a rough measurement of the force with which its heart pumped blood, although it was a rather high blood pressure, undoubtedly due to the horse's excitement. The difference between this crude Hales procedure and the devices developed and used by Wood and Lambert seems akin to the difference in warfare between the cross-bow and the atom bomb.

There was also the clinical electromyographic laboratory, where devices were employed for measuring the velocity of impulses in nerves. These measurements were useful in determining certain faults in nerve-muscle function and muscle weakness. One of these disease conditions bears Clinic names—the Lambert-Eaton syndrome.

Ear oximetry determined the oxygen content of arterial blood by a device that measured the color of blood in the ear vessels.

In all this work Wood and Lambert not only were physiologists, but also in a real sense they were bioengineers. One notable publication of Dr. Wood appeared not in a medical or scientific journal, but in the *Annals of Biomedical Engineering.* He named his laboratory the biodynamics research unit.

Any account of Mayo accomplishments without the mention of the name of Mayo's physiologist Dr. Charles F. Code could be justly labeled most inadequate. In some three and one-half decades he was author or coauthor of some three hundred published papers, about half of which one could relate to the Medical Sciences Building. Working on animals and men, he solved a number of problems relative to the adrenal glands, the liver, and diseases of the skin. But his major efforts related to the digestive system, including secretions, motility, digestion, and absorption, under both normal and abnormal circumstances. He clarified much of what happens to food from the mouth to the anus, from swallowing to defecation, in health and in disease. In all this he brought together the Clinic patient's problems and the experimental laboratory. A student once said of him, "If ever there was a man who brings the bedside to the laboratory, and the laboratory to the bedside, it is Charlie Code."

Most appropriately, he achieved the distinction of becoming president of the American Gastroenterological Association in 1965. His presidential address dwelt in part on the historical progress and changes in medical education, practice, and research. He stated:

> Only one procedure in my laboratory is what it was 20 years ago. The surviving "facts" I learned in medical school are those related to structure—that of the body, anatomy and pathology, and that of compounds, organic and inorganic. Concepts of . . . health and disease have been changed by the advancement of knowledge. What disease do you treat now as you did 20 years ago?
>
> The effectiveness of the physician has been increased 100-fold in 40 years. As a consequence, medicine and medical research are now regarded as essential components of civilized living. They have become, in the minds of the public, indispensable parts of our American way of life. They rank with the armed forces, the water works, roadways, and travel.

It would require an entire volume to recount all the accomplishments in the Medical Sciences Building effected by Wood and Lambert and their associates Drs. C. F. Code, Ward Fowler, Fred Helmholz, and others. Indeed, a complete collection of their research publications would constitute a sizable library.

CHAPTER 17

Clinic Machinery

Here we refer not to the multiple organizational aspects of the Clinic but to the employment of numerous mechanical devices to help in patient care, education, and research. Not too long ago the available medical machinery consisted of relatively simple x-ray machines, electrocardiography for recording heart action, electroencephalography for recording some aspects of brain function, and not too much more. We might liken all this to an old Model T Ford automobile. And now we have spacecraft and atomic energy. We have progressed equally in machinery available to all aspects of medicine, with abundant computers and autoanalyzers that do everything from determining certain factors in brain disease to sending a detailed bill to a discharged Clinic patient.

The advantage of all this in medicine is an increased precision and the virtual elimination of the factor of human error. Attempting to understand and explain these complexities sometimes tempts one to agree with the skeptic who ventured, "To err is human; to really foul things up requires a computer."

The author's introduction to some of the machinery occurred when he asked a question at the patient registration office. "When did Conrad Hilton first come to the Clinic?" He thought there might be a telephone call to the quarters for storage of patients' histories, with a return call ten or fifteen minutes later. Not at all. The woman stepped to a small machine like a typewriter sitting on a desk and punched numerous keys, spelling "Conrad Hilton." Almost before she finished there appeared an image on a small screen, with data about the man. She punched some keys on another machine and said, "Conrad Hilton first came here in 1961." All this took about ten seconds. Or perhaps it was as much as fifteen.

Some of this complicated machinery has been described elsewhere in this volume: the heart-lung bypass machine employed in open-heart surgery and the artificial kidney. Here we may commence with developments of relative simplicity, proceeding then to the complexities challenging ordinary human comprehension.

Telephones

First let us look at our old friend the telephone. Again, figures tell the story better than words. In the late 1960s there were some twenty-four hundred telephones in the Mayo Clinic complex, excluding hospitals. Per day there were approximately twenty-eight thousand telephone calls, about half of which were within the Clinic and the other half were incoming and outgoing. This amounted to almost one per second of a working day. Computerized machinery handled the great majority of calls, without participation by a telephone operator.

The elaborate automatic mechanical facilities to meet this need were supplemented by the four to six months on-the-job training of telephone operators. Telephone calls requiring personal handling numbered some eight thousand per working day. This might involve a request to speak with Dr. Hoffman. Since there were four doctors with this name, the telephone caller clarified the problem by saying, "I want to talk to the Dr. Hoffman with red hair." A call for Red Butt wasn't from a prankster but from a patient who wanted Dr. Hugh Butt. There might be a call for the Dr. Cain with white shoes, or the caller might want to know why there was a two hundred dollar difference between the fares of two airline flights. There might even be a telephone request for Dr. Incor. Incor happened not to be a doctor, but was the Inquiry Correspondence Service. The question asked might be, "How far is it from El Paso, Texas, to Rochester?" Or, "What is the altitude in Rochester?" "I need to know the ancestry of a doctor whose name begins with *R*." "May I speak with the department of mythology?" "What is the name of your doctor who is interested in Egyptian artifacts?"

Naturally, almost all the calls passing through the telephone operators were of an immediately understandable nature, such as a request for a Clinic appointment or to speak with Dr. Raymond Randall.

The clinic operators are asked to place overseas calls for staff members. Some of the places called in one week (much later, in 1982) included Jerusalem, South Africa, Sweden, Jordan, Guatemala, Saudi Arabia, Russia, Japan, Iran, and Venezuela.

The telephone operators were instructed to have a sense of humor, resourcefulness, and certainly courtesy. Alice Schoenrock, the telephone supervisor, told the operators, "You must have the dignity and confidence which will project the proper image of the Clinic."

Pagemaster

The Pagemaster is a device for contacting needed Clinic doctors whose immediate whereabouts might not be known. Clinic doctors carry or wear small receivers. The system is activated by a telephone operator who sets the desired doctor's call signal on the dial of a transmitter and turns on the switch. The person being paged will hear a humming signal on his receiver. He then calls the Clinic's telephone operator immediately to get the message. The signal is repeated every twenty seconds until the person paged responds. Each doctor's receiver picks up only his own signal. The call can be transmitted to a radius of one mile. Years later Motorola developed a paging system that had a range capacity of eight to ten miles.

Tube System

A system of air tubes was installed to provide direct communication between eighteen stations in the Clinic buildings and Methodist Hospital and Saint Marys Hospital. These air tubes carry such items as patients' histories and whatever objects might need rapid transportation from one area to another. Before this development, carriers of material had to come first to the tube center and then be routed from there to the desired destination. This may be compared with improvements in ordinary home telephoning. There was a time when the telephone caller had to deal first with the company's operator before reaching the person with whom he desired to converse. Now, by direct dialing, the caller bypasses the telephone operator and immediately reaches the place or person desired. Similarly, a doctor at Saint Marys emergency room can now secure blood from the Plummer blood bank directly, with no intermediaries and with much haste.

Autoanalyzers

In the past, chemical and other tests on blood or other body fluids were carried out by technicians by hand, involving innumerable careful measurements of liquids or solids, mixing proper ingredients, weighing or counting or whatever else, all very time-consuming and always subject to human error. Machinery was designed to replace human hands and eyes, just as the heart-lung machine temporarily replaces the human lung and heart and the artificial kidney device substitutes for normal kidney function.

The first automatic analyzer was secured by the Clinic in 1957 and was used for the determination of sugar concentration in blood, important especially in recognizing and controlling diabetes. The Autoanalyzer operates by pumping a small blood sample through a tubular system. At various stages the blood is diluted, separated into its component parts, and mixed with proper reagents to obtain various measurements. All the steps of the manual method are carried out automatically. This machine can determine the concentration of sugar in the blood at the rate of fifty-three samples per hour, or nearly one per minute. During its first year in operation at the Clinic, this Autoanalyzer performed some fifty thousand blood sugar determinations. Results obtained by the machine had a precision greater than is possible with manual methods; the factor of human error was eliminated, and there was considerable saving of time and labor.

"Some of the most difficult-to-treat diabetic patients tend to have large and rapid and unpredictable changes in their blood sugar levels," according to Dr. George D. Molnar. In such cases, repeated single analysis provided inaccurate information. The Autoanalyzer could be employed to determine the blood sugar concentration and even to record the findings continuously over periods of forty-eight to fifty hours. For this a tube is placed in the patient's vein and attached to the machine. A pump draws blood at the rate of six cubic centimeters per hour and propels chemical reagents through the system. The blood sugar concentrations are automatically recorded in the form of a graph.

Mayo's second Autoanalyzer determined the urea content of urine, or more commonly of blood, providing physicians with necessary information regarding kidney function or failure to function properly. In one hour, thirty-eight samples could be analyzed. During one month alone, 3,440 such tests were made. In charge of this machinery was Dr. W. F. McGuckin of clinical biochemistry.

Autoanalysis has also been developed to determine the concentration of other blood or urine chemicals such as the hormone insulin, related to diabetes, and the growth hormone of the pituitary gland, located inside the skull. Then came the determination of the amount of the enzyme phosphatase in the blood. Enzymes in general are bodily produced chemical agents which activate and accelerate various chemical reactions of life without themselves undergoing change in the process. Saliva contains enzymes which digest starches, breaking down big molecules into much smaller ones.

Alkaline phosphatase is related to bone formation. Blood levels in children, where bone formation is rapid, are normally higher than in adults. In childhood diseases where abnormally rapid bone formation occurs, the blood alkaline phosphatase level is elevated. One of the phosphatases is also increased in quantity in cancer of the prostate gland. In many instances determination of blood phosphatase levels is of value in reaching a correct diagnosis and in determining the effectiveness of treatment.

Blood Tests

The Clinic's blood bank eventually found Autoanalyzers indispensable. The determination of the blood group of a donor or recipient in a projected blood transfusion can be determined accurately and rapidly by machinery. This Autoanalyzer can perform tests on some 120 blood samples per hour, or two per minute. In 1969 about eighteen hundred such automated tests were performed each month. By use of this machine one technician can perform about three times as many tests as could be performed by the manual method, and costly chemical reagents are reduced to about one third. All this informs the Clinic doctor what transfusions are safe, whether the blood comes immediately from a present donor or, more commonly, from supplies in the blood bank.

Red blood cell counts have always been one of the most frequently required laboratory tests requested by Clinic doctors. In this procedure there is an enumeration of the number of red cells per cubic millimeter of blood. To carry this out manually–and visually–is a bit complicated, involving drawing a small but accurately measured quantity of the patient's blood into a small tube, diluting it accurately to two hundred times the original volume, and then literally counting the number of cells in a very small volume of diluted blood. This is done on a specially prepared, microscopically ruled slide. All this requires the expenditure of one of the Clinic's most expensive assets–the time of expert technicians. So the Coulter electronic red blood cell counter came into use.

A tiny sample of diluted blood is drawn into the machine, and the count is determined by complex mechanical devices. Amazingly, the number of red cells per cubic millimeter of blood is automatically recorded by an electric typewriter on a laboratory report form. The time required for the test, including the original dilution of the blood sample, is about one minute. During the year 1960 about thirty-two hundred such tests were made per month.

The changeover from counting with the eye to this electronic method of counting red blood cells was not as simple as purchasing a new device and plugging it into an electrical outlet. Intensive studies of the new method were carried out over a period of more than a year, and the successful adaptation of the electronic counter to routine laboratory use came through the cooperative efforts of many Clinic experts. Dr. Don R. Mathieson, head of the clinical pathology laboratories, pointed out that "we had the help of the whole Clinic family, but we are particularly indebted to the Section of Engineering. Members of this section made several remarkable contributions."

Computers

A considerable number and variety of computers have come into use in the many fields of practice, research, teaching, administration, and accounting. To describe and explain all these, or even just the basic principles involved, would exceed the manuscript pages available. For some three years a number of Clinic staff members have participated in an educational program on computer applications conducted jointly by the Clinic and IBM. An outgrowth of these seminars has been the introduction of computer techniques into many areas of Clinic activity.

The IBM 1620 Data Processing System was extremely flexible and could accept many different kinds of data: numeric, algebraic, and even English words. However, the computer operated internally only on numbers, and all problems had to be expressed in such fashion that the computer could translate them into something which could be represented by numbers.

This machine, in use twenty-four hours per day, seven days a week, was soon replaced in the Harwick Building with a new IBM 7040 computer system. This machine was thirty times faster than the 1620 and far more versatile than thirty 1620s would be.

These and similar but even more complicated machines made possible the recording, relating, and storage of complicated research results and also provided solutions for various patient care problems. It must be understood that such machinery would in no sense replace medical knowledge or judgment, but could well enhance doctor-patient relationships. Machinery would relieve physicians and supporting personnel of mere routine that could be done equally well and very much faster by the computer system. Information regarding tens of thousands of patients was recorded, to be called forth when desired, usually in a matter of seconds. The benefits of such machinery lay in relieving physicians and associates of routine that could be done equally well by a computer system. In the instance of a rare disease, how many such patients has the Clinic seen in the past ten years, and what are their Clinic registration numbers? The computer answered. All this would enable the Clinic doctor to use his time more effectively, would expedite the patient's progress through the Clinic, and would extend high quality of medical care to greater numbers of patients. Increased efficiency could reasonably be expected to result in a lowering of medical costs.

Much of the business side of the Clinic has become computerized. The IBM 403 accounting machine, in response to cards punched with appropriate codes, can print itemized statements of charges to Clinic patients at the rate of one hundred lines per minute. In one year 130,000 such statements were mailed to Clinic patients or insurance companies, and before long they were prepared for every Clinic patient. These were mailed only on request or as the initial statement to patients who did not check with the business office before leaving Rochester. Some one hundred different business programs became handled by computer, including payroll, expense accounting, stockroom inventory, and engineering cost accounting.

The Clinic's data processing center consisted of much more than a machine and an operator. Besides the computer unit, the 1401 system included four magnetic tape consoles, a punch card machine that both reads and writes in computer language, a printing machine that can turn out information at the rate of six hundred lines a minute, and storage facilities for tapes and punched cards.

An example or two might clarify the usefulness of computers without attempting to explain how the machinery operates.

A seventy-year-old woman, her fingers nervously clasping and unclasping the latch on her purse, speaks quietly to a Saint Marys admissions clerk. Within seconds after the clerk pushes a button, nurses, pharmacists, and dietitians throughout the hospital know that this woman has been admitted as a patient and are making preparations to care for her.

A Rochester man arrives in the Saint Marys emergency room complaining of chest pains. He's frightened; he's had these pains before, and he's been a patient at Saint Marys before. Thanks to a hospital computer system, it takes five seconds for the emergency room admissions staff to recall all of the information necessary to admit the man to the hospital.

In the past it would have taken much longer to admit such patients to the hospital and to proceed with emergency care. And there is a bit of irony in the fact that dependence on machines actually increases the possibility of more personalized patient care.

Heart Function

The electrical discharges from the beating heart are recorded by electrocardiography in a machine long used in medical practice. The tracings made tell a great deal about the beating of the normal heart and also about numerous cardiac defects. In earlier days the electrical currents were taken from three "leads" on the body: the left and right arms and the left leg. Now there are twelve more leads from various parts of the body, providing more detailed information about heart function. The new equipment installed in the electrocardiographic laboratory in the Plummer Building can make a record in thirty seconds, as compared with twelve to fifteen minutes in past days. The importance of this development relates to the figure of two hundred electrocardiogram tracings—or ECGs—taken not each month or each week but each day.

There were many instances in which such heartbeat records were required on bedridden hospital patients who could not be moved to the ECG laboratory. A telephonic system was organized. When a patient at Saint Marys needs an ECG, a technician wheels a compact stainless steel cart into position alongside the patient's bed. The electrodes are placed into position on the patient's body. The technician plugs into the telephone jack and dials the number of the ECG laboratory. There is then a telephonic transmission, not of words, but of the electrical manifestations of the heartbeat, from hospital to laboratory, where the record is automatically recorded on paper. This telephonic procedure takes less than a minute. Involved in the design and development of this complex installation were not only Clinic physicians and engineers but also the Marquette Electronics Company and the Northwestern Bell Telephone Company.

Brain Waves

Every nerve impulse in the body and every muscle contraction produces small electrical currents which can be measured and recorded by sensitive instruments. The brain, constantly active, produces such waves. From such records, called electroencephalograms, or EEGs, much can be told about brain abnormalities, depth of anesthesia during surgery, and much else. Dr. E. G. Bickford pointed out that an electrical brain discharge pattern of diagnostic significance for a patient may occur only once in a two- or three-hour interval. But because there is no way to predict when this may occur, there must be a prolonged test. Literally hundreds of feet of paper are covered with tracings of no particular significance, and the technician must spend long hours studying these tracings to determine the presence or absence of discharge patterns useful in diagnosis.

A computer was devised which could "recognize" the electrical brain wave pattern sought. It could be coupled with the EEG recording machine so that it would turn on that machine at the proper moment. Thus, only the significant brain wave pattern would be recorded.

Ordinarily, brain wave records—EEGs—were made with the patient close to the recording devices. With the help of IBM and the Bell Telephone Company, this also was vastly modified under Dr. Bickford's direction. Eventually the brain waves of a patient were recorded in the Medical Sciences Building while the patient remained in bed perhaps a mile away. The ordinary telephone transmitted the waves from the patient in bed to the laboratory, making it unnecessary for the sick patient to travel to the laboratory. The distance capability of this telephone device was extended. In one experiment brain waves were carried by a single standard telephone line from the Rochester telephone exchange all the way to Los Angeles, then looped back into another transcontinental line to Rochester. Good replication of the tracing sent and the tracing received was achieved. "Telemedicine" was begun. Dr. Bickford stated that telemedicine enabled him and his associates to check the brain waves of bedridden patients while they remained in their homes or temporary residence in Rochester, or even in their homes far distant from the Clinic. In the latter case the requisite electronic apparatus for connection could be mailed to the patient together with instructions for attaching the electrodes so as to "catch" the brain waves.

The whole field of application of computers to medical science and medical practice continued to expand at an astonishing rate and with multiplying complexities.

Television

Television, more specifically closed-circuit TV, became such an increasingly useful tool in medicine that a TV screen no longer seemed out of place in any clinical section or laboratory. A new system of closed-circuit TV cables, useful in patient care, medical teaching, and research, was established in the Clinic-hospital complex.

An early use of the system was for transmission of x-ray film images from one area to another. For example, suppose several interpretations of an x-ray film were desired. By this system the film picture could be sent to the location of the physician whose opinion was wanted. The vision appeared on a screen in his working area, and he could return his interpretation of the x-ray by telephone. This arrangement provided the means for obtaining several opinions on a film without sending it to different Clinic locations or having those consultants visit the section of diagnostic roentgenology. Such TV connections were made between the Mayo Building, the Plummer Building, Saint Marys Hospital, and the Methodist Hospital. Other important uses of closed-circuit television were soon activated.

Television may also be employed by a surgeon operating on a patient with suspected cancer to secure immediate advice from a pathologist located in his laboratory at considerable distance from the operating room. A television camera is set up in the operating room, usually suspended above the table. It can be focused by a nurse. The pathologist sees the tumor that has been exposed by the surgeon and advises the surgeon just where to remove tissue for biopsy.

Surgical Monitors

During certain surgical procedures, especially in brain surgery, it is imperative that the surgeon and his team know continuously about the patient's blood pressure, heart function, respiratory rate, and body temperature. To measure all this continuously would require such a group as would leave no room for the surgical team. Together with IBM engineers there was developed a device to solve the problem. This was the surgical monitoring system. From instruments positioned on the patient, electrical signals were transmitted to the nearby machinery. Here such required information was converted into significant numbers which were automatically typed on an electric typewriter. These records were made visual by closed-circuit TV on a screen in the operating room. To know the patient's heart rate, for example, the surgeon need only glance at the screen instead of having a technician hold the patient's wrist and count the heartbeats per minute. To have instantly available, accurate information on such vital signs allows the surgical team to respond immediately to any untoward reaction in the patient and also to observe the patient's response to restorative maneuvers. All this is to the end of improving the care of the anesthetized surgical patient. As neurosurgeon Dr. Collin MacCarty opined:

> Careful monitoring is vital to maintain the patient in the best possible physical condition. Our management of the patient is now more accurate because it is based upon better information than has previously been available to us.

In addition to such immediate benefits, this machinery is also capable of storing data for future education and research.

Heart Surgery

After open-heart surgery, as initiated at Mayo by Dr. John Kirklin, it is necessary to make continuous observations on the functioning of the patient's repaired heart for some forty-eight hours. Some six to eight physiological variables must be measured almost continuously, such as the rate of the heartbeat and the blood pressure. For this, nurses were involved in these time-consuming physiological measurements and record keeping. Why not replace the nurse, much needed elsewhere, with a machine? A joint Clinic-IBM project provided the answer.

A computer was programmed to measure continuously the desired physiological variables and to display the values at five-minute intervals on a TV screen at the patient's bedside. The nurses and the physicians caring for the patient could see these computer-measured numbers whenever they wished. Records of all measurements and all other data entered into the computer from the patient also appeared on a printed sheet and became part of the patient's record. This data became a valuable source of research information.

Microsurgery

One of the most exciting advances in surgery has been the introduction of the microscope into the operating room.

This has opened up a new world, the world of microsurgery, and has given surgeons the means to perform operations never before possible or, in many cases, to greatly improve their performance of established procedures.

Among a few of the advances made possible or common by microsurgery are the reattachment of severed fingers and hands, the bypassing of clogged arteries to the brain, the restoration of sight and hearing, and the reversal of some sterilization measures.

Although there are differences in application from one specialty to the next, the basic function of the operating microscope is the same: to illuminate and magnify—up to thirty or forty times life size—minute structures of the body, especially nerves, blood vessels, tubes, and tubules.

The mechanism for this rests on a stand placed on the operating table. The instrument is kept sterile so that the operating surgeon can adjust the focus with his gloved hand without becoming contaminated. (There is also a process in which the surgeon can focus the camera with his feet, keeping both hands free for surgery.) The magnifying device is so paired that the surgeon's assistant can also see what the surgeon sees. The process is particularly useful when working on very small blood vessels, such as joining two of them together. The technique must be learned on animals and not on patients. The surgeon must not use the process on patients until he has learned completely how to join together two blood vessels as small as a half millimeter in diameter.

Microsurgery makes life-sized to the eye structures less than a millimeter in diameter. But what became large to the eye remained small to the hand, making technical development a matter of considerable patience, concentration, and coordination. The operative field is extremely small, the instruments are delicate, minute, and sometimes of unconventional design, and the body tissues manipulated are fine and often fragile. The surgeon's hand movements must be slow, gentle, and limited in scope, since all motion is magnified under the microscope.

All these factors render microsurgical operations of longer duration than much other surgery. But this disadvantage was much outweighed by the improvements in accuracy, skill, and results achieved.

This process is used extensively in surgical procedures involving the eye, ear, nose, and throat. Microscopes, both in operating and examining rooms, are used on about seventy-five percent of all surgical eye patients. Ophthalmology incorporates perhaps the most sophisticated techniques in microsurgery. Among the major uses are in removing cataracts, in affixing a new lens to the eye, and in transplanting corneas. In the latter category the patient's cornea has become clouded with scar tissue. This is removed, and a corneal transplant is sewed in place with sutures. The sutures employed here are incredibly fine, with a diameter less than that of a human hair, and plainly visible only through the microscope. In most such cases good vision can be restored.

Among the applications of microsurgery in ear, nose, and throat (ENT) are in repair or replacement of the eardrum or the tiny bones of the middle ear that conduct sounds into the inner ear. The larynx also is easily viewed and growths removed or injuries mended.

Neurosurgery also involves microscopic techniques. The pituitary gland lies within the skull at the base of the brain, just above the nasal cavity. Operations on this gland may be necessary in several instances; overactivity of part of the gland, for instance, results in excessive bodily growth–gigantism. In the past, surgical approach to this structure was through the skull. But now the operating microscope made it possible to reach this deep-set gland via the nasal cavity, a much safer and less traumatic approach than through the skull. Another major use in neurosurgery was in cases where a vessel supplying blood to a part of the brain became partially occluded, reducing blood flow. Using the operating microscope, a scalp blood vessel outside the skull is rerouted through the skull and attached to an artery on the surface of the brain, thus bypassing the obstructed artery and restoring vital circulation. Mayo surgeons performed one of the largest series of this kind of operation in the world. Microsurgery became an essential part of about twenty-five percent of all neurosurgery cases at Mayo.

Hands, fingers, and toes that have been amputated in accidents can now be reattached, thanks to microsurgery. The microscope allows the orthopedic surgeon to reconnect, or anastomose, the tiny vessels and nerves, commonly about one millimeter in diameter, that have been severed. Blood circulation and feeling are restored to the part.

Reproductive anatomy and function are also benefited by microsurgery. Occlusion may occur in the tiny tubes of the body that carry male sperm from the testicles to the penis or female eggs from the ovaries to the uterus. Using the surgical microscope, the urologist or gynecologist can remove the occlusion, restoring the free flow of the male or female reproductive cells. In all this, the body parts involved are much too small to be operated on successfully without microsurgery.

Use of this procedure extends to still other areas, such as transferring pieces of skin from one part of the body to another to cover defects or injuries. There was even an instance in which plastic surgeons used a portion of a man's intestines to replace part of his esophagus, which had been damaged. Further examples are manifold.

Through the ages, microscopy has been devoted to the examination of dead structures on a slide. Now it also looks on living and functioning nerves and tubes, and enables a surgeon to perform operations on body parts barely visible to the naked eye.

Radioisotopes

A radioisotope is an atom rendered radioactive, emitting rays that can be detected and measured by appropriate and complex devices. Radioisotopes have become most effective diagnostic tools. Detection of thyroid gland malfunction is a good example. The hormone thyroxine, produced by this gland, is a complex molecule containing iodine. A patient is given radioactive iodine by mouth, and the machinery measures the amount of this substance which is absorbed by the thyroid gland in its manufacture of the hormone. The rate of this iodine uptake is measured from six to twenty-four hours after the feeding. A high uptake rate by the thyroid gland indicates an overactivity of that gland—hyperthyroidism. Almost all cases of such thyroid malfunction can be detected by such means.

A multiplication of radioisotope procedures in many other fields was developed by the section of biophysics to assist in diagnosis and treatment. These include clarification of various aspects of pernicious anemia, high blood pressure, kidney artery disease, red blood cell abnormalities, localization of brain tumors, and much more.

There is a diagnostic procedure for locating small bone fractures not clearly apparent in ordinary x-rays. The patient receives an injection of a radioactive substance (technetium 99) that concentrates in bone. It does not injure the bone but renders it more clearly visible in x-rays, perhaps revealing a very small bone fracture.

A "whole body counter" was developed for determining the amount and location of radioactive materials administered to a patient. The counter involved a room measuring eight feet long, nearly seven feet wide, and over seven feet high, with lead-lined walls six inches in thickness. The patient being studied lay in this room, and machinery transmitted radiations from his body to recording devices that registered the amount and location of the radioactive elements. Primary leadership in this enterprise was provided by Drs. C. A. Owen and W. N. Tauxe.

Germ-Free Isolator

In certain biological research studies on animals, the investigator wishes to avoid any effects on the animals resulting from the presence of bacteria, which might complicate the observations made. Experimental animals completely free from all germs were desired. Such mice and rats came into being. Germ-free plastic isolators were built, with arrangements to keep all bacteria from entering. After sterilization, food and water could be passed into the chamber by means of shoulder-length sterile gloves. The air supply to the isolator passed first through glass wool fibers to make it germ-free. And what about the mice who were to live in this ultrapure cage? They must be removed from the mother before birth by cesarean section, employing all the various devices to avoid infection used in surgery on humans.

Dr. Jack L. Titus and associates employed these devices to study the rate of growth and development of body organs in germ-free mice as compared with normally reared mice. Are certain of the bacteria found in normal animals involved in or perhaps necessary for normal growth and development? The answer was partly no. From birth through weaning, germ-free and conventional mice exhibited similar growth patterns. After weaning, germ-free mice grew faster than the control animals.

However, it was learned that in our germ-infected world it is helpful for animals, including mice, to experience early minor infections, which stimulate the organism to develop antibodies to combat later, more serious infections. Animals developing in a completely germ-free environment failed to develop defenses against infections, which were combatted more effectively by normally developing animals. Germ-free animals failed to develop germ-fighting machinery found in various organs of the body, such as in certain lymph glands.

International Business Machines

In all this application of physical machinery to solving medical problems, IBM always played a major role. This organization established a plant in Rochester in 1956. Much of IBM's equipment for the Rochester project was transported by air from its plant in Endicott, New York, by the Flying Tigers, heroes of World War II who once flew guerilla-type missions against the Japanese. We may hope that such reversions from war to peace may reach applications more numerous than changes in the opposite direction.

Shortly afterward, IBM offered to work with the Clinic on various research and other projects. Through the decades the interrelationships between the two institutions were tremendously multiplied. Perhaps worthy of mention is an experience with IBM president Thomas J. Watson of New York. This was entirely unrelated to Clinic problems, but it demonstrated a good deal about the organized efficiency and eager helpfulness of this great colleague of the Mayo Clinic.

The author was in charge of an international meeting on medical education held at the Palmer House in Chicago. For this convention IBM installed machines into which interpreters submitted translations into French, German, or English as required. In the audience were earphones. If the speaker was French, a German in the audience would don earphones and set the key on "German." Every French sentence came through to him at once in German.

But on the opening morning of the meetings, the translating machinery in one of the four meeting rooms failed to function, and the single IBM mechanic could not correct the fault. The author telephoned Watson in New York. His secretary said, "He is in an important meeting and cannot be disturbed."

The author recalls, "I insisted and soon had him on the line. I explained the situation, stating that a good part of this international conference was doomed to complete failure unless something were done at once. That very Monday morning a plane with experts came down from Minneapolis and soon after noon the entire machinery for interpreters was in perfect order. That was Watson!"

As the Clinic has done over the years, Watson and IBM also participated in the development of Rochester's cultural assets. A major one was the Rochester Civic Theatre. This enterprise originated in the early 1950s as the Log Cabin Theatre, housed in the cabin of the Isaac Walton League. A real theater group to produce real plays was thought essential to Rochester. *Light Up the Sky* was, symbolically, the first production. Soon the theater moved to The Little Theatre Off Broadway, correctly describing its size and location, but a real theater structure it most assuredly was not.

Determined to organize and build a real Rochester Civic Theatre in Mayo Park, organizers needed money. IBM was one of the prospective large donors. When a plant official was approached he stated:

"We certainly wish to help with the new theatre. IBM will contribute $800, for which perhaps you could give us 8 season tickets."

The author, chairman of the committee to seek large donations, wrote to President Watson reminding him of a speech he gave in Rochester when IBM was planning installation of its plant here:

"You stated that one top reason you wanted your plant here was that Rochester is a great cultural center. The Rochester Civic Theatre is a most vital element in our city's culture."

Watson sent the theater a check for ten thousand dollars.

Engineering Section

Naturally, these multitudes of extremely complex machines for patient care and research required expert attention to ensure proper and exact functioning. This is provided by the Clinic's engineering section, originally organized in 1948. The challenge to this section multiplied with the ever-increasing intricacy and numbers of machines requiring constant care.

Requiring such attention, ultimately, were eighteen hundred units of equipment in clinics and laboratories not only of the Clinic itself but also of the two hospitals. There is round-the-clock, seven-days-a-week service on crucial equipment. Responsibilities vary in complexity from maintaining in order such surgical equipment as needles and scissors to assuring that IBM computers perform accurately. The over eight hundred microscopes in use must be kept in order. The heart-lung machine must do its work as effectively as a patient's own heart and lungs. To carry out these responsibilities, the engineering section employed ten professional engineers and thirty-three skilled technicians.

It is amazing that despite the tremendous pressures for maintaining and repairing equipment throughout the Rochester institutions, the engineering section is nevertheless able to design and produce in-

The Masonic Temple Building contained facilities for medical practice by the brothers Mayo prior to construction of the Red Brick Building in 1914.

The Red Brick Building of 1914 became the first real Mayo Clinic building.

The Plummer Building (1928).

The original Saint Marys Hospital of twenty-seven beds, built nearly a century ago.

The Mayo Foundation House, the home of Doctor Will Mayo, became part of the Clinic's facilities in 1938.

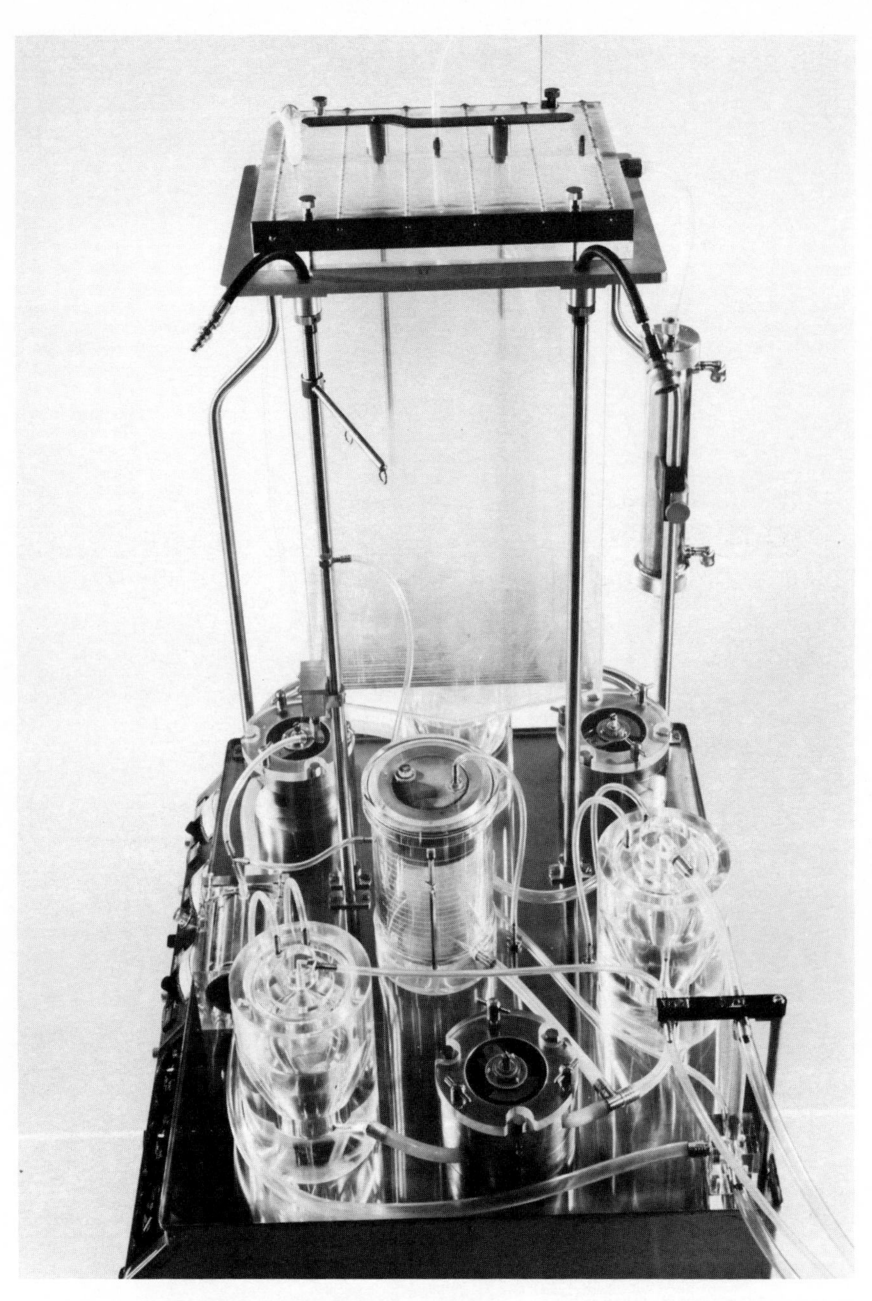

The Mayo-Gibbon heart-lung machine.

The Institute Hills Farm.

The original Medical Sciences Building.

The Damon Parkade (1962).

The Mayo Building: original ten floors built in 1955.

The Mayo Building: eighteen story construction completed in 1969.

The expanded Medical Sciences Building.

The Mayo centennial commemorative seal.

The Hilton Building for Laboratory Medicine (1974).

A patient waiting room. There are many such rooms throughout the Clinic.

The Guggenheim Building for Research and Education (1974).

dividualized, sophisticated research equipment not otherwise available. Development of new machinery is the second major function of the section, accounting for about a quarter of its time. Care is taken not to waste time designing equipment already available commercially. The need is for entirely new inventions. A major development was the Gibbon-Mayo heart-lung machine, with which a patient's blood bypasses his own heart and lungs, enabling heart surgeons to open a patient's heart and repair internal defects.

Certain microscopic research on the internal functioning of muscle cells which are about a millionth of an inch in diameter involves inserting into the cell a minute electronic probe that is about one tenth the diameter of the cell. In order to place that electrode into the cell, the tissue must be isolated from any outside movement. It was stated:

> You probably don't realize it, but the Guggenheim Building [in which the research was conducted] is vibrating all the time. Elevators going up and down, doors being slammed, trucks on the street, bulldozers and jackhammers on the construction site next door—all create movement which is transferred to this building. If we are not properly isolated from this movement we cannot possibly keep the electrode within the cell being studied.

A movement-absorbing base was constructed for experiments consisting of a sandwich of glass, wool, Styrofoam, steel, and marble (each of which absorbs a different frequency of movement) mounted atop a lead-weighted desk.

CHAPTER 18

Mayo Centennial Year

Well before the eventful year of 1964, a Mayo centennial committee was appointed and charged with the responsibility for organization of commemorative programs for the one hundredth anniversary of the birthdates of Drs. W. J and C. H. Mayo. Dr. Will was born in 1861 and Dr. Charlie in 1865. Observing a single commemorative year, rather than one for each of the brothers, was consistent with the lifelong "my brother and I" tradition of the Mayos. Throughout their lives they insisted that any honor for one properly belonged to both. Other considerations also led to the choice of 1964 as Mayo centennial year. Mayo Foundation for Medical Education and Research, one of the Mayo brothers' greatest contributions to medicine, observed its semicentennial in that year. It was truly felt by all that "an institution which forgets its past has no future."

The Mayo brothers established an institution incorporating the three indispensable ingredients of medicine: practice, education, and research. These three words were incorporated into the Mayo centennial commemorative seal as leaves growing out from the staff of Aesculapius, symbol of the medical profession. As appropriately stated by Dr. Hiram Essex, "Had the Clinic developed solely as a patient service organization it would not have attained the stature that has come from its programs of education and research." And so long ago, Dr. Will Mayo said, "It seems to my brother and myself that the crowning endeavor of a life in medicine would be to aid in the development of medical education and research."

The centennial committee chairman was Dr. C. S. MacCarty. Helping him were Drs. Burchell, Code, Johnson, Henderson, Judd, Sprague, and Mr. Schlitgus. Though the centennial committee was to coordinate all activities of the project, its members stressed that "suggestions and counsel of other members of the staff will be much appreciated." Soon a number of other staff members became very active in planning key phases of the celebration. Community leaders also planned non-Clinic observances of the occasion.

General purposes of the centennial included a reacquainting of the Clinic family with the principles of the founders in medical practice, education, and research; a review for the profession of contributions of the Mayos to medicine; and a review for interested citizens generally of the Mayos' contributions to society as a whole. Such reviews are also the purpose of this volume.

A governmental recognition of this great event came from Postmaster General John A. Granouski, who pronounced, "It gives me great pleasure to inform you that I have approved a five-cent commemorative stamp honoring the Mayo brothers and that soon we will make a public announcement."

The Past Reviewed

Let us review briefly some of the past accomplishments in medical practice, education, and research. It is felt by some that the development of cooperative group medical practice has been the most important achievement in modern medical practice. Before the Mayo brothers some group practice occurred in such charity institutions as municipal, state, and university hospitals, mostly for charity patients. But the Mayos fathered group practice for private patients, for the sick who could pay as well as for those who could not pay. And so as Helen Clapesattle said, "These were two American boys who made an obscure village a shrine of hope to suffering humanity."

Patients thronged to Rochester. Visits to the shrine numbered eighteen thousand in 1910, nearly seventy-five thousand in 1930, over ninety-seven thousand in 1939, the year both the Mayo brothers died, and more than one hundred forty thousand in 1950. During the centennial year there were nearly two hundred thousand registrations. Patient number one, under the Harry Plummer registration numbering system, registered in 1907. There followed patient number 1,000,000 in 1938 and number 2,000,000 in 1954. By centennial year nearly 2,500,000 individuals had come to the Clinic. To meet these needs there was constructed the Plummer Building, a veritable painting in stone, resembling the art of old cathedrals, completed in 1928. And then there was the recent, modernistic Mayo Building.

Readily available hospitals were essential. Saint Marys was to open October 1, 1889, just seventy-five years prior to centennial year. But according to Sister Generose Gervais, "A patient needed surgery September 30, so the hospital opened with no fanfare and cared for its first patient, who was operated upon by W. W. Mayo, father of the brothers. The first nursing staff consisted of five Sisters." The medical staff consisted of the father and his two sons. This sparsely furnished facility of twenty-seven beds could scarcely be considered a hospital. After eight persons had been admitted, the sisters had to surrender their beds to the patients. Each evening mattresses were set out on the floor for the sisters. Through the succeeding years, addition after addition was constructed, until in the centennial year there were some nine hundred beds, twenty-two operating rooms, and more than fourteen hundred nurses and other employees.

There was also the Rochester Methodist Hospital, whose beginning date goes back to 1917 when hotelier John Kahler bought the 232-bed Colonial Hotel and converted it into a hospital. Two years later he added the 130-bed Worrall Hospital, built originally as a dormitory for nurses. These two hospitals and other smaller and transitory ones were operated by the Kahler Corporation until 1954, when it sold the two hospitals to a newly formed nonprofit corporation sponsored by the Methodist Church.

Advanced education of physicians loomed no less important in the minds of the Mayo brothers than the care of the sick. The Clinic now celebrates, besides the centennial of the Mayo names, the bicentennial of the Clinic's association with the University of Minnesota Graduate School. The Mayo brothers determined to devote excess earnings to helping the sick through the advancement of medical education and research.

President George Edgar Vincent had bemoaned the fact that success in medical practice as a specialist depended almost entirely on native ability rather than systematic training, since virtually no such training existed anywhere. Vincent and graduate school dean Guy Stanton Ford saw in the collaborative enterprise in Minneapolis and Rochester the possibility of "a graduate school which will stand absolutely alone in the sphere of medical education in America." The president's dream of systematic training of specialists in medicine, made reality by the efforts of Dean Ford and Mayo Foundation Director Louis B. Wilson, anticipated a major development in the training and identification of specialists in this country.

And so, fifty years ago was established the Mayo Foundation for Medical Education and Research as part of the university. It soon became nationwide in scope, as well as international, in the training of medical school graduates seeking to become specialists in all the various fields of medicine and surgery. Such trainees, appointed for three or more years, were called fellows. The author reported:

> There are now only seven medical schools of the country which have no representatives on our fellowship roster. The international character of the Clinic-Foundation is also reflected in the considerable number and high caliber of graduates of foreign medical schools who take fellowships with us. We have been pioneers in the distinctly American system of advanced medical education of physicians for specialty practice, sponsored by the American Medical Association, the American Boards in the various specialty fields, the American College of Physicians, the American College of Surgeons and other official agencies. We see the import of the Mayo Clinic training program on the practice of medicine throughout the world. Today there are about 4,000 of our alumni distributed across the country and over the entire world.

Research and education are inseparable. Education is derived from research and education stimulates research. Fellows of the Mayo Foundation, usually interested primarily in becoming medical specialists, were encouraged to "take a minor" in some such research area as physiology, pathology, or biochemistry. Based on such work, many if not most fellows sought advanced academic master's or even doctor's degrees. It was believed that a strong research program by staff and fellows was essential not only as a responsibility to the university but also as a condition for the Clinic's survival.

At the permanent staff level, research contributions deserved a centennial celebration. To mention a few of these, which are discussed in more detail elsewhere in this volume:

The discovery and isolation of thyroxine, the hormone of the thyroid gland, by Dr. Edward C. Kendall, some fifty years ago, providing revolutionary treatment of some disorders of the thyroid gland.

The development of the PAR room, or postanesthesia recovery room, following surgery.

Work on the human centrifuge, or Big Wheel, resulting in the development of plastic garments for aviators in fighter planes to prevent blackout and death when veering upward after divebombing.

Organizing the country's first blood bank.

Perfecting open-heart surgery by shunting the blood of a patient through machinery that performed the functions of both heart and lungs during surgery inside the heart.

Originating the circular or radial unit for patient care in hospitals.

Isolation of the vital hormone cortisone, secreted by the adrenal glands, leading to the successful treatment of patients whose adrenal glands functioned inadequately to support life. For this discovery Drs. Edward C. Kendall and Philip S. Hench received the Nobel Prize in 1950.

Mirror to Man

The climax of the centennial year was a symposium called Mirror to Man, discussing human adaptation to an expanding environment, and a university convocation at which the board of regents of the university presented citations and outstanding achievement awards. There was also a concert by the Minneapolis Symphony Orchestra.

The participants of the Mirror to Man symposium were outstanding world figures:

Dr. Loren C. Eiseley, anthropologist, author of *The Immense Journey* and *The Firmament of Time*, provost of the University of Pennsylvania and former chairman of the University of Minnesota Department of Anthropology.

Dr. Peter Bryan Medawar, zoologist and experimental biologist, former Jodrell Professor of Zoology at the University of London and corecipient of the Nobel Prize in medicine and physiology in 1960 for his work on acquired immunologic tolerance in the grafting of tissues.

Dr. Rachel L. Carson, ecologist, author of *The Sea Around Us* and *Silent Spring*.

Dr. Edward Teller, nuclear physicist, author of *Our Nuclear Future*, director of research concerning planning and prediction function of the atomic and hydrogen bombs, professor-at-large at the University of California and former director of the University of Minnesota's radiation laboratory.

C. A. Doxiadis, international leader in civic planning and civic architecture, designer in charge of civic planning for the city of Philadelphia and other similar projects.

General Lauris Norstad, supreme Allied commander, Supreme Headquarters of the Allied Powers in Europe, 1956 to 1962, president of the North Atlantic Treaty Organization.

Dr. Arthur Larson, authority in jurisprudence and international law, special assistant and special consultant to the president of the United States, 1957 to 1958, director of the World Rule of Law Center at Duke University and professor of law.

Dr. Laurence M. Gould, president emeritus of Carleton College and a distinguished figure in American geographic circles, was moderator of the symposium, and Dr. O. Meredith Wilson, president of the University of Minnesota, took part in some of the proceedings.

Mirror to Man was by no means a medical symposium. It was rather a discussion of the major problems facing mankind today and how these might be met. These included war and peace, communism, population problems, government, and others. Some of the thinking of the participants is revealed in these extracts from the symposium records:

Larson: "In the Soviet Union communism is still the official ideology, but it is mostly a matter of lip service as far as the economic tenets of communism are concerned. What has really happened is that they now have capitalism, only the capital is owned by the state; it is state capitalism; it is not communism by the wildest stretch of the imagination. As to the methods of production—farming and others—they have been changed by pragmatic compromises. The incentive system is in full swing far beyond what we practice here, and in all these various ways the paper communism of Marx is unrecognizable; it is mostly window-dressing . . .

"Before the Age of Science, if you wanted to find out what the inside of the human body was like, you did not open a human body, you opened Aristotle. When Galileo, to test whether the speed of falling objects increased with their weight, dropped two balls of differing weights from the leaning tower of Pisa instead of accepting the answer contained in the books, this was considered a piece of impertinence. Today we can hardly believe this story, yet for the most part our conduct of political and international affairs is still dominated by pre-Galileo methods."

Medewar: "There is a view that medicine is abolishing—indeed has already abolished—the main causes of ill health; that the goal of medical research is to put its own practitioners out of business; that this goal will be achieved and the major task of medicine will one day be accomplished so that eventually medicine will wither away, as Lenin said the state would wither away. But some people who say this can also, in different moods, be heard to say (without any apparent awareness of inconsistency) that medicine by its very success in preserving the weak and the defective and the medically dependent is imposing a huge and growing burden on society and, in particular, on the medical services of society; that medicine, far from withering away, will, as George Orwell said the state would, become ever more pervasive and intrusive and demanding until one day all the world will become a hospital and even the best of us will only be ambulatory patients in it."

Norstad: "There is an old proverb to the effect that 'Peace is the dream of the wise, war is the history of man.' But this particular dream will persist, for its alternative is the nightmare of modern warfare with all its destructiveness. Ultimately this dream must, and will, be realized. And as Carl Sandburg said, 'Nothing happens unless first a dream.' "

Eiseley: "While I regard man as the highest form of life on this planet, let us not forget that, because in a sense he has stepped out of nature into a domain which offers enormous freedom of choice, he can also be the most evil and contemptible creature in the world. Already in our lifetime we have had two great wars marked by unspeakable cruelty, and this aspect of the step outside the safely channeled instincts of the animal world has to be borne in mind when we consider the problems of the future. We have free will."

Teller: "Peace comes from unity. I wish it could be unity of all men, but for this wonderful and grandiose aim we have, in all realism, to wait. Isolationism, on the other hand, is bad. I have in all my conscious existence considered isolationism as the greatest of evils. American isolationism contributed greatly to the first world war and to the second world war. I hope it will not contribute to the third world war. I know it will not, because isolationism, in fact, is dead. No responsible political leader in this country today is an isolationist . . ."

Concluding the two-day symposium, Dr. Gould stated,

> In summation, I think I can say for all of us here that the real crisis that faces man today is within himself more than in his environment. It is basically an intellectual one, and in all intellectual crises it has been the belief in a solution that has made a solution possible. You will leave this place not with any extravagant optimism or romantic hopes but still with sufficient faith, I am sure, from what you have heard, so that you will want to keep on trying. All of us are responsible agents of history. We cannot divest ourselves of this. Just as each day when we arise we have to make a new beginning, so civilization has to be rebuilt in every age. Life itself now depends on our building a civilization the like of which the world has not yet seen. We have had some vision of what it can be like. We look back at history, and there are some moments or some periods that shine out through all time and space: one was Periclean Athens; another was the Renaissance. I believe that the period in which you and I live and of which we speak dwarfs both of these. We are equal to all that we can understand, and to the extent that we can understand the products of science and technology and apply them for the benefit of all mankind, we have the radiant hope of another Renaissance. If it comes, it will be because great institutions like the Mayo Clinic and the Mayo Foundation and the University of Minnesota have led the way, not only in healing men's minds and bodies but also in the moral awakening which must be tomorrow.

Centennial Convocation

At the Mayo centennial convocation terminating this memorable celebration, the symposium participants each received a special citation from the university recognizing "unusual service to mankind, decisive impact upon the vision of our age, extraordinary fidelity to professional ideals," and expressing "outstanding gratitude for outstanding contributions to our culture and for generous participation in the Mayo Centennial Symposium September 16-18, 1964."

The convocation, a full-dress university session, was held, as had been the symposium, at the Mayo Civic Auditorium in Mayo Park. No assembly hall in any Clinic building was of sufficient size to accommodate the hundreds of people who attended.

An impressive academic procession proceeded up the aisle to the platform of the crowded hall. There were mace bearer, university marshall, chairman of the board of regents of the university, panelists of the Mirror to Man symposium, alumni to receive outstanding achievement awards, and others, with the president of the university terminating the procession—an inspiring array of great names, all robed in academic caps and gowns. There were the formal presentations of the mace, the symbol of authority of the president of the university, and of the national colors, involving a color guard consisting of university army, navy, and air force ROTC cadets and midshipmen.

The national anthem was sung by all. And thereby hangs a tale. In formulating the material for the printing of the final program, there arose a problem. How should "O say! Can you see?" be printed correctly. Was it "Oh say" or "O say" or "Oh (comma) say"? And where should the question mark and exclamation point be? These and related profound problems about printing the anthem finally had to be settled by the university's English department, at the author's insistence. His behavior in all this prompted a committee member to ask him:

"Victor, why do you always worry and fuss about such details whenever you are involved in the planning of any project? Things eventually work out well."

"Yes, things do work out well because I do worry and fuss about details as well as about the major aspects in planning any important project!"

A major feature of this session was the bestowing of university outstanding achievement awards on selected Mayo Foundation alumni:

> The Regents of the University, as a token of high esteem and in recognition of noted attainment by [the recipient], distinguished alumnus of the University of Minnesota, deem him worthy of special commendation for outstanding achievement . . .

The thirty-five award recipients were selected by the Clinic from the approximately four thousand alumni located all over the world. Many were heads of their universities or other institutional departments. They were:

Edward C. Boland, Internal Medicine, University of Southern California.

Randolph Lee Clark, Surgery, University of Texas.

George R. Comstam, Medicine, University of Zurich, Switzerland.

Irvin S. Cooper, Neurosurgery, New York University.

Ralph A. Deterling, Surgery, Tufts University.

Brown M. Dobyns, Surgery, Western Reserve University.

Donald M. Douglas, Surgery, University of St. Andrews, Scotland.

William W. Engstrom, Internal Medicine, Marquette University.

Thomas B. Fitzpatrick, Dermatology, Harvard University.

Piero Frugoni, Neurosurgery, University of Padua, Italy.

Grace A. Goldsmith, Internal Medicine, Tulane University.

Hirotoshi Hashimoto, Director, St. Luke's International Hospital, Tokyo, Japan.

Nicholas C. Hightower, Clinical Research, Scott and White Clinic, Temple, Texas.

C. Adrian M. Hogben, Physiology, University of Iowa.

Dwight J. Ingle, Physiology, University of Chicago.

Walter H. Judd, Author, Lecturer, and United States Congressman.

Nankumar Hemraj Keswani, Anatomy, Institute of Medical Sciences, New Delhi, India.

Paul E. Lacy, Pathology, Washington University.

Alexander Leaf, Medicine, Howard University.

Sir James R. Learmonth, Surgery, University of Edinburgh, Scotland.

Walter C. Lobitz, Jr., Dermatology, University of Oregon.

W. Randolph Lovelace II, Medical Education and Research, Lovelace Foundation, Albuquerque.

Sarah A. Luse, Anatomy and Pathology, Washington University.

Daniel F. Lynch, President, American Society of Oral Surgeons.

Walter C. MacKenzie, Surgery, University of Alberta, Canada.

Stanley W. Olson, Dean, College of Medicine, Baylor University.

Raymond D. Pruitt, Medicine, Baylor University.

Joseph E. Rall, Intramural Research, National Institute of Arthritis and Metabolic Diseases.

Edward C. Rosenow, Jr., Executive Director, American College of Physicians.

Robert F. Rushmer, Physiology and Biophysics, University of Washington.

Belding H. Scribner, Medicine, University of Washington.

Wade Volwiler, Medicine, University of Washington.

Homer R. Warner, Biophysics and Engineering, University of Utah.

C. Stewart Welch, Surgery, Albany Medical College.

Dwight L. Wilber, Medicine, Stanford University.

For each award recipient the Clinic had to submit to the university not only its recommendation but also strong support from outside Rochester, usually from authorities at the institution of the proposed recipient. In the recommendation for Dr. Walter Judd was included a letter of support from Dwight Eisenhower. After the awards were made, the author wrote Ike about Judd getting one. That great man replied most graciously stating how pleased he was about Judd's award. His letter ended with:

"Thank you so much for your courtesy in writing to me."

The author, as one of the speakers at the Mayo centennial convocation, opined:

> How have we fared throughout these fifty years? What has the University bestowed upon Rochester? What have we contributed to the renown of the University? These interrogations can be answered clearly, firmly and happily.
>
> The University has incorporated its Rochester colleagues into a community of medical scholars dedicated to a more fruitful understanding of man in health and disease. But more, the University has bestowed upon the Mayo institutions—immortality. Doctors and laboratories and clinics and hospitals die. Universities live forever. Nothing can destroy them. The oldest University represented on the stage tonight was founded during the Crusades, seven-and-one-half centuries ago, 270 years before Columbus discovered America. The University of Padua witnessed the encroaching ambitions of Frederick Barbarossa, of Napoleon, of Mussolini. The University survived the invasions of the Spaniards, the French, the Germans, the Austrians and even our own armies. It could not be destroyed by sword or cannon, by fire or plunder. The University of Padua lived through the battles of the Guelphs and Ghibellines, of emperor against Pope, of Venice against Verona, Verona against Padua. The University survives the onslaughts which tumble dynasties and governments and cultures and nations.
>
> But the immortality of a University is not an impersonal abstraction, conceived in a vacuum. It is the product of men and women, their work and their ideas, their contributions to mankind. The University is immortal because her sons and daughters made it so, because of the education and research of its students, schools and colleges and institutes. Without such life-sustaining infusions the University would also become mortal.
>
> The Mayo institutions—Clinic, Association and Foundation—endeavor to provide their full measure of the substance that bestows immortality upon the University of Minnesota.

Related Events

During the centennial year, besides the symposium on Mirror to Man and the university convocation with its outstanding achievement awards, there were medical and scientific meetings in Rochester. These ranged in importance from a few local and state groups to such national organizations as the American College of Physicians, the Central Surgical Society, the American Association of Obstetrics and Gynecology, and the Society of Neurological Surgeons. In all there were forty-two such gatherings during the centennial year—almost one per week, including the Mayo Foundation Alumni Association meeting held at the time of the symposium and the convocation.

The community and city of Rochester joined in the celebration with some twenty special events, including the dedication ceremonies for the United States commemorative postage stamps, with Postmaster General John A. Gronousri as principal speaker. The Rochester Chamber of Commerce had its own Mayo centennial committee to stimulate and assist in these many arrangements.

Rochester visitors participating in tours of Clinic facilities multiplied in the centennial year, with some seventy-eight hundred people viewing the institution in the first four months of 1964. In addition to public tours there were more than one hundred specially arranged programs, including those for visiting medical and scientific groups. The wide range of ages and interests of the many varied groups visiting Rochester called for specially tailored tours. A group of visiting nurses, for example, would probably receive detailed information about the relationship of the Clinic and its affiliated hospitals.

By a very happy circumstance, Saint Marys Hospital celebrated its diamond jubilee during the Mayo centennial year. During these seventy-five years the hospital grew from the modest twenty-seven-bed, twenty thousand dollar building of 1889, to the present nine hundred patient beds. This growth may be considered a true parallel with Clinic expansions for patient care, teaching, and research. For nearly a half century the growth of Saint Marys was directed by Sister Mary Joseph Dempsey, during which time six successive additions came into being. This included the surgical building, ultimately named the Joseph Building. Sister Mary Brigh Cassidy was in charge at the time of the jubilee and continued so for additional years.

Through the decades Saint Marys added new departments: a psychiatric unit, a rehabilitation unit, an emergency admitting section, and intensive care units to conform to the modern concept of grouping patients and tailoring specialized care to meet their needs. In its seventy-fifth year Saint Marys honored its past but maintained its commitment to the future and to continued progress in medical care.

In the years ahead, future generations at Mayo Clinic might look back with intense interest and some nostalgia to the events of 1964. For the Clinic family the centennial year led to a deeper appreciation of the institution's past and a renewed dedication to the future, guided by the ideals of the founders for nonending improvements in the care of patients, the teaching of doctors, and the acquisition of new knowledge through research.

Recess from Mayo

The termination of the author's service as director of the Mayo Graduate School of Medicine did not mark the end of his interest in the great institution. By means of publications and correspondence he kept in touch with Mayo developments during the years he lived with his wife, Maria, on the Mediterranean island of Mallorca.

As the retirement date of March 31, 1966, approached, the Johnsons were overwhelmed by the multitudes of courtesies and honors extended them. One beautiful work of art presented read thus:

> Greetings to Maria and Victor Johnson, in appreciation of your leadership in the medical and cultural progress of our community, your graciousness as hosts, and the kindness, happiness and dignity you have brought to us, from your colleagues in the Mayo Graduate School.

Equally moving and most artistically adorned was the certificate from the Mayo Clinic Board of Governors, reading:

> In recognition of his attaining emeritus status after 19 years among them his colleagues present this token of esteem and their gratitude for the many talents he has expended with such salient effect both as a scholar and the teaching of physiology, major figure in graduate medical education and gifted participant in the cultural endeavors of his community, and for the uncommon distinction which he brought to that living body of high principles which were initiated by the founders William James Mayo and Charles Horace Mayo and which clearly are now recognized as the ideals of the Mayo Clinic and Mayo Foundation.

In the half a century since the Mayo Foundation was first organized there have been three directors. Dr. Louis B. Wilson held the position for about twenty-one years. He played a decisive role in the organization of the Mayo Foundation while also functioning as director of the Clinic laboratories. Dr. Donald Balfour succeeded him and directed the foundation for a decade. He came to Rochester in 1907 as an assistant in pathology, was appointed junior surgeon two years later, and soon became head of a section of general surgery. Courtesy, kindness, dedication, and a genuine interest in physiology were hallmarks of his character. Of the author, director of the Mayo Foundation for nearly twenty years, the Clinic's publication *Mayovox* reported:

> Under his direction relations between the University of Minnesota and the Mayo Foundation have been further strengthened, the number of fellows has reached a record high and the educational program has been modified to fit the changing needs of medical education.

From the Mayo Clinic there was a certificate for "Contributions to the

Observance of the Mayo Centennial Year, 1964." The Alumni Association of the Mayo Graduate School of Medicine honored the author "for his leadership as an investigator, teacher, administrator, his warm encouragement, perceptive guidance and continuing concern for young physicians, his generous contributions of many talents to scientific educational and civic endeavors." And "The Regents and President of the University of Minnesota in recognition of devoted service express their gratitude and high esteem through the presentation of this Certificate of Merit to Victor Johnson . . . whose name is inscribed in official records for all time, as one who has contributed to our University and our State."

Two testimonials the author treasures as much as any other are the Boss of the Year award from the Rochester chapter of the National Secretaries Association and a certificate from the Mayo Clinic Fellows Association for his "contribution to the success of the Wilson Club Softball Team, Rochester Softball Association 'A' League Champions."

It was difficult for the author to answer the question, Who succeeded you? Drs. R. Drew Miller and John S. Welch continued to function in the foundation, but there was considerable administrative reorganization in the institution, along with the formation of the new Mayo Foundation. Dr. Charles F. Code became director for medical education and research and Dr. R. D. Pruitt became director of the Mayo Graduate School of Medicine. The complexities of administration were further multiplied with the development of the new undergraduate medical school. This occurred before the author returned to Rochester to resume this account.

PART III.

The Mayo Clinic Today

This section recounts the present-day (1982) situation at the institution, with the tremendous expansions in facilities and activities. This includes the development of Mayo's undergraduate medical school as a major advance in Mayo's continuing dedication to the triad of patient care, medical education, and scientific research. During these later years, the author lived in Rochester after some retirement years abroad. Available to him were Clinic publications, records, reports, meetings, and whatever else he needed, including numerous conferences with the leaders of the multiple Clinic activities.

CHAPTER 19

Mayo Medical School

At the time the Mayo Medical School opened its doors in 1972, the Clinic had actually been teaching undergraduate medical students for more than half a century. This commenced not only as part of Mayo's devotion to teaching, but also because of the desire of many medical students to come to Rochester to learn.

Medical School Roots

During the very year in which the Mayo Foundation became the first real graduate medical school in the country, the Clinic commenced teaching medical students. This was started by the head of the section of surgical pathology, Dr. W. C. MacCarty. He encouraged medical students to spend their summer vacations in his laboratories. Soon other Clinic laboratories provided similar programs. Eventually, there were also opportunities for visiting medical students to observe in clinical fields as well. One of the earliest of these was in psychiatry, under Dr. Howard Rome's direction. All this was for students during their summer vacation from medical school. These originally were not "courses" or "clerkships"; there was no stipend provided nor tuition charged, and there was no medical school credit given. Students provided their own living and travel expenses. Numerous medical school deans were informed of this program.

Sometimes such student visitors secured financial support from outside sources. But it was the Clinic's policy to reserve the right to judge the appropriateness of the source of such funds, and occasionally a request to visit Mayo with questionable financial aid might be denied. An early approved fund source was from the American Psychiatric Association.

Subsequently, a more formal program provided experience to medical students not only during the summer but throughout the entire year. This work was similar to that offered in undergraduate medical schools, entitled clerkships. Medical schools increasingly permitted elective quarters for medical students and encouraged them to seek experience and training away from the medical school campus. The Mayo Clinic was among the first of these approved away-from-campus institutions in the country. Medical school credit was given for such work. An early statement came to the author from Dr. Richard H. Young, dean of Northwestern University School of Medicine, "Our students are definitely given credit toward graduation for the work done in their clerkships at the Mayo Clinic." And the dean of the University of Pennsylvania School of Medicine stated, "We are always pleased to have our students accepted for your medical student program."

The Mayo Foundation soon provided scholarship funds for some of these medical students, aided in part by grants from the H. V. Jones Foundation and the National Institutes of Health. Some scholarships were provided by the student's home medical school.

In one early quarter of this program there were seven medical students at Mayo. Only six years later (in 1967) there were 112 visiting medical students serving clerkships in all fields from anesthesiology to urology. In effect, there was a sizable bit of an undergraduate medical school at Mayo as early as the 1960s. So the origin of the undergraduate medical school program is as old as the Mayo Foundation itself.

Early Stages

The movement toward establishing a complete undergraduate medical school commenced during the year 1966. The Clinic and the University of Minnesota Medical School formulated a plan which allowed twelve senior medical students to gain their required six months of comprehensive clinical experience at the Clinic under the aegis of the faculty of the Mayo Graduate School of Medicine. They spent their time in internal medicine, pediatrics, and some eight specialty sections. A consultant in internal medicine was appointed advisor for each student.

In essence, such a student performs all the steps in a physical examination, beginning with taking the patient's history. He suggests a tentative diagnosis and orders tests. The staff member repeats the procedures and, on the basis of his findings, evaluates the student's performance and discusses with him those areas in which the student may have erred in his judgment. One account stated:

> The student is present during examinations by members of specialty sections who might be called in consultation. He reviews the results of laboratory tests and special examinations. He participates in the final interview with the patient. He prepares a letter of findings.
>
> All of this means that in a matter of four or five days the student can follow a patient through the entire course of his examination to resolution of his problem.
>
> In all of these activities the student is under the observation of his adviser who must grade his performance. The student also makes a presentation at a section seminar.
>
> Patient acceptance of the students is very good. In fact, it is rather ego-shattering to a consultant when a patient appears disappointed if he does not see the student doctor on a return visit.

Great New Venture

Continuing and more detailed study of the advisability of adding a complete undergraduate medical school to other Mayo educational programs was approved by the governing bodies of the Mayo Clinic and Mayo Foundation. Further study was necessary regarding the goals and size of such a school, the curriculum, faculty requirements, physical needs, capital and operating expenditures, administrative arrangements, academic affiliation, and source of funds.

A commission was named by the Mayo Foundation Board of Trustees and the University of Minnesota Board of Regents to provide advice on the "wisdom and feasibility of establishing an undergraduate medical school in Rochester." The Minnesota Legislature inclined favorably toward establishing a second medical school in Minnesota and naturally focused on Rochester. And in 1969 the legislature allocated funds to the Mayo Foundation for planning and developmental activities related to a new medical school.

It seemed that it might be possible to have an entering medical school class by the fall of 1972, but only if funding and accreditation requirements were met. It was thought that the medical school project would "enhance the effectiveness of this major center in medical education and in research and in the provision of health care."

The need for additional medical schools in this country was supported by a statement of the United States Department of Health, Education and Welfare: "In numbers, our minimum goal for medicine and dentistry should be to increase school capacity to keep pace with the increase in the population in areas from which students are drawn. This would mean increasing the entering medical school class from 9,300 in 1965 to 15,000 in 1975 . . . Any medical school which can be created should be created." It was further pronounced that "assets of the Mayo Clinic and available hospitals, valued at $147 million, are available for the establishment of a medical school. These include buildings, facilities (laboratories, classrooms, equipment, records), personnel (500 medical staff, 700 residents and interns, 2,800 allied health and supportive personnel) and existing educational programs."

The Mayo Foundation considered itself morally obligated to put its experience, its prestige, and its resources at the service of society. With the existing crisis in medical manpower, establishment of a medical school seemed to be an obvious and logical extension of the foundation's overall trusteeship.

According to the Mayo Board of Development, the design and purpose of the proposed school "will express the current of reform and change which are now strongly astir in medical education. It will be as exploratory, imaginative and innovative as the purpose of such a school permits. Above all, it will seek to capitalize on those particular assets and qualities which exist to such an unusual degree in the Mayo setting."

And what about building facilities? The idea that a Mayo medical school would be housed in a separate building or buildings was properly considered to be incorrect. This educational program could well be integrated into existing lecture halls, laboratories, clinical facilities, libraries, and study rooms. Only a little remodeling was necessary to accommodate the first classes. It was anticipated that for a full four-year school with 160 students some new structure might well be needed, although such additional educational space in any new structure would be only a small percentage of the total building space already available. In a few years such additional facilities as were required became available in the new Guggenheim Building.

University Collaboration

Naturally, this tremendous project became necessarily a Clinic and university joint enterprise. This further affiliation was approved by the university's board of regents meeting in Rochester, March 13, 1970, following Mayo's own earlier approval. This joint enterprise was described as "an equal partnership of responsible, mature, independent institutions with mutual recognition of each other's independence. It provides a framework for academic and administrative ties between the university and the proposed Mayo undergraduate medical school."

> The liaison will be maintained by a committee which will consist of the University regents, Mayo Foundation trustees and central administrative officials of both institutions. The chief executive officer of the proposed Mayo medical school, the director for education, will be appointed by the regents on recommendation from Mayo Foundation to the president of the University, and he shall be responsible to the president for development and maintenance of educational programs acceptable to standards required by the regents.
>
> The University of Minnesota will grant the M.D. degree to Mayo Medical School graduates. Establishment of the school could come as early as 1972.

Dr. L. Emmerson Ward, then chairman of the Clinic's board of governors, voiced this opinion:

> This affiliation represents a major extension of the cordial and productive relationship that existed between the University of Minnesota and Mayo Foundation in graduate education for more than half a century. As two of the nation's leaders in medical service, education and research, Mayo and the University share a heavy responsibility to the people of Minnesota. The newly approved affiliation in undergraduate medical education and the allied health sciences should enable the two institutions to serve more effectively together than either could serve alone.

One significant question raised was, How will a medical school affect the Clinic practice of medicine? This question was asked with even greater urgency more than fifty years earlier when the Mayo graduate school was established and has been answered by the fact that postgraduate training of physicians has been successfully pursued in combination with the care of private patients and has, in fact, enhanced their care.

And it had to be remembered that while the undergraduate medical student would be part of a medical team, he would have no independent responsibility for diagnosis or treatment. His participation in activities related to patient care would be at all times under close supervision.

Dr. R. D. Pruitt, Mayo Foundation director for education, pointed out to the staff that the direction of planning was to have Mayo Medical School adapt to the structure of Mayo Clinic rather than the reverse. Certainly there would be some changes and adaptations in professional responsibilities of the staff, but he said these changes should be a matter of choice rather than of necessity.

"If changes are made," Dr. Pruitt stated, "our reasons should be total and institutional and not in behalf of so limited a segment of our overall responsibilities as undergraduate medical education will be. Our strength traditionally has lain, and now lies, in the basic unity of our institutional purposes. Preservation of that unity is essential. Given sufficient wisdom and determination we shall bring it off."

Site Visit

To become generally acceptable as a medical school, an institution must be approved and accredited by the American Medical Association and the Association of American Medical Colleges. And a projected new medical school, such as at Mayo, usually seeks from these agencies an evaluation of the plans for the school. So a distinguished team of physicians and medical educators accepted the invitation to make a site visit to Mayo in late 1971 to determine the probable accreditation state of the projected school. The team's reaction and their report of the survey were most favorable, so that Mayo was practically a fully approved medical school even before the first student enrolled.

In his pre-Clinic AMA days, the author frequently led such site-visit teams reviewing the prospects of proposed new medical schools. One such occasion involved a project in a large eastern city. It early became clear that the plans were far from promising in numerous respects, especially in the inadequacy of financing the proposed school's development and operation. Toward the end of the visit, the visiting team attended a dinner meeting of prominent people supporting the idea of the new medical school. During the ceremony, financial pledges were sought to support the new venture. In a very short time about forty thousand dollars were promised. The chairman beamed and sought the author's reaction to this display of financial backing. The reply was simple: "This was somewhat impressive. Could you repeat this performance every week of the year?" The projected school never eventuated.

A Tall Day

After more than five years of study and planning, involving hundreds of people and thousands of work hours, there came the Mayo Clinic's "tall day," on which occasion (November 12, 1971) Atherton Bean proclaimed:

"I am happy to have the honor of reporting that the Board of Trustees of Mayo Foundation this morning unanimously approved the opening of the Mayo Medical School in September of 1972." This historic announcement was made in Balfour Hall of Mayo Foundation House, which was jammed to capacity with reporters and supporters from within and outside Mayo, as well as lights and cameras of all kinds. Atherton Bean continued:

> People at all levels of the Mayo Institution . . . can take pride in being . . . in at the creation of a school of medicine that will train men and

women to serve the needs of mankind, and what better gift can we offer to posterity.

Dr. Will Mayo, just before he died in 1939 said, 'It was thus that my brother and I started this adventure in medical education that is now known as Mayo Foundation, and it has been a matter of very great satisfaction to us that devoted our lives to this adventure in medicine, which seems now to be bearing fruit.' Our generation, 32 years later, can be equally proud that the adventure will continue.

And on this occasion Dr. Emmerson Ward voiced these thoughts:

There is a serious and growing shortage of health manpower, particularly of physicians. We believe that any institution that can produce physicians ought to do so, and we feel that Mayo is uniquely fitted to develop a new undergraduate medical school. The addition of undergraduate medical education will strengthen other Mayo programs in medical education and research.

Mayo Clinic is not altering its traditional policy of maintaining as its primary objective the care of the patient. This in turn does not mean that our educational responsibilities will be neglected. Rather it indicates our conviction that the environment of an institution which puts patient care first is particularly relevant to the education of today's medical student in view of society's present need for physicians to take care of the sick and for medical research that is closely related to human disease.

Mayo Medical School will be an integral part of our institution. It will not be conducted as an isolated, separate function. Physical facilities of the school will, in the main, be the source as now utilized by the Mayo Clinic and its affiliated hospitals.

Staff members who are involved in this activity will bear the same relationship to Mayo as do almost all of us who now participate both in the long established graduate educational and research activities of Mayo Foundation and in Mayo Clinic's patient care responsibility.

Mayo was honored on this day by the presence of the University of Minnesota's president, Malcolm Moos, who stated, "This is a tall moment for all of us. If I were not a Minnesotan I would want to be a Minnesotan and in part because of the fierce pride that I have in this institution, the Mayo Clinic, and now the Mayo Medical School. This has been coming into place for a long time. It represents the dreams and dedication of many people. I think we all recognize that the partnership, which has ripened over 56 years with our graduate school at the University and the Mayo Clinic, now is going into a new stage. We are not sure how all these crosswalks are going to be maintained, but of one thing we are certain; we will build them stone by stone as we move ahead.

"This institution is not only a state resource but it is a national resource and indeed, an international resource."

And of course there was Dr. Raymond Pruitt, newly appointed dean of Mayo Medical School:

> We are determined to fulfill our national, or even international mission in undergraduate medical education even as for more than half a century we have discharged it in the field of graduate medical education and in the field of medical care. Our obligation as a national medical academic resource will best be discharged by deploying, in behalf of medical education, an institutional environment remarkably rich and unique to the purposes it will serve. In that environment, the medical student will encounter the finest medical care . . . skilled, integrated, personalized, compassionate.
>
> The student will find himself component to a model system. He will be a junior colleague to physicians whose professional attainment he may seek to emulate. There are some who tell us the uniqueness and excellence of our medical care will not survive the pressure of the medical student. We shall meet that challenge and patient and student alike will be enriched by the encounter.

Mayo Medical School Opens

The historic opening of the medical school occurred on September 5, 1972. The opening was simple. For entering students, there were a few days of orientation, including talks, tours, social functions, and an evening convocation. Many of the students had arrived early and had become well established in Rochester. Some found jobs in Rochester during the summer months. The first forty freshmen assembled in Mann Hall for their first class, and the first lecture in America's newest medical school was entitled "Introduction to Structure," given by Dr. A. L. Brown, Jr. Mayo's was the 110th medical school in this country. The first undergraduate medical school in the United States was founded at the Pennsylvania Hospital and the College of Philadelphia more than two centuries earlier.

A difficulty in establishing the concept of a Mayo Medical School was the complete absence of any structure bearing this title. Later in the opening year there was established the student center of the school. This old but beautiful stone structure provided numerous student facilities, although in reality it constituted but a minute fraction of space and equipment used by medical students.

Lectures were given and seminars conducted in Mann Hall and other rooms in the Medical Sciences Building, as well as on the fourteenth floor of the Plummer Building; and then two years later, additional needed facilities were provided in the new Guggenheim Building. Administrative offices were partly in the student center and also in the division of education on the Mayo Building's twelfth floor.

Admission requirements included a satisfactory score on the National Medical College Admission Test and recommendations from the premedical school, where at least three academic years of study must have been completed. Preference was given to Minnesota residents, since Mayo's was a state school. The annual tuition was a mere $1,060 for Minnesotans and $2,150 for students from elsewhere.

The major committees of the school were the admissions committee and the curriculum committee, both under Pruitt's chairmanship but with other able participants.

The entering class of forty included six women. Ten of the group were married. The students' prior training occurred in thirty different institutions. Nine of them were sons or daughters of physicians, including three Mayo consultants. All but four students were Minnesota residents, and seven were from Rochester. Student number one in the Mayo Medical School, at least alphabetically, was Mark A. Arneson of nearby Owatonna.

On the eve of the medical school's opening, Dean Raymond Pruitt stated,

> It is not our intention to rebuild Mayo institutions in the image of a medical school but, to introduce the process of education of undergraduate medical students into the setting of one of the world's greatest medical centers where the primary concern is for excellence of care of the individual patient. Within this environment, the student will have exposure to examples of those professional qualities, dearth of which has caused the alienation of patient from physician.
>
> We have an opportunity to build something different, but we do not intend, in the process of creating a new entity, to sacrifice the greatness of the past.

And former President Lyndon Johnson stated,

> This is a new day in the life of Mayo's long and honored heritage of serving, protecting, and saving the health of millions of people. The new Medical School offers great hope, not only for Minnesota and the nation, but for human beings everywhere. There can be no more laudable undertaking than training those who have chosen to devote themselves to helping their fellow man. Each member of the eminent staff of Mayo Clinic deserves a badge of honor for making a reality out of the dream and faith of the founders, the Mayo brothers. My admiration and gratitude are with all of you who will labor together for the common good and who share the vision of a brighter tomorrow for all humanity.

Faculty

Naturally, the medical school faculty consisted of Mayo staff members who already held academic posts from the university in Mayo's graduate school of medicine. Initially, about one hundred of these were assigned to devote part of their teaching to medical students. No problem was encountered here, for most of the staff was as accustomed to teaching as to caring for patients, and those selected came forward to accept this new challenge both willingly and with enthusiasm. Truly, many others, other than those listed as faculty, contributed to this new medical education. Whoever in the Clinic or its hospitals answered a question or demonstrated a procedure was a medical school teacher. Additions to the total Clinic staff had to be made in order to permit these medical school faculty members to decrease their clinical or laboratory commitments in proportion to the amount of time they devoted to undergraduate teaching.

Dean Pruitt was assisted administratively primarily by two associate deans. Dr. Ward S. Fowler, a professor of physiology in the Mayo Graduate School of Medicine, was named associate dean for academic affairs, responsible for areas of curriculum planning, selection of faculty, and the handling of certain financial and operational functions. Dr. Gerald M. Needham, a medical bacteriologist, was named associate dean for student affairs, responsible for admission of students and arranging their programs. His office kept records of student performance. Here also students were counseled, including at times when problems of performance arose.

Educational Program

Over the decades, improvements in the methods of teaching undergraduate medical students may be likened to our better and increased knowledge of human beings in health and disease. The curriculum today is centered on the person, his systems and parts, instead of on medical school departments. In medical school days not long ago, students spent every afternoon for an entire academic year dissecting cadavers, with mornings devoted to studies in various basic medical science departments such as biochemistry and physiology. There were microscopes and reagent bottles and body parts, but no patients. The cooperation between medical school departments was minimal, if not zero. Decades ago a professor of anatomy once found the author in his laboratory reading a physiology textbook and ordered him to stop because you don't read about physiology in the anatomy building.

In the first year at modern medical schools such as Mayo, there were collaborative studies in biochemistry, microbiology, hematology, immunology, infectious diseases, and growth and development. But in the main, studies centered on the various systems of the body: there were courses on the digestive system, the cardiovascular system, the respiratory system, the renal system, and the neuromuscular system. For each of these systems, the studies involved structure, both microscopic and gross, normal function, and abnormalities encountered in disease. Gross anatomy is now learned from model dissections made by graduate fellows in surgery instead of by wasting hours cutting through skin and fat and whatnot finally to reach the stomach or liver or pancreas embedded in connective tissue.

Instead of studying about the respiratory systems in the several separate departments of anatomy, histology, biochemistry, physiology, and pathology, all of these were brought together into a study of all aspects of the structure and functioning and abnormalities of breathing. Patients with pulmonary abnormalities were seen. And, of course, there were separate textbooks on the various phases of the pulmonary system. But these books were always studied as varied aspects of a body system instead of as a part of the science of physiology or biochemistry.

"Introduction to the Patient" was an important course. Throughout all instruction, there was emphasis on clinical correlations. Students saw real patients during their first week in medical school. This may be contrasted with former days, when study of a medical patient first occurred in the third year of medical school.

The second-year program continued the introduction of the student to the practice of medicine. It also included major assignments to outpatient clinic and hospital work.

At the end of the second year, the student had the opportunity to select one of a variety of educational majors or curriculum sequences. These included several fields of specialty practice such as surgery, internal medicine, pediatrics, family medicine, obstetrics, and gynecology. In these junior and senior years, the modern medical school curriculum was not very different from practices of decades ago. Here the medical student became a member of a medical team that included a staff member, one or two residents or fellows, and the student. He learned medicine in a dynamic environment in which the patient's physician examines, observes, diagnoses, and treats his patients. Lectures and seminars supplemented these practical educational experiences.

The day's work of a junior or senior medical student with patients is about as follows: he is assigned a patient, whose hospital room he enters introducing himself as doctor so-and-so. He questions the patient regarding the symptoms, recording the responses. He conducts a complete physical examination. He also writes what laboratory, x-ray, or other tests he thinks should be done and makes a tentative diagnosis if possible, as well as proposed treatment. All this is checked by a fellow and a staff member. If the patient requires surgery, the student scrubs for the operation and is at hand during the operation. This is his patient until discharge from the hospital. On outpatient services not involving hospitalization, the student functions similarly, always checked by fellow and staff. In this process, we note an improvement in the Clinic's training of graduate students; they become trained in teaching, an important factor in the training of specialists. A most important stimulus to learning is to teach.

In all this, only the first and part of the second year of undergraduate medical education is a real departure from the Clinic's familiar pattern of staff members teaching graduate medical students. Very soon the undergraduate medical student becomes a member of a medical team including staff and fellows or residents.

Decades ago the author repeatedly and strongly urged the revolution in medical education that has now taken place. He urged a teaching oriented around body parts and systems instead of around medical school departments. At a Founders Day address at the Medical College of South Carolina in Charleston, in November of 1944, he expressed these views:

> As unjustifiable as the artificial separation of the medical school professor's duties into those of teaching and research, is the equally indefensible separation of the subject matter of medicine into the obsolete watertight compartments known as departments. Our philosophy of medical education states that man's body, in health and disease, may be divided into its anatomy, its biochemistry, its physiology, its pathology, and so forth. This highly artificial subdivision of our subject matter was not planned. It was an accident—an accident of growth. At first, there was little more than anatomy in the curriculum. Anatomy gave birth to daughter sciences including physiology, which in turn produced the offspring, physiological chemistry, and later still another lusty infant, biophysics. Departments just grew, and the department system of instruction just happened. There has resulted a scramble for student time, in which every hour of student time not specifically accounted for in the curriculum is counted as fair game. The department with the most aggressive hunters captures these hours. The successful department is that which has acquired the most hours into which it then crams a maximum of detail whether or not it is relevant.
>
> A more rational and time-conserving program of study is one in which there are no anatomy, physiology or pathology "courses" at all. Instead, the anatomist, the physiologist, and the pathologist collaborate in presenting an integrated picture of the body in health and disease, in which accidental repetition is eliminated and planned repetition incorporated when required. I have participated in such a plan at another level of education, the teaching of biology to college students. The course is a collaborative enterprise in which lectures, discussions, and laboratory exercises are given by 20 men from 10 different departments, including medicine and surgery. The departmental affiliation and special interests of each instructor are subordinate to the subject matter of the year's course—biology. Frequent discussion and criticism of each other by participants in the course has led to a presentation of biology at this level which is far more effective than is possible without such close collaboration. The success and widespread adoption of such plans in college teaching are stimulating medical educators to think along similar lines. There would be an improved selection of the contents of the medical curriculum, since the material

> presented by each instructor would be subject to the scrutiny of his colleagues in other fields. The student would better grasp the total picture of medicine, since each instructor would integrate his subject with that of his colleagues in a far more effective manner than is possible under the traditional departmental course system. Student time would be conserved for reading, reflection, investigation, and the pursuit of special interests.

And behold! It eventually became recognized that the human body is not composed of anatomy, physiology, biochemistry, and pathology. It is made up of various organs and systems such as alimentary, circulatory, and nervous. The first medical school in the country to adopt this program (in 1952) was the Western Reserve University School of Medicine at Cleveland, Ohio. The Mayo Foundation's director stated, "I do not mean to imply that my utterances were responsible for this adoption, but I may claim that I anticipated and advocated this revolution in medical education."

Grading of Students

The author's concurrence with the newer developments in medical education does not include agreement with the present negative attitudes toward employing the traditional grading system of A, B, C, and so forth. At Mayo Medical School, as elsewhere in the country, such simple but most informative grading is now replaced by more elaborate reports in which the instructor briefly describes the student's performance. For example, a given Mayo student's record for some of his first year's work includes the following:

Introduction to Structure: "A determined and serious individual—he performed excellently on all tests and group sessions."

Immunology: "Mature, interested, bright and hardworking."

Microbiology: "Outstanding performance."

Musculoskeletal System: "Delightful, mature young man."

Biochemistry: "A superior student."

Neural Science: "Bright, intelligent, mature, hardworking, inquisitive mind; has a cheery, outgoing personality; he is one of the most outstanding individuals in this class."

Respiratory System: "Worked hard; very good student."

Urinary System: "Good questions, very pleasant, understands subjects very quickly; did extremely well on all the exams."

Cardiovascular System: "Good sense of humor, consistently pleasant, very good student."

Introduction to Patient: "Bright, enthusiastic, hardworking, mature, relates well to peers and faculty—will be an outstanding physician."

Might not an A or A+ tell the same story?

A recent letter by Associate Dean Joseph M. Kiely recommends a medical student for a residency he seeks. No letter grades are given. But there are some five, single-spaced, typewritten pages along the lines of the example given above.

There is no question that this system of student evaluation does paint a clear picture of a student's performance. But it eliminates the possibility of indicating a student's standing in his class, such as "upper tenth" or "upper third" or whatever.

The honor fraternity, Alpha Omega Alpha (AOA), has for many years awarded membership to the very top students in a medical school, as recommended by the dean. Mayo Medical School does not participate in this activity. The author, once national president of AOA, is not enthusiastic about this Mayo practice.

In the early 1960s, Mayo's Dr. R. Drew Miller and the author pondered the question,

> What is the relationship, if any, between excellence in medical school as indicated by high grades and excellence in the practice of medicine? Obviously, income or number of patients seen is not a good measure of a physician's quality of practice.
>
> We believed that physicians functioning as fellows or residents in clinical fields were carrying out one form of medical practice. At that time, at the Mayo Graduate School of Medicine, we offered among our residencies the standard three-year program in internal medicine, although many residents chose to remain longer, for supplementary clinical or laboratory experience. We evaluated the performance of residents carefully each quarter, and we identified the very superior among them. These were offered an opportunity to remain for an additional year beyond the normal residency period, with increased responsibility at an advanced stipend. These appointees were called "assistants to the staff." Many of them ultimately became permanent staff members.

They made the casual observation that the proportion of Mayo residents who had sufficiently high medical school grades to warrant election to AOA was much higher in the group of the very best residents than in the general residency population. This observation prompted a detailed and controlled study:

> We compared the medical school class standings of 80 assistants to the staff, whose residency performance placed them in approximately the upper 10% of residents and a group of 80 (as controls) that ranked lower as residents. The 80 pairs each contained individuals from both groups, and in each pair, both had graduated from the same school at about the same time.
>
> As compared with the controls, the group of "best" residents had generally higher medical school class standings, more "first in his class" students, more AOA members, and more "upper third."

They concluded that

> excellence of performance in medical school as indicated by high letter grades bears a significant correlation with one kind of medical practice, namely that of a residency in internal medicine at the Mayo Graduate School of Medicine. Excellent medical students are more likely to be superior physicians in this medical practice environment than are mediocre medical students.

There was a study made at Columbia University in 1952 on undergraduate (not medical school) students, relating college grades to extracurricular activities, examining the common concept that "the Phi Beta Kappa, a bookish fellow, and the big man on campus, a hale fellow well met, are two antithetical types." This study revealed that A students by and large were more likely than B students to hold at least two campus offices; still fewer C and D students were engaged in extracurricular activities.

The Columbia report further stated,

> The better a student's grades, in other words, the more likely he is to "get around" on the campus. And, conversely, the students who accumulate a long list of extracurricular activities and offices are more likely to be the better students than the poorer ones. The Phi Beta Kappa usually has a lot of interest, of which grades are only one.

The study also showed that after college, A students were found in the professions more frequently than B students, who in turn outranked the C and D students in this regard.

Even financially, students with high grades fared better. B students earned less than A students but more than C and D students. This differential obtained even though more A students entered low-salaried professions such as teaching and the clergy. "In every occupational field, it develops, the A graduates have the best earnings record. Their advantage is most pronounced in the learned (and low-paid) professions. In the high-paid professions, mostly law, medicine, and dentistry, they also have a clear advantage. Even in government jobs, they reach the top most frequently."

Medical School Student Center

This beautiful stone structure is the only building in the Mayo complex which is exclusively a medical school unit. It is the center of all the multiple Mayo structures in which medical students derive their education. Name practically any Mayo building or hospital and you have named a part of the medical school. This building was not a Mayo construction, but a Mayo purchase from the city of Rochester in the early 1970s. At that time, the structure was the one and only Rochester Public Library, preceding its present greatly expanded facilities. The center provided offices for medical school administrators, a conventional library, reading and conference rooms, as well as beautiful lounges. This is one of the finest examples of public buildings in Rochester, constructed in 1937 under the direction of architect Harold Crawford, in the Jacobean style popular at that time.

The architectural design of this relatively small Mayo Medical Student Center and its elegant interior suggest a religious edifice such as a chapel rather than a unit of a modern medical school. But perhaps these two may indeed not be antithetical. The Methodists of Methodist Hospital, the Catholics of Saint Marys, and the Clinic staff might all agree that healing the troubled soul and healing the sick patient are far from alien to one another.

Learning Resource Center

This remarkable facility is located in the student center, constituting one of the most extraordinary physical assets of the medical school. Descended as it was from a public library, the materials go beyond a mere collection of books and card catalogs. The center does indeed have books, but it also has videotape cassettes, microscopic slide collections, movies, anatomical models, medical instruments, charts, and much more to supplement mere books. Judy Lorrig, who was in charge of this unit, stated:

> Since a wide variety of learning patterns exist among students, the learning environment is being modified to accommodate these individual differences. Technology is providing new methods of delivering information to students other than the traditional lecture format; learning resource centers, where audiovisuals are utilized and stored, are being developed in response to this new type of learning.

She also voiced the opinion that traditional education, which places the major responsibility for learning on the student, is being challenged by the concept that the instructor also bears a tremendous responsibility for causing the student to learn. The learning resource center constituted a significant contribution to this teaching concept.

The main components of the LRC are ten study units located around the periphery of the main room. Each unit can accommodate two students at one time, and includes a videocassette player, a twelve-inch television monitor, and an 8 mm film projector. All the center's resources are available for students to use at their convenience. Such an approach to learning seems more efficient and economical than the traditional lecture practice.

Dr. Merlin Mitchell contributed immensely to this project. He felt strongly that various visual devices were most effective in teaching and learning. For example, if a student seeks knowledge about what a severe epilepsy seizure is like, there is "a videotape that'll stand your hair on end and get this concept across very quickly. You could never get this from just reading about it." Here there were some three hundred videotapes consisting of movie films shown on a small screen along with sound. There were also slide tapes in which microscopic slides were projected on a similar small screen, substituting for examination with a microscope. There were nearly three hundred of these also, some with sound, but others in which the student studied the slide along with reading a textbook.

The videotape program was later expanded for education in surgery, appropriately entitled "Videosurgery." In a surgical operating room there was an overhead motion picture camera with a zoom lens filming the procedure in all its details. The operating surgeon's narration was included in the resulting sound film. These videotapes were used not only for Mayo's medical students but were part of a nationwide effort at education in surgery. Subscribers to this program were medical schools, hospitals, medical practice groups, and individual physicians. All this was administered in the United States by the American Video Network. At the Clinic the surgeon Dr. O. H. Beahrs was a leader in the program. He stated that the whole process was conducted in such a way that the procedures interfered "in no way with operating room function and certainly not with the operative care provided the patients."

Family Medicine

Time was when family medicine was known as general practice, usually carried out by physicians immediately after the internship, with no special training for this work. But eventually all this changed, and family practice has become a generally recognized specialty discipline. The American Board of Family Practice became the twentieth specialty recognized by the American Medical Association. Training for certification by this board must include internal medicine, surgery, pediatrics, psychiatry, and obstetrics.

About a year after Mayo Medical School opened its doors, family medicine training was launched. In many areas of the country there was an overabundance of physicians trained and competent in such highly specialized fields as surgery, pediatrics, or obstetrics. But the number of physicians adequately trained and eager to carry on primary family care was limited in many regions.

The family medicine instruction commenced with lectures entitled "Introduction to Family and Community Medicine." But the backbone of education in this field was a preceptorship experience. This involved medical students working with preceptors, who were doctors engaged in such practice in various towns and cities throughout the Rochester area. It was felt that the best way to let the medical student know what family medicine was all about was to place him in the family physician's office, a real classroom of family practice. Mayo students spent three weeks with preceptors during the sophomore year. At first the student was merely an observer, being exposed to the "lifestyle and mood" of family practice in a small community, and there were classroom seminars at Mayo on the nature and problems of family medical practice. At the end of the sophomore year a student went for an additional period of preceptorship. Now the student could carry out some of the necessary treatment under supervision of the preceptor. Soon after this program began there were more than sixty preceptors in some thirty-seven towns in southeastern Minnesota and in nearby areas of Iowa and Wisconsin. They received no remuneration from the Clinic.

All this was but an introduction into family medicine, and the experience was part of the training of all medical students. Near the end of the sophomore year, each medical student selected a special field of interest to pursue during his last two years along with his general training in medicine at large. Those who chose the family medicine area took a six-week preceptorship toward the end of the senior medical school year. This might be with a doctor with whom they had earlier experience. During this period the student became a kind of junior partner of the preceptor and took on greater responsibility in patient care, but always under the preceptor's watchful eye. Such students were required to keep records of patients seen, and they participated in referrals of patients to other physicians or to the Mayo Clinic. The student accompanied the preceptor on all his professional activities, day and night, and he usually lived with the preceptor.

Research and Medical Education

A tremendous asset of Mayo in conducting medical education has always been the Clinic's deep devotion to research. Superior performance in research has contributed immeasurably to the excellence of graduate education of fellows or residents training to become specialists, and faculty participation in research also contributed significantly to excellence in the teaching of undergraduate medical students.

Junior medical students experienced a period of intimate exposure to the scientific methods involved in a research project. Research opportunities existed in all the medical scientific areas from biochemistry to surgical research.

There have been very naive concepts regarding the role of research in schools of medicine. Trustees say, "Our funds are so limited that they must be employed for teaching; we cannot support research." Presidents say, "Our aim is to produce practicing physicians; we leave research to the Rockefeller Institute, Harvard, the Mayo Clinic." Instructors say, "Teaching occupies my full time and energies. I am employed to teach. I have neither funds, facilities, nor time for research."

But in medical education, good teaching cannot be divorced from research. Medicine is a complex of experimental sciences and arts, and it cannot be understood unless research is also understood. The student who goes entirely through his medical course learning all the material placed at his disposal without becoming especially interested in one of the many unknowns he encounters in his studies has missed something fundamental in his education and vital to his later practice of medicine. The teacher who teaches what is known, however excellently, is remiss as a teacher unless he arouses a curiosity in his students regarding the unknown. This he can scarcely do unless he himself has been sufficiently stimulated to attempt to solve some problem at which he has at least worked earnestly during some of the time remaining after the responsibilities of classroom, laboratory, and clinic instruction have been met. This does not mean that all medical schools should try to develop ambitious and elaborate research programs. That is impossible even with normal resources of funds and individuals. It does mean that the school that considers research and teaching as separate activities, and the teacher who is not inwardly driven to do even a modest amount of research, will only partially accomplish their goals of teaching medicine. For most of our institutions and most of our teachers and most of our students, by far the greater emphasis and effort must necessarily be on mastering the known in medicine. But there must be a leavening of research to convert the dough into bread.

A well-balanced medical school program, if it carries only the flavor of research, will produce people better qualified to meet the complex problems of medical practice and better attuned to the progress that will continue to be made in the understanding and control of disease by those who devote most, if not all, their energies to unsolved problems in biology and medicine.

The author expanded on these ideas at the Second World Conference on Medical Education in Chicago:

> Past research experience by a physician who is now fully engaged in clinical practice sharpens his judgment and enhances his evaluation of the research

of others. Medicine, a lifelong study, requires the physician to keep abreast by reading the journals and listening to scientific papers. Research necessitates a struggle with data collected, requires a sifting and sorting of experimental results, insists upon a recognition of deficiencies in the supporting evidence, compels the reaching of conservative conclusions warranted by the objective findings. Experience in research warns against the pitfalls of inadequate numbers of observations, faulty controls, inaccurate measurements, the intrusion of chance, the inherent variability of biological material. Engagement in research enhances the physician's judgment of conclusions reached in medical papers he reads, sensitizes him to inadequacies of evidence, increases his wariness of exaggerated claims, tempers his acceptance of enthusiastic predictions.

Research has been called "a way of making Nature talk." But Nature guards her secrets with intense jealousy and is loath to speak. Research reveals the painful difficulty of discovery.

In this presentation in 1959, the author summarized:

Experience in research as a medical or graduate student may stimulate a continuation of some investigation throughout life. Even if the physician does no research after his formal education, his earlier experience in investigation will prove of tremendous value, because research sharpens the physician's judgments of the scientific pronouncements of others, it reveals the painful difficulty of discovery, it stimulates the pursuit of a scientific hobby. Research promotes an awareness of unobtrusive "accidental" phenomena which may be of great importance, it provides lessons in teamwork, it fosters a respect for persistent routine.

Research acquaints the investigator and physician with one of the highways of discovery leading into the unknown.

Unfortunately, there has been a great reduction in the number of Mayo fellows who seek graduate master's or doctorate degrees based primarily on laboratory research. This is not the result of any change in Mayo's philosophy about the importance of research in education. It followed regulations by the many American boards that certify to the competence of specialists in all the fields of medical practice. These regulations restrict the three-year graduate training to clinical education, leaving no time for research. The few fellows who do take academic degrees must spend an extra six or more months beyond that required for certification as a specialist by an American board.

First Graduation

Mayo Clinic historic events of magnitude have been numerous in the past century: the beginning of group medical practice on private patients, the opening of the twenty-seven-bed Saint Marys Hospital, affiliation with the University of Minnesota, the country's first blood bank, transplantation of body parts from donor to patient, open-heart surgery, plus much more recounted in this volume. Mayo's first medical school graduation deserves prominence in this record of events. On Saturday, May 29, 1976, thirty-nine Mayo Medical School graduates were awarded the M.D. degree and were transformed from students to doctors, with all the rights and privileges thereof. The first diploma was handed by Dean Pruitt to Mark Arneson of Owatonna, Minnesota.

In viewing with the graduates "this journey we have made together," the dean said, "Our position as an academic institution has been strengthened, we have shown that we can do what some outside clinics suspected we couldn't do . . . We have been companions on this stringent way, we have supported each other and have learned from each other."

Speaking further at a later annual Clinic staff meeting, Pruitt added,

> We must not be just one more new medical school. We do indeed have a great heritage. The setting of our school, the environment of our learning, is felicitous blending of research and education with the processes of medical care, but the primary mission of our Mayo institutions, of our profession, of our science, of our new school, is a mission in behalf of the humane.
>
> As we reflect on the status of our educational programs, Mayo Medical School among them, I would commend to your critical assessment the degree to which together we have made reality of our aspirations. Our educational programs are not something foreign to and apart from Mayo's traditions, purposes and goals; those programs are part of the substance overall, blended into it without flaw nor boundary, nor barricade. First there was Mayo Graduate School of 1915, in which was formalized an educational process and pattern native to a preexisting medical practice. Second, there was Mayo Medical School, designed to permit its insinuation into our institution with minimal disruption of established organization, governance and mission.
>
> I am convinced that the best of medical education derives from the surrounding in which it occurs. Moreover, I believe that Mayo provides for medical education an environment that is at one and the same time unique and superb.

To all this, it was gratifying that some seventy percent of the first graduating class had accepted residencies throughout the country for advanced training in one or another of the special fields of medicine. The general performance of Mayo students on the examinations of the National Board of Medical Examiners, as a prerequisite for medical licensure, was well above average.

At about the time of the first medical school graduation, there were 160 students in the institution. The latest entering class of 40 was selected from 1,603 premedical students who applied for appointment. Of each 40 seeking information about coming here, only one was selected for the entering class.

Financial Support

Besides the important questions, Where will the medical school be located? and Who will staff it? and How will it affect the Mayo Clinic medical practice? there was the challenge of how to finance the school. What assurance was there that Mayo could secure the thirty-three million dollars estimated as necessary to finance the operation of the school for ten years? It was imperative that planning for a medical school should proceed only if there was a fair certainty that the needed funds would be available.

This certainty eventuated, as might well be expected for any major enterprise embarked on by Mayo. The Mayo Board of Development, under the chairmanship of Dr. Kendall B. Corbin, played a leading role. Major commitments were made by three foundations.

The Hill Family Foundation of St. Paul made grants to a number of educational institutions across the north central states. Included now was a Mayo grant of $875,000 to cover a five-year period. This included the establishment and funding of Hill professorships. There was Dr. Raymond Pruitt, Hill Professor of Medical Education, and Dr. Guy Daugherty, Hill Professor of Community Health.

The Commonwealth Fund, since its founding in 1918, devoted its energies largely to community health and to general medical education and communications. From this source, Mayo secured the promise of $450,000 to be distributed over three years.

The Bush Foundation is one of Minnesota's largest and most influential private philanthropic bodies. Their grant to Mayo, to reach over a five-year period, was the largest of these three, totalling $1 million.

So the total commitments from Hill, Commonwealth, and Bush amounted to $2,325,000.

Supplementing this were government funds. The state of Minnesota agreed to provide Mayo with at least $8,000 per academic year for each Minnesota student enrolled. The total appropriation for the 1971-73 biennium was $320,000; this was later advanced to more than $1 million per year.

Then there were federal grants. The Comprehensive Health Manpower Training Act saw fit to promise $400,000. The National Institutes of Health provided some $18,000 for scholarships and loans. From individuals, including Mayo alumni, came about $2 million more; and over the next few years, further funds became available. It should be remembered that funds sought for the medical school were but supplements to what was needed for other Clinic educational activities, as well as for research.

As stated, it was originally estimated that $33 million would carry the medical school through its first ten years. But before this period elapsed, the annual medical school budget reached $4.4 million in the early 1980s. Toward this need, the state of Minnesota contributed more than $1 million based on its agreement to pay $9,000 per year for each medical student whose home was in the state. This was a significant sum, but it might be contrasted with the cost to Mayo of $27,000 annually for each of the 160 students in the school. Federal funds and student tuition helped some.

But an additional three million dollars plus was needed each year. This came primarily from earnings on the medical school's endowment fund of forty million dollars. This endowment was provided from the assets of the Mayo Foundation, which were derived in part from substantial contributions by many individuals, corporations, foundations, and other organizations and in part from other savings and investments of the Mayo Foundation over the decades.

The Mayo Clinic, the Mayo Medical School, and the Mayo Foundation were particularly grateful to numerous other endowment donors. These are listed primarily to indicate the widespread interest in this new Mayo venture: The Edmond A. and Marion F. Guggenheim Professorship from the Murry and Leonie Guggenheim Foundation; the James C. Masson Professorship in Surgery from Ruth M. Masson; The Robert H. Kieckhefer Chair in Dermatology from the J. W. Kieckhefer Foundation; the Dr. Anson L. Clark Chair in Urology from the Clark Foundation; The Stuart W. Harrington Professorship of Surgery from Dr. and Mrs. Stuart W. Harrington; the William H. Donner Professorship of Immunology from Elizabeth Donner Norment; the Serene M. and Frances C. Durling Professorship from Mr. and Mrs. Serene M. Durling; the Fred C. Andersen Professorship from the Andersen Foundation and the Bayport Foundation; the Vernon F. and Earline D. Dale Professorship from the Vernon F. Dale Trust; the George M. and Edna B. Endicott Professorship in Medicine from Mr. and Mrs. George M. Endicott and the Endicott-Bohn Foundation; the Joe M. and Ruth Roberts Professorship of Surgery from Mr. and Mrs. Joe M. Roberts; the William L. McKnight–3M Chair in Neuroscience from the McKnight Foundation and the 3M Foundation; the Paul A. and Ruth Schilling Scholarships (2) from Mr. and Mrs. Paul A. Schilling; the Jack and Elly Taylor Scholarship from Mr. and Mrs. Jack Taylor; the Lucy B. Gooding Scholarship from Mrs. J. Henry Gooding; the G. Wallace and Dorothea Peterson Scholarships (2) from Mr. and Mrs. G. Wallace Peterson; the Arthur Lee Wright Scholarship from Mr. and Mrs. Robert A. Wright; the Clara Schonlau Scholarship from Mr. and Mrs. Theodore Schonlau; the Edwin G. and Nona C. Barton

Scholarship from Dr. and Mrs. Edwin G. Barton; the Donald C. Campbell Scholarship from Mr. and Mrs. John M. Hollern; the Shirley and Herbert J. Semler Scholarship from Dr. and Mrs. Herbert J. Semler; the Ancher Nelsen Scholarship from the Honorable Ancher Nelsen.

The School Grows

Some five years after the medical school opened, there were successors to the school's original administrators. Dr. John T. Shepherd became dean. He had served as director of education of the Mayo Foundation, was active in the Clinic's board of development and its board of governors. But such administrative responsibilities had been but supplements to his scientific accomplishments, primarily in experimentation and study of the body's circulatory system. He was a physiologist holding professorships in both the Mayo Graduate School and the Mayo Medical School.

Two associates assisted him in operating the school. Dr. James R. McPherson was named associate dean for academic affairs, with responsibilities in curriculum content and Mayo staff participation in the medical school, as well as funding and budgeting. Dr. Joseph M. Kiely was appointed associate dean for student affairs, with responsibility for admission of applicants to the school and student counseling, both as regards the medical school years and the residency training plans succeeding medical school graduation.

The faculty of the medical school was drawn largely from the nearly seven hundred men and women on the professional staff of the Mayo Clinic. These consultants were members of Mayo's nine laboratory and basic service departments and nineteen clinical departments; and more than 650 fellows in all specialties are part of the health care team with whom Mayo medical students work.

The major buildings of the medical school have always been those of the entire Clinic and related hospitals, plus the student center with its learning resource center. Medical students have free access to the medical libraries with more than two hundred thousand books and thirty-one hundred medical and other periodicals. The Medical Sciences Building contained what was needed for education and research in anatomy, biochemistry, experimental and anatomic pathology, and physiology; in due time, adequate additional facilities were provided in the new Guggenheim Building for Research and Education in the Life Sciences.

CHAPTER 20

Growth Continues

The most visible sign of an institution's growth is its buildings. A photograph of the Red Brick Building of 1914, followed by one of the 1928 Plummer Building, and ending with a picture of the eighteen-story Mayo Building would be more revealing as to Clinic growth than would pages of words or figures. Similarly, pictures reveal the tremendous expansions of Saint Marys and the growth from the Colonial to the Methodist Hospital, and in the year 1972, pictures of still more new buildings and facilities imprinted themselves on the minds of Mayo planners.

There were two mental pictures of two new proposed buildings. These were to be the laboratory medicine building and the life sciences building for education and research, both to be located on the entire block south of the Mayo Building, at an estimated cost of twenty-five million dollars. For this it was necessary to demolish buildings located there: the First Congregationalist Church and the fellows' Wilson Club Building. One structure on this block was retained: the Rochester Public Library building was purchased by the Mayo Clinic and employed as a medical school unit—the Mayo Medical School Student Center, as already described.

The mental pictures of the proposed laboratory medicine and the education and research buildings were transformed into brick and stone and glass and concrete in the course of two years. They derived their names from contributors of vast sums of money for construction and equipment.

Laboratory Medicine–The Hilton Building

The hotel magnate Conrad N. Hilton contributed ten million dollars for the laboratory medicine building, which was then named for him. This was the largest single financial contribution to the Mayo Foundation to date. The primary function of the Hilton Building was to carry out a vast variety of laboratory tests for Clinic patients. Patients coming to the Clinic all required numerous chemical and other tests, primarily on the blood but also on other body fluids and parts. Adequate laboratories were provided to secure samples and specimens for this on the subway floor. Here there was also a large patients' waiting room. This really deserved to be called an auditorium or a temple, from its size and beauty. But it was properly stated that we must not allow our admiration for a beautiful medical facility to replace our appreciation of the brains and skill of the doctors and technicians using the structure.

Above the subway level of the elegant patients' lounge were five additional stories. According to Dr. W. E. Mayberry, chairman of the department of laboratory medicine, this was "the first structure at Mayo specifically designed to house clinical laboratory functions. It will provide a total organized effort to do clinical procedures efficiently and accurately, with timely reporting test results to the responsible physician."

Dr. Mayberry would probably agree that this is somewhat of an understatement, considering the complexities and multitude of the tests performed here. He correctly estimated that approximately four million diagnostic tests would be made here in 1975 and about one thousand patients daily would enter the Hilton Building to provide blood samples or other bodily substances for tests to be made. He also stated that the building "provides the most extensive diagnostic facilities in the world within an institution providing medical and surgical care. Its design and function will have wide influence upon the practice of laboratory medicine throughout the world's medical community."

Here we find the Clinic's blood bank, with all the requirements for drawing donor blood and storing it for use at the Clinic itself or at the hospitals, which also have satellite blood banks. The clinical immunology laboratory makes blood tests to determine which immune bodies patients have and what deficiencies there may be. The endocrine laboratory determines the blood content of various body hormones, such as that of the thyroid gland.

It must be recalled that multitudes of tests on patients are conducted elsewhere than in the Hilton Building. For example, in 1980 there were 626,600 diagnostic x-ray procedures and 186,900 electrocardiograms.

At Hilton the highly automated clinical chemistry laboratory analyzes the chemical composition of body fluids, particularly as regards the blood content of potassium, sodium, creatine, or sugar. About half a million such chemical tests are performed per year. In the hematology laboratory, the red and white blood cells are counted and analyzed. There are also counts of blood platelets, necessary for the normal clotting of blood, and there are laboratories for microbiology and toxicology.

The 1981 booklet—really a book—entitled "Mayo Medical Laboratories" contains some 160 pages describing available tests, with instructions for securing samples from patients. Many hundreds of tests are listed. Under the letter *A* alone, 101 tests are named, including acetylglucosaminidase A and B, allobarbital, aminolevulinic acid, antimicrobial susceptibility, and arylsulfatase A. Parenthetically, such complex medical terminology calls to mind the longest word in medical terminology, with forty-five letters in nineteen syllables: pneumonoultramicroscopicsilicovolcanoconiosis. This refers to a morbid condition in the lungs resulting from inhaling dust particles emitted from volcanos, such as silica, quartz, or slate.

This booklet, "Mayo Medical Laboratories," is not merely for Mayo Clinic use. The diagnostic laboratory resources are available to any physician or hospital in the nation. Details are given for how samples should be taken and shipped to Rochester. Under the title "Chromosome Analysis, Skin Biopsy," we read the instruction, "Wash biopsy site with an antiseptic soap (e.g., pHisoHex). Thoroughly rinse area with sterile water. Do not use alcohol or iodine preparations. A local anesthetic may be used. Biopsy is best taken by shave technique to include full thickness of dermis. Biopsy should be 3 mm by 5 mm in area. Wrap specimen in sterile gauze, moisten with sterile saline and send in sterile vial. Do not handle with hands. Send specimen on wet ice, not frozen."

About thirty thousand tests per month are done on non-Clinic patients for non-Rochester hospitals or physicians, termed clients. Such clients number well over a thousand, located primarily in the Midwest but also in the rest of the country as well as abroad. Tests performed for these clients are not routine laboratory tests which can be done in any hospital. They are those which are so complicated that adequate facilities are not available locally.

Delivered to Rochester by mail or other carriers, the samples are distributed to the proper Clinic laboratories for testing, just as though they had been collected routinely from Clinic patients, and the results are transmitted to the sender. Clients may also confer with Mayo specialists by telephone. Naturally, the Clinic must charge clients for these services. Most of the three hundred tests available cost the client well under fifty dollars each, but a few are far more expensive, involving intricate extended procedure and complicated apparatus. In 1980 the total cost to clients and their patients for these services was about nine million dollars.

This regional laboratory program is headed by Dr. Curtis Bakken, who became acquainted with this Clinic function years ago when he served in pathology and technology at St. Alexis Hospital in Bismarck, North Dakota. He recalls, "All 12 years I was at Bismarck we relied on Mayo Medical Laboratory and the Mayo Surgical Pathology Department. Mayo was our choice for two reasons: the reputation of the institution as a whole and the added personal contact . . . [in a] one-to-one relationship between the Mayo pathologist and (myself) the client."

Here we encounter another example of Mayo extending its medical comprehension to the country at large or to clients and patients anywhere in the world. This activity does not bear the name outreach, but it might well do so.

There is also a national laboratory educational program consisting of educational workshops. Dr. Dennis E. Leavelle, director of the Mayo Medical Laboratories, tells us that "more than a thousand laboratory directors, technologists, and managers have attended these workshops in the past year. These workshops are an excellent opportunity for Mayo to share its laboratory resources with our clients and at the same time provide an environment for participants to exchange ideas and experiences with fellow practitioners." He also cited the tradition of the Mayo brothers to serve not only Mayo patients but humanity in general.

Although it is but a part of the gigantic Mayo Clinic enterprise, the Mayo Medical Laboratories might well stand alone as a great medical institution; trying to understand the multiplicity and complexity of its activities, we might even venture that laboratory medicine has become as complicated as brain surgery, kidney transplants, or open-heart surgery.

The Hilton Building also houses the system for automating the reports of laboratory tests made on Clinic patients, entitled the Laboratory Information System (LIS). Laboratory tests on patients' blood, urine, or other body fluids are done primarily in the numerous laboratories on the Hilton subway floor. But such tests may also be carried out at a variety of places in the Clinic or hospital buildings. Necessarily, the results of such tests must become a part of the patient's history folder. How might this be accomplished for the many thousands of laboratory test results occurring each day? The manual system of handling laboratory paper work was fast becoming too costly and complex. Let LIS do it.

In whatever laboratory a test may be made, the result goes at once by wire to LIS by means of various automated instruments in the laboratories. The accumulated data for a given patient appears in his Clinic record folder within twenty-four hours, or sooner if priority is requested.

That Man Hilton

Conrad Nicholson Hilton was born on Christmas Day, 1877, in San Antonio, New Mexico, on the Rio Grande. As a child he worked in a part of the family house which served as a small hotel. From this, there eventually emerged a hotel empire stretching across the United States and into Latin America, Europe, the Middle East, and the Far East. Parental advice to the boy Conrad was contained in two monosyllables. His father, Gus, said, "Work," and his mother, Mary, said "Pray." In later years, to his own son, Conrad added another requisite, "You have to dream."

Thrust into the international scene by his hotel accomplishments, he became a strong advocate of international understanding and world peace in speeches and writings. An address entitled "The Battle for Peace" was published in several national magazines, and over two million reprints were requested. For this he received a Freedoms Foundation Award. He has been the recipient of honorary degrees from a number of colleges and universities. He attended Conrad Hilton Day at the Mayo Clinic when his ten million dollar gift was celebrated.

Hilton's first visit to the Mayo Clinic as a patient in the early 1960s revealed some of his remarkable attributes. The author met him at the airport and took him to the Kahler Hotel, having already made the necessary Clinic appointments. He also arranged to have one of the women in his office—"Rocky" Fay—be his guide. She would meet him in the hotel lobby each morning and conduct him about all day.

Hilton was a friendly, down-to-earth man. There was absolutely no stuffed shirt about this important personage. When Rocky spoke to a desk clerk, asking her to hasten Hilton's being seen by the doctor, he insisted, "Don't do that, Rocky. I'll wait my turn like everyone else."

Near the end of the Clinic sessions, Rocky told him:

"Mr. Hilton, I'm getting married this fall."

"Rocky, when you get married, I want you and your husband to spend your honeymoon at any of my hotels that you choose, as my guest."

Rocky was overwhelmed, naturally. She came to the foundation office saying they couldn't do this. They had too little money to go anywhere, all the Hilton Hotels would be so "fancy," and they knew nothing about hotel living. She was told:

"Rocky, you're going. Take a tourist flight to Chicago. From the airport, don't take a taxi. Take the airport bus which stops at the Palmer House, the best Hilton hotel in Chicago. Once inside the hotel, you need not spend a cent, unless you buy cigarettes or chewing gum. In the morning, telephone room service and order breakfast sent to your room. When it comes, just sign the bill. Don't tip the waiter, simply write on the bill, 'tip 15 percent.' Go to the restaurants, go to the night club, have wine, see the show and dance; and when the bill comes, just write your name and room number and 'tip 15 percent.' " So Rocky and her mate went to Chicago's Palmer House for their honeymoon.

The author had telephoned his friend, the manager of the Palmer House, explaining the entire deal and told him exactly when the newlyweds would arrive. So the couple arrived, carrying bags, hesitating and uncertain about what to do. Bellboys were waiting for them, saying, "No need to register, just come with us." They arrived at an elegant room, with much more than the comforts of home, where they spent an unforgettable week as guests of Conrad Hilton.

On a later Hilton visit to the Clinic, the author and his wife, Maria, gave a cocktail party for him at the Kahler Hotel. Since Hilton grew up in New Mexico, not too far from the Mexican border, he had learned some Spanish there. When the author introduced him to his Argentinian wife, Hilton greeted her in her native tongue, with arms around her.

Recall that all this was long before Hilton made his tremendous contribution to the Clinic.

The author also tells of this Hilton experience.

> Years later, after my retirement, Maria and I and our son, Victor Raymond, took a three-month ocean voyage to the Far East. We stopped for a few days at the Hong Kong Hilton Hotel. I had made reservations and also informed Conrad of our planned stop at his Far East hotel. We were received like royalty, finding our room adorned with orchids. There was writing paper in the desk with my name on the letterhead. There were matches with "Dr. Victor Johnson" printed on the folders; and there was a beautiful carved wood box. Inside there was a stamp saying "Victor Johnson," but in Chinese diagrammatics. The evening we left the hotel, I asked the manager to arrange for a taxi to take us to our ship. This he refused to do stating that the hotel car would transport us. A hotel bellboy came to our suite for luggage and accompanied us in the car through the long tunnel under Hong Kong Harbor to Kowloon where our ship was anchored. From the pier he carried our luggage up the gangplank to our quarters on the ship.

Seldom does one encounter such a man as Conrad Hilton; he exuded warmth, kindness, friendliness, and understanding whether it was to say "Hello" or to contribute ten million dollars to medical science.

Research and Education—The Guggenheim Building

Planned simultaneously with the Hilton Building was the even larger structure called, initially, the Life Sciences Building. Almost simultaneously with Hilton's $10 million, there came the gift of $8.5 million from the Murry and Leonie Guggenheim Foundation of New York City. So the Life Sciences Building was renamed the Murry and Leonie Guggenheim Building for Research and Education in the Life Sciences, or for short, the Guggenheim Building.

This ten-story building is not primarily related to immediate problems of diagnosis or patient care. There are a few special diagnostic laboratories on the subway level adjacent to those of the Hilton Building. The main purpose of this edifice, according to Dr. R. A. Theye, chairman of the laboratory planning committee, was "to accommodate the expanding needs for research and education, including needs related to . . . the Mayo Medical School."

For the medical school, there were lecture halls, study areas, seminar and conference rooms, laboratory space, and administrative offices for the division of education. There was a library named for that Mayo physiology great, Dr. Charles F. Code. This naming is appropriate, not only to honor Code, but also because so much of the research in Guggenheim is in the science of physiology. The major medical school lecture room was well named the Kendall-Hench Hall, after the nobelists of cortisone fame. The combination of undergraduate medical education with medical research reflected again the ever present Mayo philosophy of providing students with opportunities to participate in the work of medical research teams.

Except for the diagnostic laboratories on the subway floor, no Clinic patients need ever enter the Guggenheim Building for diagnosis and treatment. The work here is all aimed at a better understanding of the body in health and disease, including future improvements in diagnosis and treatment.

The research laboratories occupy seven floors of Guggenheim. An account of the facilities on just one floor (the ninth) would suffice to demonstrate the magnitude of this enterprise. Each laboratory here is headed by a Mayo research staff member working with research fellows and laboratory technicians. The work is done primarily on experimental animals and body tissues.

There is research on the smooth muscles of blood vessel walls, which determine, by their contraction or relaxation, how much blood will flow through blood vessels. To investigate such muscle behavior, small sections are cut from the arteries of experimental animals and placed in organ baths that contain nutrition for the living cells. Various chemical agents can be added to the baths to determine the many factors which control the diameter of blood vessels.

In the blood pressure research laboratories, studies are directed toward increased understanding of the role of the heart and the nervous system in the control of blood pressure and blood flow. Such knowledge obtained from experiments on animals increases our ability to understand and control human abnormalities in diseases of the heart and circulation leading to high blood pressure, diseases of the arteries of the heart, and heart failure.

There are studies on the mechanical functioning of the lungs, including the effects of general anesthesia and the muscles of expiration. Abnormal functioning of these muscles occurs in such diseases as emphysema and asthma.

Various aspects of kidney function are investigated: the relationship of these organs to high blood pressure occurring in patients or induced in experimental animals, the mechanisms by which body hormones regulate kidney function in health and disease, the role of the kidney in heart failure.

Ophthalmology research is devoted to causes, diagnosis, and treatment of diseases of the eye and the entire visual system, such as cataract, glaucoma, and retinal detachment. Included here is the eye bank in which human donor eyes or their parts are stored for later transplantations of such eyeball parts as the cornea or sclera for patients needing these tissues. The donors of such eyes are cadavers being autopsied. The nearest relative has signed a statement permitting the Clinic to remove usable parts of the body for various purposes such as transplantations.

So much for Guggenheim floor nine. We might simply enumerate, by title, some of the research projects on all the floors below nine: allergic disease research, immunology, pituitary hormone studies, adrenal hormone activities, biochemistry of chromosomes, electrophysiology of heart muscle, mechanisms controlling stomach contractions, neuropharmacology, neuromuscular disease, causes and prevention of stones in the urinary tract, causes of high blood pressure and hardening of the arteries, factors regulating blood pressure, and still more.

It must be noted that this is not a listing of single research projects, each leading to a published scientific paper. These are the names of laboratories in which continuous research is carried out, leading to a succession of scientific published reports.

Partly because of his many years with his first wife, the psychiatrist Adelaide, the author's interest was aroused in the laboratory of psychopharmacology, a name combining the body's mental activities and abnormalities and the science of drugs. This laboratory was directed by Dr. Elliot Richelson, a staff pharmacologist as well as a psychiatrist. But psychiatric patients were not seen here. There are studies, not on patients, but on nerve tissues and cells grown in various culture media. A number of drugs useful and functioning well in treating psychiatric patients have side effects which may sometimes be injurious to the patient receiving them.

The laboratories attempt to define the chemical processes involved here and to develop pharmacological treatments to offset such deleterious side effects. To be more precise, in Richelson's words, "Studies of the interactions of psychotherapeutic drugs with muscarinic acetylcholine receptors have yielded clinically useful data on the anticholinergic properties of tricyclic antidepressants and neuroleptics."

Much of the research in Guggenheim is carried out on experimental animals such as monkeys, dogs, cats, rabbits, and mice. Animal facilities are on the building's top tenth floor. How many animals are there? Well, for mice alone, the number multiplies into several thousands.

Besides the major financial grants from the Guggenheim family, other financial support came into being. A grant of $750,000 came from the Kresge Foundation of Birmingham, Michigan, to provide construction and facilities on Guggenheim's seventh floor for the Clinic's department of pharmacology. Here were to be carried out investigations on the actions of various chemicals on the human body and its parts, such as nerves, heart, blood vessels, muscles, and whatever else.

Touring the Guggenheim research facilities, one is amazed at the scrupulous sparkling cleanliness of everything. The corridors are as spotless as any portion of the Clinic or hospital patient facilities, and the laboratories are as clean as a well-kept, newlywed's kitchen.

It would be difficult to name any significant research project relating to the body's normal or abnormal functioning that is not being pursued at Guggenheim or elsewhere at Mayo.

Dedication

It was another tall day for Mayo and a milestone in its history when the Hilton and Guggenheim buildings were dedicated on October 18, 1974. Many voices were heard.

Atherton Bean, chairman of the Mayo Foundation Board of Trustees, termed the financial gift "a magnificent expression of the philanthropic ideals of the Guggenheim family. The late Mr. Guggenheim, who served as a sponsor for the Mayo Development Program, was deeply concerned with the health needs of the nation. In accepting the gift, we also accept the obligation to use it wisely in keeping with his wishes."

Raymond Pruitt, medical school dean, told the gathering, "There are three immediate gains which come to Mayo Medical School and Mayo

Graduate School from the completion of the Guggenheim Building. First, a set of splendid auditoriums and seminar rooms, second, a capability for expansion of student laboratories, if such expansion is deemed necessary and desirable at some time in the future, and third, the housing of those research programs in which our students will participate during their third and fourth year assignments, as will the residents and postdoctoral fellows of Mayo Graduate School who engage in research programs."

Dr. Emmerson Ward noted that the new buildings "provide Mayo with much more new space than it has ever before achieved at one time. Space, of course, provides only the setting. People who work in these buildings will determine their benefit to mankind."

Minnesota Governor Wendell Anderson, in referring to the Hilton and Guggenheim gifts, aptly quoted the psychiatrist Dr. Karl Menninger of Topeka, Kansas, as having said that "money giving is a good criterion of mental health." He added that this was certainly true of the Guggenheims and of Hilton. He also felt that "Mayo has always had an effect on the quality and health of the lives of millions of people throughout the world."

While taking pride in past accomplishments, Mayo always looks into the future, not only in medical care, education, and research but also in bricks and mortar. Despite the apparently complete amplitude of these two buildings for all time, our attention is called to the provisions in planning for the possible addition of new floors, up to a total of twenty in Guggenheim and ten or twelve in Hilton, if needed in the years to come.

Expansion of Harwick

Here we view another picture of expansion comparable to the series of photographs of the Mayo Building, Saint Marys, and Methodist Hospital. And into this expansion, as in Guggenheim, Clinic patients rarely if ever set foot, except on general conducted tours. If we were limited to one term to designate the function of the Harwick Building, that term would necessarily be *records*.

In the Harwick Building is stored one of the world's great medical treasures—the medical and surgical records of every patient seen at the Mayo Clinic since the late 1800s when the Clinic was simply known as The Mayos. These records provide present-day researchers with an enormous amount of information about the diagnosis and treatment of diseases, containing perhaps more information in one place than can be found anywhere else in the world. But this information would be practically useless without being properly organized. The important beginnings of this system commenced really with Dr. Henry Plummer's plan in which each patient was assigned a registration number that was retained for all future visits. All laboratory, medical, and surgical records for that patient were identified with that number and stored in one file, readily available on any patient revisit to the Clinic.

But much more than this was needed, particularly for research projects. All significant data in this vast collection of records of more than three million patients was computerized in the late 1970s and early 1980s. Suppose a researcher wished to review all Mayo cases of Addison's disease in the last seventeen years. In a matter of hours he would be given a computer readout listing the Clinic registration numbers and such statistics as age, sex, and geographic location of the patients concerned. In one year alone (1978), there were cross-indexed more than 700,000 diagnoses and 50,000 surgical procedures. To satisfy the thousand or more requests for patient case studies, more than 350,000 histories were identified for researchers. All this would be impossible without computers.

Merely to view this tremendous collection of patient histories is overwhelming. By actual count there are here more than 25,000 three-foot shelves, totaling some fifteen miles of shelf space, with adequate space for more histories to be filed in the future.

On the subway level, or the concourse as architects prefer to call it, there are the film archives for storage of patients' x-rays. Every patient visiting the Clinic has at least one x-ray of the chest. Many patients have still further rays. So for the 3.5 million patients who have registered at Mayo, there have been perhaps 10 million or more x-rays taken over the decades. But all these are not stored in the Harwick archives. Here are kept the films on new and former patients visiting the Clinic during only the past five years, numbering about 1.25 million people, who produced more than 5 million x-rays to be found here on an enormous set of shelves reminding us of the medical history records archives. In one month alone (January 1981), 52,015 x-ray films were received by the archives.

After five years of storage here, x-rays showing positive findings are kept at a warehouse near the IBM plant for another five years, after which most are discarded, although of course findings from all these films have been recorded in the patients' history folders. In the year 1980, there were more than forty tons of discarded x-ray films. But *discarded* is a deceptive term. They were not simply thrown away. The silver from these films was retrieved, yielding hundreds of thousands of dollars to the Clinic each year.

From this archive storage in the Harwick Building there is an elaborate pneumatic tube system which can immediately transmit x-rays requested by physicians to some twenty areas in various clinical facilities or hospital locations. Such requests number about one thousand per day. In addition, another thousand films are sent by hand directly to nearby staff members. It should be noted that all these x-ray films referred to are exclusive of dental x-rays, which are managed by the dental sections.

There is much more in the Harwick Building. There are some ten meeting and conference rooms. Offices are available for a number of Clinic business and administrative purposes, including auditing, cash disbursements, purchasing, and the credit union. There are also elaborate computer facilities.

There is a greatly expanded cafeteria and kitchen area in this building as well. The two dining areas will seat more than five hundred persons. The larger of these provides for the monthly dinner and scientific session of the entire Clinic staff. This large room overlooks a beautiful outdoor court, the new Harwick green, on which may be seen the statue entitled "Four Square Walk Through" by British sculptor Barbara Hepworth. This modernistic stone structure was given to Mayo by the family of Constantine Goulandris, who was a Greek overseas shipping executive. Several of his family had been grateful Clinic patients. The large circular orifices in this sculpture suggested to one admirer that it also might well be entitled "Four Square Throw a Ball Through." It could be used, he said, by football quarterbacks for practicing forward passes.

Franklin Heating Station

Patient care, medical education, and scientific research impose a magnitude of demands for funds and facilities. But they also need what each of us requires in his home, however modest this may be. We must have light in the darkness, heat in winter, cooling in summer, water to drink, and sometimes even elevator service. Multiply these and other personal needs by several hundreds or thousands and we approach some of the necessities for the operation of Rochester's medical complex.

To meet such needs there is the Franklin Heating Station, a name most modest for its multiple activities. This structure, with its intricate and vast machinery, is now owned by and serves Mayo Clinic, the Kahler Corporation, and Rochester Methodist Hospital. It was built at the same time as the Plummer Building in 1928 to provide heat, electricity, and tempered water for the Mayo and Kahler buildings and, much later, for the Methodist Hospital as well. Its main function is to produce usable heat and electricity. Steam for heat is the main product of the plant. Electricity and cooling capacity are its major by-products.

Franklin Heating Station was an energy conservation project decades ahead of its time. It produces steam in boilers that drive turbines to generate electricity. It converts seventy-eight percent of its fuel into other sources of energy. The steam is used to heat the buildings of the downtown medical complex. Other products besides heating and electricity include cooling, refrigeration, tempered water, cold water, compressed air, and moisture to humidify the buildings in winter as well as steam for instrument sterilization. Its chilled water provides summer air conditioning in the Mayo, Kahler, and Methodist buildings.

To carry out these winter and summer functions, Franklin burns natural gas and fuel oil. The quantities of these are tremendous. In one recent year the plant used more than 1 billion cubic feet of natural gas and 840,000 gallons of fuel oil.

But since the plant was built more than half a century ago, the use of electricity by Mayo and Kahler and Methodist has grown so that it exceeds the capacity of the plant. More and more electricity is purchased each year from the city of Rochester. The demands for cooling capacity also exceed the plant's productivity.

With the vast expansion in Clinic and hospital facilities and activities, Franklin also needs and will soon get expansion at a cost of some five million dollars. The aim here is to increase the reliability and to extend the life of the plant. The main addition will be a diesel-driven electric generator to supply power for elevators and for emergency lighting systems in the event of a power outage in the city. Other improvements will include a new tie line to the city's Silver Lake plant, which supplies a portion of the three institutions' electrical power. There will as well be water treatment equipment for boiled water, water softener equipment, and modern oil-burning equipment.

And so the Clinic will not only meet the needs of advances in medical therapy, intricate surgery, and diagnostic procedures, but it will keep the patient warm in winter and cool in summer, power elevators to eliminate stair climbing, and provide light to read a book while waiting to be seen by the doctor.

In most instances the origin of the names of Clinic buildings is obvious. These include the Harwick, Plummer, Guggenheim, Baldwin, and Hilton buildings, with names derived from Clinic greats or from generous donors. We have noted an exception to this practice in the naming of the Curie Pavilion, derived from the Nobel Prize French scientist and radiologist Madame Marie Curie, who never visited Rochester but whom Dr. Charles Mayo had met in France and admired a great deal.

And whence cometh the name Franklin? From Benjamin Franklin, who numbered among his many interests heating and electricity. He invented the Franklin stove, an ingenious device that made his living room "twice as warm as it used to be with a quarter of the wood I formerly consumed."

Since the Franklin Heating Station can meet the needs of only the downtown facilities, Saint Marys Hospital has required provision of these services by other sources.

The Subways

Rochester's northern latitude is such that the winter months are indeed frigid. Snow is plentiful. The winds become ferocious about the cluster of tall Clinic buildings. These concentrate the flow of air from the wide surrounding plains into the relatively narrow street channels. Patients coming to Rochester from all over the world, including the tropics, should not have their troubles multiplied by the harassment of cold, snow, and wind, not to mention plentiful rains. Underground passageways were early deemed essential. Decades ago, in 1921, the first of these was built, connecting the Kahler Hotel with the Red Brick Building. And over the decades, with every new building construction, further subway extensions were as necessary as were the buildings themselves.

These underground pedestrian passageways eventually connected fifteen Clinic, hospital, and hotel buildings spread out over some eleven downtown city blocks. A patient coming to snowy or rainy Rochester can go from his Kahler or Zumbro Hotel to anywhere in the considerable acreage of Clinic edifices without being outside a moment. The subway between and under these fifteen buildings lengthens to a total of nearly three miles, with a multiplicity of turns and twists and angles.

Two structures are not favored with such subway connections. One is Mayo Foundation House, which does not involve patients. The other is Saint Marys Hospital, located a good mile from the cluster of downtown Mayo buildings. At Saint Marys, the complexity of structures includes its own subway system, though this is not connected with Clinic facilities. But this speaks only for the present. Who knows? Perhaps one day there may be a subway to that essential unit also, equipped with small cars or strips of moving floorways.

The Florida Project

Mayo received a proposal to establish a branch in Jacksonville, Florida. It was made by the Jacksonville philanthropist J. E. Davis, a longtime Mayo patient and a friend who offered a substantial gift in the late 1970s to develop such a facility. Mayo has intimate relationships with numerous medical institutions in the upper Midwest. But this complex bearing the Mayo name would be located more than a thousand miles away from Rochester. In general, the city of Jacksonville enthusiastically approved the idea, with favorable reports from the Jacksonville area chamber of commerce and the Duval County Medical Society.

After some months of study, Mayo rejected the proposed project. The administration and operation of the local Rochester complex was a tremendous challenge. How then might Mayo operate a clinic so far away? Some of the other factors involved in the decision included concerns about financial risks and staffing problems in transplanting the Mayo type of practice to a distant location. There were also licensure problems for medical and paramedical personnel at Jacksonville because Florida's licensure regulations are perhaps the most restrictive in the nation.

This wise decision in August of 1980 may not be interpreted as a disinclination to expand. Already the Clinic serves the nation and the world in providing medical care for anyone from everywhere, in training specialists to improve practice throughout most countries, and in seeking control of diseases which afflict so many on this earth.

Iran

While Mayo does not wish to establish branches elsewhere, it has assisted in the planning of such independent clinics when requested to do so. This even extended to that remote corner of the earth—Iran. A dramatic sequence of events had transpired. The biggest bit of general news in the town of Rochester during July of 1975 was the visit of Fahrah Dibah, empress of Iran, along with the Iranian ambassador, the minister of science and higher education, and others, including an entourage of Iranian security and United States State Department officials. They arrived on a warm Sunday afternoon, with the goal of observing the facilities and manner of practice at Mayo in order to create and expand adequate medical care programs at home. The empress herself was personally interested in health care for children, and she toured all the Clinic and Saint Marys pediatric facilities. Numerous conferences took place.

As a supplement to this, Mayo complied with a request to send a group to Iran to survey and give advice on how they should proceed. Dr. Raymond D. Pruitt, Dr. Hugh R. Butt, and Robert C. Roesler participated in this expedition. Plans were evaluated for a Mayo-like facility in Teheran, Iran's capital. The ultimate aim was to "transfer the Mayo philosophy of excellence in patient care to the Iranian setting."

CHAPTER 21

Marching Forward

Tissue Registry

Just as it is necesssary to preserve patients' histories and x-ray films, samples must be kept of patients' body parts that have been removed during surgery or in biopsies or at autopsies. This is all done at the tissue registry in the Medical Sciences Building. The tissue registry is basically a library, but there are no books. Rather, its stock consists of surgical reports and tissues removed from patients. There are preserved tissue specimens, paraffin-coated blocks of tissue, and microscopic slides. There is material in one of these three forms from virtually every surgery, biopsy, or autopsy that has been conducted at the Mayo Clinic since 1905. There are many thousands of tissue specimens and more than six million slides, probably unequaled in any other tissue registry in the world. In one year alone (1979), the Clinic's forty thousand surgical operations and biopsies and eight hundred autopsies presented the Registry with 49,000 specimens, 47,000 surgical pathology reports, 173,000 microscopic slides, and 90,000 paraffin blocks of tissue. Slides and blocks are kept indefinitely; most tissue specimens are disposed of after twenty years. Annually, the registry gets more than ten thousand requests for materials from staff and residents, and in response it sends out about 50,000 slides and 9,000 tissue specimens.

All this material is cataloged with a sophisticated filing system of millions of cards, which allows this wealth of information to be easily and quickly tapped. The annual cost of this operation approaches a third of a million dollars.

Mayo statistical figures are always unbelievable. If one ventures a wild guess about numbers relating to patients, operations, storage specimens, x-ray films, or whatever else, one should add a few zeros to approximate the truth.

The tissue registry is useful in patient care. For example, an Iowa woman came back to the Clinic ten years after she had had a breast tumor removed. This time she had a suspicious lump on a lymph node. The question arose, Had the breast cancer spread to the lymph node, an ominous development, or was the new growth unrelated to the previous situation? The answer to this, as well as the subsequent treatment and the patient's future outlook on life, depended on information from the tissue registry.

Important though this may be, the dominant use of the facilities is for research. The extensive files allow investigative projects to be carried out that might not be done anywhere else in the world. And the orderly cataloging, filing, and availability of information may enable a researcher to carry out his work in a reasonable length of time. Without such resources, the task, as one investigator stated, "would take half a lifetime."

The registry is a great source of material for educational purposes. Examples of every kind of pathological condition can be readily compiled to illustrate cases at conferences and to teach both residents and medical students. It is a prime source of information for graduate theses written each year by students in a number of fields.

Like so much at Mayo, the tissue registry goes back to early beginnings and early Clinic leaders. Dr. Louis B. Wilson, coming to Mayo in 1905, was dissatisfied—even distressed—to find that relatively few surgical specimens had been saved from the great amount of surgery that had been done in the previous fifteen years. So he initiated the system to preserve and catalog all specimens removed at operating and autopsy tables for later reference and study. The fantastic present-day operation resulted.

Audiovisual Center

Photography at the Clinic, both gross and microscopic, is as old as any other Clinic activity, fathered here mainly by Dr. Louis B. Wilson, pathologist and first director of the Mayo Foundation for Medical Education and Research. Motion pictures and sound films eventuated. The first of these was entitled "The Mayo Clinic Library and Its Use," soon to be followed by a more complex effort called "Movement of the Heart Valves and the Origin of Heart Sounds," made on animals. One elaboration of Mayo's photographic activities was the establishment of the audiovisual center in 1969. Here the Clinic entered into a replica of a Hollywood movie set, somewhat reduced in size but sufficiently complicated in facilities to excite one's imagination.

Its aim was to bring together, in color, sound films, information about a patient or a specific disease from a variety of sources, including Clinic outpatient consultations with patients, laboratory findings, microscopic slides of diseased tissue, consultations between physicians, and patient behavior. This was primarily a documentation program, assembling such data for patient records as well as for educational purposes or even for research occasionally.

A sound film may be made on a patient who has difficulty in walking. There will be included conversations between physician and patient, physical examination proceedings, how the patient walks on arrival here, and how he progresses with treatment. Audiofilming of psychiatric patients is common, but there are also many instances of other nervous disease problems, speech difficulties, rheumatism, muscular difficulties, and much more. Collaborating in a production, there may be not only the patient and the physician but also laboratory scientists, physical therapists, and publication writers, resulting in a production script and the final movie. About two or three such complicated productions may be made in a week.

And to what goal is this effort directed? It may assist in research, and it does provide staff physicians with records of a patient's difficulties and progress under treatment. But the aim is primarily educational. And who is educated? It may be the patient himself, especially in psychiatric cases. The Clinic's paramedical personnel, such as physical therapists, nurses, or technicians, are taught how to use complicated laboratory procedures, how to inscribe pertinent information into patients' records, and how to manage patients assigned to them. The films assist in the training of residents, supplementing lecture and seminar discussions. The permanent staff members also add to their knowledge.

The films are employed extensively in teaching undergraduate medical students. In the learning resource center, students may pick films from shelves and view them at their own convenience. James Martin, in the photography area, stated, "One of the things we wanted to do was to avoid the pure lecture method of teaching, and so we determined very easily that one of the needs would be a Learning Resources Center which would incorporate all kinds of audiovisual media as an alternative to the standard lecture procedure." It must be noted that these audiovisual aids do not replace lectures or discussions but are valuable supplements to more conventional teaching procedures.

In one educational project , medical students view a sound film depicting and telling all that the staff physician has learned about the patient: the patient's complaints, the discussion between physician and patient, the examination proceedings, and the laboratory and other diagnostic findings. By design, the film lacks any suggestion of the proper diagnosis. This the student himself must make as a kind of test of his comprehension of what he has been taught. If it appears that the patient has a brain tumor, the student is expected to make that diagnosis. He should also tell in which cerebral lobe the defect lies, on which side of the brain, how serious it is, what should be the therapeutic procedure, and what is the future outlook for the patient.

The productions are employed also for the graduate education of residents and for the continuing education of physicians, not only in Rochester but elsewhere as well. Once a month a ninety-minute broadcast is transmitted to medical groups assembled in the hospitals of Winona, Minnesota, and LaCrosse, Wisconsin. The audience may consist of a hundred physicians and perhaps an equal number of nurses and other paramedicals. After each presentation there is a two-way discussion between a panel of Clinic experts in the Clinic studio and the medical audience at these locations, employing a one-way picture and a two-way audio exchange.

Besides these multiple television projects, this Clinic center still produces lantern slides to be used in illustrating educational research and other scientific presentations. Some 125,000 such still lantern slides are made annually.

Blood Donors

Just as bleeding from injuries, operations, and childbirth continue, so the need for donors of blood continues. President Nixon proclaimed January of 1972 as National Blood Donor Month to stimulate people to volunteer as donors. Supporting this effort, the Mayo Clinic blood bank stated that "donors are needed continually to supply the 7 million pints of blood that our country's hospitals will need this year . . . Observe National Blood Donor Month by becoming a blood donor."

At Mayo and its hospitals about sixty patients per day receive transfusions. For this, the Clinic must obtain some ninety liters of donor blood per day, or about twenty-five thousand liters annually. To provide this great volume of precious fluid, the Clinic has available about 8,000 donors.

Every day about 120 of these come to give blood to the bank. Even so, this provides for only about half of the Clinic's needs. Supplementary blood is obtained from the St. Paul Chapter of the American Red Cross.

Initially, all donors were paid for their blood at the rate of twenty-five dollars for each unit or half-liter. Eventually, the Blood Assurance Program was set into motion, seeking unpaid donors from the Rochester area. The main purpose here was not to save money but to get better blood, since it was found that too many paid donors had blood defects such as infections of the liver by viruses, viral hepatitis. Such blood could not be used in transfusions. It is interesting to note that Rochester area people have extremely little of this, so they constitute a most desirable source of blood. In many large urban areas, paying for blood attracts undesirable donors–winos, drug addicts, and others desperate for money. Paid blood collected from these areas has been shown to carry a much higher risk of liver infection than blood collected from volunteer donors in the same area. Mayo's volunteer donor program progressed well, and by 1980 it provided some fifty percent of all the needed blood.

It must be recalled that very often the blood drawn from a donor is not employed in its entirety for transmission to a patient. Component parts may be all that is needed. The Clinic's blood cell separator is a sophisticated machine developed by the National Cancer Institute and IBM. It is capable of removing blood from a donor and separating from it such needed components as red blood cells, white blood cells, the liquid plasma, coagulation components, and more. After separation of such blood constituents, the balance of the drawn blood is returned by the machine to the donor, who has been lying relaxed nearby. Mayo's hematologist Dr. Clark Hoagland stated, "We believe this machine has tremendous potential. Now, for the first time, we are able to give patients a transfusion of white blood cells equivalent to those present in approximately 60 pints of whole blood."

Cell Biology

Studies of the internal structure and chemistry of body cells in medicine may be traced back practically to the development of the microscope. A relatively modern version of this instrument was developed by Johannes Kepler, the great German astronomer, in 1610. By microscopy, throughout the nineteenth century there were numerous breakthroughs eventuating in increased understanding of the causes and treatment of diseases that had plagued the world for centuries. Counting the number of red or white cells in the blood and noting cellular changes produced by disease were early manifestations of the employment of microbiology.

During all Mayo history a number of groups have been involved in microscopic studies relative to patient diagnosis and care, as well as for research projects. Several of these were organized into the department of cell biology in 1979, occupying quarters in the Guggenheim, Plummer, and Medical Sciences buildings. Here there were sections of biochemistry, cell biology itself, experimental pathology, and microbiology. This department integrated such activities primarily for research purposes, much of which was in the area of cancer.

An indispensable instrument here was the electron microscope, which employs electron radiation, transforming these into tremendously enlarged visible images that can also be photographed. On such an instrument, by simply turning a little knob the image seen can be enlarged to any magnitude from fifty-five to three hundred thousand times. Another device can magnify by half a million times. Here even large molecules may be seen. An infinitely thin slice of a red blood cell, one millionth of an inch thick, is magnified to a diameter of some three to four meters. Of course, only a small portion of the slide can be seen at one time.

It is rather difficult to comprehend the real degree of such magnifications. The five hundred thousand times increase in size might be illustrated by computing that by this magnification a man six feet tall would measure five hundred miles in length. What a far cry this is from the observation two thousand years ago by the Roman philosopher Seneca, who wrote that "letters, however small and indistinct, are seen enlarged and more clearly through a globe of glass filled with water."

Eventually electron microscopy could magnify by one million times, or one thousand times what occurs with an ordinary high-powered microscope. Such magnification is comparable to expanding one inch into more than fifteen miles.

Research is conducted on cells and tissues derived not only from patients and human volunteers but from numerous animals as well, including chickens, rats, rabbits, and guinea pigs. Here there are observed the ultramicroscopic cellular and intracellular events and biochemical changes that occur under a multiplicity of circumstances, normal or abnormal. This listing could go on for pages and includes the following: effects produced by enzymes, hormones, cancer invasion, antibodies, viruses, vitamins, immunizations and vaccinations, and aging; the changes occurring in many diseases or abnormalities such as arthritis, edema, infections, liver malfunction, and leukemia; the manner of functioning of cell membranes, ovary cells involved in reproduction, and red blood cells carrying oxygen; how body cells function in various metabolic processes such as the synthesis of proteins.

The magnitude of these efforts of the department of cell biology is displayed in part by these figures: in 1979 there were eighty-nine papers published, thirty presentations at national or international meetings, seventeen lectures or seminars at other institutions, as well as twenty-seven scientific seminars at Mayo. Members of the department serve on the editorial boards of eight scientific journals. The annual budget approximates four million dollars, of which well over one half is derived from extramural sources.

In education, the twin of research, the department of cell biology is most active in both the undergraduate medical school and in the graduate school programs involving biochemistry, microbiology, anatomy, pathology, basic mechanisms of disease and others. Cell biology is internationally recognized as a unit in the complex multiplicity of scientific endeavors in medical science. There are the American Society for Cell Biology and also the *Journal of Cell Biology*.

Microscopy in Three Dimensions

In the usual electron microscopy there is made visible a single very thin slice of a tissue or a cell. The object viewed has but two dimensions, with no visible thickness. This most valuable device is now supplemented with a three-dimensional scanning electron microscope. For this device, extremely thin slices are not required. Instead, an entire small specimen can be seen all at once. Scanned by a focused electron beam, the entire structure is revealed on a screen. Magnification up to thirty-four hundred times is available. It was said that "red blood cells in bone marrow resemble morning glories blooming on a vine."

Such three-dimensional visualization of a specimen may sometimes replace the necessity for examining numerous microscopic two-dimensional cross sections of tissue. Laboratory investigators have spent untold hours slicing and viewing numerous cross sections of organisms in order to gain an understanding of their complete structure and characteristics.

The scanning electron microscope eliminates much guesswork and time-consuming labor. It was stated, "It is gratifying to see what you have been conceptualizing for so long from cross-sections. With scanning microscopy you can see the entire specimen. You can see the depth of tissue, very fine detail, the ruffles and projections of the surfaces."

Microfilm

Let us contrast the account of tremendous magnifications with a reverse process in which a given object is transformed into a very much smaller picture, a transparent microfilm. The most common object for transformation into such microfilms is the printed page. A lengthy scientific article can be transformed into a single page of small transparencies. These can be projected enlarged on a small screen, where each page can be read and copies can be made if desired.

This process may be extended to cover all the pages of a scientific journal, with the entire set of microfilms occupying but one page. The total contents of even a large book can be incorporated on one sheet.

The business office of the Clinic uses microfilm extensively in matters of accounting and payroll. Here again, material from stacks of records is made to appear on small microfilms assembled on one form. These are easily handled and are readily projected on a screen of ordinary page size to be read easily. Again, copies of the microfilms are readily available so that more than one person in the various business offices can survey the same material without moving masses of written or typed pages from place to place.

At present (1981) desired microfilms are made for the Clinic elsewhere than in Rochester. University Microfilms International at Ann Arbor, Michigan, specializes in providing "minicopies" of scientific and other journals for people or institutions who have subscribed to this service. A firm in Minneapolis provides similar aid to the Mayo Clinic business office. The clinic sends to the firm a computer record on magnetic tape, from which the microfilms are made, with as many duplicates as Mayo requests. The business office is arranging to secure machinery to make its own microfilms in the near future.

The Mayo Clinic library makes extensive use of microfilm materials: whole libraries such as the two-thousand-volume *Early American Medical Imprints 1668-1820* have been purchased, and page-by-page minicopies of journals difficult to acquire have been secured.

The obvious purpose of the procedure is to transform masses of bulky written material into easily handled, easily stored, and retrievable record formats. Jack Key, the Clinic's librarian, can display an example unrelated to Clinic functions but illustrative of microfilm potential. This he calls "the smallest bible in the world," which appears on a single card measuring about 1½ by 1½ inches. Thereon is reproduced in microscopic transparencies all the pages of the Holy Bible, starting with "In the beginning God created the heavens and the earth" from Genesis and terminating with the last words of Revelation, "May the grace of the Lord be with everyone."

Heart Transplants

Considering its great success with kidney transplants, open-heart surgery, and the heart-lung device, the Clinic decided to enter on the challenging enterprise of heart transplants. Drs. James R. Pluth, cardiovascular surgeon, and Michael P. Kaye, of the section of surgical research, renewed investigative efforts in this field in 1979. Dogs were used. The actual surgery involved presented no special problem for Mayo's experts. The major challenge was to refine procedures for counteracting the transplanted heart being injured or destroyed by the recipient's body defense mechanisms, so effective in destroying harmful foreign agents, such as bacteria, that may invade an animal's body.

For this Mayo developed rabbit antithymocytic globulin, more simply termed RATG. This injected substance can successfully counteract the strong initial rejection of the transplanted heart. But the body continues attempts at rejection so that animals, or even patients with transplants, must continue to receive the drug to suppress the body's immune responses. Although this may save the transplanted heart, it may render the recipient very susceptible to infection. A proper balance must be achieved so that the recipient does not destroy the transplanted heart yet retains anti-infection activity. The dog experiments were so successful that human heart transplants were planned to commence at Mayo in the early 1980s. Mayo's RATG was a necessity employed in heart transplants throughout the country.

The source and supply of potential heart donors presented much greater difficulty than was encountered in kidney transplants. Any healthy person can donate one of his kidneys and continue healthy with his remaining kidney. Naturally, this cannot apply to donations of a heart. A potential donor is one whose head has been sufficiently injured by a shot or an accident so that the brain dies, breathing stops, but the beating of the heart continues. Let us suppose this happens to someone in Indianapolis but his heart is needed for a patient in Rochester. This challenge has been met.

Let us say, by way of example, that a man in Indianapolis has shot himself through the head but his heart continues to beat. He is a potential heart donor. His doctors report this by telephone to the Medical College of Virginia at Richmond, which operates a center of information about potential donors of various organs, including the heart. This center has already been told by Mayo, "We need a heart donor." Virginia telephones Mayo's doctors, who fly to Indianapolis. After arranging all required legal matters, the living heart is stopped by an injection of cold solution containing potassium. The living heart is removed and placed in a cold saline solution. The doctors fly back to Rochester, arriving at the hospital about two hours after removing the heart. The donated heart is implanted into the recipient and is warmed to initiate and strengthen its beating, and surgically it replaces the recipient's failing heart. Not more than four hours may pass between removal of the donor's heart and its transplantation into the recipient.

Fortunately, this complicated procedure was not necessary at Mayo. The Clinic's cardiologists estimate that about forty patients per year might be candidates for heart transplantation. It was also determined that each month about three patients who might be potential donors are admitted to Saint Marys Hospital.

Donor hearts come from individuals who are brain dead, as might occur in an accident. Breathing has ceased, but the heart is still pumping blood. Before removing the donor heart, its beating is stopped by administering a cardioplegic solution containing potassium. As soon as the heart is transplanted, with proper blood vessel connections, this solution is washed away and the transplanted heart has recommenced its beating. The transplanted heart is completely devoid of nerves (the vagus and sympathetic) that normally help regulate the rate of the heart beat. But there remains in the recipient the hormone adrenaline, which stimulates the heart to beat faster when needed. During physical exercise by the recipient, the amount of blood pumped per beat—the stroke volume—is also increased. Exercising muscles push increased volumes of venous blood to the heart, somewhat distending the organ. Whenever the ventricle heart muscles are stretched, they contract more forcibly. Thus, during exercise the heart pumps out more blood with each beat or per minute, without need of nerve control of the heart rate. Much of this activity was studied by Mayo's physiologist Dr. John Shepherd, working experimentally on dogs whose heart nerves had been severed.

It would be remiss to omit the name and work of Mayo's Dr. Frank Mann, who performed and studied heart transplants in dogs decades ago. While human heart transplants were not even under consideration in those days, Mann thought his dog findings might eventually be of practical use in the future management of patients. They were.

While Mayo has contributed materially in helping to solve the problems of preventing the recipient's body from destroying the transplanted heart, many actual human heart transplants were in operation elsewhere. Doctors at Stanford University in California were pioneers in the field and have performed most heart transplants. Others have been performed at the Medical College of Virginia, St. Louis University, Columbia-Presbyterian, the University of Arizona, and the University of Wisconsin, as well as at several locations overseas. The total of such operations reached more than four hundred by 1980, with a recent survival rate of about fifty percent. The youngest heart transplant recipient on record (by 1981) was a nine-year-old St. Paul girl afflicted by myocardiopathy, in which her heart muscle tissue was being replaced with noncontractile fibrous tissue similar to scar tissue. She received a new heart from an eleven-year-old who died in an accident. This occurred at Mayo's sister institution, the University of Minnesota. On dismissal from the hospital, Cindy Spicer's heart was "pumping beautifully" and was "working as well as a heart possibly can" in the words of her surgeon, Dr. John Najarian. Unhappily, this girl soon died, primarily because the transplanted heart was attacked by her body defenses against foreign bodies, despite much treatment to avoid this.

Mayo's research in the field of heart transplants has been proceeding, commencing with Dr. Mann and proceeding to the discovery of RATG. But the actual transplanting of human hearts at Mayo commenced only in 1981. The first such operation did not succeed. The recipient, fifty-two years old, died during the operation because the new heart failed to pump blood through the recipient's damaged lungs.

The second heart transplant at Mayo was made on a thirty-three-year-old Michigan housewife, employing the heart of an Owatonna woman just killed in a traffic accident. This patient did well. She couldn't say enough things about the Clinic and the hospital staff. Some of her remarks were, "Rochester is the best place to be. It's become my home away from home among the wonderful people of this warm friendly city . . . I am still living with my anti-rejection medication . . . but it's hard to believe that I was so sick less than a year ago and feel so good now."

Some time after this, Sharon Jahns returned to her home in Livonia, Michigan. There was a celebration for her sponsored by the Ford Motor Company. One purpose here was to raise funds to help pay the expenses for this historic heart transplant. The happy heart recipient said, "I feel wonderful. It's amazing what a new heart can do for you."

Also doing well is Mayo's third heart transplant patient, a young man from Seattle who received a heart from an accident victim in Iowa.

Not to be dismissed lightly is the tremendous cost of a heart transplantation, reaching many thousands of dollars per case. A major factor in this cost is the necessity for the recipient to remain hospitalized with intensive care services for at least a month after the transplant.

And so Mayo has entered this field, not simply as a follower, but as one of the leaders. Drs. Pluth and Kaye state:

> Mayo has had a proud heritage in cardiac surgery and has maintained preeminence in that field throughout the years. This expertise has developed through a unique multidiscipline practice in which the various talents are combined cooperatively for the benefit of the patient. This same approach is essential for a successful cardiac transplantation program, and we are confident that with the close cooperation that has developed among our medical colleagues, further enhancement of the results of this procedure can be accomplished.

These Clinic leaders even believe that combined heart and lung transplants are on the horizon, opening a whole new vista for patients with combined pulmonary and cardiac disease.

The difficulties encountered in the field of transplantations are amazing when one considers that every normal body organ in one person functions exactly as does that same organ in another's body. Everyone's parathyroid or adrenal cortex glands function the same, secreting hormones necessary for life. How much better off would a diabetic become if he had a successful transplant of pancreatic islet tissue secreting insulin and eliminating the necessity of self-injection of insulin throughout his life. Life-saving transplantations would seem simple, but the body's inherited rejection of foreign matter makes this difficult.

Much of Mayo's research is dedicated to reducing this body hostility to introduced foreign material while still preserving the body's defense against dangerous or fatal invasions of bacteria. Mayo is working at parathyroid gland transplants and embarking on bone marrow transplants for children with fatal leukemia. Throughout medical history, there has been one eminently successful transplant procedure, if we may use that term for blood transfusions.

Bone Marrow Transplants

The interior of the body's bones contains the bone marrow. Much of this is stored fat. But far more important is the red bone marrow. Here are generated all of the body's red blood cells at the enormous rate of two million cells per second of our entire lives. The red marrow also produces most of the white blood cells. These are important in the body's defenses against infections. Leukocytes (from the Greek *leukos*, "white," and *kytos*, "cell") have the property of absorbing and digesting particles, including bacteria, just as the primitive amoeba secures and uses its food. All through the evolutionary scale, there is a persistence of this primitive food-getting reaction by specialized cells, including some of the body's white blood cells.

Like all other parts of the body, the red bone marrow is subject to disease or injury resulting in inadequate and abnormal functioning. In aplastic anemia there is a deficiency in the production of red blood cells, with a high probability of death; in leukemia, there is an excessive production of white blood cells, somewhat resembling a cancerous process. Untreated, it is also fatal. The red bone marrow may also be injured by administering radiation treatment for cancer of a body part such as the lung.

Why not consider and develop the transplant procedures that have been so successful with kidneys and so promising with hearts? Bone marrow transplants came into being, led by investigators at the University of Washington School of Medicine in Seattle. Mayo became ready to embark on bone marrow transplants in 1981. Such transplants are notably different from transplants of body organs or parts. The material to be transplanted consists of masses of bone marrow cells rather than definite structures.

A large needle is inserted into the interior of the upper margin of the hip bone or iliac crest of the donor, who is under local or, more often, general anesthesia. The sternum may also be used. The procedure is carried out in an operating room under sterile conditions. Bone marrow is withdrawn into a syringe. After proper preparation, including dilution, this mass of cells is injected into an arm vein of the recipient. It is not necessary that the transplant be injected immediately, it can be preserved for a time and injected later. Surprisingly, enough of the injection "homes" to the bone marrow, replacing the patient's bone marrow that has been destroyed by disease or otherwise. Generally, a period of one to three weeks transpires before the transplanted marrow functions adequately. During this interval, various supportive procedures are available to be employed on the patient.

In this process, matching the donor and recipient is far more complicated than is cross-matching to determine what blood transfusions are safe, and adequate procedures are necessary to prevent the recipient's body defense mechanisms from destroying the injected cells. There might even be a destructive reaction of the grafted marrow against the recipient's tissues. This also must be managed.

The bone marrow transplantation program is a multi-disciplinary effort that involves medical staff and paramedical personnel in the blood bank, hematology, pediatrics, immunology, therapeutic radiology, social service, infectious diseases, nutrition, ophthalmology, thoracic diseases, and dermatology departments, as well as nurses coordinating the care of the patients at Rochester Methodist Hospital.

It must be emphasized that even by late 1981 bone marrow transplants were still in the planning stage at Mayo. Hematologist Dr. Clark Hoagland was in charge of the development. He stated, "We are ready to go as soon as we find the first suitable patient and donor . . . If everything goes as we hope we will be able to increase our transplant numbers to one a month." And he thought that in five years the numbers might reach one a week. The first such transplant was done early in 1982; it was successful.

Animal Experiments

In all these studies, numerous animal experiments were necessary, including work on mice, rats, dogs, and monkeys. How much of our knowledge of how to control human ailments has been derived from experiments on animals! It is estimated that perhaps 100 million animals are used annually for research in the United States. This includes not only investigations in medicine but in devising new war weapons or even new facial makeups. Animals are as important a tool in medicine as are test tubes or microscopes.

Mayo's renowned neurosurgeon Dr. J. Grafton Love attributed much of his skill in delicate surgical operations involving minute parts of the human brain to what he learned from experiments he carried out on small animals during a research project as a Mayo Foundation fellow. He stated:

> During my period of fellowship training in the Mayo Foundation I decided to carry on some research and to work for a master of science degree in general surgery. I felt that this effort would enable me to better evaluate medical papers and research reported by others and that it would give me the opportunity to operate on animals, experience which would improve my technical ability. The subject of my thesis was 'The effect of phosphorus on the normal and recently restored liver following partial hepatectomy in the albino rat.' Operating on 120-gm white rats, which were under the influence of general anesthesia and removing a good portion of the liver in such a manner that they would survive, was quite an undertaking. I even explored a related problem of tying off the common bile duct to see if that would affect the poisoning of the liver after the administration of yellow phosphorus. This technique was helpful in neurosurgery, especially when I was working around the optic nerves to remove pituitary tumors, and dealing with diseases of the blood vessels in areas in which the structures are small and can be easily damaged.

Throughout medical history, opposition to animal experimentation has persisted, despite the tremendous advantages to mankind which have emerged from animal experimentation. Take diabetes alone. Today there are perhaps ten million diabetics in the world taking insulin, a product of animal vivisection. These people live reasonably well for an average of some ten years longer than they would without insulin. This totals 100 million years of human life, not including diabetics of the past no longer alive but who were kept reasonably well in the six decades since insulin was discovered.

The cause of diabetes, reported by Von Mering and Minkowski in Germany, and the treatment with insulin, developed by Banting and Best in Canada, were directly the results of experiments on dogs.

The author recalls a time in his long-ago University of Chicago days when legislation was proposed in Chicago to forbid experimentation on dogs. There was a public hearing on the proposal, attended by hundreds of people in a public auditorium. One of the speakers was Dr. Anton Julius "Ajax" Carlson, the author's chief in physiology and a collaborator in many projects in medical education and research. Here Ajax displayed his usual remarkable talents in opposition to the proposed legislation. He addressed a prominent lady in the audience, who advocated the measure, asking her to rise. She did, and Ajax expounded:

> I call your attention to this lady's lovely fur coat. Here is the history of that coat: Hunters in the wilds of Africa encountered a beautiful animal nursing six wee offspring. They shot the mother, and the babes ran and hid in the shrubbery. The mother, suffering agonies, died of hemorrhage while being transported to have her golden fur removed, to be transformed ultimately into this lady's mantle. The six cubs sought the mother in vain, wailing their misery. They all ultimately died of starvation. But it is such a gorgeous fur coat.

The proposed law was not passed.

People who oppose animal experimentation should not eat meat. Winter furs are not for them. Perhaps they should even be denied eggs for needed protein food, since that is really stealing from chickens.

During his physiology days at the University of Chicago, the author did much experimental work on hundreds of dogs, and he came to know very well their habits and temperaments, their moods and wants and responses. "When I changed surgical dressings they cooperated like human patients, lying still just as I wished." He could almost believe the lady who claimed her dog was most intelligent. She said:

> My dog understands language. When I asked him what is on the very top of a house, he said "roof!" When I asked what is on the outside of a tree, he said "bark!" And he can read. Walking along one day we passed a shining recently painted lamp post. There was a sign on it, "wet paint." And my dog did just that!

Home Parenteral Nutrition

The bloodstream serves two main purposes in maintaining the life and functioning of body parts. First, it provides body cells and organs with needed substances such as nutriments and oxygen. Second, it carries away cellular and tissue waste products. But in performing these functions, the bloodstream must be in touch with the outside world. It must first receive nutriments from food eaten and digested in the alimentary canal, and it must also rid itself of body wastes via such organs as the kidneys producing urine.

Dr. Belding Scribner has been active in both these contacts of the blood with the outside. He was a Mayo Graduate School alumnus on the faculty of the University of Washington. Regarding elimination of wastes from the blood in cases of kidney failure, he pioneered the development and use of the artificial kidney, described earlier in this volume. And in providing the blood with proper nutriments in certain diseased patients, he introduced the concept of the "artificial gut," more properly termed parenteral nutrition.

There is an inflammatory disease of the intestines in which food eaten and even digested is not absorbed into the blood in quantities sufficient to support normal life, including growth in children. This has been named Crohn's disease, after its description and analysis by New York physician Dr. Burrill Bernard Crohn. Naturally, the results are varying degrees of starvation. In this condition there are various devices and treatments employed with reasonable success. But in a very small percentage of cases, all oral means of treatment are ineffective. In such severe cases, nutriments must be administered by some route other than the diseased gastrointestinal tract. An artificial gut was needed.

Home parenteral nutrition (HPN) may be employed. In this procedure there is first a surgical process in which a catheter or tube has been inserted through the chest wall into a large vein and passed on into the interior of the right side of the heart. The tube remains so installed permanently. The outside end of the tube, protruding from the chest wall, can be connected with the machinery, which includes a pump. In this machinery there is a container of water in which are dissolved or suspended all the food ingredients needed for normal life. Not only must this include fuel for body heat and fats to be stored and amino acids for the body's production of protein tissues, but also there must be included all the necessary vitamins and salts required by the body. After adequate training at Methodist Hospital, a patient can use the process at home.

While settling for sleep, the patient on HPN hooks his tube to the pump, usually assisted by a family member who has also been trained. While the patient sleeps, the pump slowly injects the needed substances into his bloodstream. This is a slow process, unlike a normal person spending perhaps two hours a day eating food. In the HPN process, about two liters of the fluid are administered each night over a period of about ten hours.

Mayo's gastroenterologist Dr. C. Richard Fleming assumes much of the responsibility for this Clinic enterprise.

The costs of carrying out this procedure are tremendous, amounting to some twenty to thirty thousand dollars per year for the nutrient solutions alone, plus the cost of surgically inserting the catheter or tube, plus much more. But carrying out the process in a hospital is even more expensive.

It must be noted that this is not a common procedure. In fact, it is very rare compared with other Clinic statistics. Each year Mayo sees about five hundred patients displaying the Crohn's disease fault of inadequate absorption of food from the intestine into the blood. And of these five hundred, almost all are treated fairly successfully by other techniques. Only about five per year end up on home parenteral nutrition. They usually lead fairly active lives.

Artificial Pacemaker

Each normal mammalian heartbeat is initiated by a pacemaker lying in the heart's right auricle. This pacemaker not only starts each heartbeat by stimulating the heart muscle to contract, but it may also regulate the rate at which the heart beats per minute, as in exercise.

There are various heart abnormalities involving its pacemaker and resulting in a poor control of the beats of the heart. To meet this physiological defect, we again encounter complex machinery, an artificial pacemaker. This device contains a lithium iodide battery that emits stimuli to initiate heartbeats. This machine is considerably smaller than the palm of the hand. It is sufficiently small to be implanted by surgery under the skin of the right breast. There is a connection from the battery to the heart, enabling this artificial pacemaker to stimulate heartbeats, substituting for the defective physiological pacemaker. The Clinic implants into patients some three to four hundred such pacemakers per year.

It is necessary for the Clinic to observe and record the manner of the pacemaker functioning in patients who have returned to their homes. Here again we encounter the telephone. We have already seen how the telephone may be used to transmit the electrical charges involved in the heartbeat and in brain function; that is, electrocardiograms or encephalograms can be transmitted by telephone from one part of the Clinic complex to another, or to the Clinic from patients hundreds of miles away.

On departure from the Clinic, a patient is equipped with a plastic transmitter. The patient and, if possible, a member of the family are taught how to operate this device, which is complicated in its operation but simple to employ by the patient. This device reads the patient's pulse at the two thumbs and relays the electrical message by ordinary telephone to the Clinic's pacemaker center, where the heartbeats are recorded on a tracing. Sounds, a series of "blips and bleeps, like crickets chirping," are also heard. To receive these messages, telephones are available all day and night.

During the first month after implantation, patients are requested to telephone in once per week. Eventually, such calls are sent by the patient to the Clinic every three months. These calls and the records made enable the Clinic to determine whether the pacemaker is continuing to function properly. Altogether, about one thousand patients are making such pacemaker calls. Every morning the pacemaker clinic receives fifteen to twenty routine calls from patients whose heartbeats depend on electronic stimuli from implanted pacemakers. These come from all over the United States and Canada and Mexico. In 1982 the Clinic also had a few patients in Brazil, Nepal, Paris, Tokyo, Turkey, and Uruguay.

Talking about this procedure with registered nurse Sharon Neubauer, the author was impressed by the apparent simplicity of the process, no matter how complicated the machinery. While they talked, the phone rang, and Sharon said, "This call's from Saint Marys Hospital, but it could have been from Uruguay." She placed the telephone receiver on the recording device, which made tracings on revolving paper. The interruption of the discussion lasted perhaps two minutes.

Remarkably, the battery in the pacemaker lasts five to ten years before it might need replacement. Even in a five-year period, the work is astonishing. During that time, the machinery has stimulated the initiation of nearly 200 million heartbeats.

The pacemaker clinic is headed by cardiologist Dr. David Holmes. Six other Clinic physicians rotate through the pacemaker clinic, and four registered nurses take care of the beating heart telephone calls.

Continuing Medical Education (CME)

The award of the M.D. degree from a medical school and the certification as a specialist by one of the American specialty boards are noteworthy achievements for a physician. But all of this constitutes only a noteworthy commencement of medical education. Further learning is essential throughout a physician's lifetime in light of continuous medical and scientific advances in our knowledge of the body in health and disease.

During its entire history, the Clinic and its staff have been fully aware of this basic principle. To achieve these ends effectively there was established the Clinic's continuing education committee under the chairmanship of Dr. J. A. Spittell. The committee stated that "the goal . . . is to make available to physicians, continuing education programs of the highest quality. These programs should be designed to bring new knowledge, allow maintenance of professional skills, and encourage the scholarly development of the physician's potential. The ultimate objective is improvement in health care."

Over the decades this end has been sought by the Clinic through its elaborate programs of conferences, seminars, and lectures, now under the supervision of the continuing education committee. Eventually, general recognition of this necessity was incorporated into the laws relating to the licensure of physicians to practice medicine. State legislation for the continued practice of medicine by a physician required that he participate in such continuing education, without which the state withdrew its licensure. The Minnesota law required that physicians participate in a minimum of 150 hours of CME every three years.

The American Medical Association established a listing of approved educational courses for meeting these requirements for relicensure. Such programs were designated as the AMA's Category I, Continuing Medical Education credit courses. Most of Mayo's continuing education courses in all fields of medicine are in this category.

In one week alone, the Mayo Clinic bulletin listed a hundred such course meetings. All of these for which AMA approval was sought were so designated. To avoid conflicting unnecessarily with a Clinic physician's patient responsibilities, these courses were scheduled in the early morning, such as 7:30 A.M., during the noon hour, or in the late afternoon or early evening.

Such advanced medical educational opportunities met the needs of the Clinic staff. But these efforts were also extended to assist area non-Clinic physicians seeking relicensure. Three-day courses entitled "Clinical Reviews" were offered. This was a program of lectures and discussions on problems of general interest in medical fields, aimed primarily at meeting the needs of physicians engaged in family practice. It sought to help them to cope with the knowledge explosions in medicine.

In an early year of the clinical reviews program, nine hundred non-Mayo physicians attended the courses, and enrollments increased by about ten percent annually. In a three-day course, some seventy Clinic staff members might participate in lectures or conferences. These large numbers necessitated using the Mayo Civic Auditorium. The greatest number of physicians attending these sessions came from the general Minnesota area, but in one year doctors came from twenty-two states that included California, Texas, Florida, and New York. Canada and South Africa were also represented. Generally, registrants in this program were not particularly interested in the research background of new developments but rather in how new knowledge could be applied to patient care.

All of these meetings were open to any physician who wished or needed to attend. We find here still another example of the Clinic's desire to help not only Mayo doctors but also those of the surrounding area, in accord with the history-long determination to extend Clinic efforts beyond the care of Mayo patients. Physicians have been visiting Mayo since its origin, and Mayo has always welcomed them and shared with them all its knowledge and experience.

Another program reminds us of an activity of decades ago. Long before Mayo had a medical school, medical students studying elsewhere were given the opportunity to spend some time at the Clinic in various fields, supplementing their experience with patient management at their home school. Mayo eventually initiated a project much like this, offered not to medical students but to physicians in practice in the area. Such physicians could spend from four to eight weeks in Rochester. This involved not simply lectures and discussions but actual work with patients. Physicians participating in the program engaged in diagnosis and patient care in both hospital and Clinic settings under supervision of Clinic consultants. They made rounds and attended conferences and seminars. The facilities of the library, including study space, were available to them.

A further extension of this self-assumed responsibility was a project relieving area physicians of the necessity for visiting Rochester, should the care of patients in their local communities make this difficult. The Regional Visiting Faculty Program eventuated, in which a Mayo staff member visited an area community to participate in CME programs involving lectures, seminars, and hospital rounds. Soon there were twenty-two regularly scheduled continuing education programs in this format being conducted for physician communities in Minnesota, Iowa, North Dakota, South Dakota, Illinois, Wisconsin, Michigan, and Missouri.

The financing of these endeavors was assisted by charging visiting physicians tuition and registration fees for courses at Rochester and by charging the community visited in the case of our staff educational participation in education projects away from our home. But the major expenses were borne by Mayo.

It is needless to state that for the Mayo Clinic doctor, continuing education was woven into his daily and weekly regular activities. A staff member can participate in some sort of continuing education activity every day of the week and still not begin to tap the opportunities available. A consultant once described as a "bottomless pit" the number of activities set up to help physicians to keep up with the mushrooming growth of medical knowledge. The impetus here was not only continually improving medical care, but also, as stated by Dr. John Spittell, "In a place like Mayo, where the exchange of ideas and cross consultation is so frequent, you like to make sure that you are up to date in the eyes of your colleagues."

For the Clinic staff, local activities constituted perhaps the largest and most important part of continuing education, in terms of time, cost, and numbers of people involved. We might view as an example the activities of the division of cardiovascular diseases. Every Tuesday at Walters Hall at Saint Marys there is a conference for staff members interested in congenital heart disease. On Thursdays there is a coronary artery conference. On Fridays there is a clinical cardiovascular conference. At each, learning comes mainly through the reviewing of recent cases. Every Saturday morning the division sponsors a three-hour seminar at Saint Marys on a wide range of cardiovascular topics for staff, trainees, and residents.

Specialists within the division, such as electrophysiologists and pediatric cardiologists, gather to discuss matters of common interest weekly or biweekly. Monthly, the division holds a clinical-pathologic conference, a kind of quiz session in which the details of some complex or unusual cases are considered by the group and a final diagnosis is arrived at—after which a pathologist tells what the actual outcome was, and the clinical findings are related to the pathologic findings.

At a monthly conference, any deaths of patients cared for by division staff members are analyzed and discussed. There are also monthly meetings to discuss cardiovascular research topics, journal club meetings to review current articles in medical literature, and monthly meetings of the Cardiovascular Society, attended by cardiologists, pediatric cardiologists, surgeons, and basic scientists.

All this is but one example of what might be found in any special field of medicine. Writing articles or books is another means of continuing education, as well as presenting papers and engaging in discussions at medical meetings around the world. An axiom of Dr. Charles Mayo says it all: "Once you start studying medicine, you never get through with it."

Health-Related Sciences

The Clinic's devotion to teaching concentrates on the education of medical students and on graduate medical education. Residency training covers some twenty-six major fields ranging from anesthesiology to urology. There is also subspecialty education in about fifty areas from allergy to vascular surgery.

Supplementing all this, Mayo also considers it imperative to engage in the education of nonmedical persons who are so important in all aspects of medical practice. The Mayo School of Health-Related Sciences was established to meet this need. Let us examine some of these efforts.

In all such activities the Rochester hospitals are essential participants. There was for a time the Methodist-Kahler School of Nursing. By 1970 when this school closed its doors, 3,827 students had been graduated. While there is now no basic school at Mayo for training nurses, Methodist and Saint Marys hospitals do provide opportunities for practical nursing experience for several area schools of nursing, including that of Rochester

Area Vocational-Technical Institute, Rochester Community College, the College of Saint Teresa, Winona State University, Iowa's Luther College, and even the University of Minnesota. It is recognized that learning about nursing care in the classroom at these schools is essential to the nursing student. But equally important is to put into actual practice what has been learned in the classroom about patient care. This experience is provided by the Clinic and the hospitals.

About Methodist's program for nurse trainees, it was stated from Luther College, "The students here get a well-rounded experience they couldn't get anywhere else. The program is strong because of the wide variety of patients and the emphasis on restorative care. The students also have the opportunity to work with a professional hospital staff." Clinical experience is also supplemented with classroom instruction in such areas as pharmacology, medico-surgical nursing, pediatrics, and psychiatry. So Mayo continues to play an important role in the basic training of student nurses.

Methodist Hospital has an affiliation with Mankato State College in the training of students in the field of dietetics. Here again the college provides classroom and library learning, and Methodist provides experience in the working world. This course, or externship, has a five-week duration, exposing the student to what a hospital dietician does.

There is so much more in Mayo's program of education in the health-related sciences.

Cytotechnology is the microscopic study of body cells for evidence of disease. Methodist Hospital houses fifteen Mayo Clinic staff cytotechnologists. Among their functions is the training of this science. In the twelve-month-long training program, the first six months are didactic and the second six months are spent reviewing slides of cell samples. The students study cell slides and use available patient histories to arrive at the best cytologic diagnosis. Cytotechnologists work closely with pathologists.

When the students finish the program they are expected to screen forty slides in four hours, looking for individual cellular changes that may indicate disease. They will also be eligible to take the national board examinations given by the American Society of Clinical Pathologists.

The cytotechnology department at Methodist Hospital may have up to six students per year. To be considered for the program, students must have completed a two-year academic education at an accredited college or university with fourteen hours of biology or biology-related sciences.

Mayo's Nurse Anesthesia Program offers training to already registered professional nurses who have had experience in critical care nursing. This is a two-year program carried out at the Methodist and Saint Marys hospitals. There is a total enrollment of about forty, although perhaps ten times this number apply for this training, not only from the Rochester area but from elsewhere in the country. Throughout their clinical experience they work in the hospital operating rooms under the guidance and instruction of physician anesthesiologists and graduate nurse anesthetists who are certified nurse anesthetists.

Occupational therapy is also taught. Among other things, this process assists patients to carry out reasonably normal activities after being handicapped physically or mentally. Occupational therapy training involves first a four-year college educational program, after which the student must have three months of practical or internship training dealing directly with patients. This Mayo provides for students from a number of regional colleges and universities. Involved here may be teaching a patient with a new joint replacement how to write or to button his shirt. There is work with patients to restore movement and function in injured or diseased joints and limbs. To this activity, in the care of Mayo patients, is now added the training of a limited number of students seeking to become registered occupational therapists.

Physical therapy is the treatment of disease and injury by physical means, such as light, heat, cold, water, electricity, massage, and exercise. This is particularly needed in a patient with arthritis or one who has undergone orthopedic surgery. Students from across the nation apply each year to be accepted in this unit of the Mayo School of Health-Related Sciences. Such applicants already have a college bachelor's degree with a heavy science orientation. For each incoming class, forty students are chosen. The program has a twenty-one-month duration. Sixteen states were represented in the 1981 physical therapy graduating class.

Respiratory therapy is needed in patients with breathing difficulties related to asthma, bronchitis, emphysema, or whatever. Students in this field learn to assess patients with breathing problems by means of several tests and also to use equipment that provides oxygen or assists respiration. In this enterprise there is an affiliation with Rochester Community College. This is a twenty-one-month program with an initial nine months at the college, with an emphasis on biological sciences. Then follows twelve months of clinical and technical education. By 1981, there were 140 graduates from the course.

One of the latest health-related training programs is in radiography, or x-ray technology, in collaboration with Rochester Community College. This is to be a twenty-four-month curriculum with nine months spent at Rochester Community College in concentrated classroom instruction plus a fifteen-month period in didactic and clinical experience dealing with the various modes of x-ray technology at the Clinic and the two hospitals.

Just to enumerate the areas of activity of the Mayo School of Health-Related Sciences is impressive. In addition to the areas already described, there are training programs in clinical psychology, school psychology, speech defects, radiation therapy, laboratory technology, audiology, library management, nuclear medicine, and more.

We might ask, Why should Mayo be involved in the training of many hundreds of nonmedics, supplementing the education of undergraduate and graduate medical students? One motive is making another contribution to a high quality of medical care in the country. Such trainees carry out functions useful to the Clinic during their training, just as do trainees in Mayo's graduate medical education program.

Another motive in the program is the practical goal of securing well-trained technicians for permanent employment by Mayo or the hospitals. Virtually all members of Mayo's permanent medical staff are recruited from the very best residents or fellows completing their advanced training. Similarly, the best of those finishing training in one or another of the health-related sciences are offered employment in Rochester as important components of the Clinic's patient care enterprise.

CHAPTER 22

Hospital Services

The importance of hospital facilities is revealed by these figures for 1980. Clinic patient registrations were nearly 270,000, and there were more than 30,000 admissions to each of the two hospitals, Saint Marys and Methodist, for a total of over 60,000. This means that more than twenty percent of the patients coming to the Clinic require and get hospital care.

Seldom in the world would it be possible to find a more integrated and fruitful relationship between a Roman Catholic order and an institution with no specific religious affiliations as that which exists between Saint Marys Hospital and the Mayo Clinic. This is a supreme example of the devotion of truly religious people to the good of mankind regardless of religious affiliations. No formal contract exists between the two. Yet since its beginning, Saint Marys admits only Clinic patients, and its medical staff has always consisted solely of Mayo doctors.

Saint Marys Hospital administrator, and later executive director, Sister Generose Gervais, expressed the view that all this came about because "the right people living at the right time made the right use of the right opportunity . . . The mere fact of 83 years of continuous development and expansion of Saint Marys Hospital does not make it unique, aside from its unusual size in a community of 60,000. What is unique is its relationship with the Mayo Clinic. The two institutions have grown side by side, independent in organization, yet sharing the same objectives and facilities, and cooperating in providing service to the same people in an atmosphere of mutual respect and trust. It just has to be the greatest living example of trust that there is."

Sisters of Saint Francis

How appropriate it is that the leadership and operation of Saint Marys Hospital should be carried out by the Sisters of Saint Francis of Assisi. Like that thirteenth century saint, the sisters at Saint Marys rise above creed as a superlative example of how all religious people should view their responsibilities to deal with the ills of mankind. The hospital's policy has always been to open its doors to all people needing care, regardless of race, color, sex, financial status, religion, creed, or belief. Only the patient's medical needs determined his care and treatment.

Saint Francis of Assisi was not primarily interested in the medical aspects of people's needs, but he did work some at nursing lepers and sought to heal the sick by the laying on of hands. Being available to the needy, his presence instilled hope into the despairing. He was said to have eased even incurable illnesses; and he believed, like the sisters, that God loves everyone in the whole world, regardless of religion, and that everyone everywhere was a child of the same Father.

Saint Francis firmly believed in men and women working together to ease the burdens of people. He worked assiduously with the lady named Clare. Through the years they were loyal to each other in their work. Clare's loyalty and devotion to Francis greatly sustained him in his efforts to ease human ills. He established orders for both men and women. In all this we find the precursor of the joint efforts of nurse and doctor working together, as exemplified now at Saint Marys and the Clinic. Francis of Assisi was canonized a few years after his death in 1226 by Pope Gregory IX. Saint Marys Hospital celebrated Saint Francis's eight hundredth birthday in 1982.

Expansion Plans

Saint Marys Hospital and the Mayo Clinic are sister institutions not only in the care of the sick and in education and research. They grow together as well in the ever-expanding facilities and operating personnel. It all commenced with that twenty-seven-bed hospital, five nurses, and three doctors in 1889. This occurred despite a bit of hesitation initially by Dr. William Worrall Mayo, who thought the city might be too small to support a hospital; there was also the common public belief that one went to a hospital not to get well but to die.

But the little Saint Marys Hospital came into being with forty thousand dollars contributed by Dr. Mayo; and throughout the succeeding decades, nine additions were constructed, so that by 1980, the hospital had 949 patient beds, 32 major operating rooms, and more than 3,000 nurses and other employees, and an operating annual budget of well over fifty million dollars. The total assets of the hospital were double this amount, including the land, buildings, and equipment, as well as funds held by the hospital's trustees. It took some eighty-eight years for Saint Marys to become one of the largest private hospitals in America.

Saint Marys Hospital embarked on its tenth addition in the late 1970s. This was a tremendous building venture that would expand its facilities by one third in less than three years. It was named Project 282. This was to be one of the largest building projects in the history of Rochester. The structure would be a square city block and would contain the most modern surgical facilities in the world. The project was undertaken primarily to replace the hospital's somewhat outdated surgical facilities. The new surgical unit would cover a total area about the size of two football fields, with forty-three operating rooms. It also included a 1,164-car parking ramp, expansion of the employee cafeteria, a new emergency room, a forty-eight-bed nursing unit, and a new central service area. Included also were facilities for physical medicine and rehabilitation, radiology, and staff conference rooms. The building was to be seven stories in height.

Ground was broken in 1977, and the grand Saint Marys Project 282 was dedicated three years later. This expanded the total square footage of floor space at Saint Marys to 1,770,871, exclusive of the 346,800 square feet in the parking ramp of the unit. This totals about forty-eight acres of space, or about five square city blocks.

Financing

And what was to be the cost of this historic project? Fifty-five and one-half million dollars! And whence might this sum be derived? There were fifty million dollars of revenue bonds issued, not by Saint Marys but by the city of Rochester, which reflected the city's identification with the Clinic and its hospital affiliations. It also meant a relatively low interest rate during a thirty-year period during which the hospital would be paying back its loan. The low 5.6% interest rate was considered fantastic. Even so, the total interest payments over three decades would almost equal the sum of the fifty million dollar loan itself.

The bond issue received a double A rating from Standard and Poor's and Moody's rating service. This double A rating was a sign of safety and security for investors. Saint Marys was only the second hospital in Minnesota to gain such a high rating. The first was Rochester Methodist Hospital. Undoubtedly, the association of these hospitals with the Mayo Clinic contributed to the favorable rating.

Perhaps eighteen percent of the new structure consisted primarily of Mayo Clinic facilities. Consequently, the Clinic contributed some thirteen million dollars to the project.

Dedication of Project 282

There was a grand ceremony of dedication of the new structure on September 27, 1980. Presiding over the session was Sister Generose Gervais, a most able administrator at Saint Marys Hospital. She succeeded Sister Mary Brigh in this post. Participating were Rochester Mayor Chuck Hazama, as well as the executive director of the Minnesota Hospital Association and the chairman of the board of trustees of the Catholic Health Assembly. The Clinic side of the project was presented by Dr. W. Eugene Mayberry and Stephen F. Keating, chairman of the Mayo Foundation Board of Trustees. Keating stated, "This superb medical facility is more than a building. It is an act of faith that the medical center at Rochester will endure and prosper."

Surveys were conducted of the–shall we say–monument. The surgical operating rooms were particularly impressive. Here there were vacuum systems to eliminate exhaled anesthesia gases and a sophisticated air-conditioning system to filter bacteria. In most operating rooms the air was circulated at the rate of twenty-five times per hour. There was a pipe system that provides major rooms with water to warm or cool patients' blankets and a floor cleaning system that pumped antiseptic on the floors and vacuumed it away. Besides the general operating rooms there were special ones for such needs as orthopedic, cardiac, neurologic, pediatric, urologic, otolaryngolic, dental, gynecologic, and plastic surgery.

Interestingly, the operating room galleries were abandoned. In the past these served to educate thousands of visiting physicians, as well as Mayo graduate and undergraduate medical students seeking to learn more about surgery by direct observation. Eliminating these historic facilities reduced the risks of bacterial infection. But as has been the practice at Mayo, a given educational opportunity which might be discarded was replaced by something better. A closed-circuit television system was established, permitting observers located away from the operating room to witness the surgical procedure in much greater detail than was possible when observing from a post in an operating room gallery.

As speaker at the dedication of this addition to one of the largest private nonprofit hospitals in the world, Stephen F. Keating referred to the unique triads of Rochester. There is the triad of patient care, medical education, and research, as well as the triad of Saint Marys Hospital, Rochester Methodist Hospital, and the Mayo Clinic. He described Saint Marys Hospital's new wing as a magnificent medical component of the Rochester medical complex with its almost twelve thousand men and women participants and added that the new building is admirably adapted to the quarter of a million patients who come to Mayo each year for medical care. Saint Marys Hospital now has a total bed space of approximately one thousand.

The brochure for the dedication program pronounced this Saint Marys Hospital philosophy:

> Saint Marys Hospital is a tertiary care hospital sponsored by the Sisters of Saint Francis of Rochester, Minnesota. It participates with Mayo Clinic and Mayo Foundation and Rochester Methodist Hospital as an integral part of a private, not for profit medical center devoted to comprehensive medical care, to medical education, and to medical research.
>
> The philosophy of Saint Marys Hospital is based on the philosophy of the Roman Catholic Church and the Judeo-Christian principles of the sacredness of human life and the dignity of persons as God's highest creation. It embodies a commitment to respect the dignity of every person and the inherent value of human life and to achieve excellence in the provision of medical care and in the promotion of health.
>
> In the provision of patient care, appointment of the medical staff, employment of personnel, and enrollment of students, Saint Marys Hospital makes no distinction because of age, race, creed, color, sex, socioeconomic status, or national origin.
>
> Saint Marys Hospital strives to provide total care of patients, addressing their spiritual, physical, and emotional needs. Every reasonable effort is made to preserve life, to minimize pain, and to cure or relieve illness and disability. Concurrently, the reality of death is accepted, and the dying patient and family are supported in preparing for the end of physical life in an atmosphere of peace and confidence in God.

We might also quote William James Mayo: "What we accomplish in the future will not be due to bricks and mortar, but to the soul and spirit that reside within Saint Marys Hospital."

Naming the Edifice

Multitudes of the personnel of Rochester's magnificent medical enterprise, as well as Rochester citizens, hoped that the tremendous Project 282 would be named at this ceremony after the great Sister Mary Brigh. She served for twenty-two years as the third administrator of Saint Marys and remained after retirement in 1971 as consultant to the hospital. But the proposed naming of the edifice was kept a close secret.

Early in the dedication procedures it became apparent to an acute observer that the hopes for a Mary Brigh naming would eventuate. There were some eight or ten people on the platform and each of their names appeared printed on the program, except for one. Sister Mary Brigh was seated on the platform without being named in the program brochure. She must be there because she would be needed when David Leonard, chairman of Saint Marys Hospital Board of Trustees, would announce the name of the new building; and Leonard did announce the name of Sister Mary Brigh Cassidy.

The announcement was greeted by a grinning shake of her head by Sister Mary Brigh. She was hugged by Sister Generose, accompanied by a continuous din of applause from the packed lobby where the ceremonies were held.

Sister Mary Brigh was rated as one of the most capable hospital administrators in the nation. She obtained her master's degree in hospital administration from the University of Chicago. She was listed in *Who's Who in America* and won a number of awards. She held membership in the American Hospital Association and many professional and advisory councils at state and federal levels. On her retirement in 1971, Pope Paul VI awarded her the Benemerenti Medal for Accomplishment.

It was said of her that she never took herself too seriously but she always took her job seriously. No matter how busy she was in her eighteen-hour-a-day administrative duties, she always made time to visit the sick. She might drop into a patient's room late in the evening with a glass of milk or a sandwich. Indeed, she might well be compared with Florence Nightingale.

At the time of her retirement she stated, "We have only today in which to work, to pray, to dream, to plan, to help build a better world . . . We have learned and we have taught. We have shared with others and they have shared with us. We have instigated change and lived with its outcomes. We have healed and in the process found healing. That is as it is, that is as it will be.

"The younger people who follow us will face new challenges, employ new methods, design new tools and techniques. I believe they will demonstrate no less dedication of purpose."

The American Hospital Association gave Sister Mary Brigh a Distinguished Service Award (1981). Among the statements in the award document were these:

> It is a unique and rare phenomenon when the personality of an institu-

tion and its administrator become so entwined that it is inconceivable to think of one without seeing the face of the other. So it is with Saint Marys Hospital of Rochester, Minnesota and Sister Mary Brigh Cassidy.

Sister Mary Brigh has shown the amalgam of strengths necessary for effective hospital leadership. She combines compassion with hard-driving business sense, practicality with vision and toughness with grace.

In the larger world of health care, she has given her talents to the American Hospital Association, the Minnesota Hospital Association, the Catholic Health Association of the United States and dozens of community groups, colleges and associations. These associations benefit from her energy and vision while she has served in every job that needed her indomitable spirit, from committee post to governing board to president.

Emergency/Trauma Unit

One unit of the Mary Brigh Building was incomplete at the time of the dedication. The emergency room opened its doors to patients in February of 1981, replacing previous, inadequate emergency facilities. Some thirty percent of the hospital's annual patient admissions of thirty-thousand enter through the emergency room, later renamed the emergency/trauma unit. Some of these are in critical condition with life-threatening injuries or illnesses, such as accident victims or people who have suffered stroke or heart attacks. A trauma area handles patients with less serious injuries such as cuts, fractures, and sprains. The facility can handle twenty-six patients at one time and has an ambulance bay which can handle six ambulances simultaneously. The unit serves eleven counties in southwestern Minnesota and northern Iowa. It is a federally designated trauma center for this area. Every day an average of 110 people come to this facility for medical care.

And who was the first patient to enter the new emergency room when it opened? Who came first to the largest and best equipped emergency unit in the nation? Was it a victim of an automobile collision or an epileptic in severe convulsions? Not at all. It was a child with an earache.

Regarding this development, Sister Mary Brigh said, "It took a while for people to get used to the idea of going to the hospital instead of staying at home and hurting. It also took a while for them to get used to the idea of going to the doctor instead of having the doctor come to them. But before long, our Emergency Room was filled to overflowing. Emergency care was becoming an established part of hospital practice."

The emergency/trauma unit staff classifies their patients into one of the four following categories:

(1) Critical patients are those who are admitted in a state of life-threatening illness or injury. These are patients with depressed vital signs who normally would not survive if not given immediate care. Between

three and four percent of all emergency/trauma unit patients are in this category.

(2) Next is the urgent/serious condition—for example, those who have sustained severe trauma or heart attacks. About twenty percent of all emergency/trauma unit patients are classified in this category.

(3) The urgent/not serious group includes those who need care for such things as minor head injuries. This is the largest category and accounts for fifty to fifty-five percent of all emergency patients seen.

(4) Finally, there is the not urgent/not serious group, which includes those with minor puncture wounds, sore throats, or colds for example.

Regarding the emergency medical services at Saint Marys, there was the pertinent statement that "when you're giving this kind of emergency care, it's a bit like skiing downhill, you just don't relax."

Rehabilitation Unit

Occupying the entire third floor of the new Mary Brigh Building is the rehabilitation unit. Here we find victims of brain or spinal cord injuries and brain or neurological diseases that have impaired their physical functioning. They are not in the acute stages of medical crises. They have recovered from the acute conditions. Many of them have come to Saint Marys via the emergency/trauma unit in the aftermath of accidents or sudden medical crises such as strokes. By the time they arrive on the rehabilitation unit, the need is for adaptation to the results of such crises.

They may need to relearn such basic skills as dressing, eating, or bowel and bladder training. They have to relearn use of muscles that need strengthening. They may have to learn how to use adaptive devices that will help them in the performance of daily tasks. They may need to learn to stand and walk again, how to transfer in and out of wheelchairs, or how to perform personal care skills to prevent medical complications such as infections. They may have to acquire new job skills and learn how to relate to their families in the wake of a devastating alteration in lifestyle.

Dr. Gudni Thorsteinsson, director of the unit, says, "Rehabilitation is a very complex process. It is seen as the result of a team approach. Instead of 'recovery' we aim to maximize what a patient has—we'll deal with anything that relates to that individual's independence.

"Beyond the necessary physical readjustments, often the most difficult task is dealing with the emotional holocaust that follows an injury or illness that results in significant physical impairment. The rehabilitation effort must thus focus on the anger, the denial, the grief that these individuals and their families go through."

The team of experts who care for rehabilitation patients is led by a physician who coordinates the efforts of all the team members and prescribes a highly individualized program of treatment for each patient. The members of the team include nurses, physical therapists, occupational therapists, recreational therapists, medical social workers, psychologists, speech therapists, vocational counselors, patient family educators, and other people with special skills.

Among the members of the team are rehabilitation nurses. From the time a patient enters the unit until he is discharged, one nurse assumes primary responsibility for that individual's care. The nurse integrates input from other team members, practices physical skills and evaluates progress.

All this is a long-term process, lasting for perhaps three months or even as long as a year. These services are rendered at Saint Marys Hospital to about four hundred patients per year. It is anticipated that eventually rehabilitation training may be useful in a number of diseases apart from those of the brain and spinal cord, such as in patients with cardiac disease or cancer.

Numbers

Mathematical figures often impress themselves on a thinking mind. Figures are often more eloquent than words. There is the number of two million per second—the number of our red blood cells destroyed and replaced continuously throughout life. There is the lesser figure of two minutes per day, which is the increase in the sunrise to sunset period from December 21 to June 21 each year.

Saint Marys Hospital also presents interesting figures. The department of pharmacy dispenses a daily average of 840 drug orders. There are more than 3,000 employees. The annual payroll totals $45 million. More than 29,000 surgical procedures are performed each year, including some 900 open-heart operations. The department of dietetics serves nearly 4,000 meals each day, with forty percent of the hospital's patients on special diets. Dietary instructions to patients are given in seven different languages.

Assisi Heights

There sometimes arises the question, What is the relationship of Assisi Heights to Rochester's medical activities, since Saint Marys Hospital is operated by the Sisters of Saint Francis of Assisi? Assisi Heights is "a city seated on a hill," built in 1955 in northwestern Rochester. It is a motherhouse providing living and retirement quarters for the sisters of Saint Marys, but this is only a small fraction of the Assisi Heights activities and responsibilities.

It is a center for all the Saint Francis sisters of the area, whatever may be their daily activities as school teachers, church functionaries, nurses, or whatever else. There are training facilities for sisters-to-be, a community college, a magnificent chapel, an infirmary—really a small hospital—meeting quarters, and much more.

Eventually there was formed here the Christian Community Center, devoted to numerous religious activities and gatherings, not only for Roman Catholic but also for Protestant and other church groups.

Assisi Heights is a tremendously worthwhile enterprise. Though it is not intimately related to the medical activities of the Clinic, it does provide significant aid to the sisters of Saint Marys Hospital, who enthusiastically support the numerous activities of the Assisi Heights organization. Sister Mary Brigh, so important in the development of today's Saint Marys Hospital, was also active in organizing and carrying to completion the Assisi Heights plans.

Regarding the magnificent extensive edifices here, comparable to Rochester's Clinic and hospital structures, there is the following statement made by Edward A. Fitzgerald, bishop of Winona:

> The location of the motherhouse on Assisi Heights is fitting too from the Franciscan point of view. Many who have had the privilege of visiting Italy and making a pilgrimage to Assisi, birthplace of Saint Francis and center of his tremendous undertakings for God, have remarked on the similarity of location of the new motherhouse and the great basilica of Saint Francis of Assisi. Both crown a hilltop. Viewing each, one sees first the chapel and then those sections of the building radiating from the chapel. Both are of Italian Romanesque architecture, both are of similar color stone and have roofs of warm red tile. Both were built for God's glory and, for this reason, it is fitting that they be beautiful, suitable and enduring.

Rochester Methodist Hospital

The imposing structure of Rochester Methodist Hospital was as important to the Clinic's activities as was Saint Marys Hospital. Its downtown location immediately adjacent to the Mayo Building was a considerable asset in many ways. For example, all Rochester hospital patients needing radiation therapy were housed here, only a short subway distance from the Clinic's underground Curie Pavilion.

In 1979, the Methodist Hospital celebrated its twenty-fifth anniversary, at which Justice Harry Blackmun delivered the chief address. Recounted on this occasion were some of the noted accomplishments of the institution. There was the assembling of several downtown separated hospitals into one unit. Blackmun urged the staff "not to lose the spirit of the old buildings now that you have the new building." Here also was incorporated the nation's first round units in which patients' rooms radiated from the central desk of nurses and attendants instead of being spread out in a long corridor. At Methodist also occurred the first use of the Mayo-Gibbon heart-lung machine, enabling Dr. John Kirklin to operate within the heart on patients with serious cardiac defects.

Such complex surgical devices might be contrasted with unbelievable simplicity in other areas of the hospital's history. There was a time when the hospital's daily earnings of thousands of dollars were carried to the First National Bank in a huge zipper bag, with nothing untoward ever happening.

In Blackmun's words, "The hospital came into being . . . because it is the product of time, and the talent and devotion of many people . . . and I suspect it came into being because the sun is meant to shine and because the hospital was meant to be."

The eight hundred beds at Methodist were somewhat fewer than at Saint Marys, but patient admissions in 1980 were about equal, with 30,100 at Methodist and 30,300 at Saint Marys. Employees numbered over two thousand and per year more than a million meals were served to patients. Methodist's operating budget reached the figure of nine hundred thousand dollars per week as compared with Saint Mary's one million dollars per week. We might compare these dollar figures with the financial activities of the Mayo Clinic, in which income from all sources and expenditures for all purposes amounted to about five million dollars per week.

Adding the figures of the Clinic, Saint Marys, and Methodist, we arrive at a budget of one million dollars for every day of the year, including weekends. This translates into eleven dollars per second, day and night, week after week, month after month. It is almost unbelievable that such an enormous enterprise operates in a city, or town rather, with a 1980 population of 57,855.

One unit of the hospital's activities was somewhat new in Mayo history—the alcoholism treatment unit. Clinic psychiatrist Dr. Robert M. Morse stated that "a number of us were concerned that the kind of treatment we were able to afford our alcohol-addicted patients wasn't doing the job. We were treating the complications of alcoholism, not the disease itself." At the same time, Methodist Hospital administrative staff members were also considering developing an alcoholism treatment facility. The project came into being in 1972 at Methodist's old Colonial unit, where alcoholics could be housed. A multidisciplinary treatment program was developed that commenced with medical and psychiatric evaluation of the patient and of his addiction history. The program included group therapy, individual and family counseling, lectures to aid patients to understand their affliction, social and recreational activity, and a physical exercise program. The principles of Alcoholics Anonymous were introduced, and patients were encouraged to join an AA group on discharge. Patients were housed here from anywhere from three to six weeks.

It was felt that one of the most important developments that might arise from the program would be to help demonstrate both to the public and to the medical profession that alcoholism is a disorder that may be successfully and appropriately treated in a general hospital.

Nurse Shortage

A tremendous national shortage of nurses developed in the entire country in the late 1970s. Large medical complexes in many states so reported. California alone announced nursing vacancies numbering ten thousand. Newspapers in Minnesota, and even in Rochester, carried advertisements for nurses from as far away as Colorado and Texas. The number of nursing school admissions and graduates in the United States showed no growth. In many nursing schools there was also a shortage of teachers, which further caused fewer nursing students. And many graduating nurses preferred options other than hospital nursing, such as working in schools, in industry, in public health, and in nonhospital clinics. Nurses could go to almost any place and just about name and define their jobs.

The Rochester hospitals were naturally affected, and numerous efforts were developed to meet the problem. There was aggressive recruiting. Word was spread about the high quality of nursing care being practiced in Rochester; the nursing work was interesting, stimulating, and challenging. Mailings were sent out to potential graduates and advertisements placed in newspapers of nursing school campuses.

The Methodist Hospital sent recruiting teams to visit schools in Minnesota, the Dakotas, Iowa, and Wisconsin, carrying the message that Rochester Methodist was a good place to be a nurse.

A Saint Marys recruitment project also functioned. In 1981 hospital representatives visited more than eighty schools, career days, job fairs, and conventions in a nine-state area from Montana to Michigan. The hospital also expanded its advertising for nurses in college papers and nursing journals.

An improved and somewhat revolutionary nurse scheduling was also put into effect. For example, it was arranged that nurses did not spend more than half their time on evening and weekend shifts. This was contrasted with the practice in many hospitals of scheduling much more of a nurse's time on evening or weekend duty.

The Methodist Hospital developed a "float staff" of nurses. Members of this unit could basically name their hours to fit into their own family responsibilities at home. Without this arrangement possibility, many trained nurses stayed at home entirely or found other jobs. Nurses in the float staff once numbered more than one hundred.

And "minishifts" were put into operation in which nurses with family responsibilities in their own homes could work as nurses on a four-hour basis, often only once a week. As one nurse put it, "This way I can be home with the kids while they're growing up and still keep my fingers in nursing so I can come back full-time later."

Another arrangement attractive to full-time nurses was to have a given patient remain continually under the same nurse's care from entering until leaving the hospital. A nurse could thus follow the complete progress of the patient in this "primary nursing" project.

Neither of the Rochester hospitals provides complete basic nurse training. But the management of Clinic patients with their vast variety of medical problems constitutes what might be called postgraduate nursing training. And, in addition to this, both hospitals offer numerous in-service training programs for their nursing staff. Saint Marys provided a specialist to help the staff nurses to continue their education and develop themselves in their practice. Such advanced educational opportunities constituted a significant stimulus for ambitious nurses to seek employment in the Mayo hospital complex.

A major factor in solving the nurse shortage problem was the warm relationship between Clinic staff members and nurses. Mayo physicians generally agreed with this statement by a Georgia physician:

> Physicians can no longer expect nurses to carry their charts around, write all their verbal orders and be the "humble servant of the master . . ." A little time and effort spent at being considerate (rather than condescending), at being patient (rather than pompous), at educating (rather than rebuking), at being friendly and courteous (rather than aloof), and at expressing our gratitude will pay untold dividends for us and our patients . . . We can pay them twice what they deserve, but if we don't treat them as the professionals they are, we will always have a nursing shortage.

In the words of a veteran Methodist nurse, the nurse-physician relationship "can determine whether a nurse stays in hospital nursing or in nursing at all . . . Today, very frequently, the physician expects and wants the nurse to go on rounds. Some don't start until the nurse is with them. They do ask for input on patients in general. That's very rewarding; you feel like a part of the team, that your advice is valuable . . . We let the doctors know any concerns we have about the practice and they let us know any concerns about nursing care. We also work at communicating what the role of the nurse is." And the staff member listens.

Mayo's participation in the training of student nurses from various nursing schools was also aided, for such students became aware of the many desirable aspects of working in the Mayo complex.

As a result of these and many other efforts, the Rochester hospitals were affected by nursing shortages not quite as badly as elsewhere in the nation's hospitals. In one year the nurse turnover was thirty percent at Methodist and thirty-six percent at Saint Marys, as compared with a fifty percent average for the nation at large. No Clinic patients were turned away or had delayed admissions because of nurse shortages, thanks to the tremendous efforts to attract nurses made by the two hospitals.

CHAPTER 23

Advanced Diagnostic Facilities

Time was when all the outpatient care needs of the Mayo Clinic were fulfilled in the Plummer Building. But when this was moved to the new Mayo Building all the vacated Plummer space was soon put to full use, including the vast library located on the upper floors. Much of the remainder provided housing for a variety of complex diagnostic and research tools that are also extensively available in the Hilton, Guggenheim, and Medical Sciences buildings.

Heart Function

Extensive space and machinery provided the needs for electrocardiography in which records are made of the electrical discharges emanating from the heart during its blood-pumping work. Here about forty technicians employ the elaborate devices for making such heartbeat records. About six hundred electrocardiograms are made daily at the Clinic and the two hospitals. This number also includes tracings submitted to Mayo from regional hospitals and laboratories via telephone.

In the Clinic laboratories, these electrical impulses from the heart are directly transmitted into an IBM-1800 computer that processes the data, relates them to information stored in its memory, and renders an interpretation in narrative form, automatically typed.

Electrocardiograms are often carried out prior to, during, and following exercise by a patient on a treadmill or a bicycle ergometer. In use also is the Holter ECG which has been called "a walking ECG monitoring unit." Five electrodes placed on a patient's chest are connected to a tape recorder which can be carried over the shoulder. Recorded on this tape is every heartbeat of the patient per twenty-four hours, numbering about one hundred thousand. This tape is played back on a device in which abnormalities of the tracing indicating the nature of the faulty heart action are readily detected and interpreted.

There was also developed an ambulance-hospital ECG system. In Rochester or nearby, when someone has collapsed, perhaps on the street, an ambulance hastens to the site to pick up the patient and take him to a hospital. But minutes or even seconds are important. Immediately on taking the patient into the ambulance, machinery is connected that transmits ECG tracings to the Clinic, whence instructions are sent back to the ambulance. So the victim receives appropriate emergency treatment by skilled technicians in the ambulance minutes before the patient is delivered to a hospital. This process saves many lives.

The transmission to the Clinic of the electrical impulses of the beating heart from Rochester hospitals and regional medical centers seems rather simple when compared with an amazing experiment carried out in 1971 by Mayo in collaboration with the United States Department of Commerce. In this, the heart's electrical discharges were transmitted to the Mayo laboratories from Sydney, Australia, by radiotelephone. In the electrocardiogram laboratory these ECG impulses were processed by a computer whose interpretation was sent back to Sydney. The entire process was accomplished in about three minutes. It was stated that "the significance of the experiment lies in the fact that if the procedure will work between Sydney, Australia and Minnesota, U.S.A., it will work between any two points on earth."

Invaluable as electrocardiography has been in detecting the nature of cardiac abnormalities, there is more machinery related to this vital organ.

Clinical Phonocardiography

As this name clinical phonocardiography implies, the process relates to studies and recordings of heart sounds that have been heard by diagnostic physicians for centuries. Originally, this hearing process consisted of the physician placing his ear on the patient's chest over the heart. The stethoscope was invented by the French physician Rene T. H. Laennec in about 1817. It first consisted of a simple paper cylinder, and a later model was a hollow wooden tube about twelve inches long, with flared ends, allowing the examiner to catch the heart sounds into one of his ears. Today's stethoscope, leading the sounds into both ears through flexible rubber tubings, was developed by George Philip Camman in 1840. Cardiac irregularities, such as valve defects, are often revealed by a stethoscope. Of course, the stethoscope is used to hear sounds from parts of the body other than the heart, such as the respiratory system.

In phonocardiography, heart sounds are transmitted from the chest wall through a flexible tube leading the vibrations into a complex device that actually records the sound waves. During the process the waves can also be seen on a small screen. The device reveals exactly at what stage in the cardiac cycle the sound actually originates, enabling the examiner to diagnose more accurately just what a cardiac abnormality might be. There is also the written record of these events, which can be examined later by other physicians without directly examining the patient again. The device is especially useful in detecting inefficiency of the heart valves or malfunction of the large arteries leading from the heart. And it is educational to the examining physician. He can compare these recordings with what he previously detected by touch and sight and hearing, and learn from the comparison.

Phonocardiography is used far less frequently than is electrocardiography. About twenty patients per day lie under this machine to reveal what the heart and its valves may or may not be doing.

Echocardiography

As the name might suggest, in this device the heart echoes back waves transmitted to it from outside the body. These are ultrasound waves, which are vibrations of the same physical nature as sound but with frequencies above the range of human hearing. Adult humans can hear sounds with wave frequencies from 15 to 15,000 vibrations, or cycles, per second. Children might hear sounds even higher in pitch, perhaps up to 20,000 cycles. Interestingly, dogs can hear waves above the frequency detectable by the human ear, so ultrasound whistles can result in the dog hearing the sound while the human hears nothing.

Mayo's echocardiography device uses ultrasound cycles as high as 2.5 million vibrations per second. These waves are produced in machinery by electrical charges impinging on certain crystals, which respond by emitting the very high frequency ultrasound waves that impinge on the heart and are echoed back. This new medical diagnostic tool had been used a long time in engineering problems such as detecting flaws in metals.

The ultrasound echoes from the heart are not only electrically recorded; they are also made visible to the eye on a small screen where the actual beating of the heart can be seen. So we have a complex of interacting waves: electrical, ultrasound, and light. The visible picture details are not as clearly outlined as in an x-ray picture, but they can be accurately read by experts in this field. The resulting motion pictures are derived primarily from the ultrasound echoes reflected from interfaces within the heart where structures of different densities are in contact, such as the interface between blood and heart wall or between blood and heart valves. Some fifteen to twenty-five tests are performed daily.

The information revealed is amazing. This includes the thickness of the heart ventricular walls, the internal dimensions of the heart chambers, the volume of blood ejected at each heartbeat, the presence of tumors or clots within the heart chambers, and patterns of cardiac malfunction which are not revealed by electrocardiography, phonocardiography, or other devices.

Brain Waves

As already recounted, activity in many body parts, such as nerves or muscles, is accompanied by electrical discharges. Such an indication of activity is relatively simple in a single nerve. The electrical waves emitted by the beating heart are more complex but not nearly as challenging as the electricity generated by the functioning human brain, with its many millions of active nerve cells and nerve fibers.

Electroencephalography is the recording of electrical brain waves. There are electrical contacts with twenty-two points on the outside of the head, leading the brain currents into the complicated recording machinery. The tracing or record that emerges is naturally very complex. Recorded are sixteen parallel, horizontal tracings, one above the other on a large sheet of paper, which facilitates diagnosis and becomes part of the patient's record.

This procedure is particularly useful in cases of brain tumors. It does much to indicate where in the brain the tumor is located, informing the brain surgeon about where to carry out his operation. In patients with convulsive seizures, such as epilepsy, the exact location of the brain abnormality may be shown. A variety of attacks of unconsciousness or comas also modify brain waves, providing useful information about the location of the defect caused by disease, injury, or poisoning and resulting in fits of unconsciousness. Brain waves are also modified in certain metabolic diseases involving distant organs such as the liver.

Some fifty to seventy such tracings are made each day in the main laboratory or at the two affiliated hospitals. Included also are tracings submitted to Mayo from outreach facilities in the nearby towns of Austin, Hibbing, and Winona. These are made on patients by technicians trained by Mayo but employed locally. They record the electroencephalograms and send them to the Clinic for diagnosis.

Vascular Laboratory

In the vascular laboratory are procedures that determine the adequacy of the blood circulation in the limbs, often primarily in the legs. The most common patient complaint necessitating such studies is discomfort or pain in the leg muscles on walking rapidly or uphill, as occurs in some elderly people, especially those devoted to excessive cigarette smoking. There is a treadmill on which the patient walks rapidly without going anyplace. Diagnostic machinery attached to the patient records various aspects of the circulation, including electrocardiograms of the heartbeat, which might determine whether the fault lies in the heart.

Cuffs on the ankles are inflated and determinations are made of just how much cuff pressure will stop blood flow into the arteries of the feet. The procedures determine just what abnormal functioning is involved in causing pain on walking rapidly. Is the defect in a narrowing of the arteries, in the nerves, or in the muscles themselves? All this can be determined by the machinery, but always involving the expert procedures and observations of the physician supervising the study, assisted by trained technicians. Even abnormalities of the patient's gait on the treadmill may be informative. In patients with blood vessel narrowing in the leg, disturbance in gait does not appear until leg pain and distress are experienced, whereas in nerve disorders, the patient's gait is abnormal from the time his treadmill walking begins.

There are tests for vascular disease other than those employed in treadmill exercise. Ultrasound waves of very high frequency may be directed into any surface area of the body where deficient circulation is suspected. The reflected ultrasound can be converted into audible sound waves that may be delivered to the investigator by earpieces, earphones, or speakers, or they may be recorded on charts. Red blood cells in motion so affect the ultrasound waves as to provide information about the velocity of the flow of blood in the vessel being examined, and therefore about the adequacy or inadequacy of blood flow to numerous body parts, especially the arms and legs. Blood pressure and blood flow can even be determined in the arteries of the fingers or toes.

Plethysmography measures changes in the volume of a body part with each heart beat. Cuffs may be applied at various positions on the arms or legs. Volume changes in the extremity part with each heartbeat are recorded from pressure changes in the cuff, providing more aid in the assessment of the arterial circulation in the limb.

There are instruments for rapidly determining skin temperature changes in the fingers. This involves immersing the fingers in ice water for thirty seconds. The device then records the skin temperature, determining not only the temperature reduction produced by the ice water but also the time it takes for the finger to return to its preimmersion temperature. Normally, such return to the previous temperature occurs in three to eight minutes. In certain abnormalities of the nervous control of blood flow through smaller arteries (Raynaud's disease), the return to preimmersion temperature may require twenty minutes or longer. The procedure assists materially in the diagnosis of defects in arterial blood flow and what should be done about them.

Thus far this account has related primarily to defects in arteries, large or small, and to the nervous control of vessel diameter. But there are also defects of blood flow in veins, often caused by thrombosis, the formation of blood clots in the vessels. Ultrasound tests can also often identify such impairments of venous blood flow.

It must be noted that all these studies in the vascular laboratory are what is termed noninvasive. There is no invasion into body parts: no skin or other incisions and no injections. As stated by Dr. P. J. Osmundson, in charge of these procedures, "noninvasive tests . . . can be performed quickly and repeatedly, . . . involve little or no risk to the patient, . . . and can be done at moderate cost."

Coagulation Laboratories

In view of the importance of the circulating blood, it is not surprising that elaborate mechanisms have been evolved to combat blood loss should a blood vessel chance to be ruptured. One of nature's devices in invertebrates has been to produce spasms of ruptured vessels, that is, strong contractions of the injured blood vessel walls that serve to pinch off the opening. In vertebrates, the same end is served by the coagulation or clotting of blood, which everyone has observed in his own blood escaping from a ruptured vessel. When blood is drawn from a vein into a beaker, it remains liquid for only a short time. It is converted into a semisolid gelatinous mass, or clot, in some four to eight minutes. This interval is referred to as the clotting time.

There are some twelve factors within the blood and the body tissues involved in ensuring the clotting of blood following injury. Constituents in the juices of any body tissue can initiate clotting on injury. One aspect of the process is the disintegration of our blood platelets, which comprise one of the formed and microscopically evident elements of the blood. Platelet disintegration when blood is shed releases chemicals that initiate clotting. Failure of platelets to so disintegrate is involved in the hereditary disease hemophilia, characterized by faulty coagulation and excessive or even fatal bleeding on injury.

While defective blood clotting may result in death, there is an equal danger from an excessive clotting tendency, resulting in clots developing within blood vessels, occluding the movement of blood. Serious tissue damage may result. Depending on the body part or organ where such clotting or thrombosis occurs, the results may seriously impair the functions of the body parts involved. The end result may be death.

Mayo's extensive coagulation laboratories are equipped to render some fifty tests relating to coagulation of blood. Not too many clinic patients display such deficiencies. Perhaps ten examinations are done per day on patients with either faulty or excessive blood clotting.

Here again one views the inseparability of patient care and basic research, so increasingly evident in the Clinic's multiple medical activities. The major activity of the coagulation laboratories is research into the causes and possible control of either defective or excessive blood clotting. Mayo is one of the country's largest centers for the study of hemophilia.

In the library of the coagulation laboratories we find several dictionary-sized, bound volumes containing reprints of publications by Clinic investigators in this field, entitled *Collected Papers on Blood Coagulation.* These recount the efforts to arrive at controls of coagulation, whether such clotting may be at either of the extremes of deficiency or overactivity of our body's blood-clotting machinery. Such research has greatly expanded medicine's understanding and control of these blood-clotting abnormalities.

Pulmonary Function

Laboratories are provided for tests and examinations on patients in whom there is interference with breathing, usually by mechanical obstructions somewhere in the breathing passageways from the throat to the depths of the lungs. Such partial blocking of air channels can be produced by a variety of abnormalities. In bronchitis there is acute or chronic inflammation and swelling of the walls of the smaller air passages. In pulmonary emphysema there is increase beyond normal in the size of the final air pockets, loss of lung tissue, and retardation of air flow. A number of other abnormal conditions produce these effects, hampering the in-and-out movement of air.

In testing patients with such problems, a variety of mechanical and electronic devices provide the needed information. Almost simultaneously there may be electrocardiograms and measurements of arterial blood pressure, the oxygen content of blood, the pressure of air in lung cavities, the flow of air at the mouth, the chemistry of expired gas, the vital capacity or volume of air exchanged in either normal or very deep breathing, the blood hemoglobin content, the speed with which air is expelled, and even more, including electroencephalograms of brain waves when needed. Some of these studies have been used to great advantage in patients who have trouble breathing while asleep, due to obstruction of the air passages in the throat.

In four laboratories with thirty-two technicians and innumerable machines, it is possible to detect what disease may be involved and how severe the condition is. Some seventy Clinic patients undergo these tests each day. But the Clinic also provides similar services to patients who may never come to Rochester.

The Mayo Medical Services Program assists local doctors in thirty-four areas of Minnesota, Iowa, Wisconsin, Illinois, Ohio, and Missouri. A patient located rather far away breathes into appropriate apparatus attached to his body to test his breathing function. These devices transmit electronic waves by telephone to the Rochester laboratories, where the test results are recorded on Clinic apparatus. In this way, the complicated findings permit Clinic doctors to make accurate diagnoses on patients who have breathing malfunctions and whom the diagnosticians have never seen.

The basal metabolism unit for measuring the rate of oxygen consumption by the body also serves in some pulmonary function studies. Only about two such measurements are made per day. This may be contrasted with the former extensive use of basal metabolism measurements in diagnosing malfunctions of the thyroid glands unrelated to breathing difficulties. Twenty years ago some forty basal metabolism tests per day were made on suspected thyroid patients. Now this has been replaced with chemistry tests determining the blood content of the thyroid hormone thyroxine. Here we note one of the few examples of diminishing rather than increasing activities in a medical procedure, but only because this basal metabolic rate (BMR) test has become obsolete. In the entire complex of the pulmonary function laboratories, there is one bed in one small room for the few basal metabolism studies needed for all the Clinic or hospital patients.

In these highly computerized pulmonary function laboratories there is considerable research carried on, supplementing patient diagnostic studies. Here the mechanical and biochemical functions of breathing are studied on small experimental animals such as guinea pigs and rabbits, as well as on human volunteers. This important research activity is carried out under the able direction of Dr. Robert E. Hyatt.

In certain pulmonary function tests patients must breathe cylinder-stored gas. Mercury is used in the pulmonary function laboratories to determine the amount of oxygen, carbon dioxide, and nitrogen in this cylinder-stored gas. Patients breathe these gases during certain pulmonary function tests.

But despite its usefulness, mercury can be harmful if inhaled or swallowed in quantity. Therefore, measurements are taken of mercury vapor in the laboratory air. This procedure is aimed primarily at protecting Clinic technicians from being injured. This mercury vapor in the air breathed is not particularly significant for patients spending relatively short periods here, but it may be dangerous for technicians spending daily hours breathing the air. Therefore the mercury vapor must be removed.

Here we find but one of the Clinic's efforts to protect their employees from danger. In the area of occupational injury or illness, Mayo has a remarkable record. For every three job-related illnesses that occur in other health service institutions in the United States, Mayo has only one. The severity of these cases is also less at Mayo. The number of work days lost at Mayo from on-the-job injuries and illnesses is about one fourth of the national average.

Radiology Amplified

We owe the original discovery of x-rays to the German physicist William Konrad Roentgen on November 8, 1895. X-rays, sometimes also called Roentgen rays, are based on the electromagnetic discharges emitted from electrons existing in high numbers in all forms of matter. News of Roentgen's discovery spread like wildfire and applications were made almost immediately, especially in the realm of medical diagnosis. Roentgen became the first recipient of the Nobel Prize in physics in 1901. The transition from this finding to Mayo's elaborately expanded devices for looking inside the body might be likened to the advancement in transportation from the canoe to spacecraft.

Although the usual x-rays are most informative and indispensable to medicine, there are certain limitations. A patient arrives at the Clinic with complaints and symptoms suggesting the possibility of a tumor in the pelvis. X-rays reveal the shadows of an abnormal mass. But the total mass and shape of the tumor and its relationships with the adjacent normal structures are not clearly revealed. To overcome much of this difficulty the Clinic's department of radiology acquired and subsequently improved computerized tomography scanners, or CT scanners, in the early 1970s. And just what does this complex machinery do?

The scanner presents visible images and makes pictures, not of the entire body thickness but of thin sections of the body. These slices may be as little as two millimeters in thickness, although thicker slices are more commonly used. For the patient with the pelvic tumor, a series of images is made of several successive and adjacent cross sections of the area involved. The various dimensions of the foreign mass are revealed. Also shown are the intimate relationships of the tumor and immediately surrounding body structures, such as the bones of the hip. Structures are revealed which are virtually invisible on standard x-rays. It is almost as if a surgeon might have made an exploratory operation of the area. But in this case the patient has not even been touched by the observer.

Such horizontal cross-section images can be made of any part of the body from head to foot. The examiner may see any body part he wishes. This process is particularly useful in locating brain tumors. The scanner shows not shadows of the entire head but a succession of views of slices of the brain and skull, revealing the exact size, and shape, and location of the tumor. In this manner, CT scanning presents views of the inside of the living brain that were never before obtainable. This procedure largely replaces an examination in which air was injected into the brain to outline structures for better x-ray viewing, a procedure involving hospitalization and possible serious damage.

The first scanner took about two minutes to complete the scan of a slice of the body. But if the patient or the involved body part moved during the process, the resulting image would be blurred. Subsequently, new Clinic scanners could complete a scan in only three or four seconds so that image spoilage was practically eliminated from body movements, even those of breathing, since most patients could easily hold their breath for the short time required.

During this procedure the examining physician is not at the patient's side. He is in a nearby room viewing what is to be seen on a small screen. The transmission of precise information about the patient's body parts to this screen is accomplished by numerous complex computer systems. The computers reconstruct the images of the body slices. X-ray-like films for further study and for the patient's record also result.

In this complex elaboration of relatively simple x-ray pictures, more than one hundred patients per day are studied. About half of these observations are brain scans. During a recent six-year period some eighty thousand CT scanning examinations were made, more than in any other medical center in the world. The magnitude of the Clinic's total radiology activities, including common x-rays, is partially revealed by the number of Clinic staff members engaged in this activity. There are more than forty Clinic consultants involved as members of the department of diagnostic radiology.

CT scanning has been called the greatest advance in diagnostic medicine since Roentgen's discovery of the x-ray. Like Roentgen, the inventors of CT technology were also awarded a Nobel Prize in 1979. These were the English Dr. G. N. Hounsfield and the American Dr. A. M. Cormack. Although CT scanning did not originate at Mayo, improvements and extensions of the device have eventuated in the radiology department, largely under the leadership of Drs. Patrick F. Sheedy and Glenn Forbes.

Elaborate and complex as are the computerized tomography scanners, there is still more to come. Dr. Sheedy ventured that although a plateau may have been reached in CT technology, much further promise may be seen in a new device developing at Mayo that has the capacity of visualizing the actual motions of various body parts depicted on a screen. This might be likened to motion pictures replacing still slides.

Dynamic Spatial Reconstructor

The concept and planning of the dynamic spatial reconstructor, or DSR, has been a project mainly of the biodynamic research unit in Mayo's physiology department. Some ten years have been involved in this development. It was a joint enterprise of several minds so that no one person can be named as primarily responsible, although Drs. Earl Wood and Erik Ritman played leading roles. Collaborating also were the section of engineering and the division of cardiovascular diseases, as well as the departments of radiology and pathology. Parts of the apparatus were borrowed from oil-well drilling technology and image intensifiers used in many fields, including astronomy.

The DSR is located in the Medical Sciences Building, where occurred the historic development of the human centrifuge resulting in the antigravity G suit and the high-altitude oxygen mask for World War II fliers. Let us look at this massive seventeen-ton structure, the only one of its kind in the entire world, although it was felt that there might eventually be a device like this in most large medical centers.

The DSR gantry, built for Mayo by the Raytheon Corporation of Waltham, Massachusetts, somewhat resembles a very thick-walled cylinder fifteen feet in diameter. The central open space within the cylinder is about three feet in diameter. Here may lie a patient or an experimental animal. The thick walls of the cylinder are designed to contain twenty-eight x-ray tubes and twenty-eight image intensifiers. The entire machine, including the gantry, is about twenty feet long. During an examination the cylindrical gantry is made to rotate once in every four seconds, although the subject under study lies quietly with no motion. During each five seconds, about the time for five heartbeats, there are tens of thousands of low voltage x-ray cross-section pictures taken. During this brief period, the previously described CT scanner could produce but one cross-section image of a body slice.

Each time the twenty-eight x-ray guns fire, data for up to twenty-four cross sections of tissue are collected, with each cross section being about one fiftieth of an inch in thickness. All this is transferred to a screen that can be watched or recorded. Here can be seen various movements of interior body parts such as the beating of the heart, the action of the heart valves, and breathing motions. Even the flow of blood in vessels can be observed.

All this is a potential improvement on exploratory surgery. A surgeon opening the chest cannot see the actions of the heart valves, but DSR can reveal this. The body and its parts are transparent. Furthermore, the patient observed lies relaxed and quiet, with no pain or even discomfort, and hears little or nothing of the vast machinery in operation. X-ray exposure to the patient required for one set of 240 parallel cross sections is only about twice the amount of an average chest x-ray.

A physician visitor to the biodynamics research unit is amazed to see on a television screen a dog's heart that is isolated, tipped, sliced open mathematically, displayed in a cross-section form at any specified level or angle, enlarged at any desirable spot, and dissolved until only the arterial tree remains. All the while the dog's heart continues to beat normally and the dog has not been touched. A nonsurgical vivisection has been performed. A patient's heart likewise could be selectively removed from the chest and examined electronically without disturbing the wide-awake, relaxed person.

A considerable number of computers are involved in the process, including computerized tomography. There are devices for conversion of x-ray images into numbers for computer input. Mayo's computer scientist Richard Robb directs the computer aspects of the DSR project, "blending theory and hardware to make possible visualization of moving human organs." As principal investigator for the DSR computer development he shoulders a heavy responsibility.

Dr. Erik Ritman stated that the procedure "will be like doing exploratory surgery on an awake patient–painlessly." Regarding this historic development, Dr. Wood modestly said, "We just kept doing what came naturally." He also explained that "the moving three-dimensional x-ray image can be speeded up or slowed down. It can be backed up for replay in much the same way as a replay in a sporting event . . . By enabling doctors for the first time to see motions of the heart, lungs and circulatory system in three dimensions, the DSR will open a broad new vista for investigations in the fields of diagnostic medicine and physiology, furnishing significantly more information faster and often with less risk than many existing tests." Wood also remarked that the DSR was "the most sophisticated, technical, complicated and exciting research project" he ever worked on.

For diagnostic purposes, looking inside the heart as if it were cut open but still functioning can reveal valvular defects, narrowing or blood clotting in heart blood vessels, or the extent of heart muscle damage after a heart attack.

Funding for this project, initially $3.1 million, was provided by a grant from the governmental National Institutes of Health. Additional funds were needed for further developments, some of which came from the American Heart Association and the Rippel Foundation of New Jersey. The yearly operating budget of the Clinic's biodynamics research unit, responsible for the DSR, was $1 million, derived mostly from federal research grants. Full completion of this enterprise is anticipated in the near future, with extensive use partly for patient diagnosis but mainly for research to be carried out on both patients and animals, amplifying our understanding of the functions and derangements of the heart, lungs, and blood circulation.

Fiber Optics

Light travels through air in a straight line unless it encounters a transparent area of density different from air, such as glass. A lens can bend light rays. But until recent years it was difficult or impossible to induce light rays to turn in a curve around corners. Fiber optics does just this, enabling physicians to see directly into the interior of various body organs such as the colon, intestines, stomach, lungs, and more. This applies mainly to body parts having hollow interiors that open to the outside, such as the air passages of the lungs or the alimentary canal.

A fiber-optic instrument, or fiberscope, consists of bundles of glass fibers that may be two or three feet long. But each fiber is microscopically thin, measuring a mere one hundredth of a millimeter in diameter, or about the same as the diameter of a human red blood cell. It requires tens of thousands of such fibers bundled together to make a fiberscope of less than half an inch in diameter. The Japanese have been leaders in the development of these instruments and perfecting techniques for their use.

There are two all-important properties of such a fiberscope. It is most flexible and can be bent in many curves without breaking the glass fibers. And it transmits light waves around any number of corners or curves. So a fiberscope may be inserted through a patient's anus to any desired part of the large intestine. Light is carried from outside illumination to the end of the scope. Looking through the device, the physician can examine the lighted inner wall of the large intestine wherever he wishes, simply by looking through the tube. A device enables him to turn the end of the scope, pointing it at whatever he wishes to see. He can see as many small areas inside the large intestine as if he had done a complicated surgical operation, opening the colon and examining its inner surface. This procedure may be employed when a standard x-ray has revealed a small growth or tumor. Now the physician can examine the growth directly. But there is more. The fiberscope is equipped with devices which can cut off a bit of the growth, which can then be taken out with the scope. A small polyp might be completely removed. Microscopic slides may be made of this tissue bit to determine whether it is cancerous or nonmalignant. Through all of this, the patient is lying relaxed on the table. The examining physician may even turn the fiberscope to the eyes of the patient, who may directly see the small growth just as if his open intestine were lying before him.

Prior to such examination of the colon's interior, the patient must go through a two-hour process of emptying the large bowel of all of its contents. He takes volumes of diarrhetic solution until eventually what he evacuates into the toilet is as clear as water, with no feces or food fragments.

Photography is a useful adjunct. A camera can be focused through the fiber-optic bundle on the lesion, recording on film what the physician sees. Even more useful is videotape, which combines comments of the examiner with motion picture photography of the defect, and the removal of a piece it. This is of superb value in Mayo's teaching activities, which the Clinic always compounds with patient care.

Initially, fiber optics was employed for examinations of interior parts of the alimentary canal. But it was soon used also for parts of the air channels of the lungs, seeking to locate accurately a small lung tumor that might have been revealed previously by x-ray. And it was also used when cancerlike cells were discovered in a patient's sputum. The bit of tissue removed in the fiber-optic examination would reveal whether the growth was really cancerous.

In lung cancer there were some seventy-thousand deaths per year in the early 1970s. It is the leading cause of cancer deaths among males. The overall percentage cure was a discouraging ten to fifteen percent. However, when a small cancer growth is detected and localized by fiber-optic methods, the survival figures improve to about ninety percent. In its studies on the early detection and localization of lung cancer, Mayo received financial support from the National Cancer Institute. Dr. David R. Sanderson, in charge of these Clinic studies, stated, "Our goal is to improve the chance of cure for all."

CHAPTER 24

Cancer

Cancer is second only to heart disease as a killer of people. In the United States about 690,000 new cases appear each year. There were 385,000 cancer deaths in our country in 1977. At the Mayo Clinic, of the more than a quarter of a million patients seen annually, about one tenth have cancer, either just diagnosed in new patients or in patients coming back for further study and treatment of previously diagnosed cancer. This means that on each working day about one hundred cancer patients register at the Clinic.

Comprehensive Cancer Center

The United States Congress passed the National Cancer Act in 1971. This provided for the establishment of fifteen comprehensive cancer centers in the country. The Mayo Clinic was one of these. Is Mayo's cancer center housed in its own building? Not at all. As is true of the medical school, this is an institutionwide project, including the patient care units, laboratories, research facilities, and hospitals. It involves all aspects of the Clinic's cancer work from diagnosis, surgery, chemical therapy, microscopic examinations of cancer tissue, and very much more. The primary purpose of the cancer center is to provide the best possible care to today's cancer patient and, by research, to the patient of tomorrow.

Detection, prevention, and all types of treatment are involved. Of the permanent Mayo staff, about two hundred can be identified as having a major or total commitment to cancer. Divisions of the Clinic's center included developmental cancer research, medical oncology, therapeutic radiology, surgical oncology, cancer center statistical unit, cancer rehabilitation, cancer outreach, and community relations, each of which is related to both cancer treatment and research. Heading this tremendous enterprise is Dr. Charles G. Moertel, internationally renowned cancer authority. Also active in this enterprise is Dr. Joseph Kiely, especially in cancer conditions affecting the blood, such as leukemia.

Dr. Lee Clark of Houston's M. D. Anderson Hospital and Tumor Institute stated, "Some medical centers such as the Mayo Clinic, although not devoted exclusively to cancer, were offering the best therapeutic measures available." A major justification for this assertion is that Mayo sees more cancer patients than most medical centers elsewhere.

And here again we find Mayo extending its facilities and knowledge to a wide area by the development of the North Central Cancer Treatment Group (NCCTG). This consists of a multidisciplinary group of cancer specialists in seven states from Illinois to Montana and from Nebraska to the Canadian border. The aim here was to improve cancer diagnosis and therapy for regional patients who may never see the Mayo Clinic. Mayo cancer specialist Dr. James Ingle, chairman of the NCCTG, pointed out, "The earlier cancer is diagnosed and treatment begun, the greater the likelihood of significant benefit. More than 80 percent of cancer patients are first diagnosed and their treatment begun at the community level. This is where research needs to be done."

Regarding this enterprise, Dr. Lloyd Everson, a medical cancer specialist at Fargo, North Dakota, stated:

> There is a good working relationship between Mayo and the community clinics. And the cornerstone to why it works is mutual respect. We realize that we can't set up a big research program like Mayo has and Mayo realizes that they can't see all the cancer patients there are.
>
> The reality is that the cooperative basis is the only basis on which patients can be well treated.

The National Cancer Institute has been so impressed by the success of the NCCTG that they are now developing a national program modeled after the NCCTG, according to Dr. Charles G. Moertel, director of Mayo's comprehensive cancer center.

Cancer Detection

Detection and diagnosis of cancer, for the most part, begins with the physician taking a careful history from the patient and making a thorough physical examination. But there is a multiplicity of devices for cancer detection beyond this, in addition to the traditional x-ray examinations of body parts.

Microscopic examinations of sputum may reveal cancer of the lung. For this, the National Cancer Institute founded a Cooperative Early Lung Cancer Group, of which Mayo's lung project was a member.

For suspected cancer of the breast, records like x-ray films may be made by using ultrasound waves instead of x-rays, employing the Mayo-developed computerized tomographic (CT) ultrasound scanner. Breast cancers smaller than a centimeter in diameter have been identified with this ultrasound technique. Such small tumors may escape detection by ordinary x-rays. The size is significant because the earlier cancer is detected, the better the chances of cure. In cases where breast cancers are one centimeter or less in diameter when they are removed in surgery and where there is no evidence of the cancer having spread, there is an eighty percent survival rate after five years. A considerable advantage of using the CT ultrasound diagnostic facility is that it does not involve exposure of the patient to x-rays, which in themselves may be harmful.

Pancreatic cancer, the fifth most common cause of cancer death in the United States, is most difficult to detect. The pancreas is not accessible to ordinary palpation by the examining physician, hidden as the gland is in the depths of the abdomen, and there are rarely any clear symptoms or signs of pancreatic cancer, such as bleeding into the intestinal tract, which could be revealed by analysis of the feces. Here again the CT ultrasound scanner may reveal the presence of carcinoma of the pancreas.

Under study also is a procedure employed on patients with suspected lung cancer or on patients whose sputum tests show cancerous or precancerous cells emanating from the lungs. Such a patient is administered a substance (hematoporphyrin) that has two unusual features. It becomes concentrated in rapidly growing tissue such as cancer, and when illuminated with violet light, it becomes fluorescent. Such light given off by the substance can be electronically converted into ordinary sound waves. The examining physician can hear the presence of sound waves emanating from a cancer that might be difficult to detect by other means. Cancer can be heard!

It is possible that similar devices may also be employed in the detection of tumors of the urinary bladder and the brain. The complexity of this procedure is partially revealed by the terminology employed: electronic audio equipment and a chemical working substance can detect bronchoscopic hematoporphyrin fluorescence, employing a fiber bronchoscope.

In uterine cancer, there are revealing microscopic examinations of smears taken from the uterine cervix. Early urinary bladder cancer may be revealed in patients with urological complaints, such as having a bit of blood in the urine. Here, freshly voided, blood-stained urine is processed through a micropore filter. The cells on the filter may reveal the presence of cancer to the examining pathologist.

Research is also under way on cancer of the bone. Studies are made of the blood of patients with this malignancy. The efforts here are to seek evidence in the blood to assist in determining whether bone cancer has recurred after treatment and whether the cancerous growth has spread into new areas.

Medical Oncology

Surgery has been historically the major attack on cancer, and it will probably continue for some time to be one of medicine's primary weapons. But there is much more than surgery. Let us look at the medical oncology unit of Mayo's Comprehensive Cancer Center. This enterprise occupies much of the Mayo Building's twelfth floor, where staff members determine how the patient should be treated, either after surgery or in instances where surgery is not possible, as in patients with widespread metastatic cancer. One such treatment approach employs the administration of anticancer drugs. Available here in twenty-two treatment rooms are some eighty chemical agents ranging from adriamycin to vindesine. Patients here are ambulatory or in wheelchairs. Bedridden hospital patients receive their chemical therapy at the hospitals. During one month alone (January 1981), 686 patients received 1,458 treatments in the medical oncology unit. Such chemotherapy is often an auxiliary to surgery, hopefully impairing the further growth of cancer cells without significant damage to other body cells. Some of this therapy is still in the experimental stage to determine effectiveness against human cancer. But such usage is employed only after the drug has been proven safe in animal experimentation.

In assessing the possible usefulness of anticancer drugs, two things must be determined. First, is the drug harmless to normal body cells? And second, does the drug destroy cancer cells? The National Cancer Institute at Bethesda, Maryland, studies many thousands of such possible therapeutic agents. This is done on animals such as mice with cancer induced by transplanting into them cancer tissue and cells derived from human patients. Of the tremendous number of such drugs tested, only a small fraction become considered as possible effective anticancer agents. The most promising of these are reported to the nation's comprehensive cancer centers, including Mayo, where further testing proceeds. There are studies in which cancer cells are grown in cultures and the effects of the anticancer drug are observed microscopically. Much of this study is carried out in collaboration with Dr. John S. Kovach. Again, a great deal of the work is conducted on mice and rabbits having artificially induced cancer. The aim is essentially to ascertain three things: Is the drug nontoxic to normal body tissue? Is the drug destructive to cancer cells? What dosage levels are most effective? With satisfactory answers to these questions, as supplied by the animal experimentation, the studies proceed to human cancer patients to determine safe and effective dosages.

Radiation Therapy

Evaluation of the cancer patient may indicate the need for radiation therapy instead of chemotherapy. Patients requiring this are treated in the underground Curie Pavilion, with its thick, protective concrete walls. They may receive radiation either by external beams or by administration of radioactive chemicals. For example, consider a patient with cancer of the thyroid gland. This gland takes up iodine from the blood, which is needed in the gland's manufacture of the hormone thyroxine. Radioactive iodine administered to such a patient is absorbed by the diseased gland, where its radioactivity is destructive to the thyroid cancer. Such treatment may supplement previous surgical removal of the tumor, following which bits of cancer tissue may still remain in the gland. But even without such surgery, the cancer may be completely destroyed by the radioactive iodine.

Radioactive phosphorus is used in the cancerlike disease of polycythemia vera in which the bone marrow produces excessive numbers of red blood cells with a possible fatal termination. This condition cannot be treated surgically, since bone marrow is widely distributed throughout the body. Radioactive chemistry must be employed. Physiologically, the bone marrow absorbs phosphorus from the blood. So radioactive phosphorus given the patient is also absorbed by the bone marrow, where its radiation suppresses the excess production of red blood cells.

The therapeutic radiology division at Curie is employed for all Clinic patients needing x-ray treatment. Some of these are ambulatory and others come in wheelchairs or reclining on wheeled carts from the Methodist Hospital, which is only a short subway distance from the Curie. Patients at Saint Marys Hospital requiring such therapy are transferred to the Methodist Hospital. In radiation therapy, some 150 treatments are administered each day.

A recent construction at Curie is a complete surgical operating room that makes possible the administration of x-ray therapy directly on the organ from which the surgeon removes a cancerous growth. This unit is mainly employed to administer x-ray therapy to cancerous tumors that are explored by a surgeon but are too complicated and extensive to remove satisfactorily.

In all radiation therapy there must be every precaution against excessive radiation reaching exposed parts of healthy people such as doctors, nurses, technicians, and other employees involved in administering radiation to patients. Fortunately, most of the body's normal cells are more resistant to damaging radiation than are cancer cells. Proper radiation kills the cancer cells, leaving normal body cells undamaged. But excessive radiation can itself cause cancer, as occurred on the hands of doctors and others in the early days of radiation therapy. Perhaps more dramatic were the many thousands of Japanese who survived our atom bombing but later displayed fatal cancer.

Even the ultraviolet rays in sunshine may cause cancer of the excessively exposed skin, especially in tropical areas. Such skin cancer is relatively rare in mild temperate climates, but it does occur, especially in summertime outdoor workers such as farmers. It can readily be treated surgically or by radiation. This phenomenon has led to an interesting evolutionary theory. Skin cancer is rare in negroes, even in hot areas of the world, since the pigmented skin screens out this potentially dangerous radiation. Over the multitudes of centuries, evolutionary mutations toward skin pigmentation represented a distinct advantage in natural selection, with the resulting improved survival of negroes in tropical Africa and the establishment of darker races.

In all cancer treatment, there is study as well as treatment. To quote Dr. David Ahmann, chairman of the division of medical oncology, "First, give the individual patient absolutely the best we've got to give; second, learn from what we're doing so maybe we can do better with the next patient . . . Do we add this drug at this point in the treatment? When does radiation come? When surgery? How is it all combined?"

Cancer Education

One of the many responsibilities of a comprehensive cancer center is to get the facts about cancer to as many people as possible. The cancer center has a committee for education of the public about cancer, or CEPAC for short. The Clinic cooperates with the Minnesota Cancer Information Service, to which any person can telephone for advice. These queries may range from How dangerous is excessive cigarette smoking? to I have cancer. I plan to visit my children and their families. Is it alright if I kiss my grandchildren? Would they catch it from me?

There is a new mouth self-examination procedure taught to patients for the detection of oral cancer. Breast cancer is the most common malignancy in women. An important function of CEPAC is teaching breast self-examination to women. In men, cancer of the lung is a top cancer killer, with excessive cigarette smoking as a causative factor. One in ten who smoke more than a package of cigarettes in a day will develop cancer, as people are informed by the Mayo lung project. Therefore, heavy smokers should either quit the habit or have sputum cytology examinations and chest x-rays at least once per year. Even employing this lung cancer detection device, the outlook is not particularly promising.

Although the Mayo Clinic was not involved, the state of Minnesota enacted one of the nation's most stringent no-smoking laws in 1975. In any public place whatsoever smoking was prohibited, except in restricted areas bearing such notices as "Smoking Permitted." In all areas without such a notice, smoking was prohibited even without a no-smoking sign. This applied to all places where people might congregate: railway stations, restaurants, waiting rooms, rest rooms, railway cars, passenger busses, or whatever.

It is important to teach patients about cancer, but it is equally important to submit such knowledge to practicing physicians generally. All these should know that it is relatively simple to detect early cancer of the uterine cervix by making microscopic examinations of smears taken from the cervix in PAP smears. Yet multitudes of possible uterine cervix cancer victims have never had such a test.

Involved in this complex educational responsibility is the rehabilitation unit of the comprehensive cancer center, whose aim is to help restore a cancer patient to self-sufficiency or gainful employment, learning to "live with cancer." This is commenced the day a patient's cancer is diagnosed. Such psychosocial activity supplements the basic need of survival in cancer patients and helps them return to a useful, fulfilling place in society.

In young children, the most common form of cancer is acute lymphatic leukemia, with its accelerated production of one kind of white blood cells. It can become rapidly fatal without such adequate treatment as is now available. Fortunately, the condition is not common. Of the total of 690,000 new cancer patients seen in the country each year, a little less than one percent are in the pediatric category. But even with treatment, emotional rehabilitation is important, with psychiatric social workers and nurses aiding the child to live with his illness.

As with so much at Mayo, we find the roots of these endeavors embedded in the long-ago concepts of the original Mayos. Back in 1925, Dr. Will Mayo asserted that "rehabilitation will become a master word in medicine."

Cancer Research

Perhaps it could have been done ten years ago, but today it is impossible to summarize adequately all that is cancer research at the Mayo Clinic, involving some seventy members of the clinical staff and some thirty basic scientists, including immunologists, geneticists, pathologists, microbiologists, biochemists, cell biologists, plus many more. Patient therapy is closely linked with research, as by noting the results and pharmacological effects of drug or radiation therapy. A basic essential for success in the use of anticancer drugs is that the drug must be transported within the body to the cancer site. On arrival there, it must be absorbed through cell walls by the cancer cells. Just how all this is done is being studied. The complexity of such work is revealed in part by the terminology of these esoteric procedures: fluorescence spectography, nuclear magnetic resonance spectroscopy, and electron spin resonance.

Besides observations on patients, this work involves animal experimentation and microscopic—really ultramicroscopic—studies of body cell behavior. We must learn how cancer-inducing substances and anticancer materials work inside the cell at the molecular level. Animals are fed or made to breathe or otherwise exposed to the many known carcinogens in the environment, such as those in the air we breathe, the water we drink, the food we eat, or the tobacco we smoke. These might be asbestos fibers or microscopic bits of metal. The ultramicroscopic intracellular results are observed. Efforts are also under way to develop possible vaccines against cancer.

It is suspected that environmental factors may cause something like one half of all the cancer in the world. The National Cancer Institute has determined that perhaps one fourth of our cancer fatalities might be prevented if we change our lifestyle by not smoking and by dietary and other alterations when these become fully known. It is interesting that the tobacco industry, which spends some $300 billion annually in advertising, is a completely acceptable business enterprise in America, even though the government warns us of the dangers of its products on every package of cigarettes and every bit of newspaper advertising.

There are microscopic and microchemical studies of the effects of cancer-inducing chemicals on animal cells. Some animals are "immunized" with anticarcinogenic substances and then given cancer-producing agents and the cellular results observed. Investigators seek to learn in mice why normal lymphatic tissue exposed to radiation has a capacity to repair itself while tumor lymphatic tissue fortunately does not do so.

Using intricate techniques, important study is taking place on what occurs not inside the human body, not inside an organ, but within the interior of body cells, trying to determine why body cells "go wild" in cancer. Mayo's cell biologist and biochemist Dr. Thomas Spelsberg found that cancer-inducing substances that enter body cells somehow play on the intracellular mechanisms for cellular division and reproduction. The cell begins to divide uncontrollably. It was reasoned that the most realistic attack on cancer might be directed toward protection of the cellular interior parts from the action of such chemicals. This involves examination of the pathway by which chemicals are transported within the body cells and their entrance into and effect on the cell's genes and chromosomes.

Much of this work is done in cell or tissue culture. Electron microscopes magnify by two hundred thousand times, which is about fifty times as great as an ordinary high-power microscope. The microchemistry involved is revealed in part by the employment of various tissue stains. But this must be supplemented by intramolecular chemistry studies.

Funding for cancer research from extramural, non-Clinic sources amounted to $7.318 million in 1977. This was about twenty-seven percent of Mayo's total research budget.

And what have been the results? There have been no great "breakthroughs" but some "grind-throughs." There have been "promising results" and "exciting results." There is no sure cancer cure within our grasp. We know that we can produce cancer in animals by administration of certain viruses, but virus causation remains to be determined in human cancer. But we all recognize that we must continue to seek what answers there are to be found in research for the hundred diseases we call cancer. Let us continue to work hard, and let us even have some hope like that of the former Mayo pathologist Dr. Arnold L. Brown, who stated, "I would not advise my grandson, if I had one, to be an oncologist. I don't think he'd be very busy."

Cancer Treatment Group

Mayo joined with eight community clinics in the upper Midwest to form a new group that allows smaller clinics to enter the front lines not only of cancer treatment but also of research. This enterprise was stimulated by the observation of the Clinic's cancer specialist Dr. James Ingle in the late 1970s that "when you look at a map of cancer centers across the country you see a large void in the north central area." This observation resulted in the formation of the North Central Cancer Treatment Group, involving eight centers in Minnesota, Montana, Nebraska, North Dakota, and South Dakota. Mayo's comprehensive cancer center coordinated this group's activities and offered a variety of support and advisory services:

whatever chemical treatments were employed at Mayo were made readily available to all group members, and the results of such treatment were assembled by the Clinic as part of its cancer research activities; much information was provided, since there were annually many thousands of new cases of cancer diagnosed in the area, apart from those seen at the Clinic. Mayo has charge of all record keeping, statistics, drug procurement, and fiscal management for member institutions. The Clinic also offers supporting services in pathology, laboratory studies, and publications. In addition, there is available an advisory group of eight physicians with expertise in various areas of cancer care.

Serum Bank

This is but an abbreviation of the full imposing title: Mayo National Cancer Institute Serum Immunodiagnostic Bank. It is primarily a research facility in which are stored samples of human blood serum, which is the residual liquid remaining after blood has clotted. Most of these serum samples are derived from the blood of Clinic patients with either benign or malignant tumors anywhere in the body, as well as from some normal patients. As its full name indicates, this is a joint enterprise of the Clinic and the governmental National Cancer Institute. The goal is to provide researchers with material useful in developing blood tests to detect or follow the progress of cancer.

In the tenth year of this project (1981) there were more than 393,000 vials of serum stored in ninety large freezers in the Plummer and Hilton buildings. These freezers maintain a temperature of seventy-five degrees below zero centigrade.

Most of the research seeks to test blood samples for what are called "tumor markers," or substances in the blood which might indicate the likely presence of cancer somewhere in the body. As of today, very few tumor markers have been discovered. But the work continues. The bank director, Dr. Vay Lilang W. Go, explains, "Suppose a Mayo consultant wants to find and study a possible tumor marker for breast cancer. He requests vials of blood serum from women patients . . . who have undergone surgery for breast cancer. With the computer it's a simple task to identify such a group." The researcher is soon provided with his request.

Mayo investigators who use the serum bank material come from a wide spectrum of departments: medical oncology, microbiology, rheumatology, neurology, gastroenterology, clinical chemistry, nuclear medicine, thoracic diseases, and others.

The project serves not only Mayo research teams but many others as well. The serum in storage is derived not only from Clinic patients but from other National Cancer Institute centers across the country, and besides Mayo's use of the serum in Rochester, it is available to others. In one recent year alone, more than sixty thousand vials of frozen serum were supplied to cancer centers in eleven countries. Some 234 investigators from Mayo and elsewhere have tapped these resources.

All this involves a tremendous amount of paper work identifying the source and nature of each of the tens of thousands of serum samples. Naturally, all this is computerized. By these means, researchers using the bank samples have access not only to the quality controlled serum samples but also to all pertinent information about the patients providing the samples.

The Mayo National Cancer Institute Serum Immunodiagnostic Bank, the largest in the world, has become an outstanding international research resource.

CHAPTER 25

Patient Care

So much of this volume has been devoted to research and education that we must remind ourselves that patient care is the primary function of the Clinic. During the last five years of the 1970s, more than a million and a quarter patients came to Mayo for diagnosis and treatment. Of these, about one fourth were new patients and the remainder had been at the Clinic before. Throughout the years the ratio of new to old patients has declined. The annual number of new patients has not changed much in thirty years, but the number of return patients has greatly increased. And the continued demand for services is such that a new patient seeking an appointment here may have to wait four months, despite the tremendous facilities for patient care. Of course, emergency cases are seen as the need demands.

And just who are the patients who come to Mayo? What are their occupations? Is Mayo a clinic for the rich, as was implied in a newspaper article? Not at all. A study of this matter was conducted by the Clinic's section of information processing and systems. There emerged some three hundred occupational categories from account clerks to zoologists. There were butchers, bakers, and cabinetmakers. Of the more than a quarter of a million Mayo patients in 1979, the most common occupation listed was housewife, numbering 34,205 and constituting nearly thirteen percent of the total numbers. The second and third most common categories were farmers and nurses. Patients came from every stratum of society and from every category imaginable: athletes, baby sitters, bus drivers, butlers, detectives, editors, garbage collectors, gardeners, laborers, lifeguards, locomotive engineers, miners, reporters, salesmen, secretaries, sheriffs, teachers, writers, and whatever else you might name. True, there were also business executives, oil well owners, judges, governmental leaders, and millionaires. But these were inadequate in numbers to designate Mayo as a mecca for the moneyed.

Clinic Facilities

As our knowledge of the body in health and disease increases, the provisions necessary for patient diagnosis and care are multiplied. For all patient visits to Mayo, there was a total of thirty-one clinical sections in 1980. These deserve to be listed. In internal medicine we have allergic diseases, cardiovascular diseases, dermatology, diagnostic radiology, endocrinology, gastroenterology, hematology, infectious diseases, medical genetics, nephrology, neurology, oncology, pediatrics, pediatric cardiology, physical medicine and rehabilitation, preventive medicine, psychiatry and psychology, rheumatology, and thoracic diseases. For surgery there are sections of anesthesiology, cardiovascular surgery, colon and rectal surgery, dentistry, neurological surgery, obstetrics and gynecology, ophthalmology, orthopedics, otorhinolaryngology, plastic surgery, thoracic and vascular surgery, and urology.

And corresponding with all these outpatient clinical facilities there are duplicate sections in the hospitals, in addition to the multiple surgical operating rooms and emergency care installations.

To meet the needs of the multiplicity of patients seeking help, Mayo had (in 1980) 751 staff physicians and medical scientists, 713 physician residents or fellows, and 4,760 administrative and paramedical employees. The nonmedical staff includes members of a multitude of professions and occupations: accountants, x-ray technologists, civil engineers, receptionists, desk attendants, medical photographers, statisticians, printers, medical secretaries, dietitians, computer programmers, shuttlebus drivers, gardeners, laboratory technicians, system analysts, medical editors, animal caretakers, lawyers, seamstresses, administrators, social workers, purchasing agents, security guards, medical record clerks, interpreters, telephone operators, and librarians, to name but a few of the multiple different work designations at Mayo.

As varied as these occupations are, they all contribute to medical care at Mayo, sometimes through direct contact with patients and sometimes through nonclinical tasks that help the physician use his time and skills to full advantage. The men and women of the paramedical staff carry out their duties with dedication that stems from a century-long tradition of excellence and concern for the welfare of every Mayo Clinic patient.

So, ready to serve one thousand patients who come to the Clinic every working day, over six thousand people are at hand to meet their needs in the Clinic facilities alone.

Adding to this the medical students, allied health services trainees, and the Saint Marys and Methodist Hospital employees, we arrive at a total figure of more than twelve thousand people in Rochester devoted to patient care, medical education, and scientific research.

For all this complexity, the administrative organization staggers the imagination. The Mayo Clinic Board of Governors is the primary body. Assisting the board in its multiplicity of activities in studying planning, developing, and supervising, we find some fifty-eight Mayo Clinic committees. They deserve naming: academic appointments and promotions, appointment systems study, associate appointments, biohazards, building, clinical society, clinical practice, computer, continuing education, coordinating development, dialysis-transplant, education, electrical safety, environmental safety, emergency care, equal opportunities, extramural practice, facilities' policy, graduate education in the three areas of internal medicine and medical subspecialties (medical and laboratory specialties, surgical, and surgical specialties), health planning, health related sciences, human studies, infection, information systems, laboratory society, Mayo proceedings, editorial, medical care evaluation, medical relations and publications, medical school admissions, medical school education, Methodist Hospital intensive care, Methodist Hospital joint conference, patient education, pension and benefits, pharmacy and therapeutics, priorities of laboratory testing, professional services review, public affairs, radiation control, research, research training and degree programs, respiratory therapy, resuscitation, Rochester State Hospital joint conference, scholarship, spinal cord injury, staff development, Saint Marys intensive care, Saint Marys joint conference, surgical, telecommunications, tissue, transfusion, trips, and utilization review.

We must recall that most of the members of these committees are Clinic doctors whose primary responsibility is patient care. They willingly supplement their responsibilities in medical practice, research, and education with these often complex administrative duties. The committee list is overwhelming. Perhaps it might be compared with the committee lists of the United States Senate or House of Representatives.

Extramural Practice

Extramural practice is the name for one of the many facets of the Clinic's long-standing Outreach Program. Here Mayo helps to provide medical care, services, and education beyond Rochester's corporate limits. This does not apply to patients coming directly to the Mayo Clinic. It deals entirely with patients in their home communities. Clinic staff members visit these areas and determine patient treatment in consultation with local non-Clinic physicians. Not only is patient care improved, but the regional doctors experience advanced medical education from the visiting staff members. Extramural practice extends to some seventeen towns or communities in Minnesota and eleven in nearby areas of South Dakota, Iowa, and Wisconsin.

While the names outreach program and extramural practice are new, such activities have a long history. William Worrall Mayo, his two sons, and their associates traveled considerably to care for the sick outside Rochester. The newly named organization sought to be similarly cooperative with and supplementary to area physicians and organizations, with a renewed emphasis on regional cooperation.

Dr. Eugene Mayberry felt that Mayo's outreach programs not only provided good medical care in the area, but also that they may "possibly provide models that will help demonstrate how regional relations with major medical centers can improve access to medicine in rural areas and smaller communities." In other words, this Mayo program might well serve as a model for similar activities elsewhere in the country.

These visits by Mayo staff members are supplemented with further regional services. The Mayo Regional Laboratory Service provides help to small area hospitals in pathology work. It supplies several out-of-town organizations with complete pathology service, laboratory management, laboratory quality control, and continuing medical education programs. On its tenth anniversary in 1981, the regional laboratory at Mayo was receiving, per year, more than 362,000 tissue specimens for microscopic analysis and diagnosis. Note again that this refers not to Mayo Clinic patients but to people who may never have visited Rochester.

The department of diagnostic radiology provides complete coverage to some hospitals. All this supplements the visits of Mayo consultants not only in the major fields of internal medicine and surgery but also in neurology, oral surgery, psychiatry and psychology, audiology, physical medicine, and obstetrics and gynecology, aiding communities needing Mayo's help.

For a long time Mayo has also cooperated with the state of Minnesota in providing consultation for crippled children through the state's crippled children's clinics, in which activity Mayo consultants in pediatrics, physical medicine, otolaryngology, cardiovascular disease, and orthopedics have participated.

A unique and almost unbelievable outreach project pertaining to detection of high blood pressure was undertaken by Mayo's health care studies unit in the belief that public education can lower blood pressure. A squadron of housewives, armed with notebooks and blood pressure cuffs, made a house-to-house search for high blood pressure in the three nearby towns of Wabasha, Spring Valley, and Owatonna. Their mission was to identify everyone in the towns with high blood pressure, to inform them of the dangers of this disease, and to persuade them to see a doctor for treatment. In the initial screening, 6,900 adults were found to have high blood pressure. Follow-up studies led to the conclusion that community programs can be developed that have a significant beneficial effect on hypertension.

Another Clinic outreach activity was establishing (in 1976) the Mayo Regional Pulmonary Function Program. Pulmonary function tests provide information on lung conditions by measurements that include the volume of gas in the lungs, the rate at which air moves into or out of the lungs, and how uniformly the gas is distributed within the lungs. The tests tell much about how well or poorly the patient's respiratory activities are carried out.

Proper measurements of these lung activities are carried out in hospitals not too far away from Rochester by local technicians who have been trained at Mayo to properly employ the complicated machinery involved. Electrical signals from the local equipment are transmitted to the Mayo laboratory by a telephone system. Here computers process the signals and display the results to Mayo on a cathode-ray tube terminal.

By these means the important lung activity findings are revealed to Clinic experts almost as if the patient were being observed in Rochester. Results of the tests and their interpretation by a Mayo consultant in thoracic disease are immediately transmitted to the distant local physician. All this saves a good deal of money for regional hospitals that might not be able to install the total necessary equipment. At a considerably reduced cost, this procedure renders a service locally equal to that provided at the Clinic. As in an ordinary telephone conversation, miles of space separating the conversants are erased.

Area Medicine

The international fame of the Clinic and its devotion to the care of the sick from wherever in the country or the world they might come has not changed the Clinic's devotion to its home in southeast Minesota. The two Mayo brothers loved their home community and expended constant efforts to make it a better place in which to live and work. To all in this area they displayed friendliness, kindness, helpfulness, and loyalty. This philosophy has continued through a century of the practice of medicine and in the unbelievable growth and multitude of medical activities of the Clinic. The Clinic rates highly its special devotion to people in the home area. The programs of area medicine and community medicine attest to this.

The division of area medicine is housed in a large area on the Mayo Building's twelfth floor and is devoted to patients who come from the surrounding area of Minnesota and Iowa, excluding Rochester itself. A decided advantage in this arrangement is that there is a shorter waiting period for appointments of regional patients, being about six weeks instead of four months. Again, acute emergencies are managed with much less waiting. Patients from Rochester itself or Olmsted County are seen at the Clinic's Baldwin unit, which will be described shortly.

Another activity in Mayo's area medicine or outreach program was the Mayo electrocardiographic service. Electrocardiograms record the nature and abnormalities of a patient's heartbeat. An out-of-city hospital has a mobile cart containing apparatus to transmit electrocardiograms to Mayo laboratories. A technician places electrodes on the patient and dials a telephone number that transmits the electrical emissions of the patient's heart directly to Mayo's ECG laboratory, which contains a computer so programmed that it can interpret the ECG recording. This computer's interpretation—or diagnosis, in part—is transmitted back to the hospital where the patient lies. But first a Clinic physician examines the tracing and verifies the accuracy and completeness of the interpretation before it is transmitted to the sender.

Olmsted Community Hospital

Olmsted Community Hospital is not a Mayo Clinic unit. Located not far from the Clinic, it was established in 1955 primarily to care for patients living in Rochester and nearby. Some twenty years later there were eleven thousand patients treated annually under the supervision of some twenty-eight doctors who make up the Olmsted Medical Group. Again, this group was not a part of the Mayo staff. This was by no means considered an enterprise competing with Mayo. It was rather considered a partner, providing facilities often not readily available in the overcrowded Saint Marys and Methodist hospitals.

A. M. Keith, a prominent Rochester attorney and former lieutenant governor of Minnesota, stated, "Rochester needs a . . . family care facility. It gives an alternative to the Clinic . . . And I think it's healthy for the Clinic and for the community . . . and I think Mayo thinks so too."

The Clinic's Dr. Mayberry agreed, stating that it was important that the Olmsted Community Hospital provides "citizens of this area a first-rate hospital which offers them a choice in their medical care."

In fact, Mayo staff member Dr. W. F. Braasch was chairman of the committee that helped create the hospital in the early 1950s. Over the years Mayo has provided many consultation services to Olmsted Community Hospital patients. Eventually, Mayo provided all laboratory services for the hospital and for the Olmsted Medical Group. An extensive renovation of the hospital was completed in 1981 at a cost to Olmsted County of more than one million dollars. This venture was also strongly supported by the Mayo Clinic.

Community Child Care

One of the Mayo Clinic's first enterprises in community medicine dates back to 1944 when Dr. C. Anderson Aldrich came to Rochester to direct the Rochester Child Health Institute. Aldrich had carried out extensive observations on child development from infancy in the Chicago area. His wife said, "Andy has a genius for little babies." His interest at Mayo soon spread to the development of somewhat older, school-aged children. The purpose of the Clinic's institute was to watch over the health and emotional development of Rochester children from birth on, in attempts to understand physical, mental, and emotional growth.

Infant welfare clinics in the country had long been in existence, starting as mere feeding stations and then developing other concerns, such as how a child develops basic habits and makes adjustments to the social order. What constitutes normal growth and development? Aldrich favored observing and treating the whole body rather than its individual parts such as lung or stomach or kidneys. He established a complicated system of recording the numerous aspects of child development for individual babies in the Rochester area. This program of child care for an entire community was the first of its kind ever attempted in the country.

Involved in the project were not only pediatricians but also psychiatrists and obstetricians as well as the Rochester City Department of Health and school nurses. Aldrich authored several books, such as *Cultivating a Child's Appetite* and *Babies Are Human Beings.* By the time of his arrival at Rochester he had published some sixty-six articles on the prevention and treatment of child illness. While at Mayo he added fifty-seven more.

There was extensive national and international interest in this project on the part of physicians and investigators of child health. In one year alone (1979), besides multitudes of American visitors, there were

967 people from outside the United States who visited the Rochester Child Health Institute. Its work was cited with approval by the World Health Organization, which stated that "such work as the Rochester Child Health Institute is carrying on and the recomendation for its development elsewhere would be a fitting subject for action by the World Health Organization." Northwestern University conferred on Aldrich a merit award in recognition of his tremendous contributions to the understanding of growth and development in children, especially as regards mental and emotional aspects. Perhaps the greatest national recognition of his achievements was when he became the recipient of the Lasker Award, given by the National Committee for Mental Hygiene for "outstanding contributions to the education of physicians in the psychological aspects of the practice of medicine."

The Rochester Child Health Institute as such ceased as a distinct and separate unit soon after Aldrich's too-early death from cancer after serving only five years in Rochester. But numerous aspects of his tremendous achievements have continued and grown without the institute's name. There lives on Aldrich's spirit of devotion "to the children now growing up . . . who will be . . . the leaders of the future."

The neonatal intensive care unit at Saint Marys was devoted to the care of newly born infants with serious defects. The most common problem seen was premature births. Most of the newborns seen weighed less than 2,500 grams (5.5 lbs.). The smallest survivor (by 1975) weighed 800 grams (1.9 lbs.), and the smallest nonsurvivor weighed but 500 grams (1.1 lbs.).

Aside from prematurity, the biggest single diagnosis was respiratory distress in which the child's lungs were not well enough developed to breathe without a great deal of extraordinary effort. Other disorders included viral infections, blood problems, and hereditary abnormalities.

About half the babies seen came from seven hospitals located outside Rochester in a ninety- to one-hundred-mile radius in southeastern Minnesota and northeastern Iowa. Seriously ill infants were brought to Saint Marys from this radius in a special transporter device that is really a small box warmer with attached respiratory and monitoring equipment. In addition to serving the patient care needs for the region, Clinic staff and Saint Marys nurses conducted outreach educational programs for the seven hospitals served.

Mayo pediatrician Dr. Fredric Kleinberg was moved to venture that "the feeling of getting a desperately sick baby through in good shape and returning it to a grateful mother is just about the biggest high there is in medicine."

For a time, Mayo conducted the well child clinic and the children's health service. The first of these two provided routine examinations and innoculations for healthy children from birth through age four and offered consultations with parents. The children's health service cared for ill children up through age fourteen. In due time (1973) these two services were combined into the community pediatric service to meet the needs of area children. Of this, the head of the Clinic's section of pediatrics, Dr. Gunnar Stickler, said, "Specialists will be available to see well and sick children and to counsel families in matters of child care from birth through adolescence." An emergency care service was maintained to meet the needs of children developing serious illness after regular clinic hours or on weekends or holidays.

In addition to providing primary medical care to children, this service also taught community pediatric medicine to residents, interns, medical students, and pediatric nurse associates, registered nurses with special training in child care.

Eventually these various activities were centralized in the new community health center building which came to bear the name Baldwin Building, which is described a bit later in this volume. Here pediatric specialists provided comprehensive health care to children and adolescents in the Rochester area and surrounding communities. These services included newborn care, regular examinations and immunizations for healthy children, care for children and adolescents with acute or chronic illnesses, and counseling for problems relating to growth and development and adjustment to life's problems.

Education of Patients

Besides being treated for their ailments, patients must be taught about the nature and control of their condition, especially when the disease is serious and chronic. Much more is needed here than conversations between physician and patient. Specific courses of instruction have been developed. These cover not only a number of areas related to cancer and cancer detection in some body areas, such as the breast in women. There are organized patient education programs, which family members are encouraged to attend with the patient. These courses include instruction concerning asthma, heart failure, blood clotting, alcohol dependency, stomach ulcers, smoking, and a good deal more. There are a dozen regularly listed courses scheduled throughout each week. Instruction in some additional six areas is by appointment. Per month more than six hundred individuals attend one or more of the educational sessions of this school devoted to health education.

It was felt to be important for patients to understand as fully as possi-

The Harwick Building in 1979.

Saint Marys Hospital viewed from the northeast.

Saint Marys Hospital viewed from the west, showing the Mary Brigh unit of 1980.

Assisi Heights.

The new Rochester Methodist Hospital (1966).

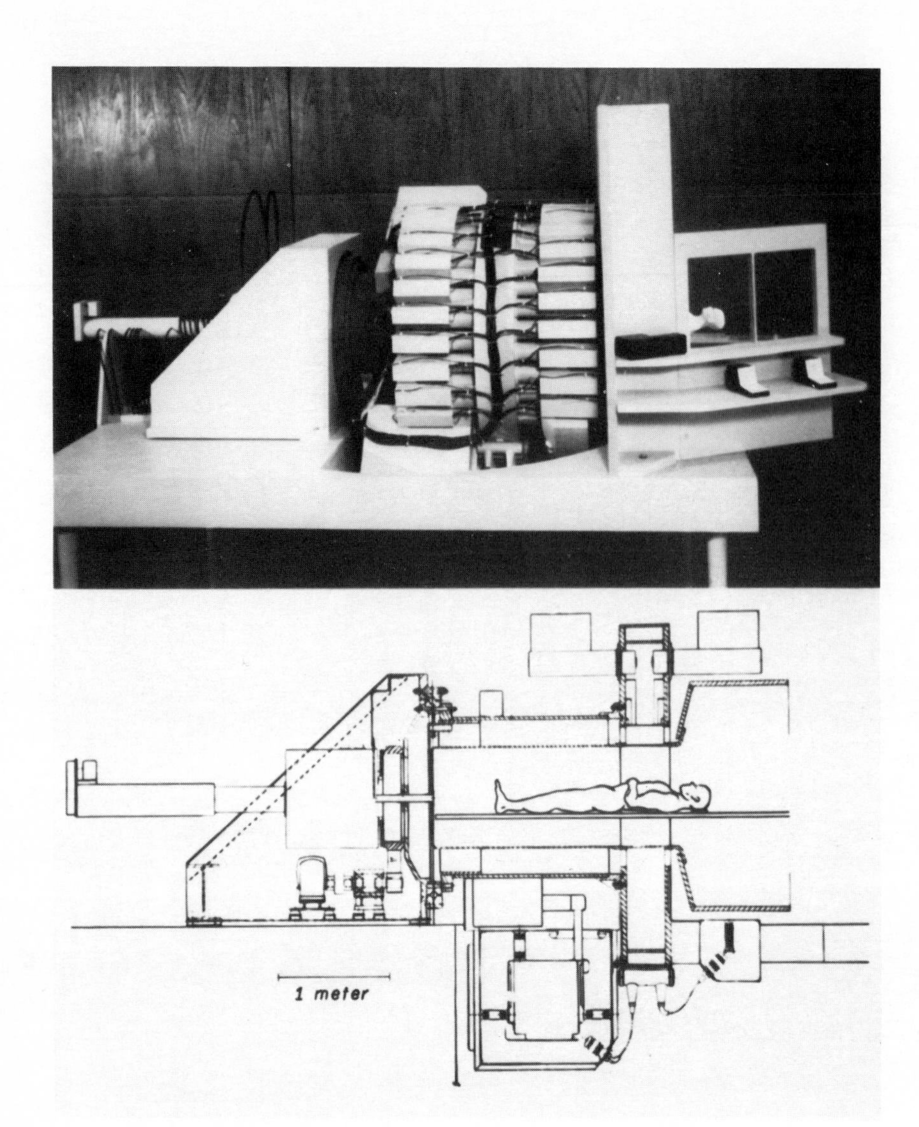

Dynamic spatial reconstructor.

The Community Health Center–Baldwin Building (1979).

An overall view of Clinic facilities, shown in light shade; included are the Rochester Methodist Hospital and Colonial Building.

Mirror to Man.

A Rochester park.

A Mayo Clinic park.

Gardens at Mayo Clinic (*above and opposite page*).

The park at Saint Marys Hospital.

ble the principles and procedures for managing their disease, since ultimately they must assume a predominant share of this responsibility on returning to their homes after the Clinic visit.

Involved in the program is a pretest to ascertain the patient's knowledge of the subject before beginning the class, followed by a classroom session taught by a trained patient educator. There are follow-up questionnaires to determine what the patient has retained and to what extent the acquired knowledge is being applied.

The program enables patients to understand so much better what the doctor has been telling them and gets them more involved in their own treatment. Registered nurses are active in these teaching activities, which frees some of the time of the Clinic's practicing physicians.

Dr. Bruce Douglass is the director of the section of patient and health education, or should we call him dean of this school? He said,

> We see health education of patients as an extension of the clinical practice of medicine. Treatment of disease, health maintenance, and health restoration all work to the same goals: to reduce morbidity, to prolong life and to improve the quality of life. Patients who graduate from these classes take better care of themselves than other patients, have fewer hospitalizations in the future and fewer visits back to the doctor.

Family Practice

Additional extensions of the outreach program are the family practice enterprises in the nearby towns of Kasson and Zumbrota. In each of these is a modest unit of the Mayo Clinic. Patients here carry Mayo Clinic registration numbers even though they may never visit Rochester. Each of these facilities is headed by three Mayo Clinic staff members who were engaged for this specific assignment. They work and live in Kasson or in Zumbrota. These units are as much a part of the Mayo Clinic as are the multiple sections in Rochester's Mayo Building.

The Kasson Health Facility was housed in a new building financed by the city of Kasson with assistance from the Clinic. Here were provided both acute and preventive medical care, laboratory and x-ray facilities, and nineteen examination and treatment rooms. There was also a special telephone link with the Clinic to provide immediate interpretations of electrocardiograms made in Kasson. In 1980, the patient visits there numbered 12,400.

The project at Zumbrota was similar to that of Kasson, and it met the needs of 9,300 patients in 1980. Representatives of Mayo and of the Zumbrota Hospital Board worked together to define the objectives of the project, among which were to provide primary care for Zumbrota area inhabitants close to where they live with easy access to specialized care, to recruit family physicians to enter practice in Zumbrota, and to provide opportunities for Mayo's undergraduate, graduate, and continuing medical education programs.

A member of the Rochester Methodist Hospital staff managed the Zumbrota Community Hospital. A diagnostic radiologist from Mayo visited the hospital weekly to provide consultative services and the Mayo Regional Laboratory Service provided coverage for laboratory procedures.

We might look on these ventures in small-town practice as completing a full century-long cycle commencing with William Worrall Mayo's family practice in the small town of Rochester. The total patient visits to these two clinics per year approximately equaled the numbers seen in Rochester in a month.

We must always remember that in the eyes of Mayo caring for patients cannot be separated from medical education. Mayo medical students may spend time at the Kasson and Zumbrota facilities. Also, work there became part of the Clinic's graduate educational program in family medicine. Unlike the Mayo staff members operating these outreach clinics, the residents continued to reside in Rochester, traveling daily to the towns. Such training in family practice was most attractive to the medical students planning eventually to carry out practice in small communities. Some twenty percent of Mayo Medical School students planned a family practice career for themselves, numbers of which were appointed to the Clinic's residency program in this field, which has become a recognized specialty in this country with the establishment of the American Board of Family Practice. Mayo's family practice residency program includes work mainly in internal medicine, surgery, pediatrics, and obstetrics but also includes work in other areas such as dermatology, psychiatry, and ear, nose, and throat. In 1981 there were twelve Clinic residents in this field.

There was also an affiliation with Saint Francis Hospital in La Crosse, Wisconsin. Mayo Graduate School residents spent much of their three-year training period in family practice at that institution, but under close Mayo supervision.

While the Kasson and Zumbrota and La Crosse projects were important in Mayo's education programs, they were but supplements to work carried out at Rochester's family practice enterprise in the new Baldwin Building. Dr. Guy W. Daugherty was an important leader in the development of these family practice projects. Well met were the outreach goals of providing needed services to area doctors and patients, evaluating the quality of medical care in small towns, developing procedures that might decrease the cost of medical care, and assisting in educational programs in family medicine. In Dr. Daugherty's view, "We have to take steps to repopulate this area with family physicians."

Community Health Center—Baldwin Building

We have seen that a century of devotion to the health and medical needs of the broad world, today and tomorrow, has never lessened the Mayo devotion to its home community. The needs of regional patients for Clinic help increased tremendously over the years with the population increase, along with a decrease in the number of family care physicians in the general area.

Over the years, while all the facilities of the Clinic were available to Rochester patients, there were several services specifically designed to care for their needs. The acute illness service provided care for adult Rochester patients with sudden illness requiring prompt medical attention. The children's health service and the well child clinic provided ample service for local pediatrics patients. In one year alone (1969) local patient registrations numbered over sixty thousand. These were first seen not only in the special sections for Rochester patients, but elsewhere in the Clinic as well. Much of the responsibility for local patients rested on the shoulders of Dr. L. A. Smith.

Further progress eventuated. The division of community medicine was formed (in 1974) under the direction of Dr. George W. Morrow to care for Rochester and Olmsted County area residents of all ages. Included in this organization were sections of internal medicine, of pediatrics, and of obstetrics and gynecology. Most of the Clinic's obstetrical patients were local area residents. Here was provided not only patient care but also support for the training programs. The health care research unit was also involved, dealing with evaluation of health care.

Dr. Morrow ventured the opinion that "this is a strong consensus move; a carefully thought out, much discussed systematic approach to the development of a health care service; . . . many individuals, departments and institutional committees, over a period of several years, have taken part in the decision and early plans to establish an expanded primary care facility in Rochester."

It became apparent almost at once that the facilities for the division of community medicine in the Mayo Building were entirely inadequate. A new building was essential, devoted entirely to the project of providing health care for all area residents, young and old. For this, the Mayo Clinic Board of Governors selected the Mayo-owned area just west across the street from the Harwick Building, and estimated the cost to be six to eight million dollars. A number of buildings at this location were demolished.

Dr. Morrow stated, "A major reason for moving community Medicine outside the Mayo Building is the need for a distinct facility which will be easily identified by Olmsted County patients as a Mayo Clinic source for providing medical care." It was also decided that there should be capabilities for obtaining x-rays and electrocardiograms and collecting blood and urine specimens, plus an adequate on-site parking structure. Dr. Morrow also voiced the philosophy that "we do not perceive the move as changing our mode of practice. The new facility will be designed primarily to offer added efficiency and greater convenience to the patient while at the same time maintaining Mayo Clinic standards for health care." The need for all this was accentuated by the fact that in 1978 there were more than eighty thousand visits to the Clinic by Rochester area patients.

All this came to pass in 1979 in the stone "five-story" community medicine building, with but three of the floors above ground. True to Mayo tradition, its architectural style was definitely different from any other medical edifice in Rochester. But it was like all others in its adaptability to the best in medical care as well as being so structured as to permit future upward expansion. Dr. Morrow tells it best: "A patient will be able to drive into the parking ramp, or be let off at the main entrance, and walk into the subway level or main floor of the building. From there the patient can go to the appropriate medical area—acute illness and obstetrics on the main floor, internal medicine on the second, pediatrics on the third.

"The x-ray and ECG test areas are both on the subway level. Here a patient requiring a chest x-ray and ECG need undress only once for the performance of both tests. If additional studies are needed, he or she can walk through the subway to the appropriate testing area in one of the adjacent buildings."

The pediatric services offered here include newborn care, regular examinations and immunizations for healthy children, care for children and adolescents with acute and many chronic illnesses, as well as counseling for developmental and adjustment problems. In obstetrics and gynecology, there is provided complete prenatal and postpartum care in either routine or complicated pregnancies.

Besides providing clinical care of patients, the new facilities also were a base for educational programs of Clinic residents and medical students following studies of community medicine, and there was also the Rochester project, devoted to research on the incidence and control of various diseases observed in local patients over some decades. We never find a breakdown of the traditional Mayo triad: patient care, medical education, and scientific research.

The community medicine building was named the Baldwin Building on receipt in 1979 of a gift of five million dollars from Jesse A. Baldwin, head of the J. A. Baldwin Manufacturing Company of Kearney, Nebraska.

This firm manufactured and dealt in various automobile parts. Baldwin was particularly adept at inventing and perfecting a tremendous number and variety of filters used in cars, such as lubricant, air, fuel, hydraulic, and cooling filters. His business ventures and financial status were marked by precipitous ups and downs. On his first visit to Mayo as a patient in 1933, he was in one of the down periods. Leaving here, he was able to pay the six-dollar-a-day hospital charge but was unable to pay his Clinic bill. He was told not to worry about the Clinic bill, "Just pay when you can." Forty-six years later, after numerous Clinic visits for checkups, he paid when he could—with five million dollars.

The dedication of the Baldwin Building was considered to be "certainly a very glad day for Mayo people and the Mayo organization . . . ," according to administrator Robert Roesler. It was considered a supreme example of the human habit of caring for his nextdoor neighbors. At the ceremony, Mrs. Baldwin stated that money given to Mayo could never replace the "many kindnesses which we have experienced at this very special place."

General Service

What group within the Clinic complex most directly influences the public's impression of the institution, other than the medical staff? In reply, one might answer, the general service section. Its staff of more than seventy considered themselves goodwill ambassadors who share major responsibility for creating and maintaining the Clinic's image to patients, visitors, and fellow employees alike.

It was felt that public relations was a primary function. General service employees fostered this end through the excellent performance of their multiple functions. The variety and number of the jobs performed is staggering. General service personnel are responsible for escorting wheelchair patients to and from appointments, providing information to patients and visitors, conducting Clinic tours, providing transportation for employees and guests, updating the lobby weather map, staffing various reception desks, operating the Clinic's parking ramp, and the list could go on and on.

Statistically, about three hundred thousand calls are received annually (that's twelve hundred daily) at the general service dispatch desk, nerve center for all general service activities. Over fifty thousand of these calls are requests for wheelchair service. Many of the rest are for routine and miscellaneous services, such as the pickup and delivery of emergency lab specimens, biopsies, patient histories, and mail.

Almost all job descriptions for general service positions require that the employee be "neat appearing, speak clearly, and be friendly and tactful in dealing with others." He must seek to "establish and maintain a pleasant, helpful relationship with the patient and visitor."

The overall attitude held by general service personnel was well expressed by an elevator starter in the Mayo Building. "I consider myself to be a goodwill ambassador." At first glance it appears that her job consisted mainly of helping patients into elevators and giving directions. "But it is so much more. I reassure patients that are frightened, and many are. I take children with chickenpox or people with claustrophobia [fear of being in closed rooms] nonstop to their floor." Janalee Holt felt that "a smile, a pat on the arm or an additional kind word can go a long way in reassuring patients that we care." Her courteous attitude has not gone unrecognized: she was recently awarded the Rochester Chamber of Commerce Courtesy Award.

Employees in general were told, "By all means, avoid thinking of patients in terms of 'cases' or registration numbers. They are individual human beings who need your help." Indeed, it may be said in general that the Mayo physician does not treat the illness of a patient. He treats a patient with an illness.

General service is also responsible for the shuttlebus service, transporting Clinic medical and paramedical personnel between the Mayo Building and Saint Marys Hospital, with stops also at several laboratories to pick up and deliver patient histories, blood and urine samples, x-rays, and more. Each day some sixty such trips are made, transporting about six hundred passengers. All of these are Clinic people, not patients.

Defective Blood Clotting

Hemophilia is a condition in which the blood fails to clot properly when needed. It is a familial hereditary disease affecting males. It is transmitted to them by the maternal parent, who carries defective recessive hereditary genes that do not affect her. But the chances of a son inheriting the abnormal gene and becoming a hemophiliac are about fifty-fifty. In this condition, much more is involved than the failure of clotting after physical injuries causing external bleeding. Very minor bumps or bruises may cause blood to seep into muscles or into joints, causing arthritis. Fortunately, it is a relatively rare disease, with only about one in ten thousand males suffering from its severe form. At Mayo, some one hundred new and returning hemophiliacs are seen annually.

The defect has been known for centuries. Occasionally it has played a part in world history. The former royal house of Spain was affected. The last czarevitch of Russia was a victim. Reports have it that much of

Rasputin's evil influence on the empress and emperor were due to his alleged healing influence on the young czarevitch's hemophiliac condition.

Studies at Mayo and elsewhere have revealed that there is no deficiency of the various major long-known elements involved in normal blood clotting, such as calcium, fibrinogen, prothrombin, or the number of blood platelets. But in hemophilia, the blood platelets fail to disintegrate properly when bleeding occurs. The various blood clotting ingredients fail to react together to produce a blood clot.

Mayo physicians have done research on hemophilia and treated patients at the Clinic for many years. Initially, whole blood or plasma transfusions from normal donors were found to be effective. Precipitates and later concentrates from normal blood plasma were developed to be used. Ultimately (1978) there was established the Mayo Comprehensive Hemophilia Center under the direction of Dr. Gerald Gilchrist. Here young hemophiliacs and their parents are taught to carry on treatment at home. At the center they learn how to inject the corrective chemical intravenously. Such injections may be needed about once a week. More commonly, patients have injections only when they have experienced some physical trauma, with or without external bleeding.

This complicated corrective chemical, antihemophiliac globulin (AHG), restores the blood clotting machinery to normal. It can be stored in a refrigerator at the patient's home or can even be carried about by the same patient for use if needed. And what might this substance be? It is a protein present in normal blood. In hemophiliacs it may be deficient in quantity or in effectiveness of operation. The compound may be extracted from blood in a blood bank, such as that at Mayo. There are also commercial preparations prepared by drug firms. But these are extremely expensive, so that most patients are instructed to use them only on injury, however minor, whether or not visible bleeding occurs.

The program of the center made unnecessary the often prolonged hospital treatment employed for hemophiliacs in former days. For reasons of distance, inconvenience, ignorance, and money, victims did not always seek care until a joint was swollen with blood. Such neglect often ended in crippling arthritis.

The treatment has been sufficiently successful so that a patient developing a serious ailment unrelated to hemophilia might safely be subjected even to complicated surgery. One of the first of these at Mayo was actually an open-heart operation to repair a complicated cardiac defect. Surgery of almost any kind would be dangerous or even impossible in an untreated hemophiliac.

Here again, the Clinic's outreach is involved. Area family physicians are trained to serve patients and families who are carrying out the home treatment they have been taught. In this there is collaboration again with the University of Minnesota, and at the Clinic the Comprehensive Hemophilia Center relies on help from hematologists, orthopedic surgeons, geneticists, oral surgeons, coagulation laboratory technicians, and more.

Let us examine two extremes in hemophilia. Walter is a severe hemophiliac. His blood lacks a factor that causes clots to form. So when he is injured, even without obvious injury, blood seeps into injured tissue until pressure from the accumulating blood stops the flow.

Walter, like all hemophiliacs, has had the disease since birth. Today, at thirty-five, he has arthritis in all his major joints as a result of numerous bleeding incidents over the years. He has had one of his hip joints replaced and needs a similar operation on his knee. He has never held a steady job because of his disease and has not married for fear of passing it on to another generation. Hemophilia has made a nightmare of his life.

Tommy, twelve, also has severe hemophilia. But you wouldn't know it from the way he acts. He rides a bike, plays softball, hikes and camps, and is active in school activities. If he bumps himself and sees or feels bleeding begin, he finds a quiet corner and infuses the clotting agent into his veins to stop the bleeding. After a few moments rest, he is off and running again. The aim of Mayo's Comprehensive Hemophilia Center is to reduce the number of Walters that might be and to multiply the Tommys.

One is tempted to ponder a bit on the word *hemophilia*. Although the condition has been known for centuries, the specific name was first used in 1828 by Professor Johann Schoenlein of Wurzburg, Germany. The most literal translation of the Greek units in the term would be "love of blood," which seems a bit out of order. It has been suggested that *philia* be translated as "a tendency toward" instead of "love" and that *hemo* be considered "bleeding" instead of "blood." This makes sense, so we have "tendency toward bleeding" instead of "love of blood."

Hypertension

High blood pressure kills many more people than any other disease. Here the arteries become thick-walled, rigid, and narrowed. About one out of every seven Americans has hypertension. It is probable that high blood pressure is the single most common disease process seen by the practicing physician. Yet one half of the people who have the condition do not know so, for they do not yet have symptoms, and only about one fourth of all hypertensives are under treatment.

The most serious complications in this condition are enlargement of the heart, heart attacks or failures, stroke, and kidney failure. These result from a great narrowing of the blood vessels, which retards blood flow to organs, bursting of the diseased vessels, or overwork by the heart in trying to pump blood through the narrowed vessels.

Treatment is partially dietary, especially avoiding salt or foods with a high salt content, such as pork, bacon, ketchup, dill pickles, and ham, or foods high in cholesterol content. Various therapeutic medicines have also been developed. But since the symptoms may be minimal or absent early in the condition, multitudes of people with elevated blood pressure deny themselves the necessary therapy.

The Mayo Clinic sees about eleven thousand hypertension patients each year. Mayo's outreach program became involved in blood pressure screening and treatment projects in several separate geographic areas near Rochester. Here the Clinic cooperates with physicians and other health care professionals in the areas. The aim is always detection, starting a treatment program and trying to make sure the patients remain in treatment. Hypertension technicians also work on these problems with patients in their own homes.

In all these efforts it was found that although people became well versed about high blood pressure, many lacked any fear of the disease, and frequently local examining physicians failed to inform their patients properly. According to the former Mayo Dr. James Hunt, "Having a doctor tell you that your blood pressure is a little high but nothing to worry about is like having a doctor tell a woman she's only a little pregnant and there's nothing to be concerned about."

Heart Attacks

Suppose a person walking the streets of Rochester is prostrated with a heart attack. Someone calls a Clinic ambulance, which may arrive within four minutes, providing immediate assistance to the victim. But during those very few minutes proper procedures performed by laymen can save many lives. Cardiopulmonary resuscitation by a bystander is needed. The first minute after the heart attack is most critical. Mayo embarked on a training of laymen to meet these needs in 1976. The Clinic's resuscitation committee offered six-hour courses to the nonmedical personnel of the Clinic and its hospitals and to Rochester people in general. The Clinic's Dr. Roger D. White stated that "our goal is to have a person in every section of the Clinic trained in cardiopulmonary resuscitation." In the year 1978 there were 498 persons attending this course, and in one session alone in 1981 there were 229 Rochester area residents participating. Laymen adequately trained are certified as competent by the Clinic. For those so certified it was recommended that they attend refresher sessions every six months.

Similar education became nationwide, partly through the efforts of Dr. White, operating through the American Heart Association as well as the Minnesota Heart Association.

And just what is taught to these students? What should one do on finding a person whose heartbeat and breathing have just ceased, and who would therefore seem to be dead? Basic life support must be carried out. This consists of administering mouth-to-mouth artificial respiration, after making certain that saliva is not blocking the air passages. Simultaneously, properly administered periodic pressure on the sternum compresses the underlying heart, causing movement of blood almost as if the heart itself were beating. So the victim's stopped heart and respiration are replaced by the activities of the resuscitator. One well-trained person can carry out both these functions, but it is better if two are on hand: one for respiration and one for heartbeat.

When the ambulance arrives, its team gives the victim advanced life support. The heart is made to beat by properly administering electric stimuli and breathing is done by use of a mask and a bag of air. Medications may also be employed. In the ambulance and in the hospital these procedures are carried out for about an hour, if necessary. If by this time the person's heart and breathing have not commenced functioning, the patient may be pronounced dead.

A study in Seattle revealed that forty-three percent of cardiac victims who were given cardiopulmonary resuscitation (CPR) within a minute after the attack survived. Only twenty-one percent survived whose first help was from the ambulance team arriving a few minutes later. Mayo's experience is essentially in accord with these statistics. And in Rochester's relatively small community, how often does this occur? About one such patient a week arrives at Saint Marys Hospital. Nearly a third of these have had the basic life support treatment within one or two minutes after the victim's collapse. The chance of survival is about twice that of victims with no CPR before ambulance arrival.

This lifesaving CPR procedure by laymen on the street or perhaps by Clinic employees is sometimes viewed with doubt by local people who may feel that training for this should be unnecessary in a city like Rochester, with its elaborate facilities for meeting any medical emergency. But a properly employed minute or two may be lifesaving. Dr. Roger White, medical director of the Mayo cardiac life support program insists that "it is the first minute that counts."

The hospital treatment of heart disease patients by cardiologists has been often supplemented with psychiatric participation. Compounded with the patient's knowledge that he has had a cardiac attack might also be his lack of understanding of the condition, fear of the outcome, anxiety, insecurity, and more. All this apprehension may dwell likewise in the minds of the patient's family, especially the spouse. It appeared essential that psychiatrists should collaborate here with cardiologists. This was done in Saint Marys coronary care unit, holding daily meetings, chaired by a Mayo psychiatrist and aimed at identifying and meeting the emotional as well as the physical needs of each patient. Rehabilitation was a prominent word. The aims and efforts in this program included (a) conveying complete information to the patient concerning the medical problem; (b) working with the patient's spouse to meet his or her emotional needs and to include the spouse in the rehabilitative program; (c) counteracting unnecessary anxiety; (d) preparing the patient to leave the hospital; to assist in this there is a library of videocassette programs about various aspects of heart attacks to be viewed by patients; (e) identifying for the patient some of the possible future risk factors, such as smoking, dietary problems, obesity, use of alcohol, and exercise habits; and (f) working with spouses and other relatives in order to meet their immediate psychological needs and to help them aid in the rehabilitation of the patient.

Involved in this program were psychiatrist, cardiologist, physical therapist, occupational therapist, dietitian, and nurses.

This rehabilitation program took a tremendous load from the cardiologist's shoulders by allowing him to concentrate on the medical aspects of the problem while other trained professionals took care of the vital rehabilitative aspects of the patient and his family.

Intensive Psychotherapy Center

As an example of the multiple types of facilities available for Clinic functions, there is the stately Georgian mansion located about halfway between the Mayo Building and Saint Marys Hospital. This structure in a general residential area in no way resembles a medical building. It served for a long time as the headquarters of the Mayo Clinic Women's Club, which eventually abandoned the house. Dr. Richard Steinhilber considered it an ideal location for the Mayo Intensive Psychotherapy Center (IPC), which came to pass.

And what happens in the IPC? Here is a unique setting in a homelike, warm atmosphere for the treatment of such psychiatric patients as promise to improve when treated at least partially, under group therapy.

These patients are not intensively ill psychiatrically, but they display one or another of troublesome difficulties such as undue worrying, depressions, anxiety states, tension headaches, marital problems, and more.

The sessions for each patient last all day, five days per week for a three-week period. There are three groups of patients, with seven or eight in each group, so that at any one time the center provides for some twenty to twenty-five percent of all the Clinic's psychiatric patients undergoing treatment of one kind or another.

This day-long program is entirely outpatient, the participants residing elsewhere, with lunch provided at the center. In each of these small groups there is a mixture of ages and sex, and the members may have quite different psychiatric problems.

Let us join one of these groups. Twice a week we meet with a psychiatrist or psychotherapist. There are discussions of the various problems of the group members, conducted by the therapist but with participation by the group members, who are encouraged to take part. Each patient discusses his own problems with others of the group, and most important, all this is recorded on videotape. When the discussion session is ended, the videotape is replayed for the group on closed-circuit television, with further discussions usually led by a second therapist. Individual psychotherapy supplements this group activity.

The major assets of the center are three: the atmosphere of a house rather than a Clinic examining room, the employment of group therapy, and the use of videotapes and closed-circuit television. In general, patients seem pleased with the results. Extremely few leave the program before completion of the standard three weeks.

This entire program commenced in a modest way in the Colonial Building of Rochester Methodist Hospital as early as 1956, but reached its full fruition at the new center in the early 1970s, largely under the direction of psychiatrist Dr. Harold R. Martin. This development at Mayo has since been copied in a few other institutions in the country.

In all this, as in every Mayo therapeutic activity, there is participation by Mayo fellows and medical students learning about psychiatric problems and their management.

Dissolving Gallstones

Along with advances and expansion of surgery there are important efforts aimed at eliminating some surgical procedures. On the one hand, there are the relatively new complications of intracardiac surgery, kidney transplants, and even heart transplants. On the other hand, in some fields medical therapy has eliminated or at least reduced the necessity for surgery. Thyroid cancer may be treated by injecting radioactive iodine, which the gland absorbs, resulting in cancer cell destruction, and there are the many anticancer chemicals that combat the disease elsewhere in the body without surgery.

Another venture has been the effort to dissolve gallstones instead of removing them surgically. The challenge here is tremendous. It is estimated that about twenty million Americans have gallstones, with about a million new cases added every year. Although many of these are symptom-free, about a half million per year undergo surgery, costing millions of dollars. Why not investigate methods for dissolving gallstones?

Gallstones are usually small, smooth, pebblelike formations in the gallbladder, the pear-sized sac connected by tubes with the liver and intestine. This sac is a reservoir in which are stored bile acids produced by the liver and important in the digestion of fatty foods. These stones are composd chiefly of cholesterol. Why not seek a means to dissolve cholesterol?

Joining several other institutions in the country, Mayo was engaged in this effort as far back as 1968. Soon afterward, the Clinic published a report on a substance called chenodeoxycholic acid, or chenic acid for short. This was developed largely under the direction of Mayo's Dr. Johnson Thistle. The substance is a normal constitutent of bile. It dissolves gallstones. A cholesterol gallstone dropped into a vial of this acid dissolved in two days, and administering concentrated chenic acid by mouth also dissolved a patient's gallstones. This chemical has the property, when swallowed, of localizing itself in the gallbladder, where it does its work.

It was deemed necessary to demonstrate whether this medical approach to the treatment of gallstones was as effective and safe as surgical removal of the gallbladder with its contained stones. Much of this work continued at Mayo and elsewhere in the country under the auspices of the National Cooperative Gallstone Study. This was an eight million dollar venture, supported by a branch of the National Institutes of Health and conducted in some ten medical centers, including the Mayo Clinic. Chenic acid was found to be harmless when given to patients. The whole treatment process takes considerable time. The pills must sometimes be taken for a period of some two years to dissolve the gallstones.

It was learned that complete dissolving of gallstones occurred in fourteen percent of patients, and there was partial dissolving in another twenty-seven percent. When rather high dosages were employed, a considerably higher percentage of good results occurred. In any case, there was a saving of millions of dollars formerly spent every year on gallbladder surgery, and also important, this treatment procedure provided an alternative to surgery in patients with heart or lung disease, which makes any surgery dangerous. As is usually the case after research of this kind, the product developed is now prepared in great quantities by drug firms.

Thus far, this account refers to stones in the gallbladder itself. Occasionally a small stone may lodge in the bile duct, the narrow tube which normally transmits bile from the bladder or liver into the intestine. This may be so located as to block completely the entire flow of liver secretions and excretions. Such obstructing stones may sometimes be removed by surgery. But here again, Mayo has developed nonsurgical attacks on the problem. Why not try to dissolve stones located in the bile duct? The drug mono-actanoin was developed and studied. It, like chenic acid, can also dissolve gallstones. But unlike chenic acid, it is not effective when taken by mouth. It must be administered directly to the gallstone in the duct. How might this be done? At least three procedures were developed.

After gallbladder surgery for gallstones it is common to leave in the bile duct a tube which extends through the abdominal wall to the outside. Should a duct stone develop, mono-actanoin can be delivered through the tube to the exact site desired.

A common procedure is to insert a needle through the abdominal wall and into the bile duct where the stone lies. Manipulating the syringe needle is directed by x-rays revealing both the stone location and positions of the needle. When the two visions meet, the drug is administered.

The third device is somewhat more complicated and is still under experimental observation. There is a device, the duodenoscope, consisting in part of a flexible tube which can be inserted through the mouth, down the esophagus, and across the stomach into the duodenum. Remarkably, there is a lighting device in which the examiner can see exactly where the end of the tube is located. Furthermore, this tube end can be manipulated and directed by the operator. It can be inserted into the duodenal opening of the bile duct and projected to the location of the obstructing gallstone. At that point, the dissolving chemical can be administered on the stone.

The Eye

The most common defects of vision are corrected with eyeglasses. A useful substitute for this is the employment of soft contact lenses made of a plastic called polymacon. Such a lens is a little smaller than a dime. An individual can put it in place in front of the cornea. This use is particularly important for people active in such athletics as football or boxing, where wearing ordinary glasses is too dangerous. But the use of these lenses extends far beyond such people. At the Clinic many hundreds of patients have been fitted with this device at all ages, from eight months to eighty-five years, although the average age of contact wearers is fourteen to thirty-five years. These lenses must be removed nightly by the wearer and subjected to boiling water to ensure absolute cleanliness.

It must be emphasized that the major use of this device was initially not to correct serious eye defects or diseases. As a substitute for glasses, it has a cosmetic effect desired by many people. Two thirds of Mayo's recipients of these lenses are women, and the wearer can readily shift from contacts to conventional glasses as might be desired.

Besides such use, the soft contact lenses were found to be a therapeutic device in various eye diseases or following eye surgery. This lens will absorb various medications and deliver them into the eye over a prolonged period.

The development of this visual aid resulted from nationwide studies under the direction of the United States Food and Drug Administration. Working on this project, the Clinic's ophthalmologist Dr. John A. Dyer headed a team of six widely known ophthalmologists, each working independently in his own medical center. More than a thousand patients took part in a two-year testing period, including about 150 at Mayo, many of whom were Clinic employees.

Dr. Dyer stated, "We found the lens to be comfortable and safe to wear, that vision was in general perfectly adequate and that there were no harmful effects to the eyes."

The anterior surface of the eye, or cornea, may lose its transparency and become more or less opaque from accident scars or from a variety of ailments, resulting in keratitis, or inflammation of the cornea. When this occurs in front of the eye's pupil, there is blindness in that eye. The only way such a visual defect may be corrected is by surgically removing the scarred piece of cornea and replacing it with a corneal transplant. The source of such a transplant is the cornea of a cadaver, such as a dead Mayo patient. Or the donor may be an accident victim with various body parts, including the eyes, being in good state. Such transplants are made using microsurgery in which the operator views the area involved via a microscope at the operating table, employing sutures about as thick as a human hair.

Because the absence of blood vessels causes the cornea to heal slowly, patients must return to Mayo for periodic checkups for about a year. Half of the stitches are removed two months after surgery and the other half after a year. Three months after transplantation, patients can be fitted for glasses or contact lenses.

Here again the Clinic figures involved are astonishing. This is not from their magnitude but from their small totals. Only about one or two such corneal transplant operations are performed per week.

Then there are cataracts. This condition consists of clouding and opacity developing in the eye lens, resulting frequently in blindness of the affected eye. The most common form of this condition occurs in the aging process—senile cataract. Removal of the opaque lens restores vision but leaves the eye without focusing power. This could be partially corrected with thick glasses or contact lenses. A process better than this was developed for implanting an artificial lens into the eye after removing the defective lens. The best such implant lenses are made of a plastic bearing the impressive name of polymethylmethacrylate, which is of light weight and optical clearness. It does not erode within the eyeball.

As in corneal transplants, microsurgery is involved here also. Several hundred such operations are done annually at Mayo and some eight hundred Mayo patients with lens implants are monitored in annual physical examinations. This is done not only for the patient's benefit but to accumulate research data on the effectiveness of lens implants.

CHAPTER 26

Computers

The extent to which computers function in patient care, education, and research is such that we must almost ascribe to these machines the ability to think like a human. Memory storage is tremendous and beyond all human endeavor. True, memory is installed in encyclopedias, but to recall past events there involves extensive search. But to assemble pertinent information from computers involves merely putting a question by pushing buttons and getting an immediate, accurate answer. The question might be, In the past fifteen years, what male patients under thirty years of age have had neurosurgery removing tumors of the brain's left frontal lobe? There is an immediate, complete, and correct answer.

It was said that computers complained of doing simple things like listing patient fees, patient registrations, or drug inventories. They preferred to make breakthroughs in the control of previously incurable diseases.

The Clinic's main computer system became located in spacious quarters in the Harwick Building. The central data system does not deal directly with studies involving immediate participation by patients. It is involved with patient records and much more, such as business office data, medical and hospital statistics, payroll, accounting, and "thousands of other duties." The computers are hooked to power lines and connected with 135 or more terminals located throughout the Clinic and the two hospitals. About forty miles of cable is involved in connecting those terminals with the computers. The largest of the computers at Harwick weighs about a ton.

Mayo's Dr. Richard Raff opines, "If a researcher has a difficult problem and can reduce it to numbers, he generally does not need to be concerned about technological assistance in studying the problem," and "It's almost impossible to predict where computer technology will be ten years from now." Computers may simply balance our checkbooks or even guide rockets to the moon.

Let us look at just a few of these "thinking machines." A number of them in use for some time have already been described. This includes the dynamic spacial reconstructor (DSR), and now there are more. Some of these are fully operative and some are in the research stage.

Heart Problems

At Saint Marys Hospital there is the coronary care unit where patients with life-threatening heart conditions receive close scrutiny. Each patient room is loaded with complex monitoring instrumentation. Functioning of the patient's heart, such as the rate of the heartbeat or the electrocardiogram tracing, is displayed on a TV screen visible to nurses, technicians, or physicians. Also displayed are such vital signs as blood pressure and the cardiac output of blood. This computer monitoring proceeds for twenty-four hours a day, revealing its findings every two minutes.

A doctor can observe from the screen all of the patient's vital signs for the past hour, the past day, or the entire length of his stay. This is revealed by the doctor punching a code on the terminal keyboard. Some complex screen displays may take less than twenty seconds to appear. It would probably take that many hours for the doctor to compile the same information by hand.

Suppose there is a patient with a very specific internal lesion of the heart. It might be helpful to know about all other past Mayo patients with a similar condition: how they have reacted, their responses to various types of treatment, and how they progressed. It would be almost impossible or tremendously time-consuming to accumulate such data without the computer.

While the computer system does not have judgment or the capability of diagnosis, it provides an immediate large background of well-summarized knowledge about a patient. It was stated that there is some potential danger in all such technology. You might "punch buttons and look at displays and forget to talk to the patient" was a warning by Dr. Byron Olney.

Diabetes

At Saint Marys Hospital there is available a complex device, the Biostater. This is basically a mechanical pancreas attached to a bed-ridden diabetic. It has a pump that withdraws two cubic centimeters of the patient's blood each hour. The machinery measures the glucose content of that blood. Such information is fed into a built-in computer. The computer in turn drives a pump to administer the proper dosage of insulin. This is essentially a mechanical pancreas, capable of continuously monitoring and maintaining normal blood sugar levels in hospitalized diabetic patients.

Might it not be possible to devise similar machinery for diabetics not hospitalized? Such patients give themselves subcutaneous injections to supply the insulin needed to metabolize sugar, protein, and fat or to store them for future use. Such injections of insulin are made before meals or perhaps twice a day. But too often the self-injection is an imprecise method that may leave the blood sugar level higher than normal sometimes, below normal at other times, and rarely just right. Might not machinery be devised in which computers function to introduce just the right amount of insulin into the body continuously, just as the pancreas does in normal people? What was needed was machinery similar in function to Saint Marys' Biostater but of relatively small size and weight. Instead of the relatively massive Biostater, there should be readily portable machinery that a patient might wear away from the hospital and that would automatically control the glucose and insulin blood level of the diabetic.

To support the effort to accomplish this end, the National Institutes of Health awarded Mayo a grant of $623,000. Studies proceeded, many of them under the direction of Dr. John Service. The goal of the project was to develop a lightweight, portable pump that would automatically administer precise dosages of insulin to its bearer, keeping blood sugar levels at or very near normal levels. A tiny computer was hooked to a small pump to control precisely the supply of insulin injected automatically through the needle imbedded subcutaneously in the subject.

It was planned that eventually the patient might "dial in" the type of meal he has eaten and the device would respond by pumping into his body the exact amount of insulin needed. Even between meals the pump should deliver insulin in a small, even rate just as a normal pancreas would do.

Research on this project initially involved animal experiments, but very soon only human diabetic volunteer subjects were employed. While all this in 1981 was still in the experimental stage, studies have advanced with sufficient success as to warrant the optimistic outlook that it might become the standard management of diabetes. Without normalizing blood sugar levels in diabetics, there may follow hardening of the arteries, gangrene, loss of vision, or degeneration of nerves.

Cancer Treatment

Radiation therapy for cancer is administered in the Clinic's Curie Pavilion. The goal is to damage or destroy the malignant tumor cells while at the same time inflicting minimal damage to healthy body cells. It was learned that differences in radiation dosages as small as five percent might seriously damage normal tissue. For this reason, the prescribed treatment programs were checked in detail by experienced technicians. Their work involved evaluating treatments proposed by the physician and suggesting alterations in the therapy. This verification process might take up to four hours. A computer system was devised which reduced this time to perhaps twenty minutes.

The elaborately named Programmed Console-12 Radiotherapy Planning System was simplified to PC-12. Into it the technician can enter and alter information, allowing the computer to do ninety percent of the brain work otherwise necessary. Safer and more effective radiation therapy for cancer resulted.

Patient Appointments

In the course of questioning and examining a patient, the physician decides what laboratory, diagnostic, therapeutic, and other tests are needed. The central appointment desk (CAD) was responsible for scheduling by day and by hour where the patient should go for these procedures ordered by the physician. Working with the physician's orders, the schedulers needed quota cards from the requested examination sites, but also much more. There was a headful of complex rules and exceptions to the rules. For example, tests involving dyes could not be scheduled on the same day as tests involving isotopes; no x-ray involving barium should precede an x-ray of the lumbar spine. Yet the schedulers did a remarkable job of juggling, shifting, and rearranging to come up with the right schedule. This proceeded to meet the needs of over 5,500,000 new and returning patients over a thirty-one-year period.

But as the Clinic grew, this task became harder and practically impossible. The number of patient tests available climbed to about 1,200 in 1976. The number of tests and x-rays ordered for patients surpassed

1,700,000 in that year. All this began to overpower the CAD. Procedures were changing so rapidly that CAD doubted its ability to function at the high level of other Clinic activities. An automated computer system was deemed essential.

The readjustment was most complicated but eventually completed in the early 1970s. The computer's inner knowledge of all the pertinent information and data was combined with the punched-in needs for a patient's tests. A computer printer tied to the terminals produced three copies of a patient's schedule in some five to ten seconds. One copy was for the patient, one for the desk where the test was to be made, and one stayed at the CAD.

Among the numerous advantages of the computer system was that once the schedule was made, it was stored in the computer. If the patient lost his schedule it could easily be called up again from the machine. Under the manual system it would have to be entirely redone by the CAD people. All the rules and regulations governing the tests were stored in the computer and the pertinent items were delivered to the patient with his schedule. For example, it might inform the patient to eat nothing on the morning of the test or to take three enemas before the test.

Chemical Analyses

Another sophisticated product of computer technology bears the impressive name of gas chromatograph mass spectrometer. It can identify and measure the quantity of various compounds in blood, serum, and urine. It can also identify drug compounds in unlabeled or foreign pills brought in by Mayo patients.

Patterns for 7,900 biological compounds are stored in the computer's memory. Of these, 5,900 are components of body parts, 360 are drugs that are commercially available, and the remaining 1,640 are compounds found in the environment. The ability to identify drugs rapidly is important when a patient is brought into a hospital emergency room after taking an overdose of an unidentified drug, samples of which are carried by the patient. By this machinery, the drug is identified and proper therapy may be instituted.

Slide Production

Here we refer mainly to slides made to be used for projection onto a screen to illustrate a scientific presentation. The audience may be medical students learning basic facts or a scientific assembly listening to a research presentation. Each year more than twenty thousand documented projection slides are made at Mayo for various professional purposes. To prepare such slides by hand is an overwhelming task. This problem was met by the Clinic's medical graphics section, employing a machine manufactured by the General Electric Corporation. This was a computerized complex called Genigraphics, or production of charts. The resulting color slides might well be called computer-generated artwork.

Let us suppose a staff member wishes a slide to illustrate the age distribution of patients with a given disease. He has figures showing these facts that he has also obtained from a computer. But figures alone are less instructive than charts that translate the figures into images, just as the picture of a person tells you more about him than do data on his height and weight.

In the problem before us the percentages of patients with the disease being illustrated are best illustrated by a series of columns, one for each age group. There may be a low column for ages ten to twenty, a taller one for ages twenty-one to thirty, and a higher column for the next decade of ages, in which group the disease was found to be most frequent.

The request for the slide must be accompanied not only by numerical figures but also by instructions regarding the colors desired on the slide, such as a blue background and yellow columns. Or perhaps the slide might depict an oval representing one hundred percent and divided into parts like pieces of a pie, each piece of a size to represent proper percentages in the various age groups, such as three percent in ages ten to twenty, twenty-three percent in the next decade, and so on, with each piece of pie appearing in a separate color.

All these decisions are fed into the computer by experts manipulating a keyboard or using a digital pen. The operator calls up words, images, and graphs from the computer's memory. Multiples of existing drawings in the files of medical graphics have been programmed into this computer memory.

The pertinent data for the slide desired that has been fed into the machine emerges from the complex as a picture on a small screen. Changes may be made until the desired total effect is achieved. Then the final image decided on is converted into the colored transparent lantern slide.

Such a slide production can be produced in about fifteen minutes with the Genigraphics machine. Formerly, it might take five people working for two or three hours to get the same result.

Besides such transparent color slides to be projected on a screen, black and white charts and illustrations are made to illustrate a scientific paper to be submitted to a scientific journal for publication.

Foods

How does a hospital efficiently plan nutritious, appetizing meals for hundreds of patients—and even employees—every day? Rochester Methodist Hospital does this with the help of a computer called FOODS, which term is really an acronym of food operators ongoing data system. And what functions does this computer system perform? It maintains current information on the hospital's food inventory, records purchase costs, provides precise recipe instructions, and computes the nutrient content of each food item. It compiles a "grocery list" for the purchase of foods.

It provides Mayo physicians with an analysis of nutrient quantities consumed by individual patients whose diet must be monitored. In the past, hospital dietitians normally analyzed patient food intake.

Mass Spectrometry

The mass spectrometer is a computer analysis instrument that can identify almost any compound in nature, down to the specific number and types of atoms. It is the most powerful instrument in the world to analyze the organic constituents of matter. It can analyze liquids, solids, or gases. These might be drugs, hormones, organic acids, carbohydrates, toxic agents, fats, or whatever else. Relatively small mass spectrometers are not unusual in medical institutions. Mayo has four of these devoted to specific routine chemical analyses. But the Clinic's new and very large Kratos machine, recently added to Mayo's research arsenal, is for much more extensive projects. It was stated that to use the Kratos for examining material derived from patients would be like using a battleship to go fishing.

The Kratos is a research device. It has an unsurpassed sensitivity for incredibly small amounts of matter. A grain of sugar, it was stated, "would be more than enough material and would be like using a shovel full of sugar for normal chemical analysis."

In analyzing substances the spectrometer breaks down the compound by bombarding it with electrons. It then propels the resulting charged particles through a magnetic field. Based on their mass, the particles fall onto a detector much as particles in a stream fall to the stream bed according to their weight and the speed of the current. A computer analysis identifies the matter's molecular structure. The machinery produces a graphlike record, almost as if it were the compound's fingerprint. This is compared with a catalog of known compound "fingerprints." The entire process takes about five minutes.

An important research use is to determine how and why the body parts interact with various drugs and other organic compounds. Involved are patients who react adversely to anesthetics, the preservation of a transplant in the recipient's body, how cancer producing substances carry out their destructive activity, and the detection and isolation of chemical compounds involved in numerous diseases. It is believed that the specific and sensitive measurements of biochemical compounds is essential in medical research. Says Dr. Ian Jardine, "The mass spectrometer has enormous capacity to achieve that goal."

The system was financed by a five hundred thousand dollar gift from the Grainger Foundation of Skokie, Illinois. Members of the Grainger family have been longtime Mayo patients and supporters of Mayo education and research programs.

Along with the mass spectrometer we might mention other machinery. There is an image-processing device for automatically enumerating the number and variety of white cells in a patient's blood sample, replacing the counting done by a technician peering through a microscope. Each day about five hundred such tests are made.

Other machinery makes some two thousand microscopic slides per month. Indeed, machinery serving medicine has progressed in complexity and usefulness as have the most intricate procedures now employed in surgery of the brain or heart.

Medical Drawings

Mayo has a huge collection of medical art, with something more than sixty thousand anatomical, surgical, and pathological drawings done by medical artists since 1903. These are used in scientific publications and to make lantern slides for illustrations in lectures. It may well be the largest such collection in the world. These drawings visually interpret complex body problems and methods to solve them, as in various surgical procedures. Use of this vast collection of information was limited for a long time because information on what was available in it could be gotten only by a time-consuming manual research of card index files. Eventually all this information about the drawings was entered into a computer system including such information as the anatomical area involved, the name of the investigator or surgeon involved, and the date and place of the medical publication employing the picture.

With the computer system a staff member needing an illustration in an article being prepared for publication need only to call the Mayo medical library with a description of the kind of drawing he wants. The computer will provide a printout of references on all art on this subject.

The consultant can then either refer to the published work to see if the art is suitable or look at a print of the picture on file. When a suitable piece of art is thus found, medical graphics provides a print or a slide for the consultant's use.

For example, a Mayo surgeon desires illustrations of heart surgery for a book chapter he has written. The computer provides him with a list of illustrations from which he may select those he can use. By this system, there is a tremendous reduction in the number of new drawings to be made. About 150 to 300 drawings are used from these files every month. Even so, the number of new drawings per year is now about 700.

Robert Benassi, head of the Clinic's medical graphics section, said that although many of the drawings in the file are old, in many cases they are still useful. "Anatomy hasn't changed over the years," he said. To illustrate his point he pulled from his file a recent request for a drawing done about 1910 for Dr. William Mayo.

Laboratory Information System

The LIS has been mentioned previously in the account of the laboratory facilities in the Hilton Building. Deserving of further consideration is the magnitude of the computer aspects of this enterprise. It automates information from the thirty-two thousand tests daily carried out in the multiple laboratories of the entire Mayo complex. It provides physicians and other medical personnel with well-organized reports of laboratory test results for individual patients. Such results are either fed directly into the computer by various automated instruments in the laboratories or entered manually on computer terminals by laboratory employees. This eliminates the handling of thousands of individual test report slips each day and decreases the potential for clerical error on the reports.

Test results for individual patients are printed on computer-generated reports that consolidate on one sheet all the information formerly carried on numerous individual test report slips. By this means tests on a patient done in perhaps six laboratories are brought together on one printed report.

Another amazing feature of the system is the provision of age-, sex-, and race-related normal values for the hundreds of analytical procedures involved in patient study. An alerting system automatically calls the physician's attention to any abnormal test result.

Remarkable though all of this may be, we hear this opinion of Dr. Michael O'Sullivan, chairman of the department of laboratory medicine: "Human endeavor and communication are essential to patient care. They will never be surpassed by the computer."

Patient History Location

The storage area in the Harwick Building for the 3,500,000 patients' histories dating back to the turn of the century has already been described. But at any one time, from 120,000 to 180,000 of these histories are out of this permanent file. We do not refer here to instances of removal of a history from the file when a former patient returns for further Clinic services. The reference is rather to the multiple other uses for which patient histories are employed. Such histories circulate around the entire Rochester medical complex. They could be at a physician's desk, with a research worker, with a medical secretary, at the business office, in a hospital, at medical statistics—actually in any of hundreds of places for a great variety of legitimate reasons.

Keeping track of the location of so many thousands of histories presented a tremendous problem. Time was when this was done with little paper slips called charge slips, which indicated where a history was at any moment. With over one hundred thousand histories in circulation, and with over six thousand changes in location in a day, the volume of slips handled was staggering.

But then history location entered the computer age. Now when a call comes to medical records for a given history, a clerk in location file punches the keys of a computer terminal. On a screen there flashes the current location of the history. If the caller wants the history sent to him, the request is keyed into the computer, a request slip is automatically printed, and the history is soon on its way unless it is still needed at its former location.

Despite the huge volume of histories out of file for good reasons, if someone wants a history, it can be produced by history location in two or three hours, or as fast as half an hour in an emergency.

Biodynamics Research Unit

A major function of the biodynamics research unit relates to the computer aspects of the dynamic space reconstructor, which takes fifteen thousand cross-sectional images of body parts per second. Dr. Richard Robb was the principal investigator in developing a computer powerful and fast enough to handle the torrents of information that this DSR generates.

Dr. Robb ventured to predict in the "wildest sense" that DSR in the future may be able to measure the chemical composition and chemical reactions within the body in addition to its anatomy. It might even record nerve vibrations from the central nervous system. He goes on to say, "People outside Mayo recognize individual success within this institution, and the successes of groups like our own, but rarely do they understand or appreciate the degree to which the environment in which we work contributes to our success. I just don't think there is another institution in the world where a DSR could be built as quickly, well and economically. Nowhere else can you find this Mayo blend of patient care, research and education together with collaboration of colleagues, not only within a given department but across departments, that is able to foster blue-sky projects like the DSR into being." He also ventured, "It's almost impossible to predict where computer technology will be ten years from now.

CHAPTER 27

Lay Administration

Considering the multiplicity and complexity of the Clinic's statistics that have been cited, one's imagination seeks answers to the questions about the magnitude and expertise of the administrative functions involved in the organization. We dare not say that these may be compared with such medical advances as open-heart surgery, kidney transplants, or brain surgery. But throughout all this, we find the same devotion to superlative performance.

The account here relates primarily to the multiple nonmedical problems faced by the Clinic. Much of it is borrowed from reports by Robert Roesler, chairman of the Clinic's department of administration, who ranks as one of Mayo's truly great lay leaders.

Beginnings

In the early days when the Doctors Mayo practiced general medicine and surgery, they did their own bookkeeping, made their own collections, and attended to the correspondence relating to the Clinic and its business. As the practice increased, assistants were added to the office staff, and the Mayos were gradually relieved of some of these responsibilities.

Shortly after moving to the Masonic Temple Building, the Mayos decided they needed a manager to take over the collecting of fees, bookkeeping, banking, and payroll. In March of 1902 they named to the post of business manager William Graham, who had been a city justice in Rochester. William Graham was a member of a family of thirteen children. One of his sisters was Edith Graham Mayo (wife of Dr. Charlie), and one of his brothers was Christopher Graham, the first internist at Saint Marys Hospital and an early medical associate of the Mayos. In his later years William Graham was known affectionately as "Uncle Billie" by many of the staff and paramedical personnel.

Graham carried on the work of the office without any regular assistance for several years. His appointment seemed to make little change in the method of collecting, which was highly informal to say the least. Each doctor set his own fees and took the money from those who paid on the spot, putting it in his pocket or in a table drawer, to be turned over to Graham at the end of the day, together with a scrap of paper on which he jotted down the names of those who had not paid. Every afternoon each member of the staff stopped at the business office and emptied his pockets of money and of these little scraps of paper. The charges were then entered into what was known as x-ray ledgers, ponderous and difficult to handle. Graham struggled with this awkward system, which must have produced many inaccuracies in billing patients.

The business office itself was certainly not imposing, being a single room eight by twelve feet in size. There was a counter where patients were interviewed, a safe that held the ledgers, and a small table for processing outgoing mail.

The purchasing system of the day was also highly informal. Whenever someone in the group wanted something he simply ordered it or obtained it at a local store and charged the purchase to the Mayo Clinic. There was no record of the transaction until the bill was received.

Harwick Appears

After living with these loose business methods for several years, during which the professional work was increasing, Dr. W. J. Mayo sought and found (in 1908) that great administrator, Harry J. Harwick. This was a most significant event in the history of Mayo administration. As a young newcomer, Harwick met a great deal of resistance to his installing a new billing and collecting system. Eventually the system was accepted, and there was a decrease in the frequency with which a farmer's livestock or grain was accepted in payment of a bill. Introduction of an orderly purchasing system also required Harwick's best tact and diplomacy, but gradually this system also was accepted and expenditures came under better control.

Harwick's sound judgment, his unquestioned integrity, his skill in interpersonal relationships, and his broad outlook won for him the admiration and confidence of the Doctors Mayo, their early associates, and the scores of staff members who came later. The story of Harwick's career is almost the entire history of administration at Mayo. He was a key element in the story for forty-four years. He was the pioneer who translated into an effective reality Dr. Will's concept of a partnership in administration between physicians and their lay associates. This concept has served the Clinic well and is one of the reasons for its success.

Harwick, that "man of steel and velvet," stated that the

> lay administrator of a medical institution . . . must be able to find a practical harmonious balance between medical ideals and philosophies on the one hand and reasonable sound business methods on the other . . . it seems to me that the greatest single measure of a lay administrator is the degree to which he relieves physicians of the ever increasing problems of group practice management . . . the principle that a layman may have a place in a medical institution—and if he measures up, a responsible place—was early recognized and put into practice by one of the greatest of medical administrators, Dr. W. J. Mayo.

Eventual Organization

The Clinic's department of administration is now a group of laymen organized into divisions, sections, and units, responsible to the board of governors of the Mayo Clinic and the board of trustees of the Mayo Foundation. Broadly speaking, the department offers advice and counsel on a wide range of financial and administrative matters. Its members provide administrative support to the professional departmental structure of Mayo and also to the extensive Mayo committee system. In addition, the department is responsible directly for a considerable number of specific functions, such as the recruitment and maintenance of a superior paramedical staff.

This group of lay persons exists at Mayo in order to do for the medical and scientific staff, for patients, and for research and education programs those tasks that it is not necessary for the physician or scientist to perform, as well as those tasks that the physician or scientist is not trained to perform. This is simply a sensible application of the principle of division of labor, a principle the Mayos recognized and applied early in the evolution of Mayo Clinic.

The recruitment of competent Clinic administrators reached an importance not too unlike the evolvement of staff members dealing with patients. These were derived from banks, business firms, the Rochester school system, university faculties in law and business administration, law and accounting firms, and whatever.

The major components of the department of administration are several divisions. Listing these recalls describing the elements composing a heart-lung machine. These divisions are fiscal services, personnel, benefits, and medical social services, public affairs services, research systems services, administrative services, educational administrative services, and also facilities, planning, construction, and maintenance services. Within each of these divisions are several sections, each attending to special problems. For example, the fiscal services division contains these separate sections: accounting, business office, finance analysis and planning, and investments and internal auditing. Altogether, the divisions of the department of administration include a total of more than thirty special sections, each with its own administrative head. All these units report their findings, conclusions, and recommendations to Robert Roesler, the Clinic's chief administrative officer. What a startling development all this is from the two-man administrative staff of seventy years ago!

We might compare all this with a listing of the dozens of clinical sections treating patients in all the multiple areas of medicine. And it must be emphasized that all these administrative functions do not include the many problems relating to the intimate relationships between doctor and patient or between teacher and student. In the medical practice, teaching, and research areas, there are numerous Mayo committees consisting of staff internists, surgeons, and researchers. One could number some sixty of these, ranging from academic appointments and promotions to utilization review.

There was one administrative procedure which might even be labeled cute. In the years following World War I there was a recession throughout the country, and payments from patients were sometimes slow. A mail collection service was established under the direction of a lawyer, A. Lee Bower. It has always been a Mayo policy never to sue a patient to collect an unpaid account. However, to encourage delinquent patients to pay overdue Clinic bills, Bower used a special letterhead, "Lee Bower, Lawyer." Many prompt payments resulted.

A very early administrative pattern involved the appointment of a lay administrator as secretary on many Clinic committees dealing primarily with matters relating to patient care, education, or research.

Drs. Will and Charlie once described the Mayo Clinic as a medical democracy. The committee system bears out this concept.

Legal Department

In such a tremendous organization as the Mayo Clinic, one might well expect to find a strong legal department. This is indeed the case. And what are its functions? With the one thousand patients per day seeking medical care in Rochester, it would seem natural that there might be many instances of complaints and lawsuits charging malpractice. While the department is indeed concerned with such matters, its responsibilities extend into numerous other activities.

Each year there are over 100,000 new laws from various legislative bodies in the United States, and federal agencies produce more than 35,000 new regulations each year. Naturally, only a relatively small number of these pertain to medical and related activities. But the legal department must keep abreast of these few. The Clinic's professional activities and business relationships might be involved.

In one year alone almost seventy patient histories per day were under consideration, mainly for insurance companies, claims agencies, and law offices. The department encourages lawyers to come to Rochester to take depositions so that they will not subpoena the Mayo doctor to go to some distant place of a trial to testify. This clearly saves much time of doctors. And many times every day the Clinic lawyers consult with staff members or other employees, not only about medically or other institutionally related problems but also about personal problems. The department attempts to deal with these questions by helping to decide whether a lawyer's services are necessary or whether some relatively simple solution is available that the person can handle by himself. The Clinic's lawyers believe that a troubled employee is not very useful to the institution. So they start this person on the path to a solution; this is good for the individual and for the institution.

There are relationships with several closely affiliated corporations, such as the Rochester Airport Company, attempting to maintain or even improve aviation transport service for patients. And maintaining proper relations with non-Rochester institutions in the Clinic's outreach program also requires legal aid. There is necessary collaboration with the Minnesota State Board of Medical Examiners, the State Board of Health, and other regulatory agencies affecting medicine in general or Mayo specifically. The Clinic's development program, seeking outside funds, demands much legal department time. The Clinic's legal chief, Gregg Orwall, stated, "I personally am spending between a quarter and a third of my time on such matters."

Naturally, there are complaints of malpractice against Mayo. Here there is aid from the Clinic's accounting section to function much as an insurance company handling claims, evaluating potential or actual claims, establishing and reviewing reserves, and attempting to minimize generally the effect of such matters on the institution or on Clinic individuals.

During the decades 1960 to 1980 there were concluded eighty-two lawsuits against the Clinic for malpractice. Of these, twenty-nine were settled out of court and forty were dismissed. Only thirteen actually came to court action, and of these the Clinic lost only three. One of the largest malpractice lawsuits against Mayo was for two million dollars. The Clinic won this case. Rereading these figures we see that during a twenty-year period the Clinic lost only three cases in court.

There is also litigation other than claims of malpractice, such as claims that equipment designed by Mayo was defective. There are sales tax problems, contests regarding wills leaving money to the Clinic, real estate matters, and much else.

In all these legal activities Mayo owes much to the expertise, effectiveness, and judgment of the Clinic's chief counsel, Gregg Orwall.

Tremendously helpful also was the care taken by Clinic doctors to explain to patients and their families the risks involved in certain treatments, especially in complicated surgery. For example, neurosurgeon Dr. Grafton Love regularly noted in a patient's history record the trouble that might be encountered. He also recorded in the history that he had so informed the patient and family and had secured consent to proceed despite possible injurious complications.

We also find this account by the heart surgeon Dr. John Kirklin:

> Early in 1955, five patients were identified for the initial use at the Mayo Clinic of a pump-oxygenator for cardiac surgery. They were selected after careful review of a large number of patients who needed open heart operations for otherwise ultimately fatal heart disease, for which no other kind of surgical treatment would be possible. Each family was told that we would use a new and hitherto unproven method with which we had extensive laboratory but no clinical experience. We explained the risks, imponderables and possible benefits of the operations.

In malpractice lawsuit matters, the legal department was obviously greatly aided by the nationwide and worldwide appreciation of the Clinic's record of unexcelled superior performance in all fields of medical practice.

CHAPTER 28

Finances

Figures relating to any of the Clinic's activities are staggering, whether this be the thousand patients per day who come to Mayo, the twelve thousand Rochester people engaged in some aspect of medical care, the nearly four million laboratory tests performed annually, or whatever else we might look into. The dollars involved are especially overwhelming.

Income and Expenditures

The average total revenue to the Clinic from all sources exceeds five million dollars – not per year or per month but per week. Most of this is derived from patient fees. The remainder comes from grants, contracts, investment income, and contributions. This pertains to the Clinic alone. Let us add here the combined income from all sources received by the two hospitals, which amounts to nearly two million dollars per week. So, into the entire medical project of Mayo, Saint Marys Hospital, and the Rochester Methodist Hospital, there flows in seven million dollars per week, or one million dollars every day of the week. This may be translated into about eleven dollars per second, day and night, week after week, month after month.

Naturally, much of this income is derived from surgery. Here again we encounter amazing figures. On a single day (July 21, 1981) there were

134 surgical procedures at Saint Marys Hospital and 111 at the Methodist Hospital, for a total of 245 major and minor operations and other procedures requiring a surgical operating room.

And, of course, the outflow of money equals the income. Almost all of the Clinic's annual revenue of $276 million in 1980 was devoted to patient care, education, and research. Additions to land and facilities totaled a bit over $25 million. Strictly for patient care the year's Clinic expenditure was about $194 million. For rendering these services the Clinic received about $209 million in patient fees. Thus, for every dollar paid by a patient, there was a surplus of a bit over seven cents. About two thirds of all the money received by the Clinic from all sources comes from patient fees. We must always remember that none of the profits from patient care goes into anyone's pocket. It is all used for medical education and research.

Approximately seventy-five percent of all Mayo's financial outflow is used for compensation and benefits paid to its professional and paramedical staff.

Research expenditures in 1980 were about forty million dollars and educational expenses about twenty-six million dollars. These funds arose from patient fees and outside sources, including gifts from thousands of individuals, from scores of foundations, estates, and trusts, and from numerous governmental agencies.

Most of the twenty-six million dollars devoted to education was employed to finance the advanced training of more than eight hundred physicians and scientists. The remainder was devoted to the undergraduate medical school, continuing medical education programs for physicians seeking licensure renewals, and the health-related sciences programs.

But the securing of funds from outside the Clinic was essential. This responsibility rested largely on the Mayo Board of Development, under the chairmanship of Dr. Emmerson Ward. Nearly fifteen million dollars came from this effort in 1980.

The Mayo Development Program commenced eleven years ago. It set a goal of seeking $100 million, which sum was reached in seven years. This outside help played a key role in helping to pay for launching the undergraduate medical school, for funding professorships, scholarships, and fellowships, and for a good deal more.

Fund raising was also a major function of the Doctors' Mayo Society, although the society also sought to engender widespread understanding of Mayo's purposes and accomplishments.

This organization was initiated under the leadership primarily of Dr. Dwight L. Wilbur of San Francisco, emeritus trustee of the Mayo Foundation as well as one of the Clinic's most outstanding alumni. Membership was offered to those of the Mayo Alumni Association who signified their intent to make an initial gift of one thousand dollars to Mayo and to contribute at this level annually, or to provide twenty-five thousand dollars or more through their estates. All this was to be used to support educational and research activities of the Mayo Foundation. In just a few years (1981) the members of the Doctors' Mayo Society numbered 181. About two thirds of these were in the one-thousand-dollars-a-year category and the remainder pledged to leave Mayo twenty-five thousand dollars in their wills.

In support of its fund-raising efforts there was issued in 1969 a booklet whose title reflects Mayo's concept of its responsibility – "Trusteeship of Health." Here was described the Mayo institutions, their functions and their goals and their needs for financial aid. It was pointed out that Mayo activities in education and research were expensive but produced no income. Federal funds from various agencies assisted, but even with such grants Mayo provided $1.50 for every dollar of federal funds in support of research, and $9.00 for every federal dollar in support of education. Funds from elsewhere than government were needed and sought and granted.

In 1981, nearly eleven thousand patients, medical staff, alumni foundations, corporations, and other friends contributed $17,610,865 to strengthen Mayo's program in medical education and research.

Highlights of the year included the following:

Jesse and Fern Baldwin of Kearney, Nebraska, gave $5 million in capital stock of A. J. Baldwin Manufacturing Company.

The late Marjorie C. Nichlos of Chickasha, Oklahoma, made gifts of securities with value of more than $2 million.

A significant new fund in cancer research, along with the establishment of Mayo's sixteenth endowed professorship, was provided through a $3 million bequest of Purvis F. Tabor of Decatur, Illinois.

The Kresge Foundation made a grant of $400,000 in support of renovation at Institute Hills Farm, Mayo's research animal facility.

Continued major gift support was received from Mr. and Mrs. Albert Borchard of Los Angeles for a research laboratory in membrane biochemistry and from Mr. and Mrs. Bruce Rappaport of Geneva, Switzerland, toward the clinical-investigator program which they established.

An additional grant from the Grainger Foundation of Chicago aided further development of the Grainger Mass Spectrometer Center.

The Fraternal Order of Eagles continued its support of Mayo cancer research with gifts totaling $155,000 from the 1981 Eagles Cancer Telethon in Rochester.

The Doctors' Mayo Society, a leadership-giving organization of Mayo alumni, added 15 new memberships during the year, bringing the total to 188.

The Leo and Alexandra Kissam Scholarship in Mayo Medical School was endowed from the estate of Leo T. Kissam of New York City.

Other major gifts were received from Mr. and Mrs. Philip N. Fortin, Billings, Montana; the Oscar G. and Elsa S. Mayer Charitable Trust; Eugenie M. Bolz, Madison, Wisconsin; Mr. and Mrs. Roy E. Meyer, Red Wing, Minnesota; Helen C. Levitt, Sioux City, Iowa; Mr. and Mrs. Ross D. Siragusa, Chicago; the Ernest J. Svenson Foundation, Rockford, Illinois; and the estate of Charlotte F. Atwood, Peoria, Illinois.

In all this money-raising effort we recognize the important role played by the board of trustees of the Mayo Foundation. About half of the thirty board members are from the Mayo Clinic and half are public members, consisting of prominent people, including business executives from all over the country.

No single source of revenue is neglected, though it be a tiny fraction of the total needs. For example, silver is recovered from the x-ray developing process and from old x-rays about to be discarded. This silver reclamation project produces about six hundred thousand dollars per year.

The total Clinic assets in 1980 were just over $353 million. Nearly half of this, or about $155 million, consisted of land, buildings, and other facilities. Investments reached about $110 million. Let us total the property values of the three major units of Rochester's medical enterprise. We add Methodist's $110 million, Saint Marys' $145 million, and the Clinic's very conservative estimate of $155 million to reach the total sum of $410 million. Recall that this does not include equipment, some of which is enormously costly. If we add all this, we approximate a total of half a billion dollars.

Worthy of note is the matter of the costs to patients for the Clinic care they receive. On this subject the Mayo Foundation's Atherton Bean stated, "I think we can say that Mayo has done its job very well in this area. The increase in the Mayo medical services index over the past five years is about half the increase in the Consumer Price Index and half the increase in the medical component of that overall index."

Income Tax

Although it involves relatively little Clinic money, there is one financial service of the Clinic that impresses itself very deeply on the personal life of staff members, quite apart from salary. The Clinic provides assistance in preparing the annual extensive and complicated state and federal income tax forms. No—the Clinic doesn't *assist*—it does the whole job; the staff member assists by providing significant figures. All this is under the general supervision of Robert Carolin of the Clinic's accounting department. Employed in this welcome service are representatives of firms of certified public accountants. Involved also is a complicated computer system. Annually this service is rendered to more than nine hundred "voting staff" members, including physicians, scientists, administrators, and other specialists. It is not available to employees generally or to students, whose income tax problems are not too complicated.

The total annual cost of this enterprise to the Mayo Clinic approximates a quarter of a million dollars.

The author recalls that he spends perhaps an hour each year in March with the same lady, Sharyn Kiehne: "She continues to be familiar with my special tax problems and became my personal income tax agent, but not paid by me."

Supplementary Figures

Besides dollars, there are many other numbers telling much about the magnitude of Rochester's medical enterprise. What about the size and the multiplicity of the structures involved? Here we refer to the total floor space, taking into account the number of floor levels in the buildings. The total for all units is more than six million square feet. Translated into acres, we find that there are 73 at Mayo, 55 at Saint Marys, and 13 at Methodist, for a total of 141 acres of floor space. This is more than one fifth of a square mile. It equals about sixty square city blocks of the size of the block on which the Mayo Building stands.

Since we are engaged in statistics about dollars and acreage, let us examine 1979 Mayo figures in other areas. During that year the Mayo Medical Museum hosted 107,680 visitors, the section of photography produced 216,635 slides, and ten vehicles assigned to general service for messenger and passenger service were driven a total of 168,653 miles.

In addition to its slide production, the section of photography made 127,631 prints and enlargements and 1,029 portraits in the past year. The audiovisual center produced 169 television programs and 288 audio recordings.

General service's two receptionists at the Rochester Airport assisted 6,065 wheelchair patients and 72 ambulance patients during arrival or departure. Another 323 patients were helped on or off aircraft, and 89 were assisted in the airport's first-aid rooms.

General service guides conducted a total of 803 Clinic tours for 25,742 persons. These included 509 public tours for 17,612 visitors, 240 special tours for 6,908 visitors, and 29 orientation tours and 25 two-day orientation tours of 846 and 376 new Mayo people, respectively.

Mayo administrators conducted 185 tours of the Clinic and affiliated hospitals for 1,336 visiting physicians and guests. The physicians were from ninety-six states and foreign countries and represented eighty-five specialities.

In that year there was a total of 19,029 guests attending functions at the Mayo Foundation House, including the following: dinners were served to 8,250 persons and luncheons to 2,695; another 2,160 guests were present at receptions, 1,573 at meetings and lectures, 2,426 at teas and coffees, 938 at gatherings of women's groups, and 987 on tours.

There were 650,000 diagnostic x-ray procedures and more than 3,5000,000 laboratory tests. Circulation of the *Mayo Clinic Proceedings* reached 84,000 per month.

Purchasing issued 39,096 purchase orders last year, an average of 152 per day. According to a study conducted for the month of June 1979, the Mayo stockroom received an average of 28 deliveries and 766 items per day. These items were delivered around the Clinic an average of 57 times daily.

Clinic copy machines made a total of 17,840,428 copies in 1979: 7,900,428 on machines in the duplicating unit and another 9,940,000 on copiers around the Clinic. The duplicating unit also made 18,865,056 impressions on its printing presses.

Systems and procedures reported that 1,493 Clinic forms were reprinted without revision in 1979, 310 were revised, 62 were deleted, and 181 were initiated.

In 1979 the Mayo Medical Library circulated 594,756 published materials, including books, journals, articles, and photocopies of uncirculated items. The library also filled 29,733 requests for reference information, supplied 3,596 copies of Mayo author bibliographies, and ordered 13,535 books. There were 3,291 journal titles on the library shelves that year.

Even the Clinic's lost-and-found efforts might deserve a moment. Yearly, some twenty-six hundred forgotten items find their way to this service. These may include coats, boots, bras, toys, glasses, jewelry, purses, or you name it. It might even be a plastic cast for an injured arm. Less than half of these are recovered by their owners. Valuable unclaimed articles are kept for some three years, then sold. The money is used to help needy patients. Cheaper items are given to charity after six months.

A bit of mathematics enables us also to translate into figures the extent of the service provided patients by the elevators in the Mayo Building. Here there are twelve elevators, six going to floor eleven and six to floor nineteen. They travel continuously all day long without interruption. Despite patient entrance into and exit from the elevators, it taks an average of but 2.5 minutes to go the three hundred feet from subway to top floor, or 5 minutes for a round trip between subway and eleventh floor. We arrive at a total of some 147 miles per working day as the combined distance travelled by these dozen elevators.

Recall that this does not include the staff and employee elevators in the Mayo Building or those in Plummer, Hilton, Guggenheim, Medical Sciences, Harwick, and elsewhere. Were we to add these to our calculations, we would undoubtedly arrive at a figure of at least two hundred miles per day or one thousand miles per working week. Expanding this, we find that the Mayo Clinic elevators in one year travel some fifty thousand miles, a distance equal to twice around the earth.

No figures relate the Clinic's expansions over the years better than an account of the stipends paid to first-year fellows or residents beginning their graduate medical education. These stipends per year were $900 in 1940, $2,400 in 1960, and $19,150 in 1982.

Citing these numerous statistics in terms of millions of dollars and millions of copies made by duplicating machines and hundreds of thousands of patients seen leads us to refrain from mentioning further figures relating to the size of the earth, or the solar system, or the universe.

CHAPTER 29

Art at Mayo

The Clinic has always felt that providing adequate facilities for patient care must be supplemented with creating an environment that would be aesthetically pleasing to patients, visitors, and those who work in the buildings.

The first Clinic building (1914) was derived from Georgian architecture. Its lobby suggested an outdoor court with a fountain and a marble balustrade. The Romanesque-style Plummer Building (1928) is an art form in itself, with richly ornamented walls, ceilings, and floors throughout. Marble floors and sculptured bronze doors enhance the dignity and serenity of this building. The architects, under Plummer's unfailing scrutiny, relied heavily on ornamentation to create the character of that structure.

With the Mayo Building there began an art program somewhat apart from architectural design. Robert Roesler, chairman of the Clinic's department of administration, stated that "when the Mayo Building was in the early stages of design, it was apparent that it would not be practical to attempt to create a structure similar in character to the 1928 [Plummer] Building. The artisans were not available, and even if they had been, the cost would have been prohibitive." But that art should be an integral part of the new structure was never questioned. Dr. Samuel Haines, then chairman of the Clinic's board of governors ventured, "Art forms were to be of interest to patients who might study them while waiting to see the doctor, to visitors accompanying patients to Mayo and certainly as important, they were to make the working environment more pleasant for Mayo personnel."

Warren T. Mosman, art consultant from the Minneapolis School of Art, collaborated with the Mayo building committee, architects, and artists to develop an overall art theme which would reflect a philosophy of the essential dignity of man. Mosman stated, "In all ages, man has made things first to be useful and then he has made them beautiful."

Mirror to Man

On each of thirteen floors of the Mayo Building there is a mural covering one large wall of the patients' waiting room. The general theme is "Mirror to Man," depicting some major activities, achievements, and philosophies of man. These works of art were to portray many phases of mankind's living. They remind one of the value of his literary heritage, of his home, of his concepts of freedom. They point out his enjoyment in the observation of nature, his need for companionship, and his desire for knowledge. Each of the artists was carefully chosen for his or her grasp of the visual and philosophic problems involved.

The artists were selected after an international survey. Those chosen visited Rochester, saw the Mayo Building, discussed their approaches, and submitted sketches to the building committee. One early sketch included three hooded, fearsome-looking figures. The artist was asked if he could possibly interpret his original idea and yet employ some more cheerful symbols. Cheerfully, the artist could and did.

On the main floor of the Mayo Building is *Man's Relation with Nature* by the English artist John Pifer. Of this mural, Pifer stated, "Man is not nature's master, nor is nature man's. They often appear to be at war with each other because they are always reversing the role of conqueror and conquered . . . man makes his claim on the land and there is always something to show that man has been there. Man and nature enrich each other always; and all change is ripeness and not destruction."

Other titles in this "Mirror to Man" art project are: *Man and the Energies, Man and the Art Form, Man and the Home, Man's Musical Heritage, Man's Responsibility to Others, Man's Desire for Companionship, Man and Discovery, Man and Creativity, Man and Plant Forms, Man's Literary Heritage, Man and Sea and Sky and Earth,* and lastly, *Earth and Spring, Summer, Fall.*

Sculpture

Sculpture also integrates works of art with architecture. On three outside faces of the Mayo Building are works which also interpret the Mirror to Man concept of the indoor murals. The bronze sculpture on the north facade, *Man and Freedom,* depicts a man in a classical graceful pose. The whole figure, straining upward, represents a search for fulfillment and dignity. The open, frank face looks toward the sky; the muscles push upward; the entire torso leans forward to depict the effort of striving for freedom. Of this work the Croatian-born sculptor Ivan Mestrovic stated, "We are compelled to condense man's concept of love and freedom in one figure, which is equal to condensing a treatise of the subject in an epigram of a few words . . . to all living beings, and in the first place to man . . . individual freedom is the most precious."

Four figures depicting *Man and Achievement* may be seen on the eastern outer wall. One of these is the *Thinker or Dreamer,* symbolizing the philosopher, artist, leader, or scientist, an enlightened man who enlightens others. Another figure presents *Makers or Doers,* representing the number of people involved in making, building and producing goods of all types. Then there is the mother and child depicting care, education, faith, and religious attitudes and concern for the welfare of those who might depend on others. And lastly the *Purveyor or Transporter* represents farmers and shippers. The important role of those involved in the assembling of produce is expressed by a man gathering in a net.

The creator of these four figures, the Lithuanian William Zorach, became a major American sculptor with works in the Chicago Art Institute, the Metropolitan Museum of Art, the Radio City Music Hall, and the United States Post Office Building in Washington.

On the south facade we find *Man and Recreation* in three groups. There is a pair of bicyclists, a typical family unit during a joyful moment, and three bathers. These are by the American sculptor Abbott Pattison, whose other works are on display at art centers in Chicago, New York, Washington, Saint Paul, and Israel.

Besides these sculptures on the outer walls of the Mayo building, there is other statuary in the courtyards at corners of the Mayo Building. These were installed a number of years after the statues on building walls. One depicts the demigod of the sea, Triton, blowing in his conch shell and surrounded with a large round pool of water. Two other courtyard statues are most modernistic. One, entitled *Conchiglia,* Italian for "shell," is as complex a shell as might be imagined. It could be called "The Complexities of Life." It is the work of the Italian sculptor Pericle Fazzani. The second is *With Compassion He Listened to All* by the Mexican artist Victor Salmones. These two cast bronze works were given to the Clinic by Mr. and Mrs. A. H. Meadows of Dallas, Texas.

Art Program

The Mayo Art Program extended also into Clinic structures of recent years, such as Harwick and Guggenheim and Hilton. Here we find oil paintings, small sculptures, mosaics, tapestries, water colors, pencil drawings, and photographic color prints. There is also a small collection of pre-Columbian ceramic pottery from Costa Rica. In the Guggenheim Building is a structural relief by Rochester artist James Kern, depicting *Search for Truth*. This theme was suggested to him by the motto which William J. Mayo kept on his desk: "They loved the truth and sought to find it."

Art tours were arranged for patients and visitors with time on their hands. Brochures and handbooks were produced for those who might wish to take a self-conducted tour of the Mayo art collection. Robert Roesler, member of the art committee stated, "We want the program to provide uplift. The program should enhance the environment and complement efforts of all Mayo people as they strive to serve patients and visitors effectively in a warm, compassionate, understanding and very human way. The program is a part of the totality of the patients Mayo experience."

Gardens

Groundkeeping is another aspect of art at Mayo. There are trees and shrubs, lawns and hedges, bushes and flowers. Nowhere in any square foot of ground space about any of the Clinic buildings is there to be found a lack of greenery and plantings. The flowers are such that there are bright cheerful blooms from spring to fall. The most outstanding gardens and lawns are to be seen in the beautiful park adjoining the Harwick Building.

In a national contest, the Mayo Clinic grounds won the grand award in its division of hospitals and medical institutions. This contest was sponsored by the Professional Grounds Management Society. The award was based not only on landscape design and outstanding plantings but also on good maintenance of the grounds. The judges for awards were from a national nurseryman's association, university and college grounds specialists, and the lawn and seed industry.

Saint Marys

Equal in beauty are the grounds about Saint Marys Hospital, with its courts and fountains and lawns and beautiful blooming gardens. When the hospital was built in 1889 it stood on seven acres of land just west of Rochester's city limits. At the time, the hospital was small and the property it occupied was large; there was plenty of room for a vegetable garden, a chicken yard, and enough wooded terrain to provide a pleasant if infrequent retreat for the sisters and staff.

Today Saint Marys is well within Rochester's city limits; the hospital is now very large and there is much less room for wooded retreats and vegetable gardens. Throughout the decades, however, Saint Marys has maintained a sense of its rural beginnings. Carefully and with determination, the hospital has preserved large open areas of greenery, trees, and flowers in the belief that pleasant surroundings are an important factor in people's health and well-being.

The planners were "cognizant of the fact that the grounds are the first thing our guests will see when they visit us. The surroundings, therefore, must be pleasant, inviting and uplifting."

There are three large courtyards. A sculpture, a statue, or a plaque here and there throughout the grounds are ever-present reminders that this is a hospital conscious and proud of its past. There is even a picnic area with wooden swings, inviting guests or patients or even staff to enjoy a time in the sun.

Throughout the nine decades that these grounds have provided the setting for Saint Marys Hospital, they have been altered and redesigned to make way for new buildings and the needs of new generations of patients and staff. But through all of those changes the beauty has remained. Today the grounds still proclaim Saint Marys as a retreat, a refuge, and a place of comfort.

In the words of the great Sister Mary Brigh Cassidy, "The true mission of a hospital must be not only to treat a specific illness but to care for the whole person—to delight the senses, to provide a warm, comforting environment, to minister to the spirit. The effect of a beautiful painting in a patient's room, the view of a sparkling fountain, even the refreshing sense that comes from a clean and shiny corridor—all of these can have an impact upon health. As a hospital, we realize that we touch our patient's health for better or worse from the moment he or she arrives on the hospital grounds until the moment of departure."

Any account of art at Mayo may not exclude the structure and grounds of Methodist Hospital and Mayo Foundation House, or the Plummer House, which is really a castle, famous for its beautiful rose garden.

CHAPTER 30

Mayo's Future

As Mayo begins a new decade, we might review briefly the existing status of the Clinic's historic triad of patient care, education, and research.

The Triad Today

Translating some annual figures into per day numbers we arrive at the following: patient admissions, 1,000; diagnostic x-ray procedures, 2,400; laboratory tests, 14,000, and electrocardiograms, 650. Recall that these figures are not per month or per week, but are for each working day.

To meet the multiple needs, the Mayo permanent staff of physicians and scientists numbered 729. For every one of these there were more than 8 additional workers, numbering 6,132. These included associate consultants, research associates and trainees, but mostly paramedical staff. All this brought the total number of Mayo Clinic people to 6,861.

The personnel at Rochester's two hospitals reached 5,490. So there results the total figure of more than 12,000 men and women involved in Rochester's medical enterprise of patient care, education, and research.

Of the 1,000 patients coming to the Clinic daily, nearly one fourth became admissions to Saint Marys or the Methodist Hospital. Such patient admissions reached annual numbers of 30,300 for Saint Marys and 30,100 for Methodist. Days of patient care totaled more than half a million in the two hospitals in 1980. The hospital beds available number 972 at Saint Marys and 798 at Methodist.

So much for medical care. In the area of education, Mayo could count a total of 1,343 individuals in training, about half of whom were medical school graduates in specialty training. The remainder were research fellows, health-related sciences trainees, and medical students. Interestingly, while Mayo undergraduate students totaled 167, there were even more than this number of medical students from other schools in the country who spent some time at Mayo as clerks in clinical fields supplementing the training of their home schools. This is a pronouncement by many medical schools of their regard for the high quality of Mayo's patient care and its training of students in clinical medicine.

Involved in the multiple research programs were a total of 859 people, the majority of whom were paramedical personnel.

The tremendous advances in patient care, education, and research may be recalled by a review of the section titles of this volume. Among these are America's first blood bank, Kendall's isolation of the hormone cortisone resulting in a Nobel prize, aviation research employing the Big Wheel, the radial hospital concept, open-heart surgery, kidney transplants, heart transplants, the undergraduate medical school, employment of computers, and so much more.

All these Clinic developments took place in these successive Mayo structures: the Red Brick Building of 1914, which "would surely do us for all time," the artistic, magnificient Plummer Building of 1928, and the original Mayo Building of 1953, with its top floors added in the late 1960s. Might this "surely do us for all time"? Patient number 3,000,000 was seen in 1974 and patient number 3,500,000 in 1980. Will patient number 4,000,000 come in 1986? Where will he be seen?

And besides the purely clinical buildings there were also the related important and indispensable structures: the Hilton Building for Laboratory Medicine, the Guggenheim Building for Research and Education in the Life Sciences, the Harwick Building with its stupendous mass of stored medical, surgical, and laboratory records of patients, the Baldwin Community Health Center, the Medical Sciences Building mainly for research—and whatever else. We may add to this the tremendous expansions of hospital facilities commencing with Saint Marys' twenty-seven-bed hospital of nearly a century ago.

Thinking of the Clinic's vast size, an anonymous staff member thought thus: "Big doesn't always mean better. Big sunflowers are not better than small violets. But bigness can also be better and great. A big Easter lily is greater and better than a small dandelion. Let us think of the Clinic in terms of Easter lilies rather than sunflowers."

It is amazing that all these developments and expansions still do not immediately open the doors to all the demands of people seeking the superior medical care offered by Mayo. A new patient asking for his first Clinic appointment may have to wait some nine months to be seen, unless it is an emergency case, in which event it is attended to immediately.

Funding

Reviewing expenditures in 1980, for education there was about $26 million, for research about $40 million, and for patient care about $175 million. Another $25 million was spent on additions to land and buildings, including Mayo facilities in the new Mary Brigh unit at Saint Marys plus a variety of remodeling projects in the downtown Clinic complex. Additional expenditures brought the grand total for the year to $276 million.

Summarizing these figures into percentages, we reach the following: sixty-three percent for patient care, fifteen percent for research, nine percent for education, nine percent for land and facilities, and four percent for miscellaneous expenditures.

Elsewhere, it was pointed out that these expenditures amount to about $5 million per week. This is supplemented with a weekly budget of $1 million for each of the two hospitals, resulting in a total of $7 million per week or $1 million per calendar day.

The major source of these funds, as might be expected, was from patients, totalling $209 million, or about seventy-six percent of the total Clinic income. The remaining income was derived from grants, contracts, contributions, and investment income.

A basic principle in Mayo financing in the past and projected into the future is that Clinic earnings in excess of cost should be employed for education and research rather than going into staff pockets. Late in his life, Dr. Will Mayo recalled about himself and his brother: "In 1894 we had paid for our homes, and we considered the advisability of a plan, which we finally put into execution, of living on one-half of our earnings, saving from that what we could for ourselves, and the other half investing and reinvesting as a fund with which we could eventually do something worthwhile for the sick. It was the growth of this fund that produced the Mayo Properties Association." They wished to employ such funds for developing "better care of the patient, research which would reduce the amount of sickness and higher medical education of the graduate type." This principle will never cease to function in the Clinic's future.

Group Practice

It must never be forgotten that the group practice of medicine involving private patients was a major Mayo contribution in medical history. As early as 1910, Dr. Will told the graduating class of Rush Medical College:

> As we men of medicine grow in learning we more justly appreciate our dependence upon each other. The sum total of medical knowledge is now so great and widespreading that it would be futile for any one man . . . to assume that he has even a working knowledge of any large part of the whole. The best interest of the patient is the only interest to be considered, and in order that the sick may have the benefit of advancing knowledge, union of forces is necessary . . . It has become necessary to develop medicine as a cooperative science; the clinician, the specialist, and the laboratory workers uniting for the good of the patient, each assisting in the elucidation of the problem at hand, and each dependent upon the other for support . . . Individualism in medicine can no longer exist . . . The internist, the surgeon, and the specialist must join with the physiologist, the pathologist, and the laboratory workers to form the clinical group, which must also include men learned in the abstract sciences, since physics and biochemistry are leading medicine to greater heights. Union of all these forces will lengthen by many years the span of human life.

At a much later stage in his life Dr. Will voiced these thoughts relative to group practice:

> Each individual member of the staff should remember that his future is tied up with that of every other individual member; that it is only as a collective community that the Clinic will be able to maintain its high place in the eyes of the people and of the medical profession, and will be able to go forward with its work.
>
> Just to each worker, with careful selection of its members, maintaining its University connection, the Mayo Clinic will go forward in the future as it has in the past and will represent a form of organization of the medical profession of which we all may be justly proud.

Dr. William Worrall Mayo may well have had group medical practice in mind when he said to his sons, "No man is big enough to be independent of others."

The Patient at Ease

Mayo's renown for its effective management of the diseases of patients has always been a major factor in the success of the institution. Extremely important also has been the most personal attitude toward patients displayed by the staff and everyone else at the Clinic. A big business man going through the Clinic kept asking himself, "What makes this place 'the best'?" He had had medical treatment in large naval and veterans hospitals and "was fully prepared for mass medical treatment on a nonpersonal basis. To the contrary, I was made to feel by each doctor, nurse and technician I contacted that I was an important patient to them and they were there to help me. This was a great feeling. I was one of some

1,000 customers that day, each feeling he or she had the greatest problem to be solved, and yet I was made to feel that my problem was important to the Clinic and to me."

Naturally, this attitude toward patients originated with the Mayo brothers. When Dr. Donald Balfour was offered a permanent post in the early years of the century, Dr. Will Mayo said to him, "We'd like to have you stay with us, Balfour. We think you're the kind of man we want here. We've noticed that patients like you; they come back to say good-bye to you when they're ready to leave."

The Mayo philosophy has always been, and will continue to be, to treat not the illness in a patient, but to treat the patient with an illness.

As stated in the 1978 Britannica health annual, "For those for whom care is provided in the Clinic's outpatient facilities, treatment is efficient, effective and most important, humane. Everyone from physicians and therapists to the aides that change the linens in the examination and treatment rooms, exudes compassion and everything at the Clinic from the records rooms, with the bustling staff of blue-smocked workers to the tasteful non-threatening decor seems designed to increase efficiency and put the patient at ease."

To put the patient at ease must and will continue into future days.

University Relations

Mayo's relationship with the University of Minnesota changed in late 1982. The Mayo Foundation became an independent degree-granting institution by virtue of approval by the Minnesota Higher Education Coordinating Board. The state agency approved Mayo's request to grant the M.D. degree and the Ph.D. degree in biomedical sciences. A request to grant the M.S. degree in biomedical sciences is pending. Mayo will be working with accrediting bodies to complete the change, which is expected to take about two years.

Members of the Mayo Foundation Board of Trustees and the University of Minnesota have been meeting for more than a year to discuss ramifications of the change in the Mayo-University academic affiliation. Speaking for Mayo, W. Eugene Mayberry, chairman of the board of governors, said, "We expect this longstanding warm relationship between the two institutions to continue but on an informal basis."

On reaching this decision, both institutions expressed gratitude for the many decades of past intimate relations, decades that had rendered strength and renown to both institutions.

Tomorrow

Let us listen to the opinions of various Mayo leaders regarding the future. Stephen F. Keating, chairman of the Mayo Foundation Board of Trustees, stated, "We have at Mayo an important national resource which should be utilized as effectively as possible in the national interest . . . In the extension of our institutional commitments in the years ahead the trustees believe that Mayo has the potential to innovate constructively and to provide responsible leadership. The process of change must be continuous and it must be orderly, grounded in the capacity for reasoned deliberate response that has characterized Mayo since the beginning."

And in the words of Dr. Leo F. Black, director of research of the Mayo Foundation, "The future holds a bright challenge for all of us. There are many diseases about which we know very little. Solutions will be slow and tedious, but solutions can be found with continued research.

"With public and private support working together, we believe that future research will be very productive and will conquer many diseases that affect mankind today."

A major leader at Mayo in recent decades has been Dr. John T. Shepherd. He was once Mayo's director for research, and at this time he is director for education, dean of the medical school, and a member of both the Clinic board of governors and the foundation board of trustees.

We may listen to his thoughts regarding the importance and necessity for continuing in research. "If we fail to invest in research . . . we will soon find that the medicine we practice will be that of yesterday and not of tomorrow . . . I am persuaded that within this decade our scientists will find answers to some of the most stubborn of human ills, and that those who will be here in 1990 will be freed of some of the diseases for which we have no answers today."

Superior leadership qualities are reflected in these opinions of Dr. Eugene Mayberry, chairman of the Mayo Clinic Board of Governors:

> Progress in the practice of medicine at the Mayo Clinic has been steady yet dynamic. The pattern has evolved through deliberate consideration of a single question: what is best for our patients?
>
> Mayo Clinic has a history of important contributions in the area of research. We are organized in such a way that the scientists work in close collaboration with clinical investigators and practicing physicians and surgeons. New knowledge, gained through research, is quickly brought to the care of patients.
>
> As Mayo Clinic faces the future and pressures of growth continue, it must continue to keep in balance practice, education and research; it

> must remain vigilant yet responsive to increasing governmental regulation over activities; must ever guard the ideal of service and the primary and sincere concern for the individual. Mayo Clinic must continue to recognize that responses to future needs and change are most likely to be effective and wise if made in consideration of the principles and ideals of the founders.

Robert Fleming, chairman of the department of administration, ventured to predict the future in numerical terms. He looked ahead to the year 2000, and looked behind to note the rate of past growth. He anticipated that patient registrations would increase from the 1980 number of 255,190 to 300,530 in twenty years. The combined medical center staff, including all employees of the Clinic and hospitals, he expects to increase from the present 12,351 to about 21,000. This includes growth in numbers of Mayo staff doctors from 729 to 1,224.

To meet these needs there would be required a fifty percent increase in hospital beds, either as additions to the present Saint Marys and Methodist, or in entirely new structures. Fleming even ventured that the Mayo Clinic itself might need the equivalent of another twenty-story Mayo Building. This might result in a new structure, replacing the Damon parking ramp, or an addition to the Hilton Building, or wherever else.

At one time Dr. Mayberry recalled how faulty a prediction for the future might be. He stated that it was anticipated by some that at the death of the Mayo brothers, "grass would grow in the streets of Rochester."

He goes on to say:

> As we look forward to the next decade we must pay particular attention to maintenance and improvement of the quality of our programs in practice, medicine, education and research. We must be innovative and continue to be leaders with these programs.
>
> Doctors Will and Charlie Mayo were attuned to change. They believed it was appropriate for each succeeding generation to make its own plans and way. I believe that if they were with us today they would approve of the progress of this institution. They would recognize their goals and ideals at work now. We must continue to make this so.

A summary of all these views may be found in the following expressions of the Mayo Clinic Board of Governors and the Mayo Board of Trustees:

> Mayo Clinic, Mayo Foundation, Mayo Medical School, Mayo Graduate School of Medicine, and Mayo School of Health-Related Sciences, collectively a private trust for public purposes, in cooperation with associated hospitals, exist for these purposes:
>
> To offer, to both the sick and the well, comprehensive medical care of the highest standard through a coordinated and integrated group practice of medicine.

To offer outstanding young men and women opportunities for education in clinical medicine, in the sciences related to medicine, and in all the allied health professions; and to contribute thereby to improved standards of medical care, and to broader availability of medical care, in this country and in other countries.

To advance and enlarge knowledge and skill in medicine, and the sciences related to medicine, through research directed toward a broader understanding of man in health and disease, prevention of illness, and diagnostic and therapeutic measures applicable to disease.

Following the principles and ideals of the founders, Dr. William James Mayo and Dr. Charles Horace Mayo, these objectives in medical practice, medical education, and medical research are to be attained without regard to race, color, creed, sex, national origin, or economic status, and upon the ideal that our first obligation is to our patients. There shall be no financial benefit to any staff member, officer, or employee beyond reasonable compensation, and only such returns to the institution as will safeguard its future. The resources of the institution shall be used only in achievement of the purposes stated above, and in keeping with the highest moral, ethical and legal standards.

Index